"Through an in-depth, critical engagement w.   ...raham Kuyper's theological ethics, Matthew Kaemingk shows why and how commitment to Jesus Christ should issue in a political pluralism marked by hospitality to and solidarity with Muslim neighbors."

— JOSHUA RALSTON
University of Edinburgh

"While engaging lived realities and introducing us to actual people impacted by those lived realities, Matthew Kaemingk provides a compelling vision for Christian faith to serve as a bridge, not a barrier, to loving the many different neighbors we live alongside within our contemporary pluralistic context. This extraordinary book is of tremendous import for the big questions the church needs to ask in this complex cultural moment; at the same time it affirms the significance of the small, daily ways Christians can love their neighbors through their regular lives and callings. I wish all Western Christians would engage with Kaemingk's exceptionally readable and timely book as they wrestle with what it means to be a Christian called to love with generous hospitality in our pluralistic culture."

— KRISTEN DEEDE JOHNSON
Western Theological Seminary

"In this compelling work Matthew Kaemingk asks what Amsterdam has to do with Mecca, and the answers he finds turn out to have implications the world over. . . . The charity and clarity on display here will challenge Christians to think more deeply, and to act more responsibly, in response to the call to live peacefully and faithfully with Muslim neighbors."

— JORDAN J. BALLOR
Acton Institute

Christian Hospitality and Muslim Immigration in an Age of Fear

Matthew Kaemingk

WILLIAM B. EERDMANS PUBLISHING COMPANY
GRAND RAPIDS, MICHIGAN

Wm. B. Eerdmans Publishing Co.
2140 Oak Industrial Drive N.E., Grand Rapids, Michigan 49505
www.eerdmans.com

27 26 25 24 23 22 21 20 19 18   4 5 6 7 8 9 10

ISBN 978-0-8028-7458-0

Library of Congress Cataloging-in-Publication Data

Names: Kaemingk, Matthew, 1981- author.
Title: Christian hospitality and Muslim immigration in an age of fear /
    Matthew Kaemingk.
Description: Grand Rapids : Eerdmans Publishing Co., 2018. | Includes
    bibliographical references and index.
Identifiers: LCCN 2017035977 | ISBN 9780802874580 (pbk. : alk. paper)
Subjects: LCSH: Hospitality—Religious aspects—Christianity. | Emigration
    and immigration—Religious aspects—Christianity. | Missions to Muslims. |
    Christianity and other religions—Islam. | Islam—Relations—Christianity.
Classification: LCC BV4647.H67 K34 2018 | DDC 261.2/7—dc23
    LC record available at https://lccn.loc.gov/2017035977

For Heather

Love them as yourself,
for you yourselves were foreigners in Egypt.

LEVITICUS 19:34

Contents

CONTENTS

Foreword

A cab ride on a recent trip to Ottawa, the Canadian capital, turned into a theological adventure. A little bleary-eyed at 4 a.m., I wasn't exactly craving conversation; but that didn't deter my cabbie. An immigrant from Afghanistan who has lived in Canada for twenty-seven years, he was happy to sing the praises of the city and the country. There was a certain irony to this that made me smile quietly in the back seat: this Muslim man was taking proud ownership of the country I had left. On a warm morning in May, he practically hymned the delights of skating on the Rideau Canal in February. He was excited about the prospects of the Ottawa Senators, at that time vying for a spot in the Stanley Cup final. He was grateful for his daughters' education, one of whom had gone on to become a nurse. He had fond memories of a boyhood spent at a summer home in the cool mountain regions of Afghanistan. When I asked if he ever got back to Afghanistan, he began to tell me about the recent wedding of one of his daughters there. This is where the conversation took a decidedly theological, one might even say prophetic, turn.

His praise of Canada and its opportunity slid into a trenchant criticism of the libertarianism and licentiousness he'd seen become "normal" over the three decades in his new homeland. While he was grateful for opportunities, he was forthrightly critical of a creeping secularism that marginalized faith and celebrated promiscuity; you could feel the temperature in the cab begin to rise. His disappointment with the progressivist orthodoxy of Canadian society was palpable, and he eventually apologized for the "French" (that is, expletives) he spoke in anger. This, he emphasized, is why his daughter had found a partner elsewhere.

ix

But in the middle of his critique of secular liberalism, he articulated what I, as a Christian, heard as a robust, affirmative theology of creation. He shared a vision for the goods of sex and marriage and friendship and community, how these creaturely blessings could be better enjoyed within boundaries, how constraints were gifts. I quietly added my "Amen," and when I said how much my Christian faith concurred with his Muslim faith on these matters, the cab was a little outpost of camaraderie that seemed a million miles away from the politics I was returning to when my plane took off for the United States.

Granted, this kind of encounter is more frequent in Canada than the United States. Muslims constitute 3 percent of the Canadian population, 5 percent of the population of Ontario, and almost 8 percent of Toronto's cosmopolitan population. But this is precisely why Matthew Kaemingk's study in this book is so prescient for us. By taking the Netherlands as a case study, Kaemingk is, in a sense, engaged in time travel. To see the dynamics of Muslim immigration and Christian response in the so-called progressive Netherlands is an opportunity to glance at a possible future for North America—a glimpse that is both a cautionary tale and a laboratory to consider how things could go differently.

This is just one of the many reasons I'm grateful for *Christian Hospitality and Muslim Immigration in an Age of Fear*. Even more significantly, this is a book centered on an audacious claim: that theology can help us learn how to live together.

But not just any theology. In fact, Kaemingk here challenges the failure of the theological imagination to really grapple with difference. Dominant schools of thought are locked in a binary imagination that either underwrites hegemony or blithely diminishes difference in the name of a vague sense of inclusion. The failure of Christian theology to articulate a complex, nuanced affirmation of plurality and difference too often translates into heretical nationalisms or naïve, progressivist assimilationism. Both have failed, Kaemingk shows. Thus he points us to a neglected stream of Christian thought that has pluralism encoded in its very DNA. The dominant strains of theological thinking have failed us on these questions: issues around immigration and Islam have engendered hatred and fear, anger and misunderstanding. Kaemingk points us to a theological reservoir we've missed; drinking from it can nourish the church to be an outpost of kingdom hospitality in ways that are sophisticated and beautiful, realistic and hopeful.

So this singular book does two things at once: it shows the real-world relevance of Reformed public theology while also making a constructive contribution to a pressing question that continues to dominate the headlines. This isn't just more prolegomena and throat-clearing; this is a Christian ethicist tackling a real, difficult, practical question with the resources of *theology*. Kaemingk doesn't pretend to be a policy expert, nor does he take his academic credentials to be a license to freelance as an activist. The (limited but constructive) role of the ethicist and theologian here is diaconal: offered in service of those involved in legislation, policy, NGOs, activism, and the quiet, quotidian works of mercy that constitute the church's hospitality.

This book is a sign of both a renaissance and maturation of Reformed public theology. No longer focused on simply articulating "principles," and no longer directed merely to an "inside-baseball" tribe, this is careful, constructive work done *from* the tradition rather than merely *about* it.

That said, this book is also an excellent introduction to this Reformed tradition of public thought—but it's an introduction on the move, so to speak. Instead of a series of static portraits, Kaemingk's book is more like a wildlife documentary: He shows you this Reformed tradition in the wild, as it were— engaged in a particular problem, in a particular context, with all of its foibles, and failures, and insights, and initiatives.

This is also why I hope *Christian Politics and Muslim Immigration in an Age of Fear* is read widely, both within the church and without. Kaemingk's work demonstrates the enduring relevance of a Christian public theology that challenges both revolution and totalitarianism. I especially hope non-Christians will read this as a peek into the robustly Christian rationale for being hospitable neighbors. Kaemingk shows that the best Christian theology engenders pluralism, not theonomy. As he summarizes: "Kuyper's Christological sovereignty did not make him a theocrat. Naming Christ as sovereign is something altogether different from naming *Christians* as sovereign." I can think of a long list of journalists who need to understand this point. Actually, I can think of a long list of *Christians* who need to understand this point.

In this book Kaemingk is also making an important contribution to the advance and development of public theology more broadly, with implications beyond the specific question of Islam and immigration. In a chapter that is both illuminating and moving, he reminds us that Christ is more than a King. Drawing on under-appreciated voices like Herman Bavinck and Klaas Schilder, Kaemingk invites us, provocatively, to follow "the Naked Slave-King between Mecca and Amsterdam." He points to the significance of the church as the site where the Spirit nourishes a *desire* for pluralism "in our bones." He emphasizes the importance of habit-forming practices that would make us *want* to follow the Naked Slave-King in humility, walking vulnerably alongside our neighbors. In this way, Kaemingk invites us to think of our public lives beyond the categories of creation and common grace, taking us back to the cross itself. "The hospitality of the cross," he emphasizes, "is normative for every aspect of public life." Here is a public theology that is ecclesial and cruciform, complex and gracious. In short, here is the public theology we need today.

JAMES K. A. SMITH

Acknowledgments

It is humbling to consider the number of colleagues, scholars, friends, family members, mentors, and institutions who all have contributed to the completion of this project. I am truly grateful for the generous support I have received on both sides of the Atlantic.

Many thanks to my academic mentors Richard Mouw, George Harinck, and Kees van der Kooi. In unique and thoughtful ways all three provided wise counsel, gentle criticism, and faithful encouragement from beginning to end. Scholars from numerous institutions generously agreed to meet with me and guide me in a wide variety of disciplines and research arenas. From Fuller Theological Seminary I received thoughtful guidance from Erin Dufault-Hunter; from Calvin College, James Bratt, John Witvliet, and James K. A. Smith; from the Vrije Universiteit in Amsterdam, Govert Buijs, Stefan Paas, Sander Griffioen, Martien Brinkman, and Henk Vroom; from the Theologische Universiteit in Kampen, James Eglinton, Ad de Bruijne, and Barend Kamphuis; from the Universiteit van Amsterdam, James Kennedy and Markha Valenta; from Kirby Laing Institute for Christian Ethics, Cambridge, Jonathan Chaplin; from the Center for Public Justice, James Skillen and Gideon Strauss.

During my time in the Netherlands, numerous individuals generously agreed to advise me, provide thoughtful feedback, and sit for focused interviews. My thanks go to Cees Rentier, Ramin Saqeb, Cees Sybrandi, Shawky Hafez, Maarten de Vries, Annemarie Krijger, Serge de Boer, Jan Schippers, Ab Klink, Meg Finnerud, Joanne Smit, Cornelie Scheeres, Gert and Rita Hunink, Doutje Lettinga, Wouter Beekers, Chad Parker, Albert Hengelaar, Gert-Jan Segers, and many more who could not be listed. To my Muslim and Christian friends in Amsterdam who have asked to remain anonymous, I give you thanks, as well.

The warmth and generosity my family received in Amsterdam from the van der Kooi family was truly unmatched. Kees and Margriet, Tineke and Said, Keimpe Kees and Ilse, Nynke and Arjan, Anne-Lotte and Jesse—our sincere thanks to you all. While I was busy writing about hospitality, you were busy showing it.

My research in Amsterdam and Los Angeles could not have taken place without the financial support of a number of generous institutions. My thanks to Fuller Theological Seminary for the Merlin Call Fellowship, to the US State Department for the Fulbright Scholarship, to the Vrije Universiteit in Amsterdam and the Stichting De Hunderd Gulden Reis for the travel grant, to the Theologische Universiteit Kampen for the research sabbatical, and to the Acton Institute for the Calihan research grant.

A number of colleagues and friends provided a wide variety of theological, political, and ethical questions and insights that are addressed in this book. While their names are not listed in the footnotes, the pages are shot through with their wisdom and insight. Special thanks to Edward Yang, Cory Willson, Tim Blackmon, Jeffrey Riddell, Matthew Carpenter, David Arinder, Chris Moore, and Ryan Moede. Thanks as well to Jan van Helden, Alissa Wilkinson, James K. A. Smith, Robert Joustra, Bob Covolo, Stewart Graham, and Daniel and Krista Carter who each read large sections of this work and provided extensive and excellent feedback.

And finally, thanks to my family. To our parents, who have provided us with generous support throughout this process and, indeed, throughout our lives. To our sons, Calvin, Kees, and Caedmon, my sincere appreciation to you for patiently enduring the omnipresence of your father's laptop computer. And finally, to my wife Heather, for everything and more, I thank you. I am undeserving, overwhelmed, and ever grateful for your love in my life.

Soli Deo Gloria

My Enemy, Too

> [Faith] was, no doubt, the source of fanaticism and persecution, but it was also, I suggest, the source of a new conception of freedom. Liberty of conscience was born, not of indifference, not of skepticism, not of mere open-mindedness, but of faith.
>
> JOHN PLAMENATZ[1]

Since the end of World War II, millions of Muslims have migrated into Europe and North America. By air, land, and sea their arrival has ignited a series of fierce public debates about religious freedom and tolerance, terrorism and security, gender and race, and so much more. As thousands of Muslims stream into the West, they carry more than ancient traditions, beliefs, and cultures; they carry an ancient question as well. How can diverse people live together?

This book wrestles with this ancient question through the lens of a very contemporary issue—Islam's growing presence in the West. As an American Christian working in the field of Christian ethics, theology, and politics, I am regularly asked to take sides in this so-called clash of civilizations. With every terrorist attack, immigration ban, cartoon controversy, burqa debate, and fresh conflict over a newly built mosque, I (along with many other Christians) am presented with a series of familiar questions. How should Western Christians respond to their new Muslim neighbors? Can Islam and Christianity peacefully coexist? Are there limits to religious freedom and tolerance? How much religious diversity can a single nation withstand?

---

1. John Plamenatz, *Man and Society*, vol. 1 (New York: McGraw-Hill, 1963), 50.

The questions do not stop. With every new controversy, discussions about Muslim immigration and integration grow in intensity, emotion, and complexity. In popular debates the demand to pick a side and match our neighbor's outrage only seems to grow.

The two sides of the debate quickly polarize and fragment. One side declares that Islam is inherently peaceful and good—the other that it's inherently violent and evil. One claims that interfaith dialogue, awareness, and diplomacy will lead to peace—the other claims that peace will be found only in higher walls and tougher policies. One side prescribes a posture of open acceptance and tolerance—the other of aggression and antagonism. While there certainly are more moderate and nuanced approaches, these two simplistic narratives dominate the public debate in Europe and North America.

These two popular responses to Islam in the West agree on very little. That said, there are three points on which they seem to cohere. First, they both believe the solution to be relatively clear and straightforward. Second, they both believe the state should be the primary agent in their proposed solution. Third, they both speak as if there are only two possible solutions—only two possible ways of dealing with the politics of difference. In other words, Western citizens *must* accept the given dichotomy. They must either select the antagonism of right-wing nationalism or the romanticism of left-wing multiculturalism.

This book constitutes not only a Christian critique of these two problematic responses, but a proposal for an alternative path forward—a third way. Uncomfortable with the solutions of the right and the left, many thoughtful Christians are tempted to simply cobble together a contingent sort of middle way, a moderate mixture of the two responses to Islam. This book is not that. This book argues that what is needed is not an amalgamation of two broken approaches. Instead, I propose an alternative way forward, a different way of seeing and responding to the challenges and opportunities of Islamic immigration in the West.

The book is written for two groups of people. First, it is written for Christians who sense a deep need for an alternative response to Islam that begins and ends with Christian conviction—not the simplistic ideologies of the right and left. Second, this book is written for non-Christians who are interested in peering over the religious fence, as it were, and exploring how some Christians are attempting to live peacefully and faithfully in an increasingly diverse, fragmented, and fear-driven world.

Deep, Close, and Fast: The Globalization of Difference

As the wheels of globalization turn, different ways of life—long isolated—are being thrown together at an ever-increasing rate. As difference only increases in its depth, proximity, and speed, the pressing question of how to live amid such difference only increases. Around the globe religious and secular communities alike are being forced to reexamine how they respond to differences that are increasingly deep, close, fast.

Islam in the West is an issue that confronts Jewish, Christian, liberal, Buddhist, cosmopolitan, socialist, and—of course—Muslim communities. This particular work is meant to serve the Christian community as it wrestles with the issue. The book makes no attempt to direct Buddhists or Jews, liberals or multiculturalists on how they should respond to their Muslim neighbor. This is not a book of universal ethics; it is a book of Christian ethics.

For a growing number of Western Christians, their relationship with Islam is no longer theoretical or abstract—it is a lived reality. Muslims—who used to be viewed exclusively through the lens of a CNN satellite feed—are moving into Christians' cities, neighborhoods, companies, and even their own homes and families. For Christians walking the streets of New York and London, Los Angeles and Paris, Chicago and Amsterdam religious pluralism is no longer an academic pursuit—it's a live question.

The response of an ethicist to Islam's growing presence in the West—if it is to have any moral weight at all—must wrestle with lived reality and the raw challenges of life on these religiously diverse city streets. If my ethical response gets lost in abstract discussions of difference and fails to address the very real sense of existential anger and fear, complexity and confusion that actual citizens experience, then my ethical response does not deserve a seat at the table.

While this book will challenge right-wing nationalists on a number of points, it must affirm their critical insight on the following point: Muslim immigration presents very real and very deep cultural and political challenges to the Western status quo. Right-wing nationalists are absolutely correct in their charge that leftist politicians and academics have failed to fully recognize or wrestle with the reality that Muslim immigrants are bringing real challenges and real questions to the future of Western culture and politics. Nationalists are absolutely right to call leftists to account. This book will therefore seek to avoid the left's fatal mistake of pursuing the romantic dream of a multicultural West without recognizing the deep challenges and counting the real costs of such a proposal. Dismissing those on the right as nothing but racist and Islamophobic has long been a convenient and lazy way for those on the left to avoid discussing the real challenges of multiculturalism.

Taking the dangers of academic abstraction seriously, I have decided to begin my own ethical response by paying close attention to how this issue has taken shape on the streets of Europe. As an American ethicist and observer, I believe that three primary reasons demonstrate why I believe my fellow Americans need to pay attention to the lived European experience with Islam. First, Europe has been wrestling with the question of Islamic immigration and integration for much longer than the United States. Second, Europe has a higher concentration of Muslims than the United States (roughly 8 percent of the population compared to 2 percent). Third, Christian responses to Islamic immigration in the United States often parrot the secular perspectives of either right-wing nationalism or left-wing multiculturalism—they lack a *uniquely* Christian response to the issue. American Christians need an outside perspective, a fresh approach, a different angle—one that actually emerges out of their own Christian conviction. Looking across the Atlantic, I believe that I have found exactly that. In the pages that follow I will explore and develop this small but potent Christian resource for thinking about religious diversity and freedom that charts a promising third way forward. The final section of this book will explore the issue of Islam in America, but only after we have paid close attention to the lessons of the European story.

European Secularism Challenged

[T]he arrival of Islam has reopened the file—up to now considered "case closed"—on the relationship between Church and State.

JOCELYNE CESARI[2]

Europeans don't need to read Peter Berger's *The Desecularization of the World* to know that "religion is back" in the modern public square.[3] Every day Europeans see, hear, smell, and literally bump into public religion on the streets of Paris, London, and Amsterdam.[4] The growing numbers, visibility, and strength

2. Jocelyne Cesari, *When Islam and Democracy Meet: Muslims in Europe and in the United States* (Palgrave Macmillan: New York, 2004), 65.

3. Peter Berger, *The Desecularization of the World: Resurgent Religion and World Politics* (Grand Rapids: Eerdmans, 1999).

4. For in-depth anthropological and sociological explorations of encounters between

of Islam in what was thought to be secular Europe has been deeply unsettling for Europeans who believed the old secularization thesis.[5]

Since the 1960s, the number of Muslims living in Europe has risen dramatically.[6] The original push and pull of their migration to Europe was economic. In the wake of World War II, the burgeoning industrial and service sectors of Western Europe experienced remarkable levels of growth. As demand for cheap labor increased, European leaders initiated immigration agreements with countries in North Africa, Asia, and the Middle East. Labeling these immigrants temporary guest workers, European states did little to encourage their integration into European society. It became common for governments to set aside separate neighborhoods and buildings to house the guest workers. An early policy goal was to isolate and maintain immigrant languages, cultures, and beliefs in order to make their eventual return home as smooth as possible.

These economic migrants were followed by successive waves of political asylum-seekers fleeing a variety of oppressive regimes and civil wars. By the end of the 1970s, European leaders began to realize that these temporary guests were rapidly becoming permanent residents. This realization touched off a wide range of policy discussions in the 1980s and 1990s about how European governments might help these immigrants integrate into European life.

Around the turn of the century, a seismic shift began to take place in European politics. The previously quaint religious beliefs and cultural practices of these immigrants became a matter of significant, urgent, and even heated debate throughout Europe. Up until this point, discussions about Islamic immigration and integration had largely been reserved for European bureaucrats. This all changed with the turn of the century. Suddenly the place of Islam in Europe took center stage in public debate.

Muslims and non-Muslims in Europe see Hakan Yilmaz and Çagla E. Aykaç, eds., *Perceptions of Islam in Europe: Culture, Identity, and the Muslim "Other"* (London: Tauris, 2012).

5. Philip Jenkins, *God's Continent: Christianity, Islam, and Europe's Religious Crisis* (Oxford: Oxford University Press, 2007).

6. These studies include helpful summaries of the history of Islamic immigration in Europe and unique insights into different aspects of the debate that followed: Andrew Geddes, *The Politics of Migration and Immigration in Europe* (London: SAGE, 2003); Gallya Lahav, *Immigration and Politics in the New Europe* (Cambridge: Cambridge University Press, 2012); Craig Parsons and Timothy M. Smeeding, eds., *Immigration and the Transformation of Europe* (Cambridge: Cambridge University Press, 2006); Jocelyne Cesari, *When Islam and Democracy Meet: Muslims in Europe and the United States* (New York: Palgrave Macmillan, 2006); John Esposito and Francois Burqat, eds. *Modernizing Islam: Religion in the Public Sphere in the Middle East and Europe* (New Brunswick, NJ: Rutgers University Press, 2003); Paul Scheffer, *Immigrant Nations* (Cambridge: Polity Press, 2011).

Secular Europeans found themselves returning to a series of old questions on religion and politics that had long been resolved in their minds, questions like: What is the proper relationship between religion and politics? What are the limits of religious freedom? Is it possible for deeply religious people to be tolerant and democratic? Do states need to enforce a set of national values and beliefs? The utter dominance of secular liberalism in Europe during the twentieth century created the impression that the questions of faith and public life had all been laid to rest and that the problem of public religion had been solved.

In this sense, a small group of veiled Muslim women walking down the Champs-Élysées confront the young, secular Parisians they pass with a series of questions many of them have never asked during their young lives.[7] The women's veils directly challenge the public dominance of their modern secularism. It is an understatement that many Europeans have begun to notice the challenge.

Exposing the "True" Islam

[I]n placing man where God had been, we took as our task the unveiling of reality.

MARKHA VALENTA[8]

The liberal firebrand Ayaan Hirsi Ali knew exactly what she was doing when she produced the controversial film *Submission.*[9] Filmed in the Netherlands

---

7. Hilal Elver, *The Headscarf Controversy: Secularism and Freedom of Religion* (New York: Oxford University Press, 2012); Jonathan Laurence and Justin Vaisse, *Integrating Islam: Political and Religious Challenges in Contemporary France* (Washington, DC: Brookings Institution Press, 2006); John Bowen, *Why the French Don't Like Headscarves* (Princeton, NJ: Princeton University Press, 2010); Jennifer A. Selby, *Questioning French Secularism: Gender Politics and Islam in a Parisian Suburb* (New York: Palgrave Macmillan, 2012); Joan Wallach Scott, *The Politics of the Veil* (Princeton, NJ: Princeton University Press, 2009).

8. Markha Valenta, "How to Recognise a Muslim When You See One: Western Secularism and the Politics of Conversion," in Hent de Vries and Lawrence Eugene Sullivan, eds., *Political Theologies: Public Religions in a Post-Secular World* (New York: Fordham University Press, 2006), 472.

9. For a critical analysis of the film *Submission,* consult Marc De Leeuw and Sonja Van Wichelen's "'Please, Go Wake Up!' Submission, Hirsi Ali, and the 'War on Terror' in the Netherlands," *Feminist Media Studies* 5, no. 3 (2005): 325–40; Iveta Jusová, "Hirsi Ali and van Gogh's Submission: Reinforcing the Islam vs. Women Binary," *Women's Studies International Forum* 31,

in 2004, Ali's drama depicts five Muslim women praying to Allah. Each of the women recalls—in graphic detail—horrific stories of abuse, incest, and rape at the hands of Muslim men. As whips crack in the background, the women plead with Allah for justice and deliverance. They receive no answer.

Texts from the Koran that demand female submission are projected onto the women's bruised and battered backs and breasts. The women repeatedly plead for divine intervention. Their deity's deafening silence presses them to a point of existential crisis. Should the women remain under the harsh law and submission of religion, or should they seek the liberation of the West? While the women's faces are veiled, their exposed breasts and backs voyeuristically reveal to Western audiences the cuts, bruises, and naked truth of Islam's brutality and backwardness.

On their broken skin, Ayaan Hirsi Ali attempts to project the true nature of Islam as an insidious movement of misogyny and violence. Muslim men, never seen or heard from in the film, are portrayed as sexually aggressive, disgusting, and violent. Muslim women, robbed of clothes and agency, are depicted as confused, helpless, and trapped in a religion of abuse and subjugation. The message is patronizingly clear. For men, Islam cannot inspire restraint—only violence. For women, Islam cannot inspire resistance—only submission.

Ayaan Hirsi Ali's film was clearly aimed, not at Muslims, but at enlightened Western audiences. She hoped to supply an answer for Westerners who always wondered to themselves, "What is going on under my neighbor's veil?" Her film promises to let audiences in on a horrific, yet tantalizing, secret. Beneath her veil, your Muslim neighbor is crying out to you. Every day she is pleading with you: Oh, Westerner, please bring me safety, liberation, and enlightenment!

As the five women cry out to Allah, European audiences know that the women will receive no answer. They know that the West alone has the power—no, the burden, to answer the women's prayers. In eleven short minutes, *Submission* asks Western audiences a simple question: Will you have the courage to stand up to Islam? Will you speak out for these women?

Making their bare breasts and backs her own personal canvas, Ali paints a vivid picture of the clash of civilizations between the forces of secular good and religious evil, Western peace and Eastern violence.[10] The bodies of these

---

no. 2 (2008): 148–55; Aysel Morin, "Victimization of Muslim Women in *Submission*," *Women's Studies in Communication* 32, no. 3 (2009): 380–408; Liz Fekete, "Enlightenment Fundamentalism? Immigration, Feminism, and the Right," *Race & Class* 48, no. 2 (2006): 1–22.

10. Samuel Huntington, *The Clash of Civilizations and the Remaking of World Order* (New York: Simon & Schuster, 1996).

Muslim women constitute the binary battlefield in a new cultural conflict. Two irreconcilable cities are constructed in this film—religious and violent Mecca versus secular and peaceful Amsterdam.

In this clash between Mecca and Amsterdam, audiences are presented with clear choices: religion or reason, barbarism or civilization, the medieval or the modern, religious violence or secular peace. The self-proclaimed Voltaire of Islam, Ayaan Hirsi Ali states loudly and clearly to her audience: Either you are with the secular us or you are with the religious rapists. Which side will you choose? In eleven short minutes, *Submission*'s fierce logic is made clear. The clash between the forces of Mecca and Amsterdam is real. A choice must be made.

The Politics of Integration

> Unless the liberal state is engaged in a continuing dialogue with the religious community, it loses its essential liberalism. It becomes simply and dogmatically secular.
>
> ROWAN WILLIAMS[11]

It is no surprise that how one frames the Islamic question will greatly influence the eventual answer. It is true that some Europeans have received Islam's arrival as an opportunity to reflect and to ask themselves "How must we change in order to welcome Muslims?"[12] This, however, has not been the prevailing response.

For most Europeans, the Islamic question is, quite simply, "How must Muslims change in order for us to welcome them?" This is why the public rhetoric around the word integration is so central in European debates about Islam.

In short, the bulk of Europeans do not approach Islam asking a *philosophical* question about how one lives with Islamic difference. They approach Islam by asking a *political* question: "How can my government more effectively neutralize Islamic difference?" Framed in such a way, the European debate over Islam is largely one of means, not ends.[13] The political end is taken for

11. Rowan Williams, "Is Europe at its end?" (Forum debate presented at the Sant'Egidio International Meeting of Prayer for Peace, Palais de Congress, Lyon, France, September 12, 2005), http://www.archbishopofcanterbury.org/958 (accessed November 5, 2009).

12. Luca Mavelli, *Europe's Encounter with Islam: The Secular and the Postsecular* (London: Routledge, 2012).

13. Jonathan Laurence, *The Emancipation of Europe's Muslims: The State's Role in Minority*

granted—the political goal is a creation of a *European* Islam. The goal is a new Islam that can be closely managed by European states and accepted by European culture. For most Europeans, therefore, the Islamic question concerns the efficient integration (read: assimilation) of the Muslim. What, in other words, are the best practices for the governmental integration of Islam? How will government teachers, government social workers, government laws, and government programs effectively mitigate Muslim difference?

Quite simply, many Europeans do not consider Islam a question to be pondered—they consider it a problem to be solved. This is why Europeans do not look to philosophers or ethicists to help them reflect on the question; they look to politicians, social workers, and teachers to solve the problem on their behalf.

Of course, one can find exceptions to this dominant European approach to Islamic integration. One can find radical Europeans who call for either the outright acceptance of Islam or its outright expulsion. Such voices, however, are in the minority. Most public discourse is focused on the question of how European governments can inaugurate the integration, reformation, or modernization of Islam—with all of the patronizing Eurocentrism these three terms imply.

During the 1980s and 1990s, European governments largely encouraged citizens to have patience with their efforts to integrate and domesticate Islam. Officials argued that the historical process of Islamic modernization and secularization simply needed more time. In the wake of 9/11, the murder of Theo van Gogh, and other high-profile clashes between Islam and the West, Europeans steadily grew resistant to their leaders' calls for patience and tolerance. Across Europe, extreme right-wing and nativists parties rose up to question the assumed wisdom of multiculturalism.

In recent years, Europeans have increasingly called for more assertive and aggressive solutions to the problem of Islam.[14] In dutiful response, politicians

---

Integration (Princeton, NJ: Princeton University Press, 2012); Ayhan Kaya, *Islam, Migration, and Integration: The Age of Securitization* (London: Palgrave Macmillan, 2009); Ariane Chebel d'Appollonia and Simon Reich, eds., *Immigration, Integration, and Security: America and Europe in Comparative Perspective* (Pittsburgh: University of Pittsburgh Press, 2008); Christian Joppke and John Torpey, *Legal Integration of Islam* (Cambridge, MA: Harvard University Press, 2013).

14. Right-wing populist parties throughout Europe have skillfully capitalized on this shift in public opinion against Islam. See, for example: Christina Schori Liang, ed., *Europe for the Europeans* (Burlington, VT: Ashgate, 2007); Ruth Wodak, Majid KhosraviNik, and Brigitte Mral, eds., *Right-Wing Populism in Europe: Politics and Discourse* (London: Bloomsbury, 2013); Mabel Berezin, *Illiberal Politics in Neoliberal Times: Culture, Security, and Populism* (Cambridge: Cambridge University Press, 2009); Simon Bornschier, *Cleavage Politics and the*

proposed and implemented a wide range of tougher economic, educational, political, and bureaucratic methods to quicken the integration of Muslims into European society. Some of these methods have been soft and subtle. Others have been hard and harsh. As nativist patience wanes, political carrots often gave way to sticks.[15]

Advocates of softer carrot-based integration methods argue that Muslims will naturally assimilate if they are first allowed to taste the good fruit of modern European life. They insist that the government must give Muslim immigrants the means to learn, work, and consume like other Europeans. Through education and consumption, Muslims will naturally come to identify with and desire a European way of life. These voices often recommend propping up moderate Islamic organizations and leaders in the hopes that three things will occur: First, funding moderate Muslim leaders will strengthen their hands against radicals. Second, by building funding partnerships, the state will be better equipped to monitor and ultimately control Muslim organizations. And third, funding these organizations will cultivate new Muslim leaders who can act as moderate liaisons between Muslims and the European state.

In opposition to these carrot-based strategies, the more aggressive stick-based advocates stress the importance of a muscular European response. They emphasize the importance of law and order, cultural conformity, governmental surveillance, and a wide range of restrictions on Islamic practices and organizations. Advocates of European strength stress the importance of a national identity, traditions, history, and culture. Discussions center around how states can protect national values through constitutional documents, civil ceremonies, and bureaucratic machinery. The importance of a national school system in which these national values will be taught is often stressed. Arguments surface as to whether headscarves are acceptable in public spaces for students, police, judges, and courtroom officials. Debates emerge as to whether strict prohibitions should be placed on Islamic minarets, calls to prayer, ritual animal slaughter, veils, circumcision, and more.

Debates between soft and hard integrationists quickly become heated. The heat, however, obscures a critical point of consensus. Both sides assume that Islam is the problem. Islam—not Europe—must change.[16] Europe is taken for

---

Populist Right: The New Cultural Conflict in Western Europe (Philadelphia: Temple University Press, 2010); and Raymond Taras, Xenophobia and Islamophobia in Europe (Edinburgh: Edinburgh University Press, 2012).

15. Ariane Chebel D'Appollonia, Frontiers of Fear: Immigration and Insecurity in the United States and Europe (Ithaca, NY: Cornell University Press, 2012).

16. Peter Morey and Amina Yaqin, Framing Muslims: Stereotyping and Representations

granted. Europe is the end of history. Europe has settled, once and for all, the fundamental questions of sex, family, politics, religion, and the good life. The proper task of the European state is to educate Muslims on the answers they have already found.

A Casualty in the Clash

Europe could be considered the Chosen Land for the Clash of Civilizations argument.

JOCELYN CESARI[17]

Theo van Gogh worked with Ayaan Hirsi Ali, serving as the director of the film *Submission*. One morning, a few months after the film's release, Theo got on his bicycle and rode through the streets of Amsterdam. Mohammed Bouyeri rode his bicycle alongside van Gogh, pulled out a semi-automatic pistol, and fired. Knocked off his bicycle, van Gogh stumbled across the street and hid behind a car in an attempt to flee his attacker. Bouyeri calmly followed the wounded director, continuing to fire as van Gogh pleaded with his attacker, "Don't do this!" The director finally collapsed to the ground.

Bouyeri approached van Gogh and fired the last of eight bullets into his body. The director of *Submission* fell silent. The attacker pulled out a Kukri machete and, in front of more than fifty witnesses, attempted to decapitate his victim. Failing to completely sever the head, Bouyeri kicked the body a few times before plunging a filet knife into his chest. Attached to the knife was a death threat for Ayaan Hirsi Ali.

Bouyeri calmly inspected his work and walked into a nearby park. He left behind, on the streets of Amsterdam, the lifeless body of the great-grand-nephew of Vincent van Gogh. The Netherlands, land of tolerance, looked on in shock.[18]

---

after 9/11 (Cambridge, MA: Harvard University Press, 2011); John Bowen, *Blaming Islam* (Cambridge, MA: MIT Press, 2012). John Esposito and Ibrahim Kalin; *Islamophobia: The Challenge of Pluralism in the Twenty-First Century* (Oxford: Oxford University Press, 2011); Katherine Ewing, *Stolen Honor: Stigmatizing Islamic Men in Berlin* (Stanford, CA: Stanford University Press, 2008); Oliver Roy, *Secularism Confronts Islam,* trans. George Holoch (New York: Columbia University Press, 2007).

17. Cesari, *When Islam and Democracy Meet,* 32.

18. For an analysis of the Dutch cultural trauma that occurred in the aftermath to the van Gogh assassination, see Ron Eyerman's *The Assassination of Theo van Gogh: From Social*

"The Netherlands Is Burning"

The newspaper headline captured the traumatized zeitgeist of the nation. Like the 9/11 attacks in New York, the murder of Theo van Gogh represented a brutal attack at the very heart of the nation—the city of Amsterdam. In the minds of many Dutch citizens, the tolerant and peaceful innocence of their beloved city had been ripped violently out of their hands. This period of national shock and sadness quickly gave way to a national state of fear and finally, anger.

> First it was a mosque in Huizen—three men tried to torch it with turpentine and gasoline. Then a mosque in Rotterdam was targeted, though only the door got scorched. There was another arson attempt at a mosque in Groningen. And in Eindhoven a bomb exploded in an Islamic school. . . . Three Christian churches were attacked in Rotterdam, Utrecht, and Amersfoort. Another Muslim school, in Uden, a small town in the south, was set on fire. Someone had written "Theo RIP" on the wall.[19]

In the end more than forty mosques and churches were either vandalized or burned in the aftermath of van Gogh's murder. In his weekly editorial for *Het Parool,* columnist Theodor Holman made a simple proposal for how the Dutch could honor the memory of Theo van Gogh.

> Shut down those filthy mosques, goddamn it, where they really preach anti-Semitism and want to kill [our] kind. Throw those fucking fundamentalists out of the country! Or, better still, sew the butchers up in bags and drop them into the sea! That's the way to remember Theo![20]

While many questions remained, one thing was clear: something had changed in the progressive land of tolerance.

Drama to Cultural Trauma (Durham, NC: Duke University Press, 2008); and Ian Buruma, *Murder in Amsterdam: The Death of Theo Van Gogh and the Limits of Tolerance* (New York: Penguin Press, 2006).

19. Buruma, *Murder in Amsterdam,* 7–8.

20. Quoted in Buruma, *Murder in Amsterdam,* 228.

Theologian as Servant

How should Christians respond to all of this? The burgeoning conflict is a complex issue involving an infinite variety of questions, not only of religion, but also of poverty, race, gender, sexuality, language, globalization, and more. Out of the single question of Islam, hundreds of smaller questions quickly proliferate.

While the complexity of the issue should rightly inspire a Christian humility, it should not inspire Christian paralysis. In the face of such complexity, a sort of relief comes for the Christian citizen who recognizes that he or she has a finite role in formulating a Christian response to the conflict between Mecca and Amsterdam.

Moreover, Christian theologians like me are one small part of a much larger Christian community whose members hold a wide variety of gifts, callings, and responsibilities. No Christian—and certainly no theologian—is responsible for providing the comprehensive Christian answer to Islam in the West. This is a matter of significant relief for me.

Any Christian response to Islam's growing presence will rightly include a variety of Christian voices. It will need to include a complex assortment of Christian politicians and poets, entrepreneurs and teachers, journalists and parents, judges and musicians, sociologists and nurses. Moreover, the institutional church should not be the only organization involved in the response. Christian charities and businesses, universities and political organizations, newspapers and schools each have a role to play. If there is a vocation for the theologian amidst this conflict, one thing is certain: that vocation is limited.

So, what *is* my responsibility as a theologian in this complex and multifaceted question? What is my calling? Where is my place in this debate? The nineteenth-century theologian Herman Bavinck, speaking on the proper relationship between theologians and scientists, offers a helpful piece of insight. Here, Bavinck argues that the calling and honor of a theologian

> is not found in an elevated throne waving an all-knowing scepter over the other disciplines. Instead [theology's honor] is that she can serve the others with her gifts. In this, theology can rule only through service. She is strong when she is weak; she is greatest when she seeks to be least. She will be excellent when she seeks to know nothing save Christ and him crucified. [21]

21. Herman Bavinck, *De algemeene genade* (Kampen: G. PH. Zalsman, 1894), 53.

13

In that last line Bavinck is not suggesting that theologians do nothing but meditate on the Christ's crucifixion—though they could certainly do worse. No. Bavinck is arguing that Jesus Christ is the person through which all persons and all events should be understood. In the cross, Christians find the person and the event whose implications stretch out to the whole of life. In light of this, the theologian's task is not to give all of the answers but to equip Christians to both see the world and live in it through the reality of Christ and his cross.

Following this model, theologians should neither be silent nor supreme as they address public issues like Islam's growing presence in the West. Instead, theologians should serve their fellow Christians by providing a Christ-centered lens through which they can imagine their own answers to the complex challenges they face in the public square.

When it comes to the fight over Islam in the West, this Christocentric lens will impact the laws Christians pass, the news stories they report, the jokes they tell, the poems they write, the cartoons they draw, the courses they teach, the medical care they provide, and the injustices they protest. Christian theologians cannot and should not predict the complex ways in which this Christocentric imagination will be implemented—theologians are servants, not lords.

Moreover, while this book will interact with a variety of disciplines (including history, sociology, politics, anthropology, philosophy), it is, without apology, a work of theology. Historians will naturally wish me to spend more time examining the history, sociologists the sociology, and so on. However, being a theologian, I am primarily concerned with articulating a theological lens for life amidst this conflict.

In the pages that follow, the justice, hospitality, and grace of Jesus Christ will make up the center of my alternative response, the third way I call "Christian pluralism." While the entire book will be an extended exploration of the meaning and significance of Christian pluralism, let me make a few clarifying remarks at the outset.

Inclusivism, Exclusivism, and Pluralism

The strong exclusivist convictions that gave freedom of religion its birth can sustain it now as well.

MIROSLAV VOLF[22]

What do I mean by Christian pluralism? In the world of Christian theology, the word *pluralism* is often associated with an extended debate over the ultimate destiny of non-Christians.[23] In short, where do non-Christians go when they die—heaven or hell? Theologians engaged in such debates traditionally divide themselves into three camps: exclusivism, pluralism, and inclusivism. Briefly stated, *exclusivists* insist that only a clear acceptance of Jesus Christ will guarantee a person's salvation. *Pluralists* argue that all faiths are equally valid paths to the same God. Finally, *inclusivists* insist that all faiths will eventually be included in the true Christian faith. While these debates are complex and important, they are not the focus of this book.

This book is not primarily concerned with resolving the future question, "Where do Muslims go when they die?" It is focused, instead, on exploring the *present* question, "How should Muslims be treated while they are still alive?"

Whatever kind of Christian you are, wherever you think Muslims go when they die, a stubborn question from which you cannot run will always haunt you: "How should I treat my Muslim neighbor today?" A future resolution of the deep differences between Islam and Christianity does not resolve the deep differences that persist between the faiths today. Therefore, when you see the word *pluralism* in this book, know that it is not being used to explore a future resolution of religious differences. Instead, the word *pluralism* is used here to describe how Christians can faithfully respond to those differences in the present.

---

22. Miroslav Volf, *Flourishing: Why We Need Religion in a Globalizing World* (New Haven, CT: Yale University Press, 2015), 155.

23. See, for example Veli-Matti Kärkkäinen, *An Introduction to the Theology of Religions: Biblical, Historical, and Contemporary Perspectives* (Downers Grove, IL: InterVarsity Press, 2003); John May, ed., *Pluralism and the Religions: The Theological and Political Dimensions* (London: Cassell, 1998); Gavin D'Costa, *Theology and Religious Pluralism: The Challenge of Other Religions* (Oxford: Blackwell, 1986); Alan Race, *Christians and Religious Pluralism: Patterns in the Christian Theology of Religions* (Marknoll, NY: Orbis, 1983); Gavin D'Costa, *The Meeting of Religions and the Trinity* (Maryknoll, NY: Orbis, 2000); Paul Knitter, *Introducing Theologies of Religions* (Maryknoll, NY: Orbis Books, 2002); Keith E. Johnson, *Rethinking the Trinity and Religious Pluralism: An Augustinian Assessment* (Downers Grove, IL: InterVarsity Press, 2001).

Jean-Jacques Rousseau famously declared, "It is impossible to live at peace with those we regard as damned."[24] Such a firm declaration appears to indicate that Christians who have signed up for the exclusivist position are, from the very start, incapable of living peacefully with non-Christians. If Rousseau is right, this is sobering news indeed, given the fact that the vast majority of the world's churches favor some form of Christian exclusivism.

As a Christian theologian who holds to a version of exclusivism (with some important qualifications), I am troubled by Rousseau's charge that I am fundamentally incapable of living at peace with my Muslim neighbors. Is Rousseau right about me? Is my exclusivism a danger to democracy? Am I incapable of tolerance? Must my beliefs neccesarily drive me to violence against Islam?

This book constitutes an attempt by an exclusivist Christian to bring together two things that Rousseau contends are mutually exclusive:

1) An uncompromising commitment to the exclusive lordship of Jesus Christ.
2) An uncompromising commitment to love those who reject that lordship.

This book attempts to serve Christians who wish to defend the rights, dignity, and humanity of their Muslim neighbors without downplaying their exclusive commitment to Christian orthodoxy or the important differences between Islam and Christianity. Against Rousseau, I want to argue that my exclusive faith in Jesus Christ as the way, truth, and life is not a barrier against but a bridge to the love, respect, and honor I hold for my Muslim neighbor. Christian pluralism is a serious exploration about how to show love, hospitality, and justice across these deep differences—denying these differences accomplishes nothing.

Pluralism(s)

Discussions of multiculturalism and pluralism are often fraught with a great deal of confusion about terms and definitions. In their book *Pluralisms and Horizons*, Richard Mouw and Sander Griffioen provide significant clarity when they define three distinct forms of pluralism: cultural, structural, and directional.[25] Under-

24. Jean-Jacques Rousseau, *The Social Contract* (New York: Cosimo, 2008), 135–36.
25. Richard Mouw and Sander Griffioen, *Pluralisms and Horizons: An Essay in Christian Public Philosophy* (Grand Rapids: Eerdmans, 1993).

standing these terms will be critical to understanding how Christian pluralism offers a third way beyond the binaries of the right and left.

- *Cultural pluralism* describes a diversity of cultures.
- *Structural pluralism* describes a diversity of community structures (families, schools, businesses, organizations, states, worship spaces, etc.).
- *Directional pluralism* describes a diversity of life-directions (religions, ideologies, spiritualities, philosophies of life, etc.).

The authors then go on to outline three distinct ways in which a citizen can respond or react when they encounter these forms of cultural, structural, and directional diversity. Note, these three forms of response are ideal types; they are not meant to describe any actual people.

1) A *descriptive pluralist* seeks to faithfully describe the diversity of individuals, cultures, faiths, and institutions within a given society. Such a person wants to avoid reducing these diverse actors to a single aspect of their identity. Descriptive pluralists are committed to carefully and honestly understanding the deep diversity all around them. While their view is helpful, descriptive pluralists can tell us nothing about whether these forms of diversity are deserving of either political protection or moral affirmation. The descriptive pluralist can describe the difference but cannot help us judge it.

2) A *juridical pluralist* argues that cultural, structural, and directional diversity deserves more than description; it deserves judicial and political protection as well. Juridical pluralists come in both low- and high-grade forms. Low-grade forms insist that governments should protect diverse cultures, organizations, and faiths from undue harassment and harm. High-grade forms go even further. High-grade juridical pluralists insist that the state must also actively aid and empower these diverse cultures, organizations, and ideologies. Finally, it is important to note that juridical pluralists make no attempt to judge the moral value of these diverse actors; they are concerned with providing justice—not praise.

3) A *normative pluralist* not only wants to faithfully describe and politically defend diversity but also wants to morally affirm and praise diversity as a normative good. In short, the normative pluralist believes that deep cultural, associational, and philosophical differences not only deserve adequate description and protection, but they deserve moral praise as well. Plurality, in all its forms, calls for celebration.

Toward a Christian Pluralism

If there is such a thing, what would a Christian pluralist look like? While the entire book will explore this question, below is a basic sketch of how a Christian pluralist might respond to these approaches to diversity.

First, a Christian pluralist will—without a doubt—fully embrace *descriptive pluralism*. She will take the deep differences of cultures, communities, and faiths seriously. She will do so because she believes human beings are worthy of careful listening, analysis, and description because they are made in the image of God. At first blush, committing oneself to merely describing diversity accurately does not sound like a difficult task. That said, we will soon see that there is a consistent pattern in the West of reducing diverse and multifaceted cultures, communities, and faiths to simplistic caricatures. Soon enough we will find that the simple act of listening and paying attention to the complexity of human life is not only a critical skill; it is a virtue.

Second, on the question of *juridical pluralism*, the Christian pluralist will absolutely insist that her government protect the legal rights and freedoms of different cultures, religions, associations, and ideologies from undue harassment and harm. Even if she deeply disagrees with their philosophical direction, she will demand a generous amount of freedom for a diversity of communities, faiths, and cultures. The low-grade versus high-grade issue (whether governments should actively finance diversity) will receive a more complex answer later on. Finally, if one group is committing violence against another group, the Christian pluralist will support the state's responsibility to coercively protect the rights and safety of other faiths, communities, and cultures.

Third, on the question of *normative pluralism* the response of the Christian pluralist will be split in two. Her evaluation of cultural and structural diversity will differ from her evaluation of ideological diversity.

She will argue without reservation for cultural diversity as a normative good. She will insist that her God not only desires cultural diversity but also takes delight in pluriformity of human cultures. Moreover, she will argue that God desires and delights in structural and social diversity as well. She will be grateful for the diverse proliferation of human families, schools, clubs, organizations, universities, artist communities, and publications. She will see these communities and associations as representing the flourishing of God's creation. This does not mean that she will see no moral faults in diverse cultures and communities. It simply means that she will not see the diversity of cultures and associations as a problem that must solved—she will see it as a good that must be celebrated.

This leaves the question of religious or directional diversity. We have already stated that the Christian pluralist is deeply committed to listening to and carefully describing diverse religions and ideologies. We have already stated that the Christian pluralist will fiercely defend the public rights and freedoms of diverse religions and ideologies. That said, can she actively give praise and take delight when people choose life-directions that lead away from her God? This book stands in the historic tradition of Christian orthodoxy and assumes that the answer is "no." This book works out of the basic assumption that God has designed humanity to be in relationship with him, that only in communion with God can humanity fully flourish and find its true home.

The Christian pluralist can faithfully describe other faiths, she can passionately defend their rights, and she can even praise their many contributions to the common good. She cannot, however, take delight in the fact that they are directing their lives away from God. While she will never force everyone to follow Christ, she cannot—and will not—deny that she wants everyone to know Christ.

The pluralist's exclusive loyalty to Christ as the only life-direction and her refusal to praise the fact that other life-directions lead away from Christ will be quite unpopular today. Critics like Rousseau will argue that her exclusive following of Jesus will make it impossible for her to defend those who follow another.

According to such an assumption, Christian pluralism has an internal contradiction—an oxymoron. The assumption, quite simply, is that in order to be a good pluralist one must let go of one's own faith and one's own community. It is suggested that one should take a posture of religious ambivalence, uncertainty, and vacillation. The important thing, it is said, is that you not take beliefs too seriously. Beliefs, after all, are assumed to be a danger to democracy—not an asset. Ambivalence, not conviction, is the source of pluralism.

This book will directly challenge this assumption. It will demonstrate that a durable defense of Muslim rights and dignity depends, not on ambivalence, but on conviction. Following Christ, the pluralist is commanded to faithfully describe and politically defend Muslim clothing, literature, families, and schools. Demanding that the Christian pluralist assume a posture of ambivalence toward Christ will rob her pluralism of its foundation, inspiration, and strength. Reducing Jesus to one moral teacher among many, the carpenter from Nazereth might inspire the pluralist to love her friends—but never her enemies.

Hegemony and Uniformity

Throughout the book I will frequently use the terms *hegemony* and *uniformity* to speak about a pervasive temptation afflicting every religious and secular movement on earth. By hegemony and uniformity I mean to describe the universal human temptation to control and finally neutralize cultural, social, and ideological difference. In an age of globalization, the experience of deep, fast, and close difference naturally inspires feelings of anxiety and insecurity. Every ideology (religious and secular) struggles with an internal temptation to solve those feelings of fear by way of an enforced uniformity and hegemony.

The forces of hegemony and uniformity can be found in the Roman persecution of early Christianity, in the Muslim conquest of North Africa, in the Catholic Inquisition, in the Puritan witch hunts, in the French Revolutionary guillotine, in the Nazi Holocaust, in the communist prisons of Russia, in the Hindu persecution of Islam, in the Buddhist nationalism of Sri Lanka, and in the capitalistic imperialism of the United States. No ideology, religious or secular, is free from the temptations of hegemony and uniformity.[26]

While these overtly violent examples of hegemony can be clearly recognized and critiqued, ideologies often take a more subtle (but no less effective) path to enforced uniformity. When a dominant majority finds a minority undesirable, it can use a wide variety of slow and subtle bureaucratic forces to methodically discipline, marginalize, demean, and finally assimilate the undesired minority. Whether explosive or bureaucratic, the temptation for hegemony is pervasive. No religion, culture, or ideology can fully escape its siren call.

In the end, every community must answer a single question: "If we as a community cannot completely extinguish this temptation for hegemony and uniformity, how can we at least mitigate its destructive effects?" Different ideological communities will naturally come to different answers. This book is not interested in answering this question for all religions and ideologies.

---

26. Charles Kimball, Mark Juergensmeyer, and many others have famously outlined the many ways in which different religious movements can fall into patterns of violence and hegemony. William Cavanaugh has pointed out a significant blind spot in their analysis, the tendency of secular movements to fall into the exact same patterns of violence and hegemony. See William Cavanaugh, *The Myth of Religious Violence* (Oxford: Oxford University Press, 2009); Mark Juergensmeyer, *Terror in the Mind of God: The Global Rise of Religious Violence* (Berkeley: University of California Press, 2000); Charles Kimball, *When Religion Becomes Lethal: The Explosive Mix of Politics and Religion in Judaism, Christianity, and Islam* (San Fransisco: Wiley & Sons, 2011).

It is attempting to help one community—Christianity—think about how it might fight its own temptation for hegemony and become a positive force for deep pluralism.

Abstraction and Contextualization

In philosophical and theological discussions of pluralism, abstraction is often the order of the day. Political philosophers and theologians often speak abstractly of religion A, religion B, and religion C living together in imaginary public square X. They then articulate the extent to which religions A, B, and C are free to express a series of abstract ideas in the public square. They then articulate a series of abstract restrictions that public square X can rightly place on them.

Such abstract discussions of pluralism commonly survey the classical political theories of John Locke, Jean-Jacques Rousseau, Thomas Jefferson, John Rawls, and Isaiah Berlin and then move on to interact with contemporary theorists like Richard Rorty, William Kymlicka, Jeffrey Stout, Alasdair MacIntyre, William Connolly, and the like. Theoretical positions are clarified, analyzed, and compared. Such abstract discussions can be extremely helpful in isolating critical questions about the theoretical nature of rights and freedoms, democratic discourse, and foundational concepts like justice, liberty, and the state.

While helpful and important, these abstract discussions run the risk of reducing the issue of pluralism to nothing more than a conflict of disembodied ideas. Framed in such a way, the challenge and solution to pluralism becomes strikingly simple—outline which disembodied ideas are allowed in the public square, decide how those disembodied ideas should be communicated, and finally decide how the state should referee the exchange of those disembodied ideas.

The embodied and clothed presence of a veiled Muslim woman walking through the streets of Amsterdam shines an embarrassing light on those who would attempt to reduce pluralism to the contestation of disembodied ideas. On the streets of Paris, London, and Berlin urbanites are confronted, not simply with a contestation of ideas, but with the gritty questions of clothing, race, food, gender, family, colonial history, language, jokes, neighbor disputes, murders, bombs, media hype, and national hysteria.[27] For most Europeans,

27. For in-depth anthropological and sociological explorations of encounters between

pluralism is so much more than the mere contestation of ideas in an imagined public square. It is a messy, ineffable, earthy, and emotionally charged encounter between very different ways of living in the world.[28]

Therefore, in an effort to wade into the embodied grit of pluralism's challenge, my primary conversation partner will not be an abstract political theory or theorist but a real material context—the Netherlands.

The Netherlands: A Case Study

Why the Netherlands? Why not France, Germany, Canada, or my own country of the United States? There are many reasons, but here are a few. First, the Netherlands has one of the oldest and largest populations of Muslims in the West. Second, the Dutch experience with Islam is regularly cited (or incorrectly cited) in international debates about how the West should respond to Islam.[29] Third, the Netherlands is the most densely populated country in Europe. Packed tightly together, Muslims, Christians, Jews, secular liberals,

---

Muslims and non-Muslims in Europe see Hakan Yilmaz and Çagla E. Aykaç, eds., *Perceptions of Islam in Europe: Culture, Identity, and the Muslim "Other"* (London: Tauris, 2012).

28. The following are some examples of contemporary political theorists who have thoughtfully made this argument: Adam Seligman and Robert Weller, *Rethinking Pluralism: Ritual, Experience, and Ambiguity* (Oxford: Oxford University Press, 2012); William Connolly, *Pluralism* (Durham, NC: Duke University Press, 2005). I will return to their arguments in chapter seven.

29. Consider, for example, the following international appeals to the Dutch experience with Islam: Bruce Bawer, *While Europe Slept: How Radical Islam Is Destroying the West from Within* (New York: Broadway Books, 2006); Craig S. Smith, "In Mourning Slain Filmmaker, Dutch Confront Limitations of Their Tolerance," *New York Times*, November 11, 2004; William Pfaff, "Europe Pays the Price for Cultural Naïveté," *International Herald Tribune*, November 11, 2004; Andrew Stuttaford, "How Enlightenment Dies," *National Review*, November 12, 2004; Suzanne Fields, "The Menace of Multiculturalism: Amnesia Renders the West Unable to Defend Itself," *Washington Times*, September 15, 2005; Theodore Dalrymple, "A Wiser Holland: The Dutch, Mugged by Reality, Toughen Up on Radical Islam," *National Review*, January 30, 2006; Robert Carle, "Demise of Dutch Multiculturalism," *Society*, March/April 2006; Bruce Bawer, *Surrender: Appeasing Islam, Sacrificing Freedom* (New York: Anchor, 2010); Mark Steyn, *America Alone: The End of the World as We Know It* (Washington, DC: Regnery, 2006); Bridgette Gabriel, *They Must Be Stopped: Why We Must Defeat Radical Islam and How We Can Do It* (New York: St. Martin's Press, 2008); Abigail R. Esman, *Radical State: How Jihad Is Winning over Democracy in the West* (Santa Barbara, CA: Praeger, 2010); Bruce Bawer, "Paradise Lost in the Netherlands," *Christian Science Monitor*, May 19, 2006; Rod Dreher, "Murder in Holland: Pim Fortuyn, Martyr," *National Review*, May 7, 2002; H.E. Baber, *The Multicultural Mystique: The Liberal Case against Diversity* (Amherst, NY: Prometheus, 2008).

populists, multiculturalists, and nationalists all seem to live directly on top of each other. Every day, Dutch citizens are confronted with differences that are deep, close, and sometimes very intense. Dense cities like Amsterdam, Rotterdam, and Utrecht demand more than ideas about pluralism; they demand a deep and sustainable life of pluralism. Fourth, Dutch Muslims, Christians, and Secularists have all, in their own ways, contributed to the escalation of the Dutch conflict—none of them has clean hands. The messiness and complexity of the Dutch conflict demand more than simplistic accusations or easy solutions.

Finally—and most importantly—the Netherlands is the birthplace of a small but robust tradition of Christian pluralism. This tradition—while incomplete and imperfect—holds rich resources for Christians who wish to live a life of justice, hospitality, and pluralism in an age of fear and fragmentation.

Book Summary

The chapters of the book are organized to answer a single guiding question: What do Christians need to faithfully respond to the growing presence of Islam in the West?

- *First, Christians need to seriously wrestle with the problem.* In order to resist simplistic solutions, they must pay careful attention to the complexity and depth of Islam's challenge to the West. Chapters one and two provide a thorough analysis of how this particular conflict has taken shape on the ground in the Netherlands.
- *Second, Christians will need an alternative model to follow.* If Christians are going to avoid the dead-end solutions of the right and left and temptations of hegemony and uniformity, they will need an alternative model, a third way. Chapter three explores how the nineteenth-century movement for Christian pluralism began, how it resisted hegemony, and finally how it campaigned for pluralism. Despite the clear contextual differences, this nineteenth-century movement offers numerous critical insights for how a contemporary third way might be conceived.
- *Third, Christians will need to develop robust theological arguments against hegemony, uniformity, and assimilation.* Abraham Kuyper, the leader of the nineteenth-century pluralists, articulated a creative Christian case against all forms of religious and secular hegemony. Chapter four examines Kuyper's criticisms of political assimilation, and it explores how his

work may inform contemporary debates about Islamic integration and assimilation.

- *Fourth, Christians will need not only deconstructive arguments against uniformity but will need constructive arguments on behalf of pluralism.* Chapter five explores Abraham Kuyper's Christ-centered argument for a Christian pluralism. Kuyper depicts Christ as a sovereign king who demanded justice for all religions and ideologies under his sovereign rule—even those who denied Christ's very kingship.

- *Fifth, Christians cannot, however, simply look to the past; they must look forward.* While appreciative of Kuyper's work, the second interlude outlines three ways in which his nineteenth-century arguments for pluralism stand in need of future development. The next three chapters address these areas in light of the current conflict over Islam in the West.

- *Sixth, Christians need a complex understanding of the whole Christ to respond to a complex issue like Islam in the West.* Christians need more than Kuyper's royal picture of Christ the King. They also need Christ's hospitality, liberation, healing, and grace. They need Christ the servant and sacrifice, Christ the prophet and priest. Chapter six supplements Kuyper's royal Christology with a broader set of Christological images. It is argued that a richer picture of Christ's work will provide a richer understanding of what it means to follow him amidst this conflict.

- *Seventh, it is not enough for Christians to simply understand pluralistic ideas in their heads; they must actually desire pluralism in their hearts.* If pluralism is just an intellectual concept, if it is not deeply desired, deeply felt, it will not be able to endure the raw challenges and difficulties of life amidst this conflict. Chapter seven explores how Christians can develop the habits, practices, and desires of pluralism through worship. It will be argued that the sanctuary can act as a critically formative space in which a Christian citizen can develop the habits of the heart they need for life amidst the conflict.

- *Eighth, Christians need real examples of what real Christian action amidst this conflict looks like.* Chapter eight provides, not a single conclusive answer, but a mosaic of smaller answers. The chapter shares a medley of stories of real Christians in everyday callings seeking to embody Christ's justice, hospitality, and grace amidst the conflict. It turns out that Christian nurses and teachers, doctors and pastors, politicians and mothers, universities and churches, sewing groups and families all have a role to play in mending this conflict. None of these actors answers the question completely; none of them answers it perfectly. However, in their own finite and imperfect ways, each of them reflects some aspect of the hospitable, just, and gracious one that they follow.

As an American citizen I felt compelled to apply all of these lessons to my own American context and the American church. The recent rise of Donald Trump and the growing strength of nationalism and Islamophobia in my country only encouraged this instinct. Therefore, the final section closes the book asking what American Christians might learn from the European conflict and how they might put into practice the theological resources Christian pluralism has to offer. This final section, therefore, explores the unique challenges and story of Islam in America, the ways in which Muslims are engaging American public life, and finally how American Christians might apply the lessons of Christian pluralism in their own context.

The Tolerance of the Fundamentalist

Reverend Kees Sybrandi was not, by any stretch, a model example of interfaith awareness and tolerance.[30] When I asked him what he thought about Muslims, he complained that they had created a lot of trouble in the Netherlands. He complained about Muslim poverty, crime, urban blight, terrorism, and government dependency. A very conservative Christian, Pastor Sybrandi firmly insisted that Jesus Christ is the only way, the only truth, and the only life worth having. He insisted that Islam was a false religion and he called Allah a desert demon spirit.

Sybrandi's attitude about Islam made his response to Theo van Gogh's murder in 2004 all the more confounding. Across the Netherlands, tensions were running high; mosques and churches were being vandalized and even burned. In a curious response, Sybrandi stood up and walked to his neighborhood mosque. He knocked firmly on the door and, to the shock of the Muslims huddled inside, he declared that he would stand guard outside the mosque every night until the Dutch attacks ceased. In the days and weeks that followed, the pastor called other churches in the area, and more and more Christians joined him, circling and guarding mosques throughout the region for more than three months.

But why? What possible reason would this conservative Christian give to explain his actions? What could have motivated him, of all people, to do this?

---

30. Kees Sybrandi, interview conducted by the author, Lelystad, NL, May 5, 2012.

Sybrandi showed little awareness of the more peaceful aspects of Islam. He showed no appreciation for Islamic culture, clothing, or food. He recounted no stories of past friendships or dialogues with Muslims. Nor did he profess that as a loyal citizen of the Netherlands it was his patriotic duty to show liberal tolerance toward Islam. He was not inspired by modern dogmas of liberty, equality, or fraternity. Multicultural appeals for a celebration of difference had little pull on his heart. When I pressed him to explain his actions, to give some account for why he would defend a religion he deeply disliked, Sybrandi simply replied, "Jesus. Jesus commanded me to love my neighbor—my enemy too."

PART ONE

Mecca and Amsterdam: A Case Study

CHAPTER ONE

The Myth of Multiculturalism

Multiculturalism has been relegated to the dung-hill of history.
JEROEN DOOMERNIK[1]

In 2011, the political leaders of France, Germany, and the United Kingdom achieved something rare—unanimous agreement. They all agreed on two critical points that would have a major impact on the future of Islam in Europe. First, they agreed that the millions of Muslims living in Europe constituted a problem that needed to solved. And second, they agreed their past solution— something they called multiculturalism—had been a complete and unmitigated failure. David Cameron, then British prime minister, argued that the policies of multiculturalism have had "disastrous results"; they have "totally failed," added German chancellor Angela Merkel; and "Clearly, yes, it is a failure," concluded Nicolas Sarkozy, then president of France. Looking back on this supposed disaster, Sarkozy insisted that there was now only one solution to the Muslim problem. Muslims in France must now "melt into a single community, which is the national community, and if [they] do not want to accept that, [they] cannot be welcome in France."[2]

These politicians were not speaking out of turn; they were giving voice

1. Jeroen Doomernik, "Integrating Former Guest Workers and Their Descendants: The Dutch Case," paper given at the Trans-Atlantic Perspectives on International Migration: Cross Border Impacts, Border Security, and Socio-Political Responses Conference, University of Texas at San Antonio, March 5, 2010.

2. "Nicolas Sarkozy joins David Cameron and Angela Merkel view that multiculturalism has failed," *Daily Mail*, February 11, 2011.

to a deep and dramatic shift that had occurred in European political culture. Before this shift, during the twentieth century, criticism of immigrants or immigration policy had been largely ignored or, more accurately, suppressed. No one would discuss it. However, at the turn of the century and in the wake of a series of terrorist attacks, rising urban crime levels, and a collection of fierce controversies regarding religious freedom, the long-standing gag order began to fail. By 2011, the dam of political silence on the issue had burst completely. A series of sweeping statements about Islam raced across the European political scene. Activists, citizens, and, increasingly, politicians began to openly argue that Islam was a problem, that Muslim immigrants were failing to integrate, that they represented a threat to the European way of life, and, finally, that something called multiculturalism was to blame for all of this.[3]

Rather than the anemic and effeminate policy of multiculturalism, Europeans were increasingly demanding something David Cameron called "muscular liberalism."[4] Cameron insisted that Europe needed a more aggressive and confident form of liberalism and that the continent required an ideological posture that was not afraid to enforce secular values on religious newcomers. Politicians like Merkel, Sarkozy, and Cameron soon began to argue that Europe needed to stand up for secular liberalism and force Islam to a point of decision—either integrate or go home.

The muscular liberalism of Cameron, Merkel, and Sarkozy in 2011 is now considered quite moderate in today's European political theater. In the years since 2011, each of these leaders' center-right parties have been outflanked by the far-right on the issue of Islam. Nationalist parties have risen in the United Kingdom, France, Germany, the Netherlands, Belgium, Austria, Switzerland, Scandinavia, and beyond. For these emerging populist movements of European nativism, the old policies of multiculturalism are said to represent the naïve dreams of the past. Muscular liberalism, on the other hand, is said to be the absolute necessity of the future.

This dramatic shift in European political culture is now being mirrored across the Atlantic in American politics. A simple comparison of the rhetoric of two Republican presidents will sufficiently tell the tale. In 2001, mere days after the attacks of 9/11, President George W. Bush met with American Muslim leaders and, following their meeting, he had this to say:

---

3. A fine summary of this trend can be found in John Bowen's "Europeans against Multiculturalism," *Boston Review*, July/August, 2011.

4. Bagehot, "Muscle vs. Multiculturalism," *The Economist*, February 10, 2011.

The face of terror is not the true faith of Islam. That's not what Islam is all about. Islam is peace. These terrorists don't represent peace. They represent evil and war. America counts millions of Muslims amongst our citizens, and Muslims make an incredibly valuable contribution to our country. Muslims are doctors, lawyers, law professors, members of the military, entrepreneurs, shopkeepers, moms, and dads. And they need to be treated with respect. In our anger and emotion, our fellow Americans must treat each other with respect. Women who cover their heads in this country must feel comfortable going outside their homes. Moms who wear cover must be not intimidated in America. That's not the America I know. That's not the America I value.[5]

Juxtapose George W. Bush's posture toward Islam with that of his Republican heir Donald Trump fifteen years later. In 2016, Trump pointed to Roosevelt's decision to intern Japanese Americans during World War II as a justification for his call not only to halt all Islamic immigration into the United States but to form a national database to register and track all Muslims in the country. In addition, Trump called for a new "intense screening" process for all Muslim immigrants to ascertain their convictions regarding democracy, free speech, and American ideals.

Fifteen years earlier, Donald Trump's proposals would have been roundly condemned by both parties as bigoted and fundamentally anti-American. His presidential candidacy would have been dismissed as a fringe movement. Not in 2016. Like Europe's, American political culture has shifted dramatically on the question of Islam. Labeling Donald Trump the instigator of this dramatic political shift fundamentally misses a deeper cultural shift going on in America. Donald Trump is not its founder or inventor; he is its current voice. Trump's speeches reflect a deep and growing anti-Islamic sentiment that has been slowly building throughout American political culture since 9/11 and even before.[6]

---

5. https://georgewbush-whitehouse.archives.gov/news/ releases/2001/ 09/20010 917–11 .html

6. Influential right-wing resources on the issue include: Bruce Bawer, *While Europe Slept: How Radical Islam Is Destroying the West from Within* (New York: Broadway Books, 2006); William Pfaff, "Europe Pays the Price for Cultural Naïveté," *International Herald Tribune*, November 11, 2004; Andrew Stuttaford, "How Enlightenment Dies," *National Review*, November 12, 2004; Suzanne Fields, "The Menace of Multiculturalism: Amnesia Renders the West Unable to Defend Itself," *Washington Times*, September 15, 2005; Bruce Bawer, *Surrender: Appeasing Islam, Sacrificing Freedom* (New York: Anchor, 2010); Mark Steyn, *America Alone: The End of*

The true instigators of this anti-Islamic movement in the United States have been a collection of right-wing authors, speakers, radio hosts, and columnists. These thought-leaders have been dedicated to influencing the Republican base since the 1990s on the issue of Islam. It is these people who have been carefully preparing the political soil for a populist like Donald Trump to take root. Any cursory survey of right-wing books or articles on the scourge of Islam in America will—without fail—include a variety of references to Islam in Europe. These books point to Europe as the cautionary tale for America. They argue that decades of liberal European tolerance and multiculturalism created a dangerous situation in which Europe could be overrun by burqas, minarets, crime, terrorism, and Shari'a.

Learning from Amsterdam

Whether European or American, anti-Islamic books and articles continually point to the failed multiculturalism of a single nation to make their point—the Netherlands.[7] These authors argue that the failures of Dutch multiculturalism clearly illustrate, once and for all, that Islam must be met, not with Western tolerance, but with Western strength. Pointing to the Netherlands, right-wing leaders insist that Muslims will only take advantage of Western generosity and freedom. In return for their benevolence, Europeans can expect nothing from Islam but terrorism, crime, unemployment, and segregation.

The fierce logic of this constructed narrative is airtight. The story of an apocalyptic clash between Mecca and Amsterdam is powerfully composed. It is filled with a compelling cast of characters, including oppressed Muslim

---

the World as We Know It (Washington, DC: Regnery, 2006); Bridgette Gabriel, They Must Be Stopped: Why We Must Defeat Radical Islam and How We Can Do It (New York: St. Martin's Press, 2008); Abigail R. Esman, Radical State: How Jihad Is Winning over Democracy in the West (Santa Barbara, CA: Praeger, 2010); H. E. Baber, The Multicultural Mystique: The Liberal Case against Diversity (Amherst, NY: Prometheus, 2008).

7. Bawer, While Europe Slept. Aspects of this narrative can also be found in the following works: Craig S. Smith, "In Mourning Slain Filmmaker, Dutch Confront Limitations of Their Tolerance," New York Times, November 11, 2004; Theodore Dalrymple, "A Wiser Holland: The Dutch, Mugged by Reality, Toughen Up on Radical Islam," National Review, January 30, 2006; Robert Carle, "Demise of Dutch Multiculturalism," Society March/April 2006; Bruce Bawer, Surrender: Appeasing Islam, Sacrificing Freedom (New York: Anchor, 2010); Bruce Bawer, "Paradise Lost in the Netherlands," Christian Science Monitor, May 19, 2006; Rod Dreher, "Murder in Holland: Pim Fortuyn, Martyr," National Review, May 7 2002; and in the sources mentioned in note 6.

women, naive multiculturalists, violent Muslim men, and courageous nationalist heroes willing to die a martyr's death for the cause of European values. This constructed narrative of Mecca and Amsterdam has spread through right-wing circles in both Europe and the United States. The title of Theodore Dalrymple's article perfectly captures its platonic ideal: "A Wiser Holland: The Dutch, Mugged by Reality, Toughen Up on Radical Islam." According to articles like these, it was as if multiculturalists had been mugged by the reality that Islam is nothing but a violent and fascist ideology—one that understands nothing but the language of force.

Told and retold by nationalists in Europe and the United States, the basic narrative goes like this: once upon a time the Netherlands was the most free, diverse, tolerant, and progressive nation in the world. Innocent and naïve, the Dutch generously welcomed Muslims into their multicultural Shangri-La. Blinded by their dream of a diverse and tolerant nation, the Dutch invited more and more Muslim immigrants to come and freely express their unique culture and values. All criticism of Islam was strictly forbidden in the Netherlands. Those who questioned Islam were labeled racists and bigots by a multicultural regime of political correctness. As Islam spread, the Dutch elites provided enormous government subsidies to Islamic families, organizations, and schools. (Here is where the constructed story takes an especially dark turn.) The tolerance and generosity of Dutch multiculturalism created a dangerous subculture of Islamic extremism. Multiculturalism actually created the dangerous situation of Islamic unemployment, dependency, segregation, crime, violence, and a whole host of other social problems. The constructed story of this clash between Mecca and Amsterdam concludes with the inevitable question, "What can we learn from all of this?" The answer is simple: since Islam will only bite our open and extended hand, then all that remains now is our fist.

Amsterdam Teaches America

Geert Wilders and Ayaan Hirsi Ali, two Dutch exports, have been the most ardent international storytellers of this constructed narrative. In recent years, they have traveled throughout Europe and the United States calling for a more muscular liberal response to Islam. Together, the two firebrands have played a significant role in bringing this narrative to American audiences through bestselling books, articles, speeches, cable news, and consultations with American politicians and media.

Ayaan Hirsi Ali lives in the United States and has worked for the American Enterprise Institute, a conservative think tank in Washington. From her position, Ali has written a host of popular pieces outlining the dangers of Islam and the failures of Dutch multiculturalism. She has given numerous speeches and interviews throughout the United States warning Americans not to make the same mistake as the Dutch.

Since his rise to power in the Dutch parliament, Geert Wilders has made several trips to the United States, speaking at numerous anti-Islamic political rallies, in American megachurches, and even at the 9/11 memorial site in New York City. Wilders has made appearances on Fox News with popular hosts like Glen Beck, Sean Hannity, and Bill O'Reilly. In each case, Wilders vividly retells the dark story of Mecca and Amsterdam and warns Americans about the dangers that will befall their nation if they walk the same path.

In 2011, Wilders gave a speech at Cornerstone Church in Madison, Tennessee, entitled "A Warning to America." There in the sanctuary, he argued, "My friends, I am sorry. I am here today with an unpleasant message. I am here with a warning. I am here with a battle cry: 'Wake up, Christians of Tennessee. Islam is at your gate.'" He continues, "Do not make the mistake which Europe made. Do not allow Islam to gain a foothold here."[8] A number of Tennessee towns not far from Cornerstone Church have made national headlines for publically banning Shari'a law and the construction of new mosques. A Republican senator invited Wilders to screen his new film *Fitna* (a documentary that compares Islam to Nazism) in the US Capitol building.[9] In 2012, Wilders gave a speech at the Western Conservative Summit in Denver and warned American conservatives, "If we do not stop Islamization, we will lose everything: our identity, our culture, our democratic constitutional state, our freedom, and our civilization."[10]

In New York, Wilders argued that "Judeo-Christian and humanist civilization is far superior to any other civilizations like the barbaric Islamic civilization. We should not be afraid to say so. It is more free, more democratic,

---

8. Geert Wilders, "A Warning to America," speech given at Cornerstone Church, Nashville, May 12, 2011, http://www.jihadwatch.org/2011/05/geert-wilders-a-warning-to-america .html (accessed February 6, 2013).

9. NIS News Bulletin, "Wilders Now a Celebrity in US and Prime Minister in Poll," NIS website http://www.nisnews.l/ public/030309_1.htm (accessed February 5, 2013).

10. Ernest Lunning, "Dutch law maker brings his crusade against Islam to conservative confab," *The Colorado Statesman*, July 6, 2012, http://www.coloradostatesman.com/content /993597-dutch-lawmaker-brings-his-crusade-against-islam-conservative-confab (accessed February 5, 2013).

more tolerant than any civilization the world has ever seen."[11] In another New York speech on September 11, 2010, he addressed the burgeoning debate over the proposed Manhattan mosque. Speaking of the victims of 9/11, Wilders declared, "For their sakes we cannot tolerate a mosque on or near Ground Zero. For their sakes loud and clear we say: No mosque here! For their sakes, we must draw the line. So that New York, rooted in Dutch tolerance, will never become New Mecca."[12]

Twisted Truths

What makes these constructed narratives of Mecca and Amsterdam truly dangerous is that they are not entirely wrong. Before we explore the significant flaws in these accounts, we must undertake an honest exploration of their partial truth. First, it is absolutely true that the Dutch spent a large amount of money helping Muslim immigrants and their various cultural organizations. It is true that the overall rates of crime, unemployment, and domestic violence are higher in immigrant versus native populations. It is true that some Muslim immigrants harbor anti-Western sentiments. It is true that a few have even acted violently on those sentiments. It is absolutely true that the failure of elite government bureaucrats to recognize the deep differences between Islamic and Dutch culture has led to serious problems. It is true that the politically correct gag order on all Dutch criticism of Islam was deeply counterproductive. Finally, it is true that if Islam is going to be a part of the West it must go through some kind of self-reflection and even change.[13] While these aspects of the story are true, they are certainly no more than half the story. In recent

11. Geert Wilders, "Speech to the Gatestone Institute" delivered in New York, NY, April 30, 2012, http://www.geertwilders.nl/index.php/in-english-mainmenu-98/in-the-press-main menu-101/77-in-the-press/1781-speech-geert-wilders-new-york-april-30 (accessed February 5, 2013).

12. Geert Wilders, "NYC Speech" given in New York on September 11, 2010. http://www .geertwilders.n l/index.php? option=com _contentandtask=viewandid=1712 (accessed February 5, 2013).

13. Reflections from Islamic leaders in Europe on the future of Islam and democracy can be found in Jytte Klausen, *The Islamic Challenge: Politics and Religion in Western Europe* (Oxford: Oxford University Press, 2005). See also Tariq Ramadan, *Western Muslims: From Integration to Contribution* (Swansea, UK: Awakening Publications, 2012). Abdullahi Ahmed An-Na'im, *Islam and the Secular State: Negotiating the Future of Shari'a* (Cambridge, MA: Harvard University Press, 2008).

years, a growing group of scholars has cast serious doubt on numerous aspects of this story and its dangerous implications.[14]

In later chapters we will develop, as promised, an alternative Christian reading and response to the conflict between Islam and the West, Mecca and Amsterdam, but we cannot hope to develop an alternative response until we have first accomplished two critical tasks. First, we must pay careful attention to the complexity and difficulty of the real-life challenges that Muslim immigrants bring to the West. In opposition to those on the left, we dare not ignore the depth of the challenge nor simply prescribe a little more awareness and tolerance as a solution. Second, in opposition to those on the right, we must deconstruct the simplistic and destructive narratives of populists like Geert Wilders, Ayaan Hirsi Ali, and Donald Trump. Their myopic narratives of Mecca and Amsterdam must be challenged. Their story's fierce logic allows for only one response—force. As long as their story stands unchallenged, there can be no space for an alternative Christian response.

Let me make one final comment before we begin our deconstruction of this narrative. My criticisms of Amsterdam and my defense of Mecca in the pages that follow may give the impression that I have over-corrected and made the opposite mistake—that I am now romanticizing Mecca and demonizing Amsterdam. This is not my intention. I regard both schools of thought represented by Mecca and Amsterdam to be complex philosophical, cultural, and political movements. Both hold within themselves potentials for peace and violence, generosity and selfishness. My desire here is to correct a dangerous

14. In this section I will draw heavily on the following works: Maarten P. Vink, "Dutch 'Multiculturalism' beyond the Pillarisation Myth," *Political Studies Review* 5 (2007): 337–50; Thijl Sunier, "Islam in the Netherlands: A Nation Despite Religious Communities?," in *Religious Newcomers and the Nation State: Political Culture and Organized Religion in France and the Netherlands*, Erik Sengers and Thijl Sunier, eds. (Delft, NL: Eburon, 2010); Thijl Sunier, "Assimilation by Conviction or by Coercion? Integration Policies in the Netherlands," in *European Multiculturalism Revisted*, Allesandro Silj, ed. (London: Zed Books, 2010), 216. Jan Willem Duyvendak, Trees Pels, and Rally Rijkschroeff, "A Multicultural Paradise? The Cultural Factor in Dutch Integration Policy," in *Bringing Outsiders In: Transatlantic Perspectives on Immigrant Political Incorporation*; Jennifer L. Hochschild and John H. Mollenkopf, eds. (Ithaca, NY: Cornell University Press, 2009); Alfonso Fermin, "Nederlandse Politeke Partijen Over Minderhedenbeliejd 1977–1995," (PhD diss., Utrecht University, 1997); Marcel Maussen, "Pillarization and Islam: Church-State Traditions and Muslim Claims for Recognition in the Netherlands," *Comparative European Politics* 10 (2012); Jan Willem Duyvendak, *The Politics of Home: Belonging and Nostalgia in Europe and the United States* (New York: Palgrave Macmillan, 2011); James Kennedy and Jan P. Zwemer, "Religion in the Modern Netherlands and the Problems of Pluralism," *Bijdragen en Mededelingen betreffende de Geschiedenis der Nederlanden* 125, no. 2/3 (2010): 237–68.

imbalance in the stories the West tells itself about the conflict between Mecca and Amsterdam. Many in the West are well aware of Islam's sins. Every evening we hear news stories of Muslim terrorism, crime, bigotry, fanaticism, patriarchy, and more. Westerners rarely hear stories about or consider their own contributions to the conflict. Both Mecca and Amsterdam have contributed to this so-called clash.

Questioning Dutch Tolerance

Amsterdam lives on in the mind's eye of the West as one of the most tolerant and progressive nations in the world. The Dutch largely earned this reputation for open-mindedness thanks to three historical periods of political development: the Golden Age (1600s), the age of "pillarization" (1900–1960), and finally the age of the progressive revolution (1960s).

These three periods of Dutch history can be used to devastating effect to make a clear dichotomy between the tolerant Dutch and the intolerant Muslim. The Dutch are described as uniquely and intrinsically peaceful, open-minded, pragmatic, and playful. Meanwhile, Muslims can be described as uniquely and intrinsically violent, close-minded, dogmatic, and joyless. Once this strict dichotomy between Mecca and Amsterdam has been constructed, the fierce logic of this clash of civilizations can be allowed its full force.[15] As we will see, a closer look at these three periods of Dutch history reveals that they are not as intrinsically peaceful and tolerant as we (or they) might imagine.

Period One: The Golden Age

During the seventeenth century, Dutch Protestants became internationally renowned for the high level of freedom they afforded religious minorities and

---

15. In my deconstruction of what we might call "the myth of Dutch tolerance," it will at times appear as though I (an American author) am being unfairly critical of the Dutch people, culture, and state. This is *not* my intention. First, my own country is far from blameless when it comes to religious, racial, cultural, and political intolerance. Second, my intention is not to set up a new binary in which Islam is a blameless victim and the Dutch are an evil oppressor. My goal, rather, is to destroy a destructive dichotomy that defines one community as perfectly fit to rule and the other as perfectly fit for domination. In this new narrative, I hope to contribute to a more complex picture of the conflict in which there are no clear heroes or villains and no simple solutions of either multicultural relativism or liberal assimilation.

political dissidents living within their borders. While most European countries busied themselves with bloody religious struggles, the Netherlands tolerated a remarkable amount of religious and ideological diversity.

This unique example of early modern forbearance is certainly worthy of considerable historical note.[16] That said, a few points should at least qualify today's effusive praise for this golden age of Dutch tolerance. First, while religious minorities were permitted to gather and worship, many of them were strictly required to do so privately. The nationally recognized Protestant churches had a clear monopoly on all public forms of worship. Second, while a diversity of political opinions and writings was permitted, actual political power was reserved for the Dutch Protestant elite. Third, while political refugees and dissidents were permitted to freely publish searing critiques of foreign political and religious leaders, they were not allowed to turn their critical eyes and pens on their Dutch Protestant hosts.

Finally, historians are beginning to argue that early forms of Dutch tolerance were inspired, not simply by a benevolent Dutch spirit, but also by powerful economic and political motivations. Dutch port cities during this period were aspiring to become major international centers of commerce. Protestant merchants working in these ports cared more about a smooth exchange of goods than in a rough enforcement of religion. Protestant dogmatism, it appears, was bad for Protestant capitalism.

Moreover, the Dutch state fundamentally lacked the political power to enforce a nationwide acceptance of the Dutch Reformed religion.[17] In essence, their loose confederation of provinces and cities could not establish a rigid theocracy even if they had wanted to. Any nationwide effort to enforce a single national theology would have been expensive, destabilizing, bloody, and ultimately unsuccessful.[18] As one historian notes, tolerance in the Netherlands was not the

---

16. Notable historical examinations of this period include Hsia Po-Chia and Henk van Nierop, eds., *Calvinism and Religious Toleration in the Dutch Golden Age* (Cambridge: Cambridge University Press, 2002); and Christiane Berkvens-Stevelinck, Jonathan Israel, and G. H. M. Posthumus Meyjes, eds., *The Emergence of Tolerance in the Dutch Republic* (Leiden: Brill, 1997).

17. "Contrary to the powerful European monarchies, the Dutch Republic in the pre-1795 period lacked a strong centralized government. As a result religious conformity could therefore not be as effectively implemented as an instrument of state power and authority. After all, the Dutch Republic was a federation of principalities, and even within the Republic's constituent parts administration often was decentralized. As a result, the confessionalization of Dutch state and society arguably was less extensive than in surrounding states," Kennedy and Zwemer, "Religion in the Modern Netherlands," 241.

18. "The highly fragmented and politically decentralized nature of the Dutch Republic opened up spaces for the organization of dissident religious groups. This did not happen

result of Dutch generosity. It was instead "born of necessity" and is best understood as "damage limitation—the avoidance of unpleasantness and conflict."[19]

In fact, scanning the history of Dutch tolerance, one finds a surprisingly consistent pattern. Political power is traditionally reserved for a single dominant ideology—first Catholicism, then Protestantism, and finally liberalism. Whatever the time period, the ruling ideological group reluctantly tolerates the minorities who stubbornly persist. These weaker ideologies are expected to keep their beliefs relatively private, docile, and submissive under the reign of the dominant ideology.

In other words, the history of a tolerance in the Netherlands has tended toward repetition—not progress. Time and time again, whether the ruling elites were religious or secular, the dominant ideology begrudgingly tolerates minorities, all the while slowly working to either systematically marginalize them or assimilate them into their ideal of the Dutch national whole. Throughout its history, religious and ideological diversity in the Netherlands has consistently been understood to be a problem to be solved—not a reality to be celebrated.

This telling of Dutch history flies directly in the face of popular Dutch histories that claim a smooth historical progress from religious restriction into secular liberty. These whiggish liberal histories of tolerance fail to recognize the striking similarities between secular and religious regimes and their poor treatment of ideological minorities.[20]

Period Two: The Age of Pillarization

While pragmatic ideological dominance is the historical norm for the Netherlands, there is, however, one extremely fascinating historical exception. For a

---

everywhere. In some parts of the Republic the political reformation took the form which was usual in the German Empire and led to confessional homogeneity. In several areas in the core of the Republic, however, both in the countryside and the cities, organized groups of religious dissenters emerged. . . . Conflicts about the amount of liberty such groups were to be allowed played themselves out in different local settings and had different results," Peter van Rooden, "Dutch Way of Dealing with Religious Differences," in *Religious Newcomers and the Nation State: Political Culture and Organized Religion in France and the Netherlands*, Erik Sengers and Thijl Sunier, eds. (Delft, NL: Eburon, 2010), 61.

19. Michael Wintle, *An Economic and Social History of the Netherlands, 1800–1920: Demographic, Economic and Social Transition* (Cambridge: Cambridge University Press, 2000), 265.

20. van Rooden, "Dutch Way of Dealing with Religious Differences," 59.

brief period, between 1900 and 1960, there was no dominant ideology in the Netherlands and four distinct ideological communities actually shared political and cultural power. During this period of pillarization, no single ideology was allowed to assert national dominance.

The story of pillarization begins in the early nineteenth century as up-and-coming liberals gradually took power away from Reformed elites. Dutch liberals sought to solve the Dutch problem of religious minorities by dramatically expanding the size, scope, and disciplinary power of the state. The centerpiece of their liberalizing campaign was the establishment of a government-run school system. Through these new government schools, Dutch liberals hoped to assimilate young Catholics, Calvinists, Anabaptists, Jews, and socialists into a liberal whole. Through the schools, they would end religious superstition and create a modern liberal nation.

While ambitious, their plans of liberal assimilation failed. The liberals overplayed their hand and awakened a powerful resistance movement from Catholics and Calvinists. But here is where the story gets interesting. Rather than violently ousting their liberal overlords and taking power for themselves, the Calvinists and Catholics proposed a new model in which political and cultural power could be shared—they called it *verzuiling* or pillarization.[21]

From roughly 1900 to 1960, the Netherlands, broadly speaking, became a nation of four equal power bases or subcultures (liberals, socialists, Calvinists, and Catholics). These four pillars shared cultural and political power. None of the four was permitted to dominate, assimilate, or direct the others. This period of pillarization has been examined and highlighted by numerous international scholars as a fascinating moment in political history.[22]

21. "Dutch pillarization, purportedly so characteristically Dutch, was resisted even in its heyday by many secularists and Protestants who thought it detracted from the social unity they thought the Netherlands required," James Kennedy, "Globalization, the Nation-state, and Religious Newcomers: Reflections on Two Countries," in *Religious Newcomers*, Sengers and Sunier, 160.

22. This balance of power was famously described as consociationalism. Arend Lijphart's political analysis on pillarization as a form of consociational power-sharing inspired a number of important works on politics in divided societies. Critical works include: Arend Lijphart, *The Politics of Accommodation* (Berkeley: University of California Press, 1968); Arend Lijphart, *Democracy in Plural Societies* (New Haven, CT: Yale University Press, 1977); R. Stiefhold, *Segmented Pluralism, Consociational Democracy and Austrian Electoral Politics* (Ann Arbor: University of Michigan Press, 1973); Matthijs Bogaards, "The Favourable Factors for Consociational Democracy: A Review," *European Journal of Political Research* 33, no. 4: 475–96; Adrien S. Ellebout, *The Limits of Consociationalism* (Saarbrücken, Germany: VDM Publishing, 2008); Arend Lijphart, "Consociational Democracy," *World Politics*, 21, no. 2 (1969): 207–25.

In recent years, a few have called for a resurrection of pillarization in response to the conflict between Mecca and Amsterdam. The thinking has been that a Muslim pillar of Islamic schools, organizations, newspapers, and political parties would empower Muslim immigrants. These proposals have been roundly criticized for a number of reasons. First, there is no longer a balance of ideological power in the Netherlands. Dutch liberalism is in complete control. The traditional opponents of liberalism (Catholics, Calvinists, and socialists) are now extremely weak. They can no longer check the pervasive and dominant cultural power of Dutch liberalism. Any new Muslim pillar would likewise have to live under the hegemony of Dutch liberalism. It would not be able to meaningfully check liberalism's power.

A final reason why reviving Dutch pillarization is problematic is that it does not resolve a critical issue facing Dutch society—the divisive segregation of immigrants and natives. The old system of pillarization was great for sharing of power. It did not, however, cultivate an understanding, interaction, or affection between the ideological pillars. The pillars did not particularly appreciate one another nor did they particularly desire the other.[23] Pillarization was not the result of a generous Dutch spirit—it was a grand bargain of necessity. None of the ideologies was strong enough to dominate, so they were forced to settle for a deal. Pillarization could balance interests; it could not, however, cultivate solidarity. In a country where tensions are high and trust is low, solidarity is desperately needed.

Period Three: The Age of Progressive Revolution

More than any historical period, the 1960s loom large in the self-understanding of Dutch citizens today. The sixties are seen as the critical historical moment in which the Dutch liberated themselves from the ideological divisions and dogmatisms of the past to create a progressive liberal future together. Freed from the religious past, they would endeavor to create a cosmopolitan playground of progressive values, individuality, exploration, self-discovery, and diversity.[24]

23. "The legendary Dutch historian Johan Huizinga once wrote that although the Dutch state was very liberal and tolerant, there was nothing especially tolerant or liberal about the Dutch themselves," Henk Te Velde, "Liberalism and Bourgeois Culture in the Netherlands, from the 1840s to the 1880s," in *Under the Sign of Liberalism: Varieties of Liberalism in Past and Present,* Simon Groenveld and Michael Wintle, eds. (Zutphen, NL: Walburg Pers, 1997), 120.

24. Peter van der Veer, "Pim Fortuyn, Theo van Gogh, and the Politics of Tolerance in the Netherlands," *Public Culture* 18, no. 1 (2006): 111–24.

The progressive liberal revolution of the 1960s marked the beginning of the end for three Dutch subcultures (Calvinism, Catholicism, and socialism). In the decades that followed, the individuals and institutions of these three pillars were rapidly assimilated into the new liberal whole. The rise of Dutch liberalism to a position of near total cultural, political, and ideological control is absolutely critical to understanding the nation's response to Islamic newcomers.

As mentioned earlier, the Dutch look back on the 1960s as the end of the age of conformity and restriction and the advent of the age of freethinking, diversity, and open-mindedness. Sociologists, however, are beginning to call their liberation story into question. It turns out that the Dutch are more ideologically uniform today than they have been in any age since the Reformation. When asked for their perspectives on the issues of sex, marriage, family, economics, politics, the environment, religion, life, death, and the good life, contemporary Dutch citizens demonstrate a higher degree of moral uniformity than nearly any nation in Europe.[25] Sociologist Willem Duyvendak notes that the liberal Dutch are "much more uniform in their opinions and attitudes than in their pillarized past."[26] The 1960s created "a rather homogeneous progressive moral majority."[27] Later on we will explore this observation that liberalism appears not to cultivate ideological freedom and diversity but their opposite.

Politically speaking, the Dutch are no longer accustomed to deep or principled political difference. The liberal consensus effectively ended the philosophical debates that used to mark the contests between Catholicism, Socialism, Calvinism, and liberalism. In the 1990s, Prime Minister Wim Kok, "stated with great complacency that the Dutch welfare state was now complete and only minor technical details were left for political discussion."[28] Dutch political debates had devolved into arguments over which party was better equipped to manage the liberal state, the liberal economy, and the liberal culture.[29] No longer did the socialist or Christian leaders seriously argue that the

---

25. Paul Mepschen, Jan Willem Duyvendak, and Evelien H. Tonkens, "Sexual Politics, Orientalism, and Multicultural Citizenship in the Netherlands," *Sociology* 44 (2010): 962–78.

26. Duyvendak, Pels, and Rijkschroeff, "A Multicultural Paradise?," 138–39.

27. Duyvendak, *The Politics of Home*, 87.

28. Peter van der Veer, "Pim Fortuyn, Theo van Gogh, and the Politics of Tolerance in the Netherlands," in *Political Theologies: Public Religions in a Post-Secular World*, Hent de Vries and Lawrence Eugene Sullivan, eds. (New York: Fordham University Press, 2006), 531.

29. "The convergence-pattern we do find is by no means a small matter. Some may rejoice about it in the name of 'consensus,' but they are obviously wrong. Democracy is not the end of conflict but conflict mastered. For a society to function democratically, agreements must be

government or the market rested under the sovereignty of either God or the workers' collective. No longer did they argue that politics should be guided by the principles of scientific socialism or divine law. After the 1960s, the distinct moral philosophies of socialism, Catholicism, and Calvinism were largely absorbed into the ideology of liberalism. Socialists and Christians alike traded in their distinct moral language for the liberal language of freedom, equality, technological progress, economic growth, social care, and responsibility. In 1996, *The Economist* attempted to explain their lack of reporting on Dutch politics by blaming it on liberalism's "boring success."[30] The Netherlands considered itself finished, complete, and whole. The liberal divines surveyed all that they had conquered and created, "And behold," Markha Valenta quips, they declared "it was good."[31]

As a result of this liberal uniformity, young Dutch citizens walking the streets of Amsterdam in the 1990s had no experience living in a culture in which liberalism was contested in any meaningful way. Liberal dominance was all they knew. Young Dutch liberals had no experience with a significant segment of Dutch society challenging the cultural and political status quo.

In the 1950s, the Netherlands was considered a conservative European backwater with one of the highest rates of church attendance in all of Europe. By the 1970s, the Netherlands had largely cohered into the liberal consensus. In a remarkably short amount of time, and with a shocking lack of resistance, the Netherlands had not only caught up with but surpassed the rest of Europe in its zealous pursuit of liberalism. Soon enough, Ian Buruma argues, the Dutch began to think of themselves as the global leaders of the progressive movement. Their sense of cosmopolitan liberation from religion "led to an air of

---

established over the framework and modalities of political debate. If these agreements result in the disappearance of debate, however, democracy will also pass away. Democracy implies a diversity of opinions and choices as well as the recognition of the legitimacy of conflicts between them. Yet, if parties are no longer distinguished by anything other than insignificant differences in their manifestos and advocate basically the same policies, if citizens no longer see themselves confronted with real political alternatives, then debate ceases to have any raison d'être and the democratic framework for it becomes nothing more than an empty shell which most people, not surprisingly, prefer to ignore. Maybe the real question is not whether left-right ideology in Holland has had its day, but when and in what form it will return," Rob Eisinga, Philip Hans Franses, and Marius Ooms, "Convergence and Persistence of Left-Right Political Orientations in the Netherlands 1978–1995," *Econometric Institute Report* (1997), 20.

30. *The Economist*, October 12, 1996.

31. Markha Valenta, "How to Recognize a Muslim When You See One: Western Secularism and the Politics of Conversion," in *Political Theologies: Public Religions in a Post-Secular World*, Hent de Vries and Lawrence E. Sullivan, eds. (New York: Fordham University Press, 2006), 465.

satisfaction, even smugness, a self-congratulatory notion of living in the finest, freest, most progressive, most decent, most perfectly evolved playground of multicultural utopianism."[32]

Spiritual but Not Tolerant

They have privatized all religions and ideologies, except their own.

GERT-JAN SEGERS[33]

What happened to religion in the Netherlands after the 1960s? To use the term *secularization* might be a bit misleading. In recent years, a number of sociologists have begun to question the popular argument that religion just up and died in the Netherlands after the sixties.

A number of scholars now insist that religion was not destroyed—it was simply disembedded. According to Meerten Ter Borg, "disembedded religion" is a postmodern manifestation of religion that has broken free from bounded religious institutions, systems, and dogmatic beliefs.[34] James Kennedy describes the disembedding process as moving through three historical phases in the Netherlands since the 1960s—religion as social organization, religion as social activism, and finally religion as individualistic spirituality.[35] Understanding how today's Dutch citizens transitioned from institutional religion to individualistic spirituality will be critical to understanding their future reactions to Islamic immigrants.

According to Kennedy, during the 1960s the Dutch became convinced that traditional religion was too dogmatic and too conservative to contribute to the emerging liberal consensus. Kennedy remarks that "in a cultural environment where openness and unity were buzzwords of the first order" Christianity's boundaries "increasingly became an embarrassment."[36]

---

32. Buruma, *Murder in Amsterdam*, 11.

33. Gert-Jan Segers, *Voorwaarden Voor Vrede: De komst van de Islam, de integratie van moslims en de identiteit van Nederland* (Amsterdam: Buijten En Schipperheijn B.V., 2009), 44.

34. Meerten Ter Borg, "Some Ideas on Wild Religion," *Implicit Religion* 7, no. 2 (2004): 108–19.

35. James C. Kennedy, "Recent Dutch Religious History and the Limits of Secularization," in *The Dutch and Their Gods: Secularization and Transformation of Religion in the Netherlands since 1950*, Eric Sengers, ed. (Hilversum: Uitgeverij Verloren, 2005), 40.

36. James C. Kennedy, "Building the New Babylon: Cultural Change in the Netherlands during the 1960s," (PhD diss., University of Iowa, 1995), 40.

During the 1960s and 1970s, an astounding number of Catholics and Calvinists abandoned their churches to join with the liberal consensus. In response to this exodus, many churches became convinced that they needed to fit in with the new liberal consensus.[37] These churches quickly adopted the social activism model of religion. Here religions try to prove that they can contribute to the liberal consensus and its pet projects (such as third-world aid, nuclear nonproliferation, environmental care, the end of apartheid, and the rise of the United Nations).

The church's adoption of these causes did not have its desired effect. The more churches sought to convince their members that they were identical to the liberal consensus, the more their people stopped coming to church. Why, after all, should a person continue living in a subculture if it is no different from the dominant culture? According to Kennedy,

> The "open" churches of the 1960s won the respect of many outsiders, but they won few converts. In this time of great ecumenism—when goodness and truth were no longer confined to a particular faith—there were *less*, not more, reasons to join a church or stay in one. Ethics, morality, even faith no longer needed a church. Moreover, in a world where openness and solidarity were widely praised, the churches could only lose.[38]

By the 1980s, the social activism model of religion, having dissolved most religious institutions, gave way to the final incarnation of Dutch religion—individualistic spirituality.[39] During this historical phase, self-actualizing spirituality quickly became "the dominant religious motif in the Netherlands."[40] Here religious impulses become "more individualistic, more diffuse, less ethical in intent, and more 'spiritual' in feeling."[41] Here, Ter Borg notes,

---

37. "In the mid-1960s, most Christian leaders still believed that timely and substantive changes might staunch the human flow out of the churches—and make the churches positive and necessary institutions in society. This would entail making the churches more 'secular' and profane, more relevant to the needs of 'modern man.' And that seemed in turn to require a new, more 'open' outlook that would reflect the growing unity of the world," Kennedy, "Building the New Babylon," 158.

38. Kennedy, "Building the New Babylon," 209.

39. Pun intended.

40. Kennedy, "Recent Dutch Religious History," 38.

41. Kennedy, "Recent Dutch Religious History," 38.

religiosity is separated from both social groups and traditions. As a consequence, it seems fragmented and disembedded. . . . Its content is neither consistent, nor compulsory. . . . Here, we find fragments or clusters of religious content, loosely knitted together . . . a colourful mix of all kinds of religious ideas and beliefs and practices. . . . The believers lack any theological discipline. . . . Because the elements of content are not dogmatic, they may be easily changed. Anything can be accepted, anything discarded. There is no other criterion for acceptance apart from emotional well-being or pragmatic expectation.[42]

These spiritual Dutch are convinced that there is something more to life. And yet, these spiritualists "obviously don't particularly care about the content or the meaning of this 'more.' If there is any belief left here, it is in no way integrated with any other aspect of their daily life."[43] In this milieu, religion is declared "positive" only if it is "diffuse."[44] The chief religious virtue then is flexibility—the heart's unending embrace of fragmentation, contingency, and *bricolage*.

This is a remarkable transformation in the history of Dutch religion. For Dutch Catholics and Calvinists in the 1950s, religion was considered a sacred and unbreakable commitment to an institution, a lifestyle, and a belief system. Their faith pointed to a universal and sovereign reality. One's membership in this faith could not be altered without a traumatic rupture in one's identity. Fast forward to the 1990s, when the grandchildren of these institutional Catholics and Calvinists saw their faith as an individualistic, optional, emotional, and momentary tool for self-actualization. Their spiritual practices served their own personal needs for enlightenment, relaxation, and self-empowerment. The deep chasm between these religious grandparents and their spiritual grandchildren foreshadowed the coming conflict with Islam—a religion that takes its beliefs, morality, and community very seriously.

It is also important to note that the Dutch largely moved through these three historical periods together—as one people, one liberalizing nation. According to Kennedy, this is no surprise. For, he explains, "consensus-oriented societies like the Netherlands tend to create a broadly shared religious consensus about the legitimate place of religion in society in which each succeeding paradigm drives out the other."[45] It is no surprise, therefore, that the Dutch

---

42. Ter Borg, "Some Ideas on Wild Religion," 114–15.
43. Ter Borg, "Some Ideas on Wild Religion," 118.
44. Ter Borg, "Some Ideas on Wild Religion," 118.
45. Kennedy, "Recent Dutch Religious History," 40.

would eventually demand that Muslims reform their religion into a personal and private Muslim spirituality of diffuse feelings and experiences.

Kennedy concludes that the popular "secularization thesis, has had a huge impact on how religion has been culturally constructed and understood in the Netherlands since the 1960s."[46] Secularization and modernization "now form for the Dutch a compelling 'master narrative.'"[47] Their own particular path of spiritual progress is interpreted as the universal path upon which all religions must walk. Like them, all faiths must progress from institution to individuality, from dogma to feeling, from duty to pleasure, from ethics to empowerment. This is the natural, universal, inevitable, and proper evolutionary development of all religions.

In essence, Kennedy argues, the Dutch "see traditional, organized religion as belonging, in short hand, to the Middle Ages."[48] Their "construction of religion along the continuum 'medieval – modern'" continues to have a significant impact on how the Dutch understand Islam.[49]

A House Fit for Islam?

[The Dutch] "home" is constructed in such a way that [Islam] can never really feel a part of it.[50]

When Muslim immigrants began arriving in the Netherlands during the 1960s and 1970s, they encountered a culture that was becoming less, not more, prepared for their arrival. These modern Dutch citizens remembered their own religious past with regret and disgust. They were now being asked to welcome large numbers of immigrants for whom religion was absolutely central. Religious diversity was gone. Pillarization was finished. Ideological diversity and division had given way to the national liberal consensus. This is the Netherlands Muslim immigrants were stepping into. Instead of encountering citizens who were trained, ready, and willing to live alongside deep moral differences, the new immigrants found themselves surrounded by a progressive moral majority who desired unity and uniformity. Muslim immigrants encountered

46. Kennedy, "Recent Dutch Religious History," 29.
47. Kennedy, "Recent Dutch Religious History," 30.
48. Kennedy, "Recent Dutch Religious History," 30.
49. Kennedy, "Recent Dutch Religious History," 31.
50. Jan Willem Duyvendak, *The Politics of Home: Belonging and Nostalgia in Europe and the United States* (New York: Palgrave Macmillan, 2011), 101.

a culture that considered itself to be at the progressive forefront of human history. The foundational questions of sex, family, work, culture, and politics had been settled and put to rest by modern liberalism.[51] While Muslim immigrants could provide a quaint window into the world's past, only their Dutch hosts could provide a window into the world's future.

These new religious immigrants would be labeled medieval and would be examined through the historical lens of religious violence, dogmatism, duty, and social control. Religion was something the Dutch had courageously escaped and transcended. Islam, as a thick and ideologically distinct religious community, would be interpreted as a step backward.

Dutch Islam: Segregation, Integration, Assimilation

[The Dutch] are quite ready to extend their hands to those children, so long as they renounce the same things that Dutch progressives renounced not so very long ago.[52]

When Muslims immigrants began arriving in the Netherlands during the 1950s, their numbers and visibility were so insignificant that the Dutch largely ignored their presence. As their numbers grew in the 1960s, quiet discussions in The Hague focused on equipping these guest workers for their eventual return home. Government programs were developed to maintain indigenous cultures, languages, families, and faith until a humane return could be arranged.[53] Early on, there was no encouragement for these workers to learn Dutch or advance in their education and careers. Nor was there a desire for the immigrants to become involved in Dutch society. The living and working conditions of many of these guest workers were soon found to be below acceptable Dutch standards. Embarrassed to find such conditions in the most progressive nation in the world, politicians saw it as their duty to provide various forms of care for the workers during their temporary stay in the Netherlands.

Intentional or not, these early forms of government care communicated

---

51. "By the time Muslim immigrants began to arrive in significant numbers, religious controversies no longer structured policy alternatives and no longer formed the basis of inter-party policy competition," Doutje Lettinga, *Framing the Hijab: The Governance of Intersecting Religious, Ethnic, and Gender Differences in France, the Netherlands, and Germany* (Ridderkerk, NL: Ridderprint, 2011), 58.

52. Buruma, *Murder in Amsterdam*, 128–29.

53. Duyvendak, *The Politics of Home*, 86.

three important messages to migrant workers. First, their presence was little more than a temporary economic necessity. Second, while they fulfilled these economic functions for the Netherlands, they would be treated as objects of Dutch care. And third, the Dutch state had no interest in interacting with them as cultural, intellectual, or political partners in dialogue. Their existence in the Netherlands was limited to economic production and governmental care.

These early policies slowly began to shift during the 1970s.[54] If the goal of the first phase had been return, then the goal of the second was integration. Because the workers were refusing to leave, Dutch politicians decided that they needed to find a way to help them fit in. Early integration strategies were based on the assumption that guest workers first needed to be educated and empowered within their own ethnically specific organizations before they could achieve the ultimate goal of Dutch integration.[55] Politicians hoped that these immigrants, once empowered, would assimilate into the liberal consensus in the same way that the Calvinists, Catholics, and socialists had before them.

More and more scholars have convincingly demonstrated that the ultimate goal of these early efforts was not the multicultural protection of unique cultures but the eventual integration of those cultures into Dutch liberalism. According to Willem Schinkel, the Netherlands

> never had a "multiculturalist" policy. Its policies in the 1980s, geared toward the "preservation of cultural identity," were premised on the idea that cultural assimilation—in almost any sense the exact opposite of what can be reasonably called "multiculturalism"—would be best attained when immigrants were to emancipate starting from the strength of their own background. Once emancipated, they would cast off this background and their "integration" would be complete.[56]

54. Duyvendak, Pels, and Rijkschroeff, "A Multicultural Paradise?," 131.

55. Sunier, "Islam in the Netherlands?," 123. See also Sunier, "Assimilation by Conviction or by Coercion?," 220.

56. Willem Schinkel, "The Politicization of Culture in the Netherlands," *Metropolis M* 3 (2011) http://metropolism.com/magazine/2011-no3/realpopulism-the-politicization/english (accessed February 6, 2013). Maarten Vink adds that, "There was never any serious discussion of an unequivocal right to express their identities from an assumed symmetry of cultures. . . . The group-oriented basis of the ethnic minority policy may have reflected a 'pilllarisation reflex,' but newcomers simply lacked the necessary power basis to claim a form of cultural autonomy equal to that of the old denominational groups," "Dutch 'Multiculturalism' beyond the Pillarisation Myth," 345. Justus Uitermark submits that these initiatives did not betray "a desire to preserve or celebrate minority cultures but to make sure that ethnic communities did not fall victim to the twin processes of cultural isolation and economic deprivation. The

During the 1980s, the Dutch state focused on funding immigrant organizations that were explicitly cultural or ethnic in their orientation. Institutions marked by a religious identity were excluded primarily because "policymakers were convinced that religious organizations were ill-equipped to help immigrants form a bridge to the larger society. Religious organizations were assumed, after all, to keep people in isolation."[57]

Integration policies were driven exclusively by elite Dutch politicians and bureaucrats in The Hague. The Dutch people and—more importantly—the immigrants themselves, had no substantive involvement in these discussions. This fateful decision would contribute to an increasing sense of frustration and resentment in both communities. Muslim immigrants were told that they would be well cared for and Dutch citizens were instructed to wait patiently for the inevitable assimilation process to achieve its end. Political elites defended immigrants from criticism out of a fear that such criticism would delay the assimilation process.

Applying the political labels of multiculturalism and pillarization to these policies toward Islam is problematic for three reasons. First, multiculturalism argues that the state has a responsibility to protect the cultural integrity of minority communities. The end goal of these Dutch policies was clearly not cultural integrity but cultural integration. Second, pillarization was a system in which different ideologies were allowed to publically organize and articulate a specific set of social and political beliefs. These integration policies were never focused on the organization of Islamic beliefs for articulation in the Dutch public square. Third, while pillarization was a historical period in which elite representatives from different ideologies sat at a common table discussing a common future, these integration policies were developed without substantive representation from immigrant communities.[58]

During the 1980s, a small number of Christian Reformed scholars and activists (veterans of the old pillarized system) made the suggestion that the Netherlands attempt to form an Islamic pillar.[59] They argued that Muslims

---

sentiment that informed the minorities policy was one of anxious paternalism rather than enthusiastic multiculturalism," *Dynamics of Power in Dutch Integration Politics* (Amsterdam: Amsterdam University Press, 2012), 71.

57. Duyvendak, Pels, and Rijkschroeff, "A Multicultural Paradise?," 136–37.

58. Uitermark, *Dynamics of Power*, 73.

59. "The Danish researcher Klausen suggests that the Dutch once sought to create an 'Islamic pillar' and that this included policy measures such as funding for Muslim TV and the building of mosques as well as 'some measure of Muslim self-government.' The French scholar Gilles Kepel even suggested that the Dutch would nowadays allow 'a Muslim pillar'

should be encouraged to organize and advocate for their distinct social and political beliefs in the public square. This suggestion, however, was immediately dismissed by the majority of liberals and Christians alike, who all favored the goal of cultural integration into the liberal consensus.[60] In fact, as early as 1979, "the Scientific Council for Government Policy had already rejected the idea of creating a new Islamic pillar, fearing [Islam] would isolate itself from a secularized, individualistic society."[61]

By the close of the 1980s, these integration strategies were already considered a failure. The state's own assessment found that most of these cultural organizations "were using the money for their own benefit in an attempt to improve their organizational networks and to strengthen their communities, instead of promoting the integration process. . . . [G]overnment policies [had] the opposite effect from that intended."[62]

During the 1990s, politicians once again shifted their civilizing mission to Islam.[63] In this next stage, the Dutch state ignored ethnic communities and organizations and focused their integration efforts directly on individual immigrants. The goal here was to equip individual immigrants for participation in the modern marketplace.[64] The state hoped that economic participation would "lead to an erosion of the migrants' cultural baggage, or at least relegate

---

to function according to 'the Shari'a.' Paul Scheffer has written that 'many believed that using the means of pillarization' to integrate Muslims was 'a logical continuation of an old tradition with new means.' It is very much the question, though, who these 'many believers' were and how widespread this supposed support for pillarization actually was. In political debate, the clearest example is Kees Klop, who worked for the scientific bureau of the Christian Democrat Party and who spoke out in favor of the emergence of a Muslim pillar in an article published in 1982. He argued that Dutch history had shown that a certain level of isolation could be beneficial in the early stages of collective emancipation. Far from finding general enthusiasm for this idea, Klop's viewpoints were met with skepticism," Maussen, "Pillarization and Islam," 343.

60. "However plausible it may have seemed . . . to think about the creation of Islamic institutions in light of the Dutch history of pillarisation, in actual fact policy responses to the presence of Islam in the 1980s were barely shaped by this idea. There was never much enthusiasm to see an Islamic pillar emerge. The collapse of the pillarised society was interpreted as a result of processes of individual emancipation, democratisation and growing social mobility. The overall emphasis in policy was on participation and integration," Marcel Maussen, *Constructing Mosques: The Governance of Islam in France and the Netherlands* (Amsterdam: Amsterdam School for Social Science Research, 2009), 193.

61. Lettinga, *Framing the Hijab*, 68.

62. Sunier, "Assimilation by Conviction or by Coercion?," 222–23.

63. Sunier, "Assimilation by Conviction or by Coercion?," 225.

64. Fermin, *"Nederlandse Politieke Partijen,"* 289.

this to the non-political, private realm."[65] This market-based integration plan had some historical precedent. During the explosive economic growth of the 1960s, many Calvinists, Catholics, and radical socialists made a lot of money, and many quickly exchanged their distinct perspectives on money for the capitalistic worldview of the modern marketplace. Perhaps Muslims would follow their lead and exchange their faith for finances as well.

Throughout this entire process, the linguistic distinction between cultural integration and assimilation is reduced to a haze. Clearly the multiculturalism label cannot be seriously applied to any of these periods. The goal was not multiculturalism but monoculturalism. Thijl Sunier provides a much more accurate description of twentieth-century Dutch policy toward Islam—a "benevolent but patronizing assimilation."[66]

Cracks in the Dike

> If liberalism is going to take the ideas of liberty and toleration seriously, it must be prepared to tolerate non-liberal religions. To happily announce that liberals will tolerate liberals is to hollow out the meaning of toleration.
>
> JEFF SPINNER-HALEV[67]

This benevolent but patronizing policy toward Islam would not last forever. The public's patience with Islam's slow assimilation into Dutch culture was beginning to wane. Public criticism of Muslim immigrants during the 1980s had been expressly forbidden by liberal elites. Those who questioned the status quo were labeled as racists and bigots. In a culture that prides itself on progressivism, such labels were deadly.

In the 1990s, however, frustrations continued to grow and small cracks began to form in the dike of Dutch political correctness. In 1991, Frits Bolkestein, a member of a center-right party, gave a speech at the International Liberal Conference in Lausanne, Switzerland. In this speech, Bolkestein became the first mainstream politician to openly suggest that Islamic values clashed with liberal ones. He argued that one side or the other would ultimately need to

---

65. Sunier, "Assimilation by Conviction or by Coercion?," 220.

66. Thijl Sunier explains that in "France, assimilation is good for the Republic; in the Netherlands, it is good for the immigrant," "Assimilation by Conviction or by Coercion?," 217.

67. Jeff Spinner-Halev, "Liberalism and Religion: Against Congruence," *Theoretical Inquiries in Law* 9.2 (2008): 564.

win out.[68] Bolkestein was roundly criticized for breaking the gag order on the issue—but others would soon join his ranks.

By the end of the decade, even leftists like Paul Scheffer and Paul Schnabel were joining Bolkestein. They openly questioned, not only the immigration policies, but also the immigrants themselves. Their public criticisms "constituted a new turn in the political debate. . . . It was now possible even for those on the left to openly question the position of Islam in the Netherlands."[69] Paul Scheffer's article, "The Multicultural Drama," published in 2000, is widely recognized as a watershed moment in which the Dutch left joined the Dutch right in advocating a more aggressive policy toward Islam. Recalling the breakthrough, Scheffer states, "Everywhere I talked about it, you could notice that there were people thinking, 'Ah, finally, someone with an impeccable background who is not associated with the wrong sort (*foute*) of sympathies.'"[70] The sight of a left-wing leader like Scheffer openly criticizing immigrants and immigration policy created the necessary political cover for common citizens to vent their own pent-up frustrations with their Muslim neighbors. Likewise, Paul Schnabel's influential article entitled "Pleidooi voor aanpassing en assimilatie" ("A Plea for Adaption and Assimilation") performed a similar function.[71] Schnabel presented his Dutch readers with an embarrassing question. Tell me "exactly what have 'other cultures' actually contributed to Dutch culture, besides some restaurants, music and festivals."[72] Many of his readers had no answer.

At the turn of the century the liberal consensus was losing its benevolent patience with Islam. The assimilation process was not working. Radical solutions were needed and the politics of political correctness would no longer do.

68. Sunier, "Assimilation by Conviction or by Coercion?," 225.

69. Sunier, "Assimilation by Conviction or by Coercion?," 230–31.

70. Uitermark, *Dynamics of* Power, 90.

71. Paul Schnabel, *De Multiculturele illusie—Een pleidooi voor aanpassing en assimilatie* (Utrecht: Forum, 1999).

72. Sunier, "Assimilation by Conviction or by Coercion?," 230.

CHAPTER TWO

Marginalizing Islam

[Contemporary Dutch polls] show that intolerance is abundant
and in plain sight. Never less than a fifth, and often a third or
more describe immigrant minorities as "lazy. . . complainers. . .
intrusive. . . dishonest. . . violent. . . not law-abiding. . . selfish."

PAUL SNIDERMAN and LOUK HAGENDOORN[1]

Today the belief that cultural diversity is tearing the country apart
and that social equality cannot be achieved without strict and coercive assimilationist policies has become widely held.

THIJL SUNIER[2]

Between 2001 and 2006, a perfect storm of terrorist attacks abroad, a horrific assassination at home, a drama-thirsty media, and a charismatic cadre
of populist politicians came together to transform Dutch political culture.
This potent combination of characters, events, and cultural forces combined to completely burst the dam of political correctness and benevolent
paternalism that had been built in the Netherlands during the late twen-

1. Paul M. Sniderman and Louk Hagendoorn, *When Ways of Life Collide: Multiculturalism and Its Discontents in the Netherlands* (Princeton, NJ: Princeton University Press,
2009), 127–28.
2. Thijl Sunier, "Assimilation by Conviction or by Coercion? Integration Policies in the
Netherlands," in *European Multiculturalism Revisted*, Allesandro Silj, ed. (London: Zed Books,
2010), 231.

tieth century. In the space of a few short years, all of the pent-up fears, prejudices, and frustrations of the Dutch people were released in a series of cathartic outbursts against Muslim immigrants. The public debate quickly became Islamicized, focusing specifically on the religion of the immigrants as the root of the problem.[3] By 2006, 67 percent of Dutch citizens were convinced that there was a clash between Dutch culture and Islam. More than half believed Islam was a threat to Dutch national identity.[4] Within "every political party, there [was] a faction especially ready to respond negatively to minorities."[5]

In 2001, a charismatic populist by the name of Pim Fortuyn kicked off a nationwide debate about how the Netherlands could more aggressively monitor, control, transform, and solve the problem of Islam. The time of Dutch patience and generosity was over. Fortuyn demanded that the "rules of the game" shift yet again for immigrants in the Netherlands.[6] In the 1960s, immigrants were encouraged to isolate themselves until they could return home. Then, in the 1980s they were encouraged to participate in their own ethnic organizations. Then, in the 1990s they were told to leave their organizations and start participating in the marketplace. After 2001, economic participation was no longer enough. Now politicians like Fortuyn demanded that immigrants publically demonstrate their loyalty to, love of, and identification with "Dutch values and norms."[7] In other words, it was no longer enough for Muslims to follow liberal laws; they had to feel a love for liberal culture and the liberal values that undergirded them.

---

3. "Islam increasingly became the explanatory factor, not only for specific (collective) behavior of Muslims, but also for all kinds of societal problems they faced. This 'islamization of the discourse,' often leads to a narrowed outlook: 'when one wants to know what goes on in the head of a Muslim then one should study Islam.' All other possible explanations were in fact reduced to 'the' Islam." Thijl Sunier, "Islam in the Netherlands: A Nation Despite Religious Communities?," in *Religious Newcomers and the Nation State: Political Culture and Organized Religion in France and the Netherlands*, Erik Sengers and Thijl Sunier, eds. (Delft, NL: Eburon, 2010), 124.

4. Doutje Lettinga, *Framing the Hijab: The Governance of Intersecting Religious, Ethnic, and Gender Differences in France, the Netherlands, and Germany* (Ridderkerk, NL: Ridderprint, 2011), 12.

5. Sniderman and Hagendoorn, *When Ways of Life Collide*, 136.

6. Han Entzinger, "Changing the Rules while the Game Is On: From Multiculturalism to Assimilation in the Netherlands," in *Migration, Citizenship, Ethnos: Incorporation Regimes in Germany, Western Europe, and North America*, Y. Michal Bodemann and Gökçe Yurdakul, eds. (New York: Palgrave Macmillan, 2006), 121–44.

7. Entzinger, "Changing the Rules," 121–44.

One sociologist explains this critical shift in the following way. Muslims living in the Netherlands are now subjected to "feeling rules." Now a sense of "belonging" is required. For the Muslim

> feeling at home—has become a requirement. . . . [Immigrants] are increasingly expected to demonstrate feelings of attachment, belonging, connectedness and loyalty to their new country. . . . Emotive culturalization thus stresses the need for loyalty to the nation-state and demands proof of such feelings from immigrants . . . immigrants who do not manage to feel at home should go "home" . . . even when they are born and raised in the Netherlands.[8]

After 2001, wide-ranging new laws and initiatives were proposed in an effort to send a clear message to Muslims—embrace liberalism or leave.[9] Bans were proposed on minarets, public calls to prayer, and Muslim schools. Politicians called for restrictions on veils, arguing that they constituted a security risk. Some said veils were a barrier to social interaction and others simply declared that veils made people feel "uncomfortable."[10] Some insisted that new mosques should not be built in a "foreign" style. Immigrants applying for residency from non-Western countries were required to observe videos of gay couples kissing and pictures of nude beaches in an effort to assimilate them into a Dutch worldview.[11] One politician suggested that Muslim women should receive regular vaginal exams to ensure that they were not being forcibly circumcised. Still others suggested that Muslim councils be formed so that the state could use them to directly communicate Dutch values and expectations to Muslim leaders. Finally, some politicians suggested that Islamic schools, organizations, and mosques be regularly inspected and monitored for anti-Western sentiments.[12]

To say that all liberals agreed with all of these aggressive proposals would be an overstatement. Cooler heads, constitutional limits, and international pressure[13] usually prevailed. Nevertheless, across the political spectrum, po-

---

8. Jan Willem Duyvendak, *The Politics of Home: Belonging and Nostalgia in Europe and the United States* (New York: Palgrave Macmillan, 2011), 93.

9. Sunier, "Assimilation by Conviction or by Coercion?," 214–34.

10. Lettinga, *Framing the Hijab*, 171.

11. Lettinga, *Framing the Hijab*, 81.

12. Sunier, "Assimilation by Conviction or by Coercion?," 214–34.

13. "In May 2008, Human Rights Watch declared the [new Dutch immigration policies] to be discriminatory on the basis of international human rights law which forbids countries

litical parties in the Netherlands (right and left, secular and religious) all took a clear step toward a more muscular brand of liberal nationalism.[14] While specific motivation for attacking Islam differed, each political party claimed to be defending some good that Islam endangered, be it women, homosexuals, Dutch workers, Judeo-Christian values, artistic freedom, democracy, or Dutch culture. Whatever their reasoning, every political party would creatively develop its own unique excuse to demonize and marginalize Islam.[15] As Willem Schinkel and Friso Van Houldt have argued, all parties are now demanding cultural assimilation. Islam's distinct public presence in a liberal nation-state "is able to incite political enthusiasm across the political board: from socialists to Christian democrats to right-wing conservatives."[16]

Framing Islam: The Four Horsemen of Muscular Liberalism

Pim Fortuyn, Theo van Gogh, Ayaan Hirsi Ali, and Geert Wilders were the most prominent and successful advocates of this new "aggressive form of secular humanism."[17] Through radio, TV, film, and public debates these charismatic populists depicted an apocalyptic clash between religion and reason, oppression and freedom, the Middle Ages and modernity.[18] Each of them perfected unique and devastatingly effective ways to frame Muslims as wholly incompatible with the Dutch and as completely other. In the following section,

---

from making distinction based on ethnicity or nationality in their immigration policies" in Lettinga, *Framing the Hijab*, 81–82, n. 89.

14. Jan Rath, Astrid Meyer, and Thijl Sunier, "The Establishment of Islamic Institutions in a Depillarizing Society," *Tijdschrift voor Economisch en Sociale Geografie* 88 4 (1997), 394. See also Sniderman and Hagendoorn, 68.

15. Lettinga, *Framing the Hijab*, 51.

16. Willem Schinkel and Friso Van Houdt, "The Double Helix of Cultural Assimilationism and Neo-liberalism: Citizenship in Contemporary Governmentality," *The British Journal of Sociology* 61, no. 4 (2010): 711.

17. Alana Lentin and Gavan Titley, *The Crisis of Multiculturalism: Racism in a Neoliberal Age* (London: Zed Books, 2011), 119.

18. See Ian Buruma, *Murder in Amsterdam: The Death of Theo van Gogh and the Limits of Tolerance* (New York: Penguin Press, 2006); Ron Eyerman, *The Assassination of Theo van Gogh: From Social Drama to Cultural Trauma* (Durham: Duke University Press, 2008); Peter van der Veer, "Pim Fortuyn, Theo van Gogh, and the Politics of Tolerance in the Netherlands," *Public Culture* 18, no. 1 (2006): 111–24; Jusová Iveta, "Hirsi Ali and van Gogh's Submission: Reinforcing the Islam vs. Women Binary," *Women's Studies International Forum* 31 (2008): 148–55.

I will briefly outline the four unique frames the leaders used in their attempts to demonize Islam, making it the absolute other to Dutch liberalism.

Pim Fortuyn: Homosexual Marginalization

In early 2002, Pim Fortuyn's anti-Islamic party *Lijst Pim Fortuyn* was poised to make a dramatic sweep into power.[19] It appeared inevitable that Pim Fortuyn would soon become the prime minister. Fortuyn's meteoric rise to power was, however, not to be. He was murdered only nine days before the national election. An animal-rights activist named Volkert van der Graaf shot him outside of a radio station in Hilversum. During his brief time in the national spotlight, Fortuyn attacked Islam from a wide variety of directions. But Fortuyn was particularly adept at using his homosexuality to marginalize the Muslim other. Having emancipated himself from a Catholic, Marxist, and heterosexual past, Fortuyn had successfully transformed himself into a freethinking, playful, and promiscuous homosexual man. He was the very embodiment of the Dutch liberation story and he named this outright. Fortuyn claimed to be the very incarnation of the modern people, their leader, their father, their Moses.[20] He promised to lead his liberals out of the wilderness of Islamic backwardness into the promised land of liberal progress. Through his personal narrative, Fortuyn cast himself as the unapologetic champion liberalism needed to confront its mortal enemy—the Islamic other.[21]

19. Forutyn's most important work on Islam in the Netherlands is *Tegen de islamisering van onze cultuur: Nederlandse identiteit als fundament* (Utrecht: A.W. Bruna, 1997).

20. Peter Jan Margry, "The Murder of Pim Fortuyn and Collective Emotions: Hype, Hysteria and Holiness in the Netherlands?," *Etnofoor: antropologisch tijdschrift* 16 (2003): 106–31.

21. "Sexuality features prominently in European debates on multiculturalism and in Ori-entalist discourses on Islam. . . . [R]epresentations of gay emancipation are mobilized to shape narratives in which Muslims are framed as non-modern subjects, a development that can best be understood in relation to the 'culturalization of citizenship' and the rise of Islamophobia in Europe. . . . [In the Netherlands] the entanglement of gay rights discourses with anti-Muslim politics and representations is especially salient. The thorough-going secularization of Dutch society, transformations in the realms of sex and morality since the 'long 1960s' and the 'nor-malization' of gay identities since the 1980s have made sexuality a malleable discourse in the framing of 'modernity' against 'tradition.'" Paul Mepschen, Jan Willem Duyvendak, and Evelien H. Tonkens, "Sexual Politics, Orientalism, and Multicultural Citizenship in the Neth-erlands," *Sociology* 44 (2010): 962–78. Quotation from the abstract. Additional quotations from this work are noted parenthetically in the text.

Fortuyn successfully framed "Islam as a backward culture and a threat to his personal way of life." He powerfully captured the Dutch historical imagination when he declared that Islam had to go because "I refuse to start all over again with the emancipation of women and gays" (968).

As Fortuyn understood and demonstrated, discourses of sexual freedom offer a rich grammar to represent and reinforce an imaginary of Dutch "liberated" modernity versus Muslim oppressed tradition. . . . Gay rights discourses are so powerful in the Netherlands precisely because gay men—as unattached and autonomous subjects—stand for the ideal citizen of neoliberal modernity. (969)

Gay rights discourses have thus offered a language for the critique of Islam and multiculturalism . . . that renders Muslim citizens knowable and produces them as objects of critique. Sexuality offers a prism through which cultural contrast comes to be perceived, temporally, as the difference between modernity and tradition. The central tropes of this discourse—modernity versus tradition; individualism versus the lack thereof; tolerance versus fundamentalism—frame an imagined modern self against an imagined traditional other. (970)

Fortuyn's "sexualization of citizenship" was a powerful rhetorical strategy for "shaping an imaginary of modern individualism" (964).[22] The Dutch were defined as sexually healthy and free, while Muslims were sexually sick and repressed. As opposed to the liberated Dutch, Muslims were still sexually controlled "by tradition, community and family" (964). By framing Islam as fundamentally anti-homosexual, Fortuyn was able to frame the faith as fundamentally anti-Dutch. It was not a far step for Fortuyn to conclude that the Dutch constitution should formally restrict Islam's right to the freedom of

---

22. For a further investigation into how the rhetoric of sexual politics has been used to marginalize and demonize see Liz Fekete, "Enlightenment Fundamentalism? Immigration, Feminism and the Right," *Race & Class* 48, no. 2 (2006): 1–22. Paul Mepschen, "Against Tolerance: Islam, Sexuality, and the Politics of Belonging in the Netherlands," *Monthly Review* 102 (2009); Sarah Bracke, "From 'Saving Women' to 'Saving Gays': Rescue Narratives and Their Dis/continuities," *European Journal of Women's Studies* 19, no. 2 (2012): 237–52; Stefan P. Dudink, "Homosexuality, Race, and the Rhetoric of Nationalism," *History of the Present: A Journal of Critical History* 1, no. 2 (2011): 259–64; Robert Nichols, "Empire and the Dispotif of Queerness," *Foucault Studies* 14 (2012): 41–60; Judith Butler, "Sexual Politics, Torture, and Secular Time," *The British Journal of Sociology* 59, no. 1 (2008): 1–23.

religion.[23] Pim Fortuyn demanded that Muslims be granted their rights only after they submit to sexual norms of the dominant culture. Because Fortuyn spoke as a homosexual, a sexual community long on the underside of the dominant culture, the irony of his demand is palpable.

Still, in a land where progressive liberalism was now in the dominant majority, Fortuyn's rhetoric spread like wild fire. By the end of 2002, 46 percent of eighteen- to thirty-year-olds in the Netherlands were in favor of a zero immigration policy.[24]

Ayaan Hirsi Ali: Gender Marginalization

If Fortuyn's rhetorical strategy for marginalizing Islam was homosexuality, Ayaan Hirsi Ali's was gender. Ali skillfully wielded her own narrative of female emancipation from Islamic men to rally liberals against Islam.[25] According to her biography, Ali was raised as a devoted Muslim in Somalia and Kenya during the 1970s and 1980s. In 1992, when she was 22, Ali's father allegedly forced her to leave and marry a man in Canada whom she had never met. On her way to Canada, Ali stopped to visit family members in Germany. While in Düsseldorf, she fled and applied for asylum in the Netherlands. A brilliant and determined young woman, Ali quickly mastered the Dutch language and soon graduated from university. By 2002, Ali had renounced her faith in Islam and converted to Dutch liberalism. Based on her reports, she decided to leave Islam for a number of reasons. She has cited her fascination with European Enlightenment philosophy, her appreciation for the rationality and efficiency of modern Europe, her horror at Osama bin Laden's use of the Koran to justify his attacks on 9/11, and her personal contact with Muslim women who had experienced violence at the hands of Muslim men.

23. Sam Cherribi, *In the House of War: Dutch Islam Observed* (Oxford: Oxford University Press, 2010), 44.

24. Jocelyne Cesari, *When Islam and Democracy Meet: Muslims in Europe and in the United States* (Palgrave Macmillan: New York, 2004), 32.

25. Ayaan Hirsi Ali's major works include *The Caged Virgin: An Emancipation Proclamation for Women and Islam* (New York: Free Press, 2006); *Infidel* (New York: Free Press, 2007); *Nomad: From Islam to America: A Personal Journey through the Clash of Civilizations* (New York: Free Press, 2010). A critical analysis of Ali's political use of her own narrative can be found in Mineke Bosch's "Telling Stories, Creating (and Saving) Her Life: An Analysis of the Autobiography of Ayaan Hirsi Ali," *Women's Studies International Forum* 31 (2008): 138–47.

Ali's biography is, in many ways, perfectly constructed to appeal to the Dutch zeitgeist. The biography illustrates the superiority of Western reason and politics, the violence and backwardness of religion, and—most importantly—the emancipation of women from abusive, patriarchal, and religious men. Her narrative perfectly mirrored the Dutch vision of their own liberation from religious conservatism to secular emancipation. Ali's rhetorical gift has always been the translation of "her particular experiences into a universal discourse of liberation."[26] The more she used this narrative, the more Dutch media exposure she received. How could the Dutch not welcome, embrace, and defend a woman who shared their own story of liberation from the clutches of religion?[27]

Through Ali's compelling biography, Dutch readers could peer beneath the veil and see exactly what they had always wanted to see—a violent, oppressive, and medieval ideology. Ali's story delightfully confirmed their fears that little Islamic girls were crying out for their help. Liberal white women just had to save these girls from the clutches of Islamic men and Islamic dogma.

Theo van Gogh: Artistic Marginalization

Irony can be a healthy antidote to dogmatism, but also an escape from any blame. Outrageous or offensive statements are often followed by protestations that they were meant in jest, but only once their poisoned darts have hit their marks. Irony is a great license for irresponsibility. . . . Its destructive power can be cushioned in a narrow society where everyone knows the rules of the game. When it is exposed to outsiders with a less playful view of words, the effects can be devastating.[28]

While Fortuyn and Ali used rather serious sexual frames to marginalize Islam, Theo van Gogh used his playful, grotesque, and mocking wit. Through his hyperbolic films, columns, interviews, and jokes, van Gogh framed Islam as a joyless and artless ideology incapable of handling criticism or taking a good

---

26. Justus Uitermark, *Dynamics of Power in Dutch Integration Politics* (Amsterdam: Amsterdam University Press, 2012), 102.

27. For an exploration of how Ali's feminist rhetoric was used by the right to discipline Islam, consider Fekete, "Enlightenment Fundamentalism?"

28. Buruma, *Murder in Amsterdam*, 112–13.

joke.[29] If Fortuyn and Ali sought to incarnate the gay and women's movements of the Netherlands, van Gogh sought to embody the bohemian hedonism of 1960s Amsterdam. Rather than engage in a thoughtful dialogue with Dutch Muslims, van Gogh made disgusting and sardonic jokes at them. He called them "goat fuckers" and dismissed all criticism, claiming he was speaking as nothing more than the "village idiot." Through this behavior, Ian Buruma argues, "Theo van Gogh placed himself squarely in the tradition of abusive criticism."[30]

As a film director, van Gogh successfully framed Islam as not only against art, but also as incapable of creating it. Before his death, van Gogh produced a number of films and television shows that portrayed Islam as a religion that was fundamentally incompatible with the spirit of the Netherlands. According to Peter van der Veer,

> Discussions in Holland after van Gogh's murder focused on the intolerance of Islam, the threat of Muslim extremism, and, perhaps most significantly, Muslims' lack of humor. . . . Muslims simply could not take a joke; they took life and especially their religion too seriously. Much emphasis was placed on freedom of speech and artistic expression. The terms of the debate resembled those generated by Salman Rushdie's *Satanic Verses*, in which Muslim illiteracy in satire was identified as a sign of deep cultural backwardness.[31]

As a filmmaker and culture critic, van Gogh's principal rhetorical strategy against Islam was neither philosophical nor political: it was artistic. He used the arts to marginalize and exclude them. Van Gogh believed himself to be the platonic Dutch ideal of artistic freedom, expression, humor, and sarcasm; he successfully framed Islam as his absolute opposite.

Geert Wilders: Historical Marginalization

Pim Fortuyn and Theo van Gogh were murdered in 2002 and 2004. Ayaan Hirsi Ali emigrated to America not long after. None other than Geert Wilders

---

29. See Buruma, *Murder in Amsterdam*; Eyerman, *The Assassination of Theo van Gogh*; van der Veer, "Pim Fortuyn"; Jusová Iveta, "Hirsi Ali and van Gogh's Submission."

30. Buruma, *Murder in Amsterdam*, 98.

31. van der Veer, "Pim Fortuyn," 112.

would step into this vacuum left in muscular Dutch liberalism. Wilders lacked Fortuyn's charisma, Ali's stirring biography, and van Gogh's carefree humor. Two things Geert Wilders does not lack, however, are an acute understanding of media-driven politics and an impressive command of the well-placed sound bite.[32] While his political opponents carefully choose their measured bureaucratic prose, Wilders, the showman, seizes stage with a blistering assault of witty populist one-liners.

One of Wilder's most effective strategies of Islamic marginalization has been his cunning and creative (ab)use of history. The Middle Ages, World War II, the Holocaust, the Enlightenment, and South African apartheid all make regular appearances in his speeches. Islam is framed as both a medieval religion and a fascist political ideology à la Nazism. Those who defend Dutch Islam are Nazi sympathizers. Multiculturalists are apartheid supporters. Meanwhile, Wilders frames himself as the reincarnation of Winston Churchill, the lone courageous defender of Western civilization, freedom, and Judeo-Christian values against the forces of Islamofascism. Making this courageous stand, Wilders claims to be a walking martyr, one who has been "marked for death" by the Islamic forces of evil.[33] Akin to the brave Dutch citizens who resisted the Nazis, Wilders stands bravely for freedom against the rising Islamofascist tide sweeping across Europe.

Wilders's use of national history is, of course, selective. His rhetorical game is best described by Markha Valenta as a "politics of bad memories" or perhaps a "politics of invented memories." Wilders's rhetoric "presents us with a public 'memory' of shocking change, where an imaginary life of stable tranquility and mutuality was suddenly disrupted and scuppered by the arrival of people with values from other civilizations and cultures. This is the immigration-as-rupture memory."[34] Wilders conveniently ignores the fact that Muslims were originally invited to the Netherlands to do work the Dutch did not want to do. He conveniently forgets the long history of Dutch efforts to exploit, exclude, and assimilate those Muslim guest workers. He also ignores the long history of Dutch colonialism over Islam in Asia. In fact,

---

32. For an analysis of Wilders's rhetorical style and strategy, see Hans de Bruijn, *Geert Wilders Speaks Out: The Rhetorical Frames of a European Populist* (The Hague: Eleven International Publishing, 2012).

33. Geert Wilders, *Marked for Death: Islam's War against the West and Me* (Washington, DC: Regnery Publishing, 2012).

34. Markha Valenta, "Multiculturalism and the Politics of Bad Memories," *Open Democracy*, March 20, 2011. http://www.opendemocracy.net/markha-valenta/multiculturalism-and-politics-of-bad-memories (accessed February 7, 2013).

the first significant contact between Islam and the Netherlands was not an Islamic invasion of the Netherlands. It was the Dutch who invaded Islam. It was the Dutch who had conquered, oppressed, and colonized Indonesia—the largest Muslim nation in the world. Likewise, the present civilizing offensive Wilders advocates is not the final historical straw after years of Dutch patience and tolerance. It is nothing but a repetition of the past, the colonial echo of Wilders's ancestors who conquered Indonesia singing, "*Roeit uit dat gebroedsel, verneder die klant/Met Nederlands driekleur 'beschaving' geplant*" ("Wipe out that vermin, humiliate their nation/ Plant in them the Dutch tricolor that brings civilization").[35]

A Softer Assimilation Movement

It would be a gross overstatement to cast these four populists as the sole representatives of the liberal consensus in the Netherlands. During this same period, cooler liberal heads proposed more benevolent strategies to try to encourage Islamic reformation or enlightenment.

One softer approach was infamously posed by the mayor of Amsterdam, Job Cohen, in a series of public lectures beginning in 2002. One of his speeches, titled "*Religie als bron van sociale cohesie?*" ("Religion: A Source of Social Cohesion?"), perfectly captures Cohen's conviction that the state should empower and use Islam to moderate Muslim immigrants.[36] In essence, Cohen proposed that the government select and partner with Islamic institutions whom they deemed acceptably moderate.[37] Through these partnerships, the state could strengthen the hand of moderate Islamic leaders, inspire mutual trust, and further marginalize Islamic fundamentalists.[38] If they were carefully monitored by the state, Cohen insisted, these moderate Islamic institutions

35. Paul Scheffer, *Immigrant Nations* (Cambridge: Polity Press, 2011), 131.

36. Job Cohen, "Religie als bron van sociale cohesie? Godsdienst en overheid in een postgeseculariseerde samenleving," public lecture given at the University of Leiden, December 19, 2003.

37. Cohen's proposal is also outlined in Buruma, *Murder in Amsterdam*, 241–50.

38. The Dutch government "has sought cooperation with Muslim groups, hoping to domesticate their religion by stimulating the erection of two Muslim Councils that were officially recognized in 2005 and meet the Minister of Integration: the 'Contactorgaan Moslims en Overheid' (CMO) and the 'Contactgroep Islam' (CGI). The CMO represents the largest Sunnite mosque organizations (approximately 560,000 Muslims). The CGI represents minority Muslim communities of the Alevi and Ahmadiyya (approximately 115,000 Muslims)," in Lettinga, *Framing the Hijab*, 65.

would empower Muslim immigrants to integrate into Dutch society. Cohen argued that if the Netherlands is "falling apart," then perhaps religion could play a role in bringing it back together (under the larger liberal umbrella, of course).

As the mayor of Amsterdam, Cohen's enduring desire was to "keep things together" at seemingly any cost. His governmental embrace of moderate Islam was warm—but tight. According to Justus Uitermark, Mayor Cohen "introduced or defended many repressive measures" on the Muslims he hoped to embrace, including: "preventive searches, camera surveillance, raids. . . . The preservation of social cohesion and social peace [was] the cornerstone of his approach and central to his understanding of integration politics."[39]

It is ironic that Cohen's suggestion of funding and monitoring a new Islamic pillar was so quickly dismissed by his peers. After all, much of the Netherlands's anxiety over Islam surrounds its shadowy, diffuse, and disembedded nature.[40] Cohen's pillar proposal would have offered a way to increase the state's surveillance and control of the Islamic community—and Cohen knew it. Cohen had read his history. By increasing its funding of Catholic and Calvinist institutions in the 1960s, the liberal welfare state was able to increase its control over the religious groups, all the while weakening their religious particularity and independence.

Other soft assimilationists, like Paul Scheffer, have insisted that the Netherlands needs to more clearly outline what it means to be Dutch. Scheffer argues that a clear definition will make it easier for immigrants to fit in.[41] In other words, the state needs clearly tell them who "we" are so "they" can more easily become like "us."[42] Scheffer's arguments reflect a larger desire in the Netherlands to develop a stronger and more clearly delineated set of national values, traditions, and holidays. In recent years, some citizens have even called for a "historical canon" of great Dutch works of literature, art, and philosophy to be enshrined.[43] In a similar vein, the atheist philosopher Paul Cliteur has argued that the Dutch state should more purposefully promote "secularism" as a unifying public morality for the nation.[44] Another liberal, Afshin Ellian,

---

39. Uitermark, *Dynamics of* Power, 132.

40. See Kennedy and Valenta, "Religious Pluralism and the Dutch State," in *Geloven in het publieke domein*, ed. W. B. H. J. Van de Donk et al. (Amsterdam: Amsterdam University Press, 2006), 337–52.

41. Scheffer, *Immigrant Nations*, 115–17.

42. Sunier, "Assimilation by Conviction or by Coercion?," 226–27.

43. Scheffer, *Immigrant Nations*, 138.

44. Paul Cliteur, "*De noodzaak van morel en politiek secularism*," in *Continent op drift?*

adds that the Dutch need to exhibit a more forthright patriotic pride in their liberal constitution and liberal values. If they do this, he argues, Islamic integration will be improved.[45]

Such well-meaning arguments falter on a number of points. While the Dutch imagine themselves to be worldly cosmopolitans who don't have a nationalist bone in their bodies, it simply is not true. Duyvendak argues that Hollanders actually have a very strong cohesive sense of what it means to be Dutch.[46] Is it really true, he asks, that the Dutch are

> failing to define what they stand for? No, there is little evidence that immigrants are left in the dark by a country unwilling to reveal itself. Instead, we witness a dominant narrative that tells immigrants—and in particular those with Muslim backgrounds—that how they lead their lives is improper and maladapted, and that they therefore spoil the home feelings of the natives. The Netherlands has shown quite clearly what it stands for over these past years.[47]

There is a paradoxical sense in which the liberal consensus is devoted to opposite ends. Liberalism appears to desire that Islam be both domesticated and foreignized at one and the same time.[48] Either way, Islamic immigrants can only lose.

Femke Halsema of the *GroenLinks* political party provides an interesting final example of soft assimilation. Rather than placing an outright ban on the burqa, Halsema proposed that the state try to "'emancipate the burqa away' by stimulating women's (labour-market) participation."[49] Halsema's enduring hope is that when Muslim women become educated, rational, and upwardly mobile (like her) they will "throw off their headscarves and be completely free."[50]

Europese waarde in de schaduwen van morgen, ed. Hans Verboven (Kapellen: Uitgeverij Pelck-mans, 2010), 110–20.

45. Afshin Ellian, "Emancipation and Integration of Dutch Muslims in Light of a Process of Polarization and the Threat of Political Islam," Middle East Program Paper Series (Washington, DC: Woodrow Wilson International Center for Scholars, 2009): 15–23.

46. Duyvendak, *The Politics of Home*, 99.

47. Duyvendak, *The Politics of Home*, 101.

48. Sunier, "Islam in the Netherlands," in *Religious Newcomers*, ed. Sengers and Sunier, 126–27.

49. Lettinga, *Framing the Hijab*, 175.

50. Lettinga, *Framing the Hijab*, 176.

Whether the assimilation is soft or hard, generous or muscular, the enduring problem remains the same (Islam) as does the solution (liberalism).

Islam: Life on the Underside of Dutch Liberalism

More than any other religious group, however, Muslims seem not to be the masters of their own identity in their adopted countries. An essentializing discourse on Islam, existing on every level of society, is imposed on them from the micro-local to the international level.[51]

The term "integration" has come to mean quite different things to those who see themselves as the reference point and those who see themselves described as "the problem."[52]

According to the Dutch sociologist Oussama "Sam" Cherribi, Muslims living in a city like Amsterdam exist under "multiple points of pressure."[53] They experience *economic* pressure in a Dutch economy that is progressively outsourcing its industrial jobs. They experience *cultural* pressure to master the complex nuances of Dutch cultural expectations. They experience *religious* pressure from other Muslims to remain fiercely faithful to Islam in a secular culture whose push and pull never ends. They experience *bureaucratic* pressure from an army of civil servants coming into their homes to explain Dutch values, behaviors, and healthy family dynamics to them. They experience *intellectual* pressure from needing to constantly justify and interpret their ancient faith in a dynamic, complex, and postmodern culture. They experience *journalistic* pressure from media that consistently depict them as violent, dogmatic, and backward. They experience *internal* pressure to achieve for themselves a personal sense of honor and respect in a society that frequently demeans them. They experience *institutional* pressure when Muslim institutions are denied funding and autonomy equal to those of Christianity, Judaism, and liberalism. They experience *nationalistic* pressure to regularly and "publically express their

---

51. Jocelyne Cesari, *When Islam and Democracy Meet: Muslims in Europe and the United States* (New York: Palgrave Macmillan, 2004), 21.

52. John Bowen, *Why the French Don't Like Headscarves: Islam, the State, and Public Space* (Princeton, NJ: Princeton University Press, 2010), 247.

53. See Sam Cherribi, *In the House of War: Dutch Islam Observed* (Oxford: Oxford University Press, 2010).

disgust for radicals and their love, affection, and gratitude for the country in which they live, in a way not required of others."[54]

Cherribi argues that this multiplicity of pressures on Muslim immigrants makes the cultivation of strong, stable, and thoughtful Muslim communities extremely difficult. When combined, these pressures quickly become a "pulverizing machine that destroys the individual who happens to be Muslim and reconstitutes him or her as someone who is only a part of a larger, alienated, monolithic entity, in this case the 'Muslim threat.'"[55]

Islamic family systems find themselves "under huge strain because of [the] father's loss of status. In many migrant families this results in an inverted form of intergenerational conflict. Instead of children being dependent on their parents, the parents are in many ways dependent on their children."[56] Translating for one's father at the grocery store, doctor's office, and shop inverts the father-son relationship. The sight of one's father being demeaned and mocked by native Dutch people can destroy the relationship.

Psychiatrist Zohra Acherrat-Stitou explains that the younger generation of Dutch Muslims is not only "angry with a society that exploited their parents," but they are also "angry with their parents for failing to put up any resistance." This bipolar isolation causes some young Muslims to feel "mistreated, misunderstood, and insecure."[57] Back home in Africa and the Middle East, nuclear families are supported by a larger cultural ecosystem. In the Netherlands, nuclear families are islands. Fending for themselves, they must completely reimagine what it means to be an organic Islamic family in a sea of atomistic Dutch individuals.

Muslim immigrants clearly experience political pressure as well. Politicians routinely question their constitutional rights and attempt to curtail Islamic practices, clothing, buildings, food, rituals, schools, institutions, beliefs, and family arrangements. Of course, Muslims are allowed to defend themselves politically and legally in the Netherlands, but their defense of Islam must always be articulated using the majority's "secular language of autonomy and freedom and not in the religious language of moral reasoning that the minority uses."[58]

Liberalism has therefore made its moral language the only moral language permitted in the public square. A Muslim woman who wishes to defend her

---

54. Cherribi, *In the House of War*, 32.
55. Cherribi, *In the House of War*, 5.
56. Scheffer, *Immigrant Nations*, 11.
57. Scheffer, *Immigrant Nations*, 18.
58. van der Veer, "Pim Fortuyn," 123.

right to wear her veil must claim that she does so because she is an autonomous, rational, self-creating, self-defining individual. She must claim that she "personally prefers" to wear a veil because she happens to freely like it. Her true theological orientation and posture must remain concealed. Like a cruel joke, she is forced to parrot liberalism—even in her protest against it. As Markha Valenta notes, liberalism's "discursive and political priority forces critics to question them on their own terms. To consider the veil—or the nation—outside this framework is to risk placing oneself outside the public discussion itself."[59] The cruel irony only continues. For the more a Muslim woman uses liberal language to defend her Muslim identity, the less well integrated she is judged to be.[60]

59. Valenta continues, "This, in fact, is what has happened. On the one hand, the significant analyses of the veil not framed in exclusively modernist, Western-centric terms . . . continue to be generally marginalized and ignored by Western politicians, policy makers, journalists, pundits, and public intellectuals. And not only by them but by feminists, as well, deeply indebted as the majority are to Western humanism," "How to Recognize a Muslim," in *Political Theologies: Public Religions in a Post-Secular World*, ed. Hent de Vries and Lawrence E. Sullivan (New York: Fordham University Press, 2006), 458.

60. See a French example of this brutal irony in Bowen, *Why the French Don't Like Headscarves*, 177.

A Christian Defense of Islam?

What other reaction could the majority have but to reject Muslim immigrants? What other conclusion could they draw but to oppose cultural pluralism and press for assimilation?

PAUL SNIDERMAN and LOUK HAGENDOORN[61]

Liberty of conscience was born, not of indifference, not of skepticism, not of mere open-mindedness, but of faith.

JOHN PLAMENATZ[62]

In their attempt to explain this dramatic shift in Dutch political culture, sociologists Paul Sniderman and Louk Hagendoorn made an interesting and rather alarming statistical discovery. After conducting extensive surveys, they discovered that there is a large block of Dutch citizens who are—for lack of a better term—ideological conformists. This group's posture toward Islam, its decision to either welcome or exclude, protect or demonize the religion, depends greatly on the tide of national opinion. During the 1990s, when political correctness was *en vogue,* these Dutch conformists spoke out passionately against those who broke the laws of political correctness. Once the gag order

---

61. Paul M. Sniderman and Louk Hagendoorn, *When Ways of Life Collide: Multiculturalism and Its Discontents in the Netherlands* (Princeton, NJ: Princeton University Press, 2009), 130.

62. John Plamenatz, *Man and Society,* vol. 1 (London: Longman, 1963), 50.

was lifted by a series of terrorist attacks, charismatic populists, and a shift in media coverage, this huge bloc of conformists made a collective shift against Islam. According to Sniderman and Hagendoorn, this group of conformists may constitute as much as one-third of the population. In short, this bloc has the power to dramatically affect the social and political fate of Islam.

The questions, therefore, quickly become clear: In a public square that fears difference and desires assimilation, how will a deep diversity endure? Will a group rise up to challenge the demonization and marginalization of difference? Will a community rise up to model a life of hospitality and justice amidst deep difference?

Critical theorist Nancy Fraser argues that lasting democracy depends, not on consensus, but conflict. The common belief that democracy requires a single and homogenous set of values and culture is wrongheaded, she argues. Democracy requires, not a single homogenous public square, but a "multiplicity of publics."[63] Fraser argues that diverse communities and countercultures serve a critical democratic function. They openly challenge and question the dominant assumptions, practices, and power of the majority. Fraser warns that if the majority goes unchecked and unquestioned by these "counterpublics," the majority will inevitably grow in its destructive hegemony and pursue even more aggressive cultural uniformity.

Fraser points to a variety of marginalized groups who have served as counterpublics in recent history. She lists "women, workers, peoples of color, and gays and lesbians" as subversive communities who "have repeatedly found it advantageous to constitute alternative publics." Within these countercultures, these communities creatively oppose and challenge the dominant culture. Their communities "invent and circulate counter-discourses, which in turn permit them to formulate oppositional interpretations of their identities, interests, and needs." According to Fraser, one excellent example of this sort of counterpublic "is the late-twentieth century US feminist subaltern." This feminist community was, according to Fraser, culturally prolific. Together they produced a wide "array of journals, bookstores, publishing companies, film and video distribution networks, lecture series, research centers, academic programs, conferences, conventions, festivals, and local meeting places." Through this prolific cultural production, the feminist counterculture "invented new terms for describing social reality." These new terms directly challenged a male-dominated culture. Because of this particular counterculture,

---

63. Nancy Fraser, *Justice Interruptus: Critical Reflections on the "Postsocialist" Condition* (New York: Routledge, 1997), 85.

the male-dominated assumptions of the center, which "were previously exempt from contestation, now have to be publicly argued out."[64]

Fraser appears to have touched on something that the Netherlands—and the greater West—desperately needs, a counterculture capable of questioning liberal assumptions and liberal hegemony, a counterculture capable of defending Islam.

But there is a problem. Surveying the homogenous liberal landscape of the Netherlands, a counterpublic is difficult to find. Moreover, most of Fraser's favorite countercultures (unions, homosexuals, and feminists) have had their unique moral discourses co-opted by the rhetoric of Islamophobia.[65] In other words, each of these groups has already had its unique moral language co-opted to demonize Islam as a direct threat to the well-being of women, homosexuals, and labor unions. If the gay, feminist, and labor countercultures have been largely assimilated into the modern liberal consensus, who will challenge the majority?

A Christian Counterculture

Can we be peacemakers? Can we make a constructive contribution to this great social dispute even if our contribution is from the margins of society?

GERT-JAN SEGERS, Dutch Christian Politician[66]

As a work of Christian theology, this book has no interest in dictating to other subcultures how they should contest liberalism or defend Islam—that deci-

---

64. Fraser, *Justice Interruptus*, 81–82.

65. See Paul Mepschen, Jan Willem Duyvendak, and Evelien H. Tonkens, "Sexual Politics, Orientalism, and Multicultural Citizenship in the Netherlands," *Sociology* 44 (2010): 962–78; Liz Fekete, "Enlightenment Fundamentalism? Immigration, Feminism, and the Right," *Race & Class* 48, no. 2 (2006): 1–22; Paul Mepschen, "Against Tolerance: Islam, Sexuality, and the Politics of Belonging in the Netherlands," *Monthly Review* 102 (2009); Sarah Bracke, "From 'Saving Women' to 'Saving Gays': Rescue Narratives and Their Dis/continuities," *European Journal of Women's Studies* 19, no. 2 (2012): 237–52; Stefan P. Dudink, "Homosexuality, Race, and the Rhetoric of Nationalism," *History of the Present: A Journal of Critical History* 1, no. 2 (2011): 259–64; Robert Nichols, "Empire and the Dispotif of Queerness," *Foucault Studies* 14 (2012):41–60; Judith Butler, "Sexual Politics, Torture, and Secular Time," *The British Journal of Sociology* 59, no. 1 (2008): 1–23.

66. Gert-Jan Segers, *Voorwaarden voor vrede: de komst van de islam, de integratie van mos-liims en de identiteit van Nederland* (Amsterdam: Buijten and Schipperheijn Motief, 2009), 107.

sion is theirs. This book is concerned with the question of how the Christian community might constitute a distinct counterpublic that subversively seeks justice, hospitality, and grace for Muslims amidst the clash between Mecca and Amsterdam.

At first glance, the chances of a Christian counterpublic in the Netherlands appear slim.[67] It is a truism that the Dutch church was devastated by the forces of secularism during the twentieth century.[68] The beliefs and lifestyles of many professed Christians are indistinguishable from those of their liberal neighbors.[69] The nation's churches are deeply divided politically, theologically, generationally, liturgically, and ethnically. Many Christian organizations are either narrowly concerned with their own survival or they are focused on gaining the respect and funding of the liberal state.[70] Of course, there are points of hope for the church in the Netherlands, but on the whole, it has never been weaker.

To make matters worse, over the last decade, two Christian political parties, the CDA (Christian Democratic Appeal) and SGP (Staatkundig Gereformeerde Partij), have failed to resist the nationalists and populists in their attacks against Islam. Like the feminist, gay, and labor subcultures, Christians have seen their unique philosophy and way of life co-opted to serve Western hegemony over against Islam. With little resistance from Christians, Geert Wilders regularly declares his Islamophobic *Partij voor de Vrijheid* the defender of Judeo-Christian values. While it might be tempting to blame Christian politicians for their lack of political courage, they are all looking at polling data which indicate that many Christian voters are attracted to the populism and nationalism of Wilders's more aggressive approach toward Islam. The CDA and the SGP have lost many Christian voters over the last decade to muscular liberals like Wilders. In this light, Dutch Christianity appears either unable or unwilling to constitute a courageous counterpublic that will defend the rights and dignity of Islam.

In the remainder of this book, I seek to demonstrate that this need not be so. There is an alternative path. Christianity is capable of fervently defending those with whom it disagrees. It can speak out on behalf of deep difference. It

67. James Kennedy, *Stad op een Berg: De publieke rol van protestantse kerken* (Zoetermeer: Uitgeverij Boekencentrum, 2009).

68. Erik Sengers, ed., *The Dutch and Their Gods: Secularization and Transformation of Religion in the Netherlands since 1950* (Hilversum: Uitgeverij Verloren, 2005).

69. Kennedy, *Stad op een Berg*, 130.

70. Kennedy, *Stad op een Berg*, 255.

can be an advocate of generous religious and cultural freedom.[71] It can challenge liberal hegemony, it can contest liberal uniformity, and it can resist liberal assimilation. And it can do all of these things out of an uncompromising belief in the truth of the Christian faith. The church can do this because—as we will see in the next chapter—it has done it before.

71. One example of a recent Dutch Christian leader who has spoken out on behalf of religious freedom and peace-making in the Netherlands can be found Stefan Paas's recent work *Vrede stichten: Politieke meditaties* (Zoetermeer: Boekencentrum, 2007).

PART TWO

Christian Pluralism: A History

CHAPTER THREE

The Emergence of Christian Pluralism

Kuyperians were pluralists before it was cool.

JAMES K. A. SMITH[1]

During the nineteenth century, a small community of Christians in the Netherlands began to formulate a robust set of arguments against ideological hegemony and for ideological pluralism. Their context, while different from our own, holds within it a rich collection of theological resources for the current clash between Mecca and Amsterdam. This chapter tells their story, while chapters four and five explore their theological arguments against hegemony and for pluralism.

What makes these nineteenth century pluralists remarkable is their insistence that the state should never award special favor to any ideological community—religious or secular. The grounding for their arguments was not philosophical; it was theological. They insisted that God demanded equal justice for Catholics and Protestants, socialists and liberals, atheists and Jews alike. All ideological communities, no matter how heretical, had to be afforded the freedom to live out their ideological convictions in the public square. This meant that they would need equal access to their own ideologically grounded schools, newspapers, associations, universities, political parties, and more. These early pluralists did not do this out of mere kindness or generosity; they believed it was their Christian duty. This chapter will explore how this curi-

---

1. James K. A. Smith, "Reforming Public Theology: Neocalvinism and Pluralism," Herman Bavinck Lecture, Theological University of Kampen, June 27, 2016.

ous and creative community of Christian pluralists emerged, developed, and enacted their reforms.

Throughout this recounting, I will highlight a number of potential resources for pluralists today.[2] *Potential*, of course, is the operative word. Any appropriator of a nineteenth-century political movement must be mindful of two critical factors. First, as we will see, this early movement was far from flawless. Its members suffered from a number of inconsistences and blind spots.[3] Second, there are obviously significant contextual differences between the nineteenth- and twenty-first century conflicts over religious pluralism. With these limitations acknowledged, this chapter uncovers rich resources for Christians to imagine their own pluralistic response to the conflict between Mecca and Amsterdam.[4]

2. George Harinck, a historian and director of the Historical Documentation Center for Dutch Protestantism (1800–) at the Free University in Amsterdam, has repeatedly noted the important historical lessons that can be gleaned from this movement for the contemporary conflicts over Islam in the Netherlands. Consider, for example, Harinck's "Kuyper als medevormgever van de plurale samenleving," *De Reformatie: Weekblad tot ontwikkeling van het gereformeerde leven*, 85, nos. 10–11 (December 5 and 12, 2009): 151–53, 165–68; "Een leefbare oplossing: Katholieke en protestantse tradities en de scheiding van kerk en staat" in *Ongewenste goden: De publieke rol van religie in Nederland*, Marcel ten Hooven and Theo de Wit, eds. (Amsterdam: SUN, 2006: 106–30); *De tucht van de democratie: Over pluriformiteit en burgerschap* (Amersfoort: Wetenschappelijk Instituut van de ChristenUnie, Mr. G. Groen van Prinsterer stichting, 2005); "CDA: keer terug naar het pluralistische model van Kuyper!" *Zonder geloof geen democratie: Christen Democratische Verkenningen*, Summer, 2006: 284–95; "De actualiteit van Abraham Kuyper," *Christen Democratische Verkenningen: Themanummer "Benauwd in het midden,"* Marcel ten Hooven et al., eds. Summer, 2008: 276–80; "Gastvrijheid als sleutel voor een christendemocratische samenlevingsvisie," *Migratie in een open samenleving: Christen Democratische Verkenningen*, Hubert Beusman, Pieter Jan Dijkman, Ab Klink, and Jan Willem Sap, eds., Fall 2011: 141–47.

3. Applying the label "Christian pluralism" to this movement demands a brief defense. The twentieth-century term "pluralism" was clearly never used by this nineteenth-century movement. Though a diverse lot, most contemporary pluralists coalesce around a number of broad convictions. They each argue that the state (as much as possible) should not try to enforce any form of uniformity on its citizens (be it religious, social, cultural, or philosophical). Instead, pluralists argue, the state (as much as possible) should guard the pluriformity of its citizens from any forces of hegemony and uniformity. I give this nineteenth-century movement the label "pluralist," not to indicate that they were always consistent in their pluralistic principles or behavior (they were not), but to argue that their movement evinces (and foreshadows) many later arguments made by twenty-first century pluralists. Furthermore, this movement deserves the label "Christian," not because they perfectly embodied the person of Jesus Christ—like all Christians they often failed to follow Christ's example, but because they demonstrated a sincere, consistent, and primary intention to understand and follow Christ in their private and public lives.

4. While I could introduce the early pluralist movement by exploring a list of its central

Liberalism and the Government of Minds

The movement for Christian pluralism in the Netherlands of the nineteenth century arose in direct response to the growing ideological hegemony of modern liberalism. The flashpoint of the conflict was the national education system. Who would control the schools? Soon after they came into power in 1795, the liberals had shrewdly recognized that the nation's schools would be the critical "battleground for the minds of the young." Education was "the place" where liberals could "launch a fundamental change in society." By controlling the nation's schools, they hoped to remove the "protective barriers sheltering some parts of the population against the reforming power of the state."[5] Liberals quickly coalesced around a plan to strip private, regional, and religious schools of their autonomy and place them in the hands of the liberal nation-state.[6]

---

ideas, I think it best to begin with its birth story. My reasons are many, but for now I will limit myself to three. First, if one wishes to initiate a new subaltern of Christian pluralism between Islam and West, it would be wise to consider the successes and failures of a similar counterpublic from the past. Second, by emphasizing the *story* of Christian pluralism over its ideas, I hope to highlight the communal, cultural, contingent, and developmental nature of this and any movement for Christian pluralism. Third, the movement emerged during a time of intense national tumult. While today Dutch liberals describe Islam as a divisive, dangerous, and backward ideology threatening Dutch peace and progress, during the nineteenth century, Dutch liberals applied those exact labels to the Reformed, Catholic, and socialist communities. The twenty-first century is not the first time Dutch liberalism reacted with fear, anxiety, and aggression toward "sectarian" communities who refused to assimilate into the liberal consensus.

   5. Michael Wintle, *An Economic and Social History of the Netherlands, 1800–1920: Demographic, Economic, and Social Transition* (Cambridge: Cambridge University Press, 2000), 268.

   6. The historical overview that follows draws heavily from the following sources: Nikolaj Hein Bijleveld, "Voor God, Volk en Vaderland : de plaats van de hervormde predikant binnen de nationale eenwordingsprocessen in Nederland in de eerste helft van de negentiende eeuw" (PhD diss., Groningen University, 2007); J. A. Bornewasser, "The Authority of the Dutch State over the Churches, 1795–1853" in *Britain and the Netherlands: Church and State since the Reformation*, A. C. Duke and C. A. Tamse, eds. (The Hague: Martinus Nijhoff, 1981); Wendy Fish Naylor, "Abraham Kuyper and the Emergence of Neo-Calvinist Pluralism in the Dutch School System" (PhD diss., University of Chicago, 2006); Stanley Carlson-Thies, "Democracy in the Netherlands: Consociational or Pluriform?" (PhD diss., University of Toronto, 1993); Simon Schama, "Schools and Politics in the Netherlands, 1796–1814," *The Historical Journal* 13, no. 4 (1970), 589–610; M. Gilhuis, *Memorietafel Van Het Christelijk Onderwijs: De Geschiedenis Van De Schoolstrijd* (Kampen: Kok, 1974); Jantje Lubbegiena van Essen, "The Struggle for Freedom of Education in the Netherlands in the Nineteenth Century," in *Guillaume Groen Van Prinsterer: Selected Studies*, Jantje Lubbegiena van Essen and Herbert Donald Morton, eds. (Jordan Station, ON: Wedge Publishing Foundation, 1990); Harvey Hillson Ginsburg, "The Struggle for

Before the nineteenth century, governmental oversight of education was minimal to non-existent. Primary education was delivered through a fiercely provincial combination of private organizations, orphanages, charities, and churches. Reformed pastors often enjoyed pedagogical privileges. Local schools often asked them to oversee the theological education of students. In heavily Roman Catholic areas, local priests were (unofficially) allowed similar catechetical privileges. Local schools were to be independently established, maintained, and funded by local churches, families, organizations, and local communities. Poor children received either private scholarships or aid from local churches, or they were left without an education.

During the nineteenth century, the liberal Dutch nation-state quickly began to extend its bureaucratic reach into this vast amalgam of private schools. Through a series of ambitious reforms, private schools were seized by the state and underwent a dramatic shift in their curriculum, funding, governance, and philosophical orientation. No longer the purview of the church or local community, schools increasingly became the exclusive property and responsibility of the liberal nation-state. The philosophical orientation of the schools progressively shifted from Protestant doctrine to Protestant values, from Christian morality to bourgeois morality, from the Christian Bible to modern rationality, and from a Christian prayer to a nationalistic pledge.

There is no doubt, however, that the educational philosophy of Dutch liberalism was forged in the revolutionary salons of Paris. For the French, the revolutionary school was the critical space in which young revolutionaries could be liberated from the monkish spirit of their Catholic parents and assimilated into the beliefs, practices, and community of the Revolution. Georges Danton famously argued that French children "belong to the Republic more than they do to their parents."[7] A curriculum for children, therefore, had to be "arranged in the order of their utility to the country." Only then could the revolution "shape not only the behavior of citizens but their will, their loyalties, and their ways of understanding themselves and the world" (18). For the revolution to succeed, one Parisian minister declared, "a certain government of minds is always necessary" (37).

---

the Control of Primary Education in the Netherlands, 1848–1917" (PhD diss., Yale University, 1952); Mark T. Hooker, *Freedom of Education: The Dutch Political Battle for State Funding of All Schools Both Public and Private (1801–1920)* (Bloomington, IN: LlyFrawr, 2009); Charles Glenn, *The Myth of the Common School* (Amherst: University of Massachusetts Press, 1987). Additional references to Glenn are given parenthetically in the text.

7. Danton's speech to the National Convention, quoted in Glenn, *Myth of the Common School*, 22.

Deeply impacted by this philosophy of education, the Dutch state progressively saw itself as the exclusive arbiter of national education and the formation of young minds. State-controlled curriculums were increasingly focused on liberating children from their religious identities. The mission, in short, was to assimilate them into the liberal nation-state.

The echoes of revolutionary Paris can be crisply discerned in the comments of J. H. van der Palm and Adriaan van den Ende, who served as the first administrators of the new national school system. According to van der Palm, centralized liberal education was critical "lest rural youth remain submerged in the wallow of prejudices" (47). In an effort to control these "fanatical idiots," van der Palm declared all private and religious schools to be public (*openbaar*). With this small legislative move, he instantly brought all religious schools under the direct oversight of the liberal nation-state (48).

Van der Palm's successor, van den Eende, continued and expanded his predecessor's reforms with a nationalistic passion. With zeal, he commissioned his liberal teachers to uproot "old enmities" and instill in children "an unlimited trust and the most hearty support" in "the present government" (49). Under his leadership, the Dutch school system was shot through with "a missionary zeal" for liberal nationalism. His teachers saw themselves as "inaugurating a new order of national morality." Under his administration there "was no higher term of praise in the reports on teaching than '*ijverig*'—zealous."[8]

Throughout the nineteenth century, liberals argued for universal liberal "education and the propagation of [liberal] 'culture.'" Eventually, they promised,

> a homogenous Dutch nation would come into being, and would naturally take on a liberal character. This was the political core of the liberal school policies. The school was a nation-forming institution. [The nation] could not be divided into competing "sectarian schools" nor could it be left in the hands of a political or church party. The Liberals considered themselves alone to be *algemeen* [i.e., common, neutral, non-sectarian].[9]

Representing the height of liberal zeal, Prime Minister Kappeyne de Coppelo argued that religious schools "must be oppressed" lest their sectarian

---

8. Schama, "Schools and Politics in the Netherlands," 599.

9. Siep Stuurman, *Verzuiling, Kapitalisme, en Patriarchaat* (Nijmegen: Socialistiese Uitgeverij, 1983), 116–17.

children grow up to "be a fly that makes the whole ointment smell." Such flies, Coppelo declared, "have no right to exist in our society."[10]

The Emergence of Christian Pluralism

Religious minorities tended to respond to this new liberal hegemony in one of four ways. The first was that of *assimilation*. Here, religious individuals and institutions allowed themselves to be absorbed into the new liberal consensus, surrendering their religious particularity. The second response was that of *moderation*. Here, religious minorities attempted to hold fast to some of their convictions while modifying others to please the liberal rulers. The third response was that of *retreat*. Here, religious minorities fled the public square and attempted to construct isolated religious communities where they could practice their faith privately. The fourth response was one of *retribution*. These minorities hoped to take the country back by toppling the liberal hegemony and restoring the old Christian hegemony. These four religious responses to liberal hegemony (assimilation, moderation, retreat, and retribution) are not historically unique. They are as old as time.

What is unique is a fifth response, that of *Christian pluralism*. Unlike the assimilation and moderation models, the Christian pluralists refused to alter their religious convictions or practices to fit in with the liberal hegemony. Unlike the retreat model, the pluralists practiced their faith openly in the Dutch public square. And unlike the retribution model, the pluralists had no desire to "take back" the country and restore Christian hegemony. Instead, these early pluralists argued for the formation of a state and society in which all worldviews could publically flourish and advocate for their own unique visions for the common good. According to historian Michael Wintle, these early pluralists desired "a location for themselves within the framework of the nation at large; it was a search for legitimation, for a just and recognized place for themselves as an active, important, but unique part of the Dutch nation, past, present, and future."[11]

---

10. Abraham Kuyper, *De Schoolkwestie I. naar aanleiding van het onderwijs-debat in de kamer* (Amsterdam: J.H. Kruyt, 1875), 20–21.

11. Wintle, *An Economic and Social History of the Netherlands,* 288.

The Pluralist Platform

The first modern political party in Europe, the Christian pluralists called themselves the Anti-Revolutionary Party (ARP). Their name reflected their opposition to the liberalism of the French Revolution. They saw the French Revolution as a destructive force of ideological violence and hegemony in Europe. In 1880, the ARP published its first political platform entitled *Ons Program* (Our Program). *Ons Program* demanded that the liberal elites surrender their national ambitions of ideological dominance and respect the deep ideological diversity of the Dutch people. In opposition to ideological assimilation of the liberals, the Christian pluralists argued that

> Nothing should be forced and nothing united which is not organically one. If there are people of good will who are one in mind and spirit, let them join together and courageously confess the faith of their hearts, but let them not claim any greater unity than that which is really their common possession. Thus, with complete autonomy let groups and circles unite who know what they want, know what they confess, and possess an actual not merely nominal unity. If here and there such circles exist which share a common life-trait, let them become conscious of their unity and display it before the eyes of the world.[12]

According to these early Christian pluralists, the liberal elites had a sclerotic understanding of religious freedom. They argued that the liberal definition of religious freedom included little more than the individual right to a series of private religious ideas and beliefs. In opposition to this liberal definition, Christian pluralists insisted that true, deep, and rich religious freedom needed to take religion seriously for what it was—a public, cultural, and institutional movement within a nation. In addition to individual rights, early pluralists argued for cultural-institutional rights as well. In other words, they argued that religious individuals must be free to gather and form their own cultural institutions (schools, universities, associations, newspapers, labor unions, political parties, and so on). In short, true religious freedom had to allow religious communities to publically express and organize their own unique ways of seeing and living in the world. The early Christian pluralists knew that religions build more

---

12. Abraham Kuyper, "Uniformity: The Curse of Modern Life" in *Abraham Kuyper: A Centennial Reader*, James Bratt, ed. (Grand Rapids: Eerdmans, 1998), 32.

than convictions; they build cultures. And they build more than ideas; they build institutions.

Moreover—and this was critical—if the state wanted to fund schools, hospitals, and charitable organizations, Christian pluralists insisted that they do so equally. Liberal organizations could no longer receive preferential treatment. For example, if the state desired to address the issue of poverty, it would need to justly distribute the poverty assistance funds to Catholic, Reformed, Jewish, socialist, and liberal charities alike. These organizations would be financially rewarded based, not on their agreement with liberal ideology, but on their institutional effectiveness in alleviating poverty. The definition of effectiveness would be a matter of democratic discussion among the worldviews; no single worldview could define effectiveness alone.

In terms of education policy, the pluralists fundamentally agreed with liberals that the state had a responsibility to see to it that all children received a basic education.[13] However, they did not agree that liberalism should have exclusive ideological control over the nation's schools. The pluralists argued that true democracy was a contest of worldviews, ideas, and ideologies. If public education empowered only one worldview (liberalism), then democracy would suffer. In other words, if all children had to be trained in the liberal worldview, then minority worldviews were being forced "into an unequal struggle."[14] In opposition to this, the pluralists argued that all schools, be they Catholic, Jewish, humanist, liberal, socialist, or Protestant, had a right to equal funding from the state. In this, they insisted, "we do not beg for an alm, but stand up for our right."[15] The right to equal funding did not come without some expectations. Under the pluralists' platform, the state would enforce a number of universal educational standards in reading, writing, arithmetic, and

---

13. "Kuyper also argued that the state had a legitimate interest in ensuring a certain academic level of schooling, and towards that end had the right to provide minimum regulation of all schools. Such regulation included requiring the association to be legally formed, building safety codes, teacher qualifications, subjects taught, hours in school per week, student/teacher ratios, and the writing of an extensive curriculum plan. (*Parl.* 3:394) The content, methodology, and direction (religious context) of the curriculum were not to be regulated. He agreed to common examinations but only if they could be written and administered by committees comprising educators from every type of school. In this way, he hoped that schools could be held accountable for teaching the rudiments of learning and basic structure of knowledge, but also remain free to do so from their own perspective," Naylor, "Kuyper and the Emergence of Neo-Calvinist Pluralism," 147–48.

14. Kuyper, "Maranatha," in *Centennial Reader*, 224–25.

15. Kuyper, *Ons Program*, 673; trans. in Naylor, "Kuyper and the Emergence of Neo-Calvinist Pluralism," 261.

so on. While the state examined a school's basic educational performance, it was not permitted to evaluate the truth of a school's philosophical foundations. At no time would a school be forced to prove the validity of its philosophy before the eyes of the state.

Beyond education, the pluralists went on to challenge the liberal system of political representation. Liberals had devised a regional winner-take-all electoral system in which only the largest ideological groups received a voice in parliament; the pluralists advocated a proportional voting system. According to their proposal, even small ideological groups with as little as five percent of the national vote could still garner at least some representation in the parliament.[16]

Christian pluralists openly admitted these reforms would not always be the most efficient way to govern the nation. But, they argued, such were the demands of justice in an ideologically divided society. True justice demanded a generous legal and political state.[17] While costly, a pluralistic state was required to "treat all denominations or religious communities . . . regardless of their views on things eternal, on a footing of equality."[18]

In addition to recognizing the cost, the pluralists admitted that they were opening their country up to a real political risk. They acknowledged that wild, outlandish, and even irresponsible religions and ideologies could take root in the free soil of pluralism. Acknowledging this risk, they ultimately concluded that the best way to protect the liberty and security of their nation was to allow these wild faiths to show their fruits and compete openly in a pluralistic marketplace of ideas and institutions, for whatever "shoots up and is able to grow must be allowed to grow."[19] The danger of instability and insecurity involved in pluralism "cannot detain us, for the obvious reason that this possibility exists just as much with [hegemony] but then in a more hideous, offensive, loathsome manner."[20]

It was indeed a possibility that a terrible ideology could abuse the freedoms of pluralism to gain national power and inflict violence and destroy pluralism itself. What would the Christian pluralists do then? How would they respond? One Christian pluralist at the time replied with a rather curious declaration. He stated that if an ideological tyranny ever arose, "Leave it

---

16. Kuyper, "Uniformity," in *Centennial Reader*, 41.
17. Kuyper, "Uniformity," in *Centennial Reader*, 41.
18. Abraham Kuyper, *Our Program* (Bellingham, WA: Lexham Press, 2015), 57.
19. Kuyper, *Our Program*, 68.
20. Kuyper, *Our Program*, 36.

to Christian believers, if need be to Christian martyrs, to have the honor of demonstrating the intrinsic emptiness of [that] non-Christian spiritual life."[21]

A Monumental Task

Nineteenth-century Christian pluralists faced significant social and political obstacles to achieving their goals. First, modern Dutch liberalism (their primary opponent) was one of the most dominant cultural and political powers the Netherlands had ever known. Not since the rule of the Roman Catholic Church in the Middle Ages had a single belief system and authority had so much power across the provinces. Dutch liberalism had progressively taken control of the state, schools, universities, newspapers, cultural institutions, and organizations. Countering their power and influence would not be easy.

Beyond the strength of their opponents, the pluralists were internally weak, as well. The majority of their constituents were rural, poor, uneducated, politically ill informed, unorganized, and unengaged. At the beginning of their movement they had no major newspapers, universities, or cultural and political organizations. Most of their members did not even have the right to vote. This disparate group of farmers, factory workers, and shopkeepers was hardly the makings of a potent modern political movement.

But all this could be overcome if potent and strategic alliances could be formed with some like-minded groups. Unfortunately, alliances were difficult to make for the pluralists. Other major groups at the time, like the conservatives, socialists, and moderate Protestants, were not interested in championing the cause of pluralism. Each was holding out hope that its group would soon rise up, dethrone liberalism, and replace it with its own national hegemony. They did not want pluralism—they wanted hegemony. With these allies off the table, the Roman Catholic Church was the last remaining option. The irony was palpable. The Christian pluralist movement was made up almost entirely of Reformational Calvinists. A Catholic/Reformational coalition was almost unimaginable. How would Protestant leaders ever convince their people to enter into a political alliance with Catholics?

To make matters worse, the fledgling pluralist movement had to contend with a volley of political accusations from their opponents. Liberals accused them of secretly harboring theocratic ambitions. Conservatives argued that their reforms were costly, dangerous, and destabilizing. Christian theocrats ac-

21. Kuyper, *Our Program*, 68.

cused the pluralists of having weak Christian convictions.[22] Christian pietists argued that true Christians should not engage in worldly politics.

Still, all of these monumental obstacles could be overcome if the movement had an inspiring slogan or galvanizing issue to rouse the faithful to action. Once again, the pluralists were at a distinct disadvantage—pluralism is not politically sexy. Stump speeches for a government that respects religious diversity hardly make for a riveting battle cry. As contemporary theorist Michael Walzer has argued, political movements demand a clear vision of some total victory or some future dominance. The pluralism argument for a diverse civil society hardly fits the bill. As Walzer explains, something critical "is lost when we give up the single-mindedness" of social uniformity. Looking back on the history of hegemonic political movements there was a

> heroism in those projects—a concentration of energy, a clear sense of direction, an unblinking recognition of friends and enemies. . . . The defense of civil society doesn't seem quite comparable . . . [I]ts greatest virtue lies in its inclusiveness and inclusiveness does not make for heroism. "Join the associations of your choice" is not a slogan to rally political militants.[23]

Govert Buijs, another contemporary theorist, echoes these sentiments when he asks whether a pluralistic society can actually be politically "desirable." For many voters, he explains, pluralism seems "morally defective, a muddy complex of compromises . . . weak and effeminate . . . inefficient, time-consuming, and bothersome."[24] The battle cry of pluralists for "a form of its own for whatever has a life of its own" fails to inspire.[25]

So the question is simple. How would this movement, with all of its internal and external challenges, ever succeed in growing from a series of small house meetings in the 1830s to the crowning achievement of the constitutional reforms of 1917? The remainder of this chapter tells that story.

---

22. See Hoedemaker's criticism of Christian pluralists in Hans Van Spanning, "Van Vrije-Antirevolutionairen naar Christelijk-Historische Unie," in *De Anti-Revolutionaire Partij 1829–1980*, George Harinck, Roel Kuiper, and Peter Bak, eds. (Hilversum: Verloren, 2001).

23. Michael Walzer, "The Idea of Civil Society: A Path to Social Reconstruction," in *Community Works: The Revival of Civil Society*, E. J. Dionne, ed. (Washington, DC: Brookings Institution, 1998), 141–43.

24. Govert Buijs, "The Promise of Civil Society," in *Civil Society: East and West*, Peter Blokhuis, ed. (Sioux Center, IA: Dordt College Press, 2006), 30–31.

25. Kuyper, "Uniformity," in *Centennial Reader*, 41.

This daunting list of challenges required a charismatic and energetic leader who could tackle a seemingly impossible array of tasks. The pluralists needed a leader who could organize a potent cultural network of newspapers, churches, schools, universities, and political organizations to support the movement. They needed a leader who could *intellectually deconstruct* the liberal hegemony with a barrage of rhetorically powerful editorials, books, speeches, and debate performances. They also needed a leader who could *intellectually construct* a robust Christian defense of the pluralistic alternative. They needed a leader who could steer Christians away from the four temptations of assimilation, moderation, retreat, and retribution. Finally, they needed a leader capable of convincing this group of very conservative Christians to fight for the rights and dignity of ideological communities with whom they deeply disagreed.

The pluralist movement demanded a leader with organizational wisdom, rhetorical wit, oratorical flare, political acumen, and theological bona fides. Such a leader would most likely not suffer from indecisiveness, nuance, or humility. For better, and sometimes for worse, the pluralists had their leader in Abraham Kuyper.

Abraham Kuyper: A Theologian of Pluralism

[We tolerate] not out of indifference to God's truth, but precisely out of the firm conviction that the truth of God demands it.[26]

Abraham Kuyper's life (1837–1920) spanned the full history of the pluralist movement, from its humble beginnings in 1830s house meetings to its grand legislative successes of the 1910s. In the movement's tireless service, Abraham Kuyper worked feverishly as a church pastor, school organizer, newspaper editor, university professor, party leader, and finally, as the prime minister of the Netherlands.

While chapter five will explore Abraham Kuyper's *constructive* theological case for Christian pluralism, chapter four will examine his *deconstructive* theological case against all forms of ideological hegemony and uniformity. Kuyper himself knew that deconstruction had to come first. The Dutch—like all peoples—naturally desired ideological unity and uniformity. Deep pluralism is uncomfortable, inefficient, and unstable. Kuyper knew, therefore,

26. Abraham Kuyper, *De Gemeene Gratie*, 3: 286 (Leiden: Donner, 1902–1905).

that this natural desire for ideological conformity needed to be thoroughly deconstructed before an alternative argument for pluralism could ever gain a hearing.

The next two chapters will, therefore, present two important sides of Abraham Kuyper's life and work—the deconstructive and the constructive, the critical and the creative. Both sides are integral, not only for understanding Kuyper's project, but also for understanding the project of any Christian pluralist. In every era, pluralists must not only be able to deconstruct calls for cultural and ideological assimilation, but they must also be able to construct alternative ways of living together with deep difference. Kuyper's two political callings, the critic and the collaborator, the antagonistic prophet and the reconciling priest, reflect the paradoxical path every Christian pluralist must walk.

Before I outline Abraham Kuyper's theological deconstruction of hegemony and his construction of pluralism, a number of cautions must be noted. First, Kuyper never composed a book-length treatise on either topic. His reflections on pluralism are scattered throughout a lifetime of editorials, speeches, letters, debates, and books that span six decades of recorded work. His arguments for pluralism were in constant development. Second, even at the end of his life, Kuyper was never a pure or perfectly consistent pluralist. He continued to desire a number of small public advantages for the Christian faith in the Netherlands, such as Sunday closing laws and God-based oaths in the courts. In all, the reader must remember that Kuyper was a creature of the nineteenth century and was prone to many of the biases and blind spots every finite historical position includes. Finally, while I do my best to be historically faithful to Abraham Kuyper's life and thought, what follows is not a comprehensive accounting and analysis of Abraham Kuyper's political theology. The two chapters that follow select and develop specific aspects of Kuyper's thought that can positively contribute to the contemporary practice of Christian pluralism.[27]

---

27. For those interested in getting a more macro-level view of Abraham Kuyper's life and work, I would recommend James Bratt's recent biography *Abraham Kuyper: Modern Calvinist, Christian Democrat* (Grand Rapids: Eerdmans, 2013) along with Bratt's edited collection of *Abraham Kuyper: A Centennial Reader* (Grand Rapids: Eerdmans, 1998) and Abraham Kuyper's *Lectures on Calvinism* (Grand Rapids: Eerdmans, 1954). These pieces sufficiently capture Kuyper's theological approach to religion, politics, science, culture, and public life. The following pages are an example of the *selective* use of Kuyper's public theology for my own construction of a new Christian pluralism. I do not use everything Kuyper wrote about religious freedom, politics, or Islam. For example, when writing about the Islamic faith, Kuyper was informed by years of careful study and extended personal contact during his travels through

Why did Abraham Kuyper dedicate his life to deep pluralism? Why did he commit every ounce of his energy to cultivating ideological freedom and justice? Reading his work makes one thing clear: he did not fight for religious freedom because he believed it was a patriotic duty, a scientific given, a rational conclusion, a pragmatic determination, a constitutional requirement, or a mark of civility or nobility. At the end of the day, Kuyper fought for pluralism because he honestly believed that his God demanded it. While Kuyper rhetorically appealed to history, tradition, reason, current events, emotion, patriotism, and experience, none of these factors compared to his foundational theological grounding for plural justice and freedom. For Kuyper, ideological hegemony was not merely irrational—it was blasphemous. For, Kuyper declared, whenever religious freedom is crushed, "God's name" is "robbed of its splendor."[28]

Kuyper's argument against hegemony and for pluralism was theological in its foundation, inspiration, orientation, and articulation. For, as he explained, "though our demands [for religious freedom] sometimes resemble those of the most active radicals, they grow from different roots. . . . We expect everything, and they nothing, from the faith!"[29] This is precisely why his editorials, speeches, and books on religious freedom were shot through with biblical references, theological images, and historical appeals to the Christian leaders of the past. He reappropriated nearly every major Christian doctrine to make his case that all Christians must fight against hegemony and for pluralism. The doctrines of creation, sin, grace, Christ, the Imago Dei, the church, the Holy Spirit, election, justification, and the eschaton all make appearances in his pluralistic appeals. The prominence of these theological themes in Kuyper's work presses the point that Kuyper was, first and foremost, a theologian of pluralism. His Christian faith was not an impediment to his pluralism—it was his chief resource.

---

the Mediterranean. That said, Kuyper's comments on Islam bear many of the marks of a destructive European orientalism. My decision not to explore Kuyper's comments on Islam in this book stems from my conviction that other aspects of his thought present themselves as more fruitful places for my goal of developing a Christian approach to pluralism.

28. Abraham Kuyper, *Our Program*, 64.

29. Kuyper, "Calvinism: Source and Stronghold of Our Constitutional Liberties," in *Centennial Reader*, 316.

CHAPTER FOUR

Kuyper's Deconstruction of Uniformity

[Our reforms] do not divide the nation or break society . . . they
find the nation divided, conviction against conviction and they
reckon with this undeniable fact! . . . [The freedom] we want for
ourselves we must not withhold from others!

ABRAHAM KUYPER[1]

Religious communities will never receive justice from liberals for the simple
reason that liberals do not understand religion. This is the heart of Abraham
Kuyper's critique of modern liberalism. Kuyper believed that all of the political
problems for which liberalism is continually criticized when it comes to issues
of religion and public life emerge from a series of fundamental misunderstand-
ings about what faith is and how faith works.

This chapter will explore Abraham Kuyper's argument that modern liberalism fundamentally misunderstood three critical aspects of the life of faith:
first, that liberals wrongly believed that faith was a unique condition that was
specifically limited to uniquely religious people; second, that liberals wrongly
believed that faiths could be unified through some form of governmental program of universal education or assimilation; and third, that liberals wrongly
believed that faith could somehow be kept private (that is, out of the public
square).

1. *Pro Rege* 3:181–182. Trans. and quoted in Wendy Fish Naylor, "Abraham Kuyper and the
Emergence of the Neo-Calvinist Pluralism in the Dutch School Struggle" (PhD diss., University
of Chicago, 2006), 147.

This chapter not only examines Kuyper's threefold rebuttal of liberalism on these points, but it also presents his alternative definition of faith as a potent force that is irretrievably pervasive, pluriform, and public. First, faith is *pervasive*. Kuyper argued that all lives are faith-based, and that all human beings ground their lives on a faith in someone, something, or some idea that is unproven or ungrounded. Whether people self-identify as religious or secular, they all rely on or believe in someone or something. Whether they select a higher being, a philosophical ideal, a charismatic leader, a political movement, an object, or simply their very selves, all people have some authority (or some collection of authorities) operating in their lives. Kuyper argued that no one is free from a desire to rely on or cleave to something.

Second, faith is *pluriform*. Kuyper insisted that humanity's allegiances and belief systems are hopelessly divided and they can never be reconciled or united by any governmental force. The ideologies of the world are distinct and disparate. No terrestrial practice or institution can hope to merge or assimilate them. They are, and will remain, divided and pluriform.

Third, faith is *public*. Kuyper insisted that the faiths and ideologies of the world will consistently resist political efforts to privatize or limit their influence. Belief systems will inevitably seep in or burst out into the public square. If liberalism continued to treat faith as something that could be privatized, it would never provide religious minorities with the recognition or justice that they deserve.

While this chapter is dedicated to Kuyper's criticism of liberals, they were not the only hegemonic movement that received sharp criticism from Abraham Kuyper. Christian theocrats also felt the sharp edge of Kuyper's rhetorical knife. Because Europe was leaving Christendom, Kuyper considered liberalism the more immediate danger. Nevertheless, Kuyper continued to have strong words of criticism for those who still hoped for a return to the rule of the church. Kuyper argued that theocrats and Constantinians failed to understand the pervasive, pluriform, and public nature of faith as well. Therefore, while the majority of this chapter is focused on Kuyper's deconstructive critique of liberal hegemony, it will also explore a number of his critiques of Christian hegemony. For Kuyper, neither the state nor the church could ever solve the problem of religious diversity by either artificially transcending, unifying, or privatizing the diverse faiths of the nation.

Before I begin, a few brief remarks on my methodology are necessary. First, Abraham Kuyper never collected or synthesized his many criticisms of the liberal hegemony. The specific terms *pervasive, pluriform*, and *public* are mine, not his. They are meant to heuristically summarize and organize his many thoughts on the subject into a helpful order.

Second, Kuyper's indiscriminate and inexact use of terms like "faith," "religion," "worldview," "life-expression," and "life-principle"[2] may appear problematic, but I believe that there is a profound reason for his life-long mixture of terms. Kuyper believed that dividing ideologies into the two simple categories of "religious" and "secular" was fundamentally arbitrary and unhelpful. Examining the beliefs and behavior of Catholicism and Nationalism, Protestantism and socialism, Islam and liberalism, Kuyper found more points of commonality than difference.[3] All ideological movements—secular or religious—were, in Kuyper's mind, fundamentally faith-based. To place secular and religious movements on different planes struck Kuyper as both problematic and unjust.

Third, Kuyper's claims that all faiths are pervasive, pluriform, and public need to be nuanced. Of course one can find individuals who claim no faith, allegiance, or ideal. Of course one can find individuals who claim a willingness to have their particular faith absorbed into a larger whole. One can even find individuals who profess a willingness to keep their faith private and personal. Kuyper admits that these limited exceptions can exist for a time.[4] That said, Kuyper insists that their existence is fleeting and their influence is limited. The absence of an ultimate point of loyalty, meaning, or purpose cannot persist for long. Kuyper insists that rootless individuals and communities are particularly vulnerable to being absorbed into rising ideologies who clearly point to some foundation or direction.[5] As a species, Kuyper argues, human beings cannot

2. Consider Kuyper's *Lectures on Calvinism* (Grand Rapids: Eerdmans, 1953), where modernism, German Pantheism, Statism, and the French Revolution are placed alongside of Islam, Catholicism, and Calvinism under the same descriptive label "worldview" (or *Weltanschauung*). Additional references to this work are given parenthetically in the text.

3. In the following discussion I will allow Kuyper's concept of "faith" (*pistis*) as it appears in works like *The Encyclopedia of Sacred Theology*, trans. Hendrik de Vries (New York: Charles Scribner's Sons, 1898) to run into, mingle with, and inform his concept of "worldview" as it appears in works like *Lectures on Calvinism*. This is an interpretive choice. I allow Kuyper's discussion of terms like faith, religion, life-expression, and worldview to run together to reflect the interchangeable way in which Kuyper himself spoke about these movements. While some scholars might try to clearly distinguish nationalism and liberalism as secular movements wholly other from religious movements like Islam and Catholicism, Kuyper appeared to see more similarity than difference. Kuyper's choice to remain imprecise with these terms is therefore reflected in the following section. Additional references to this work are given parenthetically in the text.

4. See, for example, Abraham Kuyper, *De Meiboom in De Kap* (Kampen: Kok, 1913), 15.

5. "In any successful attack on freedom the state can only be an accomplice. The *chief* culprit is the citizen who forgets his duty, wastes away his strength in the sleep of sin and sensual pleasure, and so loses the power of his own initiative. . . . Only when discipline weakened and affluence slipped in and sin became brazen could theory bend what was enfeebled and

remain untethered, neutral, or pragmatic forever. The species will continually seek a point of ultimate meaning and purpose. As G. K. Chesterton wrote, "Pragmatism is a matter of human needs; and one of the first of human needs is to be something more than a pragmatist."[6] Abraham Kuyper would have agreed.

Faith as Pervasive

Human beings believe. They trust. They rely. They worship. Any anthropological system that failed to recognize that the fundamental role of *fides* in human life was, in the mind of Abraham Kuyper, seriously flawed. And yet this is exactly what many liberals had done. They had argued that faith was a temporary state which the human species could outgrow. They believed that human beings could achieve an areligious state of bare secular rationality and neutrality.

Abraham Kuyper's anthropology stood in stark contrast to this assumption. He believed that all human life is, at bottom, a faith-based endeavor. Faith, he argued, is an ineradicable *"habitus"* (*Encyclopedia*, 266) of the human species. Faith "precedes every act of thought or observation" (*Encyclopedia*, 132) and serves as the foundation upon which all "human intercourse is founded" (*Encyclopedia*, 134). All people—whether they label themselves religious or secular—live by some form of precognitive, prerational faith. These *pistic* foundations, however unexamined, provide human beings with a sense of security, purpose, direction, and confidence. Simply put, if human beings were ever going to go out and engage the world around them, they would first need to put some level of precognitive faith in their senses, reasoning, and cognition. For every human action in the world

> presupposes faith in self, in our self-consciousness; presupposes faith in the accurate working of our senses; presupposes faith in the correctness of the laws of thought; presupposes faith in something universal hidden behind the special phenomena; presupposes faith in life; and especially presupposes faith in the principles, from which we proceed. . . . (*Lectures*, 131)

Napoleon kick in the decrepit." Abraham Kuyper, "Sphere Sovereignty" in *Abraham Kuyper: A Centennial Reader*, ed. James Bratt (Grand Rapids: Eerdmans, 1998), 473.

6. G. K. Chesterton, *Orthodoxy* (London: John Lane Company, 1909), 64.

Not as if the knowledge of others rests on intellectual certainty and ours only on faith. For all knowledge proceeds from faith of whatever kind. You lean on God, you proceed from your own ego, or you hold fast to your ideal. The person who does not believe does not exist.[7]

Whether we admit it or not, Kuyper insisted, our scientific, social, and political lives are positively shot through with faith-based convictions (*Encyclopedia*, 266). A culture's faith-based assumptions about life are so pervasive that a culture's institutions, systems, and artifacts become the tangible "expression of what is central" to that culture's soul.[8]

But what did Kuyper mean by faith? From his writings it is clear that Kuyper did not simply mean a bare set of epistemological starting points, nor did he mean an abstract set of distant philosophical beliefs. Faith, Kuyper argued, is a deeply intimate, relational, and even mystical "cleaving to something" (*Encyclopedia*, 128). This "something" is not only believed, but it is beloved and sovereign. This point of ultimate allegiance cannot be proven by science, logic, or reason; it rests in the mysteries of the human heart and soul.

Standing in the tradition of Augustine and Calvin, Kuyper argues that human beings are naturally inclined not simply to intellectual beliefs but to a whole-life commitment of worship, devotion, and service. He argues that this predisposition toward whole-life faith was "implanted" in the human species at their very creation (*Lectures*, 45). Kuyper's anthropology is shot through with the conviction that human beings are haunted by an inescapable *sensus divinitatus*—a haunting sense that all of life is lived *Coram Deo* (before the face of God). In this sense, he argued, all people are engaged in a search after "something to which to cleave" (*Encyclopedia*, 277). Whether that something be Yahweh or Allah, science or reason, the nation or the market, pragmatism or materialism, the rule of the proletariat or one's own individual will, all human beings will ultimately submit to and serve someone or something. Faith is a whole-life practice, he argued, a practice "from which the mind cannot free itself."[9] "Our thinking can not help but inquire about" matters of faith (*Wisdom and Wonder*, 69). We are all looking, in our own unique ways, for "the origin, the coherence, and the destiny of things" (*Wisdom and Wonder*, 69). To be human is to be engaged in a search for that singular "point in our

7. Kuyper, "Sphere Sovereignty," in *Centennial Reader*, 486.
8. Kuyper, "Common Grace," in *Centennial Reader*, 198.
9. Abraham Kuyper, *Wisdom and Wonder: Common Grace in Science and Art*, trans. Nelson Kloosterman (Grand Rapids: Christian's Library Press, 2011), 71. Additional references to this work are given parenthetically in the text.

consciousness in which our life is still undivided and lies comprehended in its unity—not in the spreading vines but in the root from which the vines spring" (*Lectures*, 20).

While there are many potential objects of faith, Kuyper ultimately divides humanity into two categories: those who bind themselves to Jesus Christ and those who bind their lives to something else. One could attach oneself to a series of abstract philosophical ideals like beauty, justice, or truth. One could attach oneself to a community like a family, clan, race, or nation. Some bind themselves to material objects like money, sex, or some aspect of nature. One could even give one's self wholly to the practices of commerce, art, leisure, or politics. It is critical to note that, for Kuyper, all of these ideals, relationships, material objects, and practices were, in and of themselves, good and valuable things. Kuyper was not against beauty, families, money, or commerce. That said, none of those things deserved singular title of *sovereign* in a person's life. As a Christian, Kuyper insisted that ultimate allegiance could be rendered only to Jesus Christ.

Admitting that one's life rested on some sort of faith was, in Kuyper's mind, simply a matter of intellectual honesty. To deny faith's role, to claim pure objectivity and rationality, was a "culpable blindfolding" of the self (*Encyclopedia*, 152). Moderns who declared that they could transcend the super-stitions of faith and ground their thought "exclusively upon the action of the senses" were, according to Kuyper, "entirely mistaken, and allow themselves a leap to which they have no right" (*Encyclopedia*, 132). Every system of human thought pivoted on some deep fulcrum, and intellectual honesty demanded that liberals stand alongside other people of faith and "tell us where the pivot" in their lives and thought ultimately lies.[10] For is it not true, Kuyper asked, that all human beings "view things through a subjective lens and always fill in the unseen part of the circle according to [their] subjective opinion?"[11] "What natural scientist operates without a hypothesis"; does he not practice "science as a *man* and not as a *measuring stick?*"[12] For our "consciousness, our reason, and our understanding are something altogether different from a camera" (*Wisdom and Wonder*, 63). "All this" and more, "shows the utter untenability of the current representation that science establishes truth" (*Encyclopedia*, 143).

Ultimately, Kuyper argued that while liberals were aware of the super-

---

10. Kuyper, *Our Program*, trans. Harry Van Dyke (Bellingham, WA: Lexham Press, 2015), 51. Additional references to this work are given parenthetically in the text.

11. Kuyper, "Sphere Sovereignty," in *Centennial Reader*, 488.

12. Kuyper, "Sphere Sovereignty," in *Centennial Reader*, 487–88.

structure of their political ideology, the faith-based *"ground* on which the lowest points of these piles rest is not explored." He lamented that, to the misfortune of all, a self-critical investigation of liberalism's ground floor "is abandoned before it is finished" (*Encyclopedia*, 129; emphasis mine).

While Kuyper's deconstruction of modern claims to religious neutrality is now common fare in the postmodern academy, Nicholas Wolterstorff reminds his readers that Kuyper's nineteenth-century critique was delivered during "the heyday of modernism."[13] For, in "an age which swore by the supposed objectivity and impartiality of all science,"[14] Kuyper's deconstructions were considered "highly provocative and eccentric."[15] Kuyper was, in many ways, "a postmodernist born out of season."[16] His deconstructive arguments that liberals were "not blank tablets, *tabula rasa*, on which the facts of the world are inscribed"[17] would have placed him on the outer fringes of the nineteenth-century European academy. Del Ratszch, a philosopher of science, echoes Wolterstorff's evaluation, arguing that "Fifty years before many Western philosophers, Kuyper had already seen that 'values' and even metaphysical principles play a proper, ineradicable role" in academic inquiry and discourse.[18]

But Kuyper's prophetic deconstruction was aimed at more than scientific positivism. It was aimed at political positivism as well. In challenging the objectivity of the liberal academy, notes Wolterstorff, Kuyper was "challenging the Lockean model" of the liberal public square "at its very foundation."[19] For, if modern liberals did not have an exclusive claim over scientific discourse, they would not have an exclusive claim over political discourse either.

If Kuyper was right, liberalism was no longer special. It was no longer unique. It had not transcended dogma; it was one faith among many. It, too, would have to compete openly and equally in the marketplace of ideas, beliefs, and practices. If Kuyper was right, liberals in both the laboratory and the public square would have to surrender their quixotic search for the "phantom" of "neutrality."[20]

13. Nicholas Wolterstorff, *Educating for Shalom: Essays in Christian Higher Education*, ed. Clarence Joldersma and Gloria Goris Stronks (Grand Rapids: Eerdmans, 2003), 117.

14. Jacob Klapwijk, "Rationality in the Dutch Neo-Calvinist Tradition," in *Rationality in the Calvinian Tradition*, ed. H. Hart et al. (Lanham, MD: University Press of America, 1983), 98.

15. Wolterstorff, *Educating for Shalom*, 214–15.

16. Wolterstorff, *Educating for Shalom*, 208.

17. Wolterstorff, *Educating for Shalom*, 67.

18. Del Ratzsch, "Abraham Kuyper's Philosophy of Science," *Calvin Theological Journal* 27 (1992), 301.

19. Wolterstorff, *Educating for Shalom*, 208.

20. Kuyper, *Gemeene Gratie*, vol. 3 (Leiden: Donner, 1902–1905), 280. Additional references to this work are given parenthetically in the text.

In the end, Kuyper argued, Christians should actually give thanks to God for the skepticism of "Kant and his contemporaries." For, though the Kantians had "intended injury to the Christian faith," their skepticism was in fact a double-edged sword. The Kantians had providentially inserted doubt into the very heart of the modern liberal project. Because of Kant, moderns could no longer be so certain of their objectivity. This Kantian doubt, Kuyper argued, could now be used to pry open liberalism's iron doors to create a dialogical space for counter-faiths like Christianity to gain a critical voice in both the laboratory and the state (*Encyclopedia*, 675).[21]

Liberalism had promised a secular political discourse free of religious creeds and authoritative thrones. Kuyper's response was quite simple. He openly questioned liberalism's ability to keep its creeds unwritten and its thrones empty. For no human being, he insisted, could "rest content with such a bare negation" (*Lectures*, 23). When one faith is dethroned, someone or something else will inevitably be "placed on the vacant seat" (*Lectures*, 87). The human desire to believe cannot be avoided. Faith is, and always will be, pervasive. And this is why, Kuyper declared, however much the liberals "rage against dogmas, they themselves are the most stubborn of dogmatists."[22] Herein lay the most dangerous aspect of liberalism, its blindness to its own faith (*Lectures*, 51).

Faith as Pervasive: Liberalism as Religion

Throughout the nineteenth century, liberals used the pejorative labels of *dogmatic* and *sectarian* to rhetorically marginalize Catholic and Protestant communities. All the while, they themselves claimed to be beyond dogma. Catholics and Protestants were framed as a religious problem that required a secular solution.

Kuyper flipped their rhetorical strategy back on them by playfully exposing that it was, in fact, liberals who were the "doctrinaire democrats" (*Our Program*, 91). At many points in his work, he tabulates a list of liberal super-

---

21. Considering Kuyper's deconstruction of modern neutrality, the "postmodern" label seems to fit quite well. That said, Kuyper's seemingly postmodern stress on the role of subjectivity and the noetic effects of sin are balanced by a chastened confidence in the stability and order of God's creation and the continued ability of human beings to at least partially perceive creation's structures and laws by the common grace of God. A careful discussion of these more hopeful elements in Kuyper's moral anthropology will be covered at the end of chapter five.

22. Kuyper, "Modernism: A Fata Morgana," in *Centennial Reader*, 115.

stitions, taboos, and dogmatic prejudices latent within the religion of modern liberalism. He spoke of their mystical devotion to "the Catechism of Rousseau and Darwin" (*Lectures*, 189). He declared their academies to be the "sectarian schools" of modernism (*Our Program*, 192) and "counter-churches" (*Our Program*, 188). Kuyper even playfully described liberal elites as a new clerical order. For

> '*Clerus*' was what people called the class of religious people that claimed they were the only ones that knew how things were, and expected nothing from the rest of the people except to learn how things were. And now have not our liberals lent themselves to the charge of dividing the nation into a *Clerus* class who knew, and a class of lay people, who had no right to speak?[23]

Moderns had loudly declared that they alone had liberated themselves from religious ritual, confession, and clericalism. And yet, with a twinkle in his eye, Kuyper repeatedly pointed out how liberals themselves had doggedly mimicked the liturgical, catechetical, and dogmatic practices of the religion they claimed to transcend. Kuyper reveled in the irony that liberals were now copying the catechisms they had always mocked.

> How droll they had found those Sunday schools! . . . What fun they had at the expense of those "piety factories"! But now. . . Modernists distribute their own little tracts . . . [organize their own] Sunday schools [and] Societies. . . . Once they expected to celebrate our funeral; now we see them robed in what they thought were our winding-sheets.[24]

Liberalism had not transcended religious institutions—it had simply made new ones.

From this position, Kuyper argued that liberalism was not simply a new political technique; it was an "all-embracing *life-system*" (*Lectures*, 11). This new life-system made deep and far-reaching claims concerning the nature of humanity, community, authority, and the contours of the good life. To support this new life-system, liberalism had erected a broad apparatus of liturgical, educational, and political means to empower its mission to the

---

23. Abraham Kuyper, *De Schoolkwestie II. De Scherpe Resolutie En Het Decretum Horribile* (Amsterdam: J.H. Kruyt, 1875), 3. Quoted and trans. in Naylor, "Abraham Kuyper," 247.

24. Kuyper, "Modernism: A Fata Morgana," in *Centennial Reader,* 107.

Dutch people. Labeling liberalism a religion was not simply a playful game of "oratorical phraseology but simply indicating a purely logical concept" (*Our Program*, 70). Liberalism was rendering ultimate trust in modern reason, science, and individualism. Why couldn't he label such behavior religious?

In this playful rhetorical move, Kuyper was undermining a powerful dichotomy that had been constructed between so-called secular and religious movements in the Netherlands. This powerful and pervasive dichotomy effectively marginalized those labeled "religious" and empowered those labeled "secular." In deconstructing the dichotomy, Kuyper hoped to destroy the political hierarchy that it naturally produced.

William Cavanaugh, a contemporary political theologian, has spent years analyzing secular definitions of religion in modern political discourse. His findings seem to support Kuyper's conclusions that modern distinctions between religious and secular political movements are more the result of a rhetorical power play than scientific distinction.[25] When considering the common secular-religious rhetoric, Cavanaugh explains that religious political movements are commonly described as superstitious, violent, and controlling, while secular movements tend to be described as rational, peaceful, and liberating. Quite simply, religious movements are depicted in international politics as the problem, while secular movements are conveniently described as the solution. This reinforces a simple power dynamic whereby secular authorities are legitimate and religious authorities are not.

Cavanaugh deconstructs this problematic dichotomy by outlining how so-called secular political movements like capitalism, socialism, liberalism, nationalism, and rationalism have all displayed many of the same characteristics of so-called religious movements. Cavanaugh examines how secular movements have historically used their own rituals, practices, texts, and histories to control populations, suppress diversity, and inflict violence. He demonstrates how these secular movements pass on their ideological habits, practices, and beliefs to young citizens, how they demand ultimate devotion, and finally how they require the giving and taking of life to sustain their secular visions of the good life.

In the end, Cavanaugh concludes that modern distinctions between religious and secular movements appear to be little more than a rhetorical power play by which one faith (secularism) is able to marginalize other faiths. By

25. William Cavanaugh, *The Myth of Religious Violence* (Oxford: Oxford University Press, 2009).

problematizing other faiths, the liberal faith sets itself up as the rightful solution. In diagnosing everyone else as sick, liberals become the cure.

Abraham Kuyper's most recent biographer notes that he had a unique ability in the nineteenth century to "unmask the emerging modern regime of putative religious 'neutrality' as in fact a scheme of secularist hegemony."[26] Under Kuyper's schema, while liberalism would still have a voice in the public square, it would simply be one among many. Kuyper envisioned a day when liberalism would no longer be allowed to dominate or control public discourse—be it academic, cultural, or political. Having exposed the faith-based assumptions of modern liberalism, Kuyper hoped to cultivate a public square in which his own Christian belief could "take its stand" neither under nor above but "by the side" of liberalism (*Lectures*, 21).

Now that liberalism had been exposed, Kuyper concluded that the new religion had two choices. It could humbly accept its position as being one faith among many faiths, or it could openly admit its aspirations for ideological hegemony. If the new liberal religion chose the latter, Kuyper suggested that his ideological overlords "remove the Lion from the Netherlands' coat of arms, the symbol of the fiercest freedom, and set up in its place an Eagle with a lamb in its claws, a symbol of tyranny!"[27]

Faith as Pluriform

[T]he unity of the world is merely painted on the walls.
ABRAHAM KUYPER[28]

Abraham Kuyper was convinced that the faiths, ideologies, and worldviews of the human race would never come together to form a unified consensus. Until the end of time, humanity's faiths would remain irretrievably diverse and pluriform. Human beings would never bow to the same ultimate authority. They would never submit to the same ultimate law. Their lives would aim in different directions. Their souls would rest in different saviors. In light of this assertion, Abraham Kuyper declared that all movements that dreamed of creating ideological unity and uniformity were both misguided and dangerous.

26. James D. Bratt, *Abraham Kuyper: Modern Calvinist, Christian Democrat* (Grand Rapids: Eerdmans, 2013), xiv.

27. Kuyper, *De Schoolkwestie I. Naar Aanleiding Van Het Onderwijs-Debat in De Kamer*, 22.

28. "Uniformity: The Curse of Modern Life," in *Centennial Reader*, 23. Additional references to this work are given parenthetically in the text.

The pluriformity of faiths would remain a permanent feature of political life until the return of Christ.[29]

Kuyper believed that it was his Christian duty to resist both secular and religious movements that would try to unite the world's faiths through the use of political power. He insisted that secular and religious hegemons alike were asking the same wrongheaded question about ideological diversity. Their hegemonic question, "How can the state unite the nation's faiths?" needed to be replaced with the pluralist question "How can the state provide justice for the nation's faiths?" Kuyper wanted to move both religious and secular ideologues toward this pluralistic question. To accomplish this, Kuyper would need to deconstruct their misguided dreams of national uniformity once and for all. They had to accept, at long last, that they could never use the powers of the state or the church to "compel universal homage" or "bring about a unity of settled result."[30]

For Kuyper, God alone was the only possible source of ideological unity. No state, no church, no cultural movement, no school system, no scientific method, and no system of human reason could ever unite the pluriformity of faiths. God alone had claim to such authority. Terrestrial powers and institutions were all finite and flawed in their power and judgment. None of them could claim direct access to ultimate truth, justice, or authority. Humanity had severed its direct connection to all of these ultimate forms of unity when it rebelled in sin. For, "if things had not been broken," Kuyper argued, humanity's moral "consciousness would emit the same sound from all" (*Lectures*, 136). In cutting itself off from God, Kuyper declared, "an abyss in the universal human consciousness" was opened up "across which no bridge can be laid."[31] No state, religion, or scientific method could ever successfully bridge the ideological divisions.

While Kuyper accepted and defended the diversity of faiths, he did not celebrate it. Because they were the result of human rebellion, he mourned humanity's faith-based disagreements. Kuyper's negative appraisal of *pistic* pluriformity is a curious outlier in his corpus. Typically, when Kuyper encounters some form of diversity in the world, he gives effusive praise to God for

29. In this section, readers of agonistic political philosophy will find a side of Abraham Kuyper that sounds eerily similar to this contemporary perspective. While Kuyper's proximity to this tradition cannot be denied, he will betray some important differences from agonism in chapter five when we discuss his chastened hopes for interfaith dialogue, cooperation, and justice.

30. Abraham Kuyper, "The Twofold Development of Science," in *Principles of Sacred Theology*, trans. J. Hendrik De Vries (Grand Rapids: Eerdmans, 1954), 116.

31. Kuyper, *Principles of Sacred Theology*, 152.

the beautiful variety and pluriformity on display. Kuyper commonly thanks God for the variety of human persons, gifts, callings, and cultures. He revels in the kaleidoscopic diversity of animals, regions, and landscapes. Kuyper even gives thanks for the vast diversity of Christian churches, which reflect a wide variety of aspects of the manifold glory and mission of Jesus Christ. In many ways, Kuyper was enraptured with pluriformity, for he saw the glory of God most clearly reflected in the prismatic and dynamic diversity of God's creation.

However, the diversity of religions and ideologies was different for Kuyper. He insisted that human beings were called and created to worship God and God alone. They were not created for communion with many gods—they were created for One. Kuyper could never bring himself to revel in the diversity of ways in which human beings directed their worship away from the creator and toward some aspect of creation (*Encyclopedia*, 280–81). Kuyper called this split in human worship (between those who worshipped the creator and those who worshipped some part of creation) "the antithesis." Kuyper argued that because of this fracturing of humanity's one faith, because of this antithesis, "Moral consensus, the further we go, looks more and more like a mirage" (*Gemeene Gratie*, vol. 3, 181). In our rebellious state against God our "ideas everywhere separate" (*Lectures*, 131). Ideological fragmentation and division is simply the reality of life lived after the fall into sin.

Not only was the spiritual fragmentation real and permanent, Kuyper insisted, but it also would be pervasive throughout humanity's social, cultural, and political life. The impact of this fragmentation would be found, not only "in the sensations of the heart," but

> in the fabric of our thoughts, in our antipathies and sympathies, throughout our conception of life, in the way we conceive of our personal, domestic, social and political life. It exists in our science and in our art, in our jurisprudence and in our pedagogy. It penetrates everything. . . . To say that the Dutch people are of one mind and one meaning is nothing but a sentimental fantasy. . . we are not one.[32]

Kuyper argued that those who aspired to bridge these deep ideological chasms with a universal religion or morality betrayed a weak understanding of the true depths of human brokenness and sin. During Kuyper's day, liberals were optimisticaly arguing that modern science, rationality, and the liberal nation-state could overcome these ideological differences. In a similar fashion,

---

32. Abraham Kuyper, *Wij Calvinisten* (Kampen: Kok, 1909), 15.

Dutch theocrats argued that a state church—if properly empowered—could unite the divided nation. Kuyper insisted that both immanent visions of ideological uniformity were deeply mistaken. For all governments, school systems, and "even the churches, are undermined by and stained with human weakness and sin" (*Gemeene Gratie*, vol. 3, 268).

One final note: Abraham Kuyper's evaluation of non-Christian ideologies is always both deeply positive and deeply critical at the same time. It is deeply positive in that the universal human desire to worship displayed in non-Christian ideologies is not an evil thing—it is a gift from God. For, "there is no form of idolatry so low, or so corrupted" that has "not sprung from this [God-given] *semen religionis*" (*Encyclopedia*, 301). That said, Kuyper's critical evaluation still holds. While humans' urge to worship is both natural and good, their choice to direct their worship away from God is not. Kuyper still labels non-Christian ideologies idolatrous because they have misdirected their God-given worship away from the creator and toward the creation. This simultaneously positive and negative evaluation of non-Christian faiths will be critical, moving forward.

Faith as Pluriform: Against Christian Hegemony

Kuyper argued throughout his career that it was not the calling of the church to coercively unite the pluriform faiths of the world. The church, he argued, must also remain "*ipso facto* antithetical to the unity dream. . . . This is its essential character, its very nature."[33] He lamented that Christians throughout history had become enraptured by the dream of Christian hegemony. Christ alone could bridge the divisions of the human heart. Christendom was, according to Kuyper, a blasphemous attempt by the church to claim Christ's authority for itself.

Kuyper identified two distinct ways in which churches attempted to solve the problem of religious diversity. The first method was one of aggression. Here the church bridged ideological divides through the forceful assimilation of minority faiths into an all-powerful state church. The second method was one of assimilation. Here the church solved the problem by allowing itself to be absorbed into some larger national community. While these two methods, aggression and assimilitation, appear quite different, they actually rest upon some common assumptions: first, that the pluriformity of ideologies is

---

33. Kuyper, "Calvinism: Source and Stronghold of Our Constitutional Liberties," in *Centennial Reader*, 390. Additional references to this work are given parenthetically in the text.

a problem that the church must solve, and second, that the church must serve the nation by giving up something core to its identity to solve the problem of ideologicial division (either its peaceableness or its exclusive faith).

Abraham Kuyper argued that the strategies of aggression and assimilation both fundamentally undermine the radically separate, free, and distinct nature of the church of Jesus Christ. Both debased the church's integrity, castrated its preaching, perverted its mission, and ultimately sapped its power. Kuyper insisted, against both sides, that Christ had drawn a clear line of distinction between church, state, and nation "that no one can expunge" ("Calvinism: Source and Stronghold," 397). For, from the church's very beginnings, its "characteristic imprint" has been that it was "not of this world" ("Calvinism: Source and Stronghold," 390). For Kuyper, the church was called to be a distinct and voluntary community, an outpost of freedom, "within the iron ring of uniformity."[34] If the church forcefully assimilated outsiders or allowed itself to be assimilated, it would suffer a fundamental "loss of its character" ("Calvinism: Source and Stronghold," 390).

According to Kuyper, the regin of Constantine was an early example of the church forfeiting its distinct character. Kuyper lamented that in grasping the emperor's sword, the church had hoped to penetrate the world, but in actuality "the world penetrated the church" (*Gemeene Gratie*, vol. 3, 202). By accepting the empirical logic of the *Pax Romana*, the voluntary and peaceful "method of Jesus was replaced by the old method of power and violence" (*Gemeene Gratie*, vol. 3, 202).

The church's integrity and vitality depended on its independence from the state. For, according to Kuyper, the "church never sank away more deeply than when she went back to the inn and sought to become a national or state church; neither did she revive again in spiritual vigor, except when the Lord drove her out of the inn and pointed her back to the stable."[35] State-funded churches die a slow death of lethargy and torpor, Kuyper argued: "Just look at what is left of vitality in the Greek Orthodox church! Look at the piteous state of the Evangelical churches in Germany" (*Our Program*, 36). Achieving the title "national church" would

> only lead to the spiritual death of the church. . . . [It] deprives the church of Christ of its freedom of movement, which is one of its vital

---

34. Kuyper, "Sphere Sovereignty," in *Centennial Reader*, 469.

35. Abraham Kuyper, *Keep Thy Solemn Feasts*, trans. John Hendrik Devries (Grand Rapids: Eerdmans, 1928), 78–79.

conditions. It turns its pastors and teachers as if by magic into vapid and haughty magistrates. . . . This weakens the church, causes it to pine away, and numbs its spirit. (*Our Program*, 35)

The political establishment of Christianity was, in Kuyper's mind, a pyrrhic victory. For, when state churches embrace a nation of many faiths by thinning out their own faith, they drain the gospel of its central power. Kuyper loathed the banal sermons of state preachers who sought to please anyone and everyone in the nation. Kuyper complained that "We want to be inspired, not put to sleep. We seek God's glorious ordinances, not hollow words or empty phrases" (*Our Program*, 36). Kuyper regularly lamented the establishment of a national Reformed church in the Netherlands after the Reformation. He mourned that his forefathers "did not relax the ties that bound the church to the state."[36] In binding their vibrant reformational movement to the power of the govenment, the church "soon saw the stream of its life freeze over."[37]

Kuyper argued that true Christian pluralists would never "want a restoration of the state church, for we know how detrimental it is to our faith. We do not long for the church to be a schoolmistress once again." For, under state churches, "even holy ground has to be made common for the purpose of dissolving all religious differences into a 'Christianity' above confessional division" ("Uniformity," 32). For preachers paid by the state are commonly degraded to "performing sapper services for the *zeitgeist*" ("Calvinism: Source and Stronghold," 395).

Faith as Pluriform: Against Liberal Hegemony

If Christian hegemony was not an option for Kuyper, neither was liberal hegemony. One common strategy for liberal hegemony—popular in Kuyper's day and our own—is the imposition of a liberal moral language on the public square. Under such a strategy, minority faiths are still permitted to have their own private moral languages. Still, when these minority faiths enter the public square, they are allowed to speak but only by using the moral

36. Kuyper, "Conservatism and Orthodoxy: False Versus True Preservation," in *Centennial Reader*, 68.

37. Kuyper, "Conservatism and Orthodoxy: False Versus True Preservation," in *Centennial Reader*, 68.

language of liberalism. Through the imposition of a single universal moral discourse, liberals believed, and believe, that they can overcome the problem of pluriformity.

This liberal dream of binding all faiths and cultures together under a universal moral language echoes, in many ways, medieval Catholic arguments for a universal natural law. Under natural law, medieval scholastics argued, God had embedded his moral laws throughout creation and, moreover, had written those laws on every human heart. Through the use of human reason, natural law theorists argued, all people and all cultures could recognize the universal contours of God's natural laws.

Abraham Kuyper doubted both proposals for a universal moral law that could bind all faiths, ideologies, and cultures together. Whether he was responding to the universalizing claims of either liberals or Catholics, Kuyper's hesitancy rested on a single theological conviction—the fallen and perverted nature of all systems of human morality. Being a Calvinist, Kuyper believed that the moral conscience of all people had been stained by the mind-darkening or noetic effects of sin. Kuyper therefore argued that neither secular liberals nor religious Catholics could claim access to a universal morality. He insisted that any "pure knowledge and firmness of these divine ordinances has been lost as a result of sin" (*Our Program*, 33). Humanity no longer had immediate or undefiled access to universal moral laws. Human systems could, therefore, "never provide us with the criterion for justice because man's sense of justice [had been] disturbed by sin" (*Our Program*, 30). If the opposite were the case, if we were indeed free from sin, then

> political officials could discern that universal law from what they see all around them, from the run of life itself, from the way things work! Just as an experienced watchmaker gets to know the principles according to which a watch is made when he takes the watch apart . . . so in the same way governments would get to know the proper course of life through simple observation—would learn the principles that underlie those laws that are just. (*Our Program*, 33)

However, because of human sinfulness, all investigations of morality are biased in favor of the investigator.

In contrast to liberal and Catholic attempts to articulate a universal moral law, Kuyper insisted, Christian pluralists "refuse to be blinded by an illusion of certainty." Instead, they must be "content with more modest results" (*Our Program*, 38). After all, wasn't that presumptuous "striving for unity, that hankering to be one people and to have one language, majestically put down in the collapse and rubble of the tower of Babel?" ("Uniformity," 23).

If one could not access universal moral law through science or reason, natural law or natural theology, neither could one find a universal law in Holy Scripture. Kuyper declared that no reader could determine once and for all the divine ordinances from Scripture without inserting his or her own sinful motivations. No one was capable of this—no scholar, no theologian, no politician, and no church. You must remember, Kuyper insisted,

> you are dealing with sinners—with a sinner on the throne, with sinners in the assembly hall, with a sinner in his study, with sinners at the voting booth and the home. . . . [Once you recognize the reality of sin] you come to the frank admission, whether you like it or not, that the word of God, however perfect in itself, yet precisely because it finds only sinners, can never be fully understood. You will recognize that it is impossible to formulate with fixed certainty, and lay down for all ages and all countries, the principles or ordinances of justice revealed in that Word. (*Our Program*, 37)

Therefore, "If you carry on and ignore the profound significance of the fact of sin, as theocrats do, then you deem the sinner quite capable of acquiring firm, correct and keen knowledge of what God's Word reveals about civil life" (*Our Program*, 37).

While Kuyper was deeply distrustful of universal moral systems, it is important to note that he did not believe in a state of *total* human confusion, chaos, and dissent when it came to morality. Kuyper did, in fact, believe in a natural law. He did believe that all people had been created with a universal sense of right and wrong and that creation was filled with divine ordinances and patterns to which all people and cultures had access.

So how does one resolve this with Kuyper's moral pessimism? Nicholas Wolterstorff succinctly captures both sides of Kuyper's moral anthropology when he explains that it "requires a division of the question: ontologically, Kuyper agrees that there is a natural law. Epistemologically, he expects abiding disagreement about the content of natural law."[38] In other words, two things are true for Kuyper. First, all religions and ideologies feel the same God-given

---

38. Wolterstorff, "Abraham Kuyper's Model of Democratic Polity for a Religiously Diverse Citizenry," in *Kuyper Reconsidered: Aspects of His Life and Work*, ed. Cornelis van der Kooi and Jan de Bruijn (Amsterdam: Free University Press, 1999), 198.

moral laws pressing upon them. Second, because all religions and ideologies are blinded by the noetic effects of sin, they will never completely agree on the substance of those universal laws they all feel. In other words, while all religions and cultures will agree on the need for things like love, justice, fidelity, and family, because of our sin, "the actual appropriation, use and confession of [these things] will be different" (*Gemeene Gratie*, vol. 3, 233). Abraham Kuyper argues that complete moral agreement "would only be possible if there were an extraordinary, supernatural organ that could decide with absolute certainty what the revealed knowledge of God demanded in a given case. But such an organ is lacking . . . [and] any attempt to call such an organ into existence . . . [has] corrupted state and church alike" (*Our Program*, 60).

Having fallen into sin, Christians and non-Christians alike had lost the ability to fully outline the universal laws God had laid down in creation. In our sin humanity can "see the parts, pieces, and elements, but we no longer have an eye for . . . [their] unity, origin, and destiny" (*Wisdom and Wonder*, 55). Thus, Kuyper explained, just as "a dog or bird sees the bricks of a palace, the wood and plaster, maybe the colors, [the animal] comprehends nothing of the architecture, the style, the purpose of the rooms and windows, [in the same way] we stand with darkened understanding before the temple of creation."[39]

The debate between moral universalists and relativists is a common fixture in contemporary discussions of pluralism. Scholars, columnists, and politicians can often be found surrendering to either Scylla or Charybdis. In the next chapter, we will see how Abraham Kuyper attempts to equip Christian pluralists with an alternative way forward.

Modernity and the Curse of Uniformity

> Instead of the unity of an artist who uses a rich diversity of tints and colors, we are given the uniformity of a house painter who paints everything the same color.[40]

As I stated earlier, Kuyper argued that liberalism was mimicking, for better or worse, Christendom's long-standing desire for ideological uniformity ("Uni-

---

39. Kuyper, "Common Grace in Science," in *Centennial Reader*, 449.
40. Kuyper, *De Schoolkwestie I. Naar Aanleiding Van Het Onderwijs-Debat in De Kamer*, 239, in Naylor, "Abraham Kuyper," 240.

formity," 19–44). Like Christendom before it, Kuyper argued, modernity was on a crusade to establish an immanent city of God. Kuyper believed that in the new "religion of modernity" one could sense a spiritual "charm, an apparent source of order, a prophecy of peace that seduces the peoples. Once articulated and accepted as a life-principle, it is irresistible in its urgency" ("Uniformity," 35). Liberalism's dream of ideological uniformity had all of the spiritual momentum of a Christian crusade.

While Kuyper criticized medieval Christendom, he found liberalism's efforts to enforce ideological uniformity even more dangerous. Foreshadowing Michel Foucault's *Discipline and Punish*, Kuyper reasoned that while Christendom enforced uniformity through the simple and external use of the sword, modern liberalism attempts to inject ideological uniformity directly into the arteries of a nation through a complex variety of laws, institutions, civil servants, governmental offices, and policies.[41] Kuyper granted that, while we "have rightly cursed the violence" of the Middle Ages and the Roman Catholic Church, we must "not forget that the sector of our life over which the state spread its net back then had hardly one tenth the reach of our present government" ("Calvinism: Source and Stronghold," 282).

Foucault's infamous argument that modern liberalism disciplines and domesticates citizens through the complex "capillary" use of power is anticipated in the work of Abraham Kuyper. In his famous address on the curse of modern life, Kuyper claimed that liberalism was like a "powerful leaven that runs through all the arteries of life and never rests until all that lives and moves has been distorted by its fatal standards" ("Uniformity," 35). Kuyper argued that, on the whole, modern liberalism had opted for a patient and "indirect" path "through its cool and surly behavior" (*Our Program*, 67). Indeed, Christendom's

> striving for imperial unity was not abandoned by [modernity]; on the contrary, the goal has remained the same. But here is the difference. Whereas in the past that unity would be imposed upon the life of the nations externally—by the sword—today it would be insinuated into the very heart of the peoples by its own fermentation. . . . [T]he French Revolution people opted for another strategy. They prepared to take a longer road. ("Uniformity," 24)

41. Michel Foucault, *Discipline and Punish: The Birth of the Prison*, trans. Alan Sheridan (New York: Random House, 1995).

Kuyper argued that the dream of liberal uniformity was not only dangerous, but it was also impossible. Kuyper joked many times that liberals couldn't
even unite their own ranks. If one looked into the liberal camp, one found

> Optimists and pessimists. A school of Kant, and a school of Hegel.
> Among jurists the determinists oppose the moralists. Among med-
> ical men the homeopaths oppose the allopaths. Plutonists and Nep-
> tunists, Darwinists and anti-Darwinists compete with one another in
> the natural sciences. Wilhelm van Humboldt, Jacob Grimm, and Max
> Mueller form different schools in the domain of Linguistics. Formalists
> and Realists pick quarrels with one another within the classical walls
> of the philological temple. Everywhere contention, conflict, struggle.
> (*Lectures*, 131)

If modernity could not unite even its own followers, how could it possibly
hope to unite the followers of other gods?

Thus, while Kuyper attributed the diversity and division of human faiths
to a permanent state of human sin, liberals blamed the fragmentation on a
temporary state of human ignorance. These two different diagnoses produced two very different solutions. While Kuyper had to openly accept that
no ideological unity could be achieved, liberals did not. For Dutch liberals there was always a hope that ideological divisions would be overcome
through various forms of education and social work. This, Kuyper concludes,
is why the liberal

> tries to force his consciousness upon us, and claims that our conscious-
> ness has to be identical with his own. From his point of view noth-
> ing else could be expected. For if he conceded that there might be a
> *real difference* between his consciousness and ours, he would thereby
> have admitted a break in the normal condition of things. We, on the
> contrary, do not claim that our consciousness shall be found in him.
> (*Lectures*, 137; emphasis mine)

Kuyper argues that this is why the persistence of religious minorities so vexes
the liberal nation-state. These minorities' refusal to assimilate into the liberal
whole is "an insult upon the common consciousness" that liberals so desire
(*Lectures*, 27). An honest recognition of human sin and real acceptance of the
fragmentation and pluriformity of faith liberates Kuyper from the dangerous
dreams of uniformity.

Still, Kuyper deeply sympathized with the universal longs of both theocrats and liberals. He understood their desire for communal wholeness and unity. Humanity, after all, was originally created for a universal unity of spirit. The loss of that spiritual unity in humanity's fall was lamentable. It was part of human nature to lament our lack of unity. Hence, Kuyper remarked, the "mistake of the Alexanders, and of the Augusti, and of the Napoleons, was not that they were charmed with the thought of the *One World Empire,* but it was this—that they endeavored to realize this idea notwithstanding that the force of sin had dissolved our unity" (*Lectures,* 80).

Faith as Public

[E]very kind of faith has in itself an impulse to speak out (*Lectures,* 131).

Even the most radical unbeliever, if he is a logical thinker, will have to grant that it is utterly absurd for a person to take such a confession of Christ on his lips and ignore the consequences that flow directly from it for our national politics.[42]

Faith was not only pervasive and pluriform, Abraham Kuyper insisted, but it was profoundly public as well. Human beings, he argued, cannot keep their diverse faith-based convictions to themselves. Their points of ultimate commitment and ultimate loyalty will inevitably spill out of their private lives into the public square.

According to Kuyper, all worldviews, religious and secular, ancient and modern, have a missional aspect to them by which they seek to go out and influence "the tendency and construction" of public life (*Lectures,* 26). Catholics hope to move the public square in a Catholic direction, socialists hope to move it in a socialist direction, democrats in a democratic direction, pragmatists in a pragmatic direction, and so on. None of these philosophies keeps its convictions private. Human beings harbor within themselves an undeniable urge, however small, to express their faith and, more than that, to influence the behavior of others according to that faith. To ask minority communities to keep their beliefs, practices, and visions of the common good private was, in Kuyper's mind, not only unreasonable and unjust, but it was ultimately dangerous.

42. Kuyper, "Maranatha," in *Centennial Reader,* 210.

Kuyper considered the liberal definition of "religion" on this count to be deeply problematic. To define religion as a collection of private beliefs and feelings about the supernatural was, according to Kuyper, to fundamentally misunderstand the deeply public nature of faith as a complete way of communal, cultural, and organizational life.

Real faith, Kuyper argued, was a three-pointed relationship between an individual, the ultimate, and the whole world around them. Kuyper insisted that a person's ultimate, whatever that was, would not rest quietly but would start to direct an individual's relationship with the world around him or her (*Lectures*, 19–21). The ultimate would begin to take charge of how that individual would interpret, imagine, relate to, and live in the world. That ultimate would infiltrate a person's ethics, aesthetics, economic practices, and—of course—one's politics.

To illustrate his point, Kuyper went into great detail tracing how Catholicism's emphasis on the preeminence of the church (*Lectures*, 21), how Islam's emphasis on the transcendence of Allah, how revolutionary France's emphasis on the sovereignty of the People (*Lectures*, 87), how Germany's pantheistic devotion to the German *Volk* (*Lectures*, 89), and how Africa's animism each produced public structures, beliefs, and practices. As Augustine had argued centuries earlier, the structures of a particular city reflect the deepest loves of that city. In other words, the spirituality of a city cannot and will not remain private—its deepest loves will be written into its walls.

Abraham Kuyper presented a counterdefinition of faith that was far more complex and cognizant of its public, cultural, and institutional character. Institutionally speaking, Kuyper fully expected ideologies and faiths to form their own organizations and associations, their own schools and political parties, newspapers and publishing houses. Culturally speaking, Kuyper would not have been at all surprised by differing faiths developing their own cultural practices of clothing and fashion, story-telling and art, music and entertainment.

Kuyper recognized that some faiths would be more intentionally public than others. He recognized that not all faiths would develop fully formed systems of cultural practices and institutions or, for that matter, a coherent political platform. Not all faiths would develop fully formed philosophies of science, the arts, economics, or culture. Kuyper recognized that many citizens would not think out all of the public consequences of their spiritual convictions. For, he stated, "I know well enough, that countless numbers of courageous men do not think things through. Their small thought world is put together as a mosaic with stones from three political visions set next to each other."[43] Patchwork philosophies are not exclusive to postmodernity; they were well known in Kuyper's day. That said, while no one had a perfectly systematic worldview, Kuyper believed that a citizen's ultimate convictions, if they were truly ultimate, would inevitably start to spill out into the public square.

The notion of private religion was therefore a contradiction in terms. Kuyper insisted that no people of integrity could serve one master in their private life and another in their public life. For one cannot be a person of

> character and intelligence, and still allow yourself to be tempted to split your conscience in two, professing your God in one half and in the other half bowing before laws that have nothing to do with Him. That does not comport with reason, nor does it square with your conscience. (*Our Program*, 31)

Thus, to use a contemporary example, if a person claimed a private faith in the power of yoga and meditation, yet all the while in his public life he displayed an ultimate reliance on ambition and money, his faith in industry would be revealed as his true spiritual foundation. Kuyper had no patience for one who lived "as a citizen without God at one time" and a spiritual milksop the next (*Our Program*, 20). To ask a Christian to privatize his or her faith and behave like a liberal in the public square was no minor request; for Kuyper it was a command to convert.

In light of this, Kuyper encouraged Protestants, liberals, socialists, Catholics, and radicals to huddle with their own kind, develop their own particular convictions, and express them openly and publically. For "whatever you may choose, whatever you are," he argued, "you have to be it consistently . . . in your entire world- and life-view" (*Lectures*, 134).

While faiths were free to publically express themselves, Kuyper insisted that they not be free from public critique and challenge. Kuyper wanted the freedom for faiths to contest each other and hold one another accountable. For example, if a Christian politician defended the poor in parliament one day, claiming "Jesus commanded that we defend the poor," and then went on to attack labor unions, a socialist colleague had the right to challenge the possible hypocrisy.

In the end, Kuyper envisioned a diverse public square in which faiths could advocate for their convictions, could build their institutions, and could live out their unique cultural practices. Democracy demanded it. In the end, he concluded that liberalism's definition of religion as mere private spiritual-

---

43. Kuyper, *De Meiboom in De Kap*, 15, trans. in Naylor, "Abraham Kuyper," 8.

ity rendered liberals incapable of granting justice to the public and cultural fullness of faith. Liberalism's sclerotic understanding of faith as a set of private ideas lacked the public-legal resources to make space for the broad cultural practices and institutions public faiths like Christianity, socialism, and—soon enough—Islam would demand.

Pervasive, Pluriform, and Public

All three aspects of faith—pervasive, pluriform, and public—were critical to Kuyper's deconstruction of liberal and theocratic dreams of hegemony and uniformity. If faith was not truly public, leaders could hope to privatize and ultimately marginalize its voice. If faith was not truly pluriform, leaders could hope to assimilate minority faiths. If faith was not truly pervasive, leaders could claim to have transcended the biases of faith. They could declare themselves capable of ruling those still benighted by superstition. Kuyper believed that if he could successfully deconstruct each of these three misconceptions about the nature of faith, he could expose the theocratic and liberal dreams of ideological uniformity as both unworkable and unjust.

In the end, Abraham Kuyper concluded that liberalism's narrow and incomplete understanding of faith rendered it incapable of responding to the emerging religious diversity of Europe. Liberals had quite simply "not kept pace" with the change growing around them.[44] Their misguided dreams of ideological uniformity led them to construct "a model state for a fantasy nation."[45] Failing to recognize the pervasive, pluriform, and public faith active throughout Europe, the modern liberal state was quickly becoming "a sheet of ice underneath which the water has flowed away." Kuyper therefore argued that liberalism lacked "the vitality to catch up to the political evolution the nation [was] undergoing."[46]

Kuyper argued that his Christian pluralist movement would endeavor to "take up a position not behind but in front of today's liberalism; and . . . characterize that liberalism was stationary and conservative."[47] The modern

---

44. Abraham Kuyper, speech to the Vereeniging voor Christelijk Nationaal Schoolonderwijs in Utrecht, May 18, 1869.

45. Kuyper, speech in Utrecht, May 18, 1869.

46. Harry Van Dyke, "Abraham Kuyper: Heir of an Anti-Revolutionary Tradition," paper presented at the international conference "Christianity and Culture: The Heritage of Abraham Kuyper on Different Continents," Free University, Amsterdam, June 1998, 24.

47. Van Dyke, "Abraham Kuyper: Heir of an Anti-Revolutionary Tradition," 24–25.

dreams of liberal uniformity were nothing but the age-old reincarnation of Caesar, Constantine, and Napoleon. "I say," Kuyper concluded, their dreams of uniformity are "nothing but a looking backward after a lost paradise" (*Lectures*, 80).

Conclusion: Deconstructing Liberalism's Treatment of Islam

Contemporary Christians living between Mecca and Amsterdam can clearly profit from Kuyper's deconstructive project on a number of fronts.

First, Kuyper did not simply engage in an intellectual contest with liberalism; he confronted the complex cultural power of liberalism with a cultural, institutional, and political movement of his own. Similarly, contemporary Christian pluralists cannot simply deconstruct liberal ideas; they must contest liberalism's vast cultural, religious, and institutional power through the production of alternative cultural institutions and practices. A pluralist subaltern will need countering organizations, schools, universities, art galleries, and churches that contest liberalism's hegemonic dreams at multiple points. Christian artists, journalists, academics, and business leaders must embody the values of Christian pluralism in their own unique spheres of influence. Islam is being pressed, not simply by hegemonic ideas, but by hegemonic cultural networks, businesses, institutions, and practices. The cultural response of Christian pluralists must be as expansive as the cultural forces of liberal uniformity.

Second, if Christian pluralists accept Kuyper's insistence that faith is pervasive, two points are clear. First, they can no longer regard the faith of Muslim neighbors as something wholly alien from their own. Muslims, like all human beings, are responding to a universal desire to worship and serve some greater power. Our Muslim neighbors are haunted, just as we are, by a common *sensus divinitatus*. Second, if faith is pervasive, Christian pluralists must challenge liberals who claim to have transcended the superstitions and biases of faith. When liberals call for an enlightenment of Islam, when they claim to be the only ones who can provide a secular light to Islam, Christians must challenge their claims to pure neutrality and secularity.

Third, if Christians accept that faith is pluriform, they will be radically critical of any desire, promise, or attempt to assimilate Islam into European or Western culture. Governmental efforts to assimilate pluriform faiths are not only quixotic and unjust, but they also tread on a holy and sacred responsibility that belongs to Christ alone.

Fourth, if Christian pluralists accept that faith is public, they will not be surprised when Muslims express their faith through cultural practices like clothing, music, and the arts. They will not be alarmed when Muslims begin to develop institutions like schools, charities, media outlets, and even political parties. These public manifestations of Islamic convictions will be seen as completely natural. Governmental attempts to limit these expressions will be labeled both foolhardy and unjust. Moreover, liberal demands that Muslims adopt a liberal moral language in public life will be understood as deeply problematic. Christian pluralists will encourage Muslims to fully express and defend their faith publically using their own distinct moral language. Only then can a true interfaith conversation and contestation occur in public life. The imposition of a liberal moral language in the public square will be recognized for what it is, not an invitation to conversation but an invitation to conversion.

Finally, Christian pluralists must expose liberalism's attempts at Muslim assimilation as hopelessly backward. Dreams of liberal uniformity must be exposed as fundamentally incapable of responding justly to a religiously diverse and dynamic world.

Looking forward to the next chapter, we see that the deconstruction of liberal dreams cannot be the end goal for Christian pluralists. It is not enough to tear down and deconstruct. The Christian subaltern must begin to imagine and construct its alternative vision of how these pervasive, pluriform, and public faiths are actually going to live together. Creative ideas, practices, and institutions of Christian hospitality, justice, and grace will need to be devised amidst the warring cities of Mecca and Amsterdam. In the next chapter, we will analyze Kuyper's constructive pluralism and explore how his theological imagination might inspire our own.

CHAPTER FIVE

Kuyper's Construction of Plurality

I know of no other solution than to accept—freely and candidly, without any reservations—a free multiformity.

ABRAHAM KUYPER[1]

If we want to retain the idea of the nation-as-home, it needs to be a house with many rooms.

JAN WILLEM DUYVENDAK[2]

Having deconstructed the dreams of hegemony and uniformity, pluralists of all stripes must move forward to construct their own visions for a pluralistic culture and state. As pluralists make these arguments, they are commonly challenged to respond to a wide range of political, cultural, and ideological questions.

Political questions for pluralists typically include some version of the following: How will your pluralistic state distribute power equally and justly between different faiths and worldviews? How will your pluralistic state set the limits of religious freedom? Who will finally end the pluralistic debate and actually make a decision? In other words, in a truly pluralistic state, where does ultimate power lie? Can anything or anyone ever be sovereign in a pluralistic state?

---

1. Abraham Kuyper, "Uniformity: The Curse of Modern Life," in *Abraham Kuyper: A Centennial Reader*, ed. James Bratt (Grand Rapids: Eerdmans, 1998), 39.

2. Jan Willem Duyvendak, *The Politics of Home: Belonging and Nostalgia in Europe and the United States* (New York: Palgrave Macmillan, 2011), 121.

In addition to these political questions, pluralists can also expect a range of cultural questions. These often include questions like: If our national culture lacks one central religion, worldview, or system of values, what will keep our nation together? How will our culture withstand moments of crisis, fear, and violence? What, in other words, will keep our national culture from sliding back into either fragmentation or hegemony?

Finally, pluralists who come from a specific faith tradition like Islam, Judaism, Christianity, socialism, or liberalism will need to be prepared to answer additional questions from their own tradition. For example, Jewish pluralists like Jonathan Sacks and liberal pluralists like William Kymlicka are frequently asked to explain how their commitment to pluralism squares with their commitments to the traditions of Judaism and liberalism. Their Jewish and liberal peers press them to answer questions such as: Why should our community fight for communities we consider mistaken? If our community is ultimately correct about the common good, why shouldn't we strive for political hegemony? How can our community engage in a dialogue with those we consider wrong? How can we connect with those outside our moral linguistic system? Finally, pluralists can also expect their ideological communities to ask them: Does your pluralism truly spring from our tradition or have you imported it from elsewhere?

During his nineteenth-century struggle for pluralism, Abraham Kuyper fielded all of these questions from a long list of adversaries both inside and outside the Christian world. Outside the Christian world, nationalists warned that Kuyper's pluralism would lead to national fragmentation and civil war. Secularists found his religiosity to be a superstitious imposition in a properly secular public square. Fiscal conservatives argued that his pluralism would be costly and inefficient. Social conservatives argued that his reforms were too destabilizing to the status quo. Progressives argued that preserving religious diversity would impede the modern progress of the nation. Individualists saw his defense of religious communities as a dangerous revival of corporatism.

Inside the Christian world, Kuyper's antagonists were just as plentiful. Christian theocrats argued that he was abandoning the dream of a Christian Netherlands. Sectarian Christians argued he should stay out of the sinful world of politics. And finally, liberal Christians found Kuyper's refusal to support the modernization of the Netherlands embarrassing. Kuyper's pluralism was indeed criticized from every side: the right and the left, the religious and the secular.

This chapter explores how Abraham Kuyper responded to these challenges and constructed his own practical and theological defense for Christian pluralism. Be advised, the chapter is not an exhaustive historical recounting of Kuyper's thought on religion, politics, and pluralism. Instead, it is a thematic exploration of the major contours of his case for Christian pluralism that are particularly relevant to our guiding question: what is a Christian pluralist's response to the conflict between Mecca and Amsterdam?

I trust that this chapter's more thematic appropriation of Kuyper's thought will be faithful to his own dynamic appropriation of Reformed public theology. As Kuyper himself argued, theology is not a "rigid, unalterable power that [has] reached its final conclusions. . . . It only gradually reveals its power, [it] has a unique insight for every age that assumes a form suitable for every country. Precisely in this restless metamorphosis its development continues."[3] I therefore hope to look back to Kuyper just as Kuyper looked back to earlier traditions, "not to restore its worn-out form," but to faithfully reimagine its riches in a form "suiting the requirements of our own century."[4]

With that we turn to the major themes in Abraham Kuyper's theological case for Christian pluralism. We begin with his primary theological foundation—the sovereignty of Jesus Christ.

Abraham Kuyper's Theory of Sovereignty

The throne that governs the destiny of heaven and earth is not to be found down below.[5]

When irreconcilable conflicts occur, all pluralists—secular and religious—must grapple with a series of abiding questions about where ultimate sovereignty lies. In the crisis over Islam in the West, questions of sovereignty often sound like this: Who has the authority to judge Islamic beliefs, practices, and institutions? Will the state have the authority to intervene in Muslim marriages, schools, and mosques? What principles will govern the state's intervention into Muslim communities? And, finally, how will the intervention be executed? All of these questions are ultimately about sovereignty and authority. Where does the "buck stop"?

---

3. Abraham Kuyper, "Calvinism: Source and Stronghold of Our Constitutional Liberties," in *Abraham Kuyper: A Centennial Reader*, ed. James Bratt (Grand Rapids: Eerdmans, 1998), 293. Additional references to this work are given parenthetically in the text.

4. Abraham Kuyper, *Lectures on Calvinism* (Grand Rapids: Eerdmans, 1954), 41. Additional references to this work are given parenthetically in the text.

5. Abraham Kuyper, *Dagen van goede boodschap* (Amsterdam: J. A. Wormser, 1887), 32.

In diverse cultures, questions of sovereignty are inescapable. Yes, diversity, freedom, and dialogue are all critical, but eventually there comes a point where a decision has to be made. Western political theory and practice have traditionally bestowed ultimate sovereignty on one or some combination of the following entities: a state, constitution, tradition, sovereign, church, or group of voters. These various entities receive the final authority over the religions and worldviews that exist within their sovereign realm.

Abraham Kuyper's theory of sovereignty was a curious aberration in the history of modern political theory and practice. Kuyper's peculiarity can be found in his utter refusal to grant ultimate sovereignty to any mortal institution or individual. For Kuyper, no state, electorate, constitution, or religious body was deserving of ultimate authority. For Kuyper this was a matter of both history and principle.

Kuyper warned that, historically speaking, no terrestrial authority had ever or could ever sustain true pluralism. Every earthly authority could and eventually would become twisted to serve the hegemonic ambitions of a single faith. Leaders could become dogmatic, churches could go on crusades, constitutions could be altered, voters could become vengeful, cultures could become chauvinistic, and public rationalism could become irrational. All types of earthly authority were vulnerable to becoming corrupted. Because of this vulnerability, none of these mortal authorities could serve as Abraham Kuyper's trustworthy guardian of deep pluralism. History, Kuyper insisted, demonstrated that bestowing ultimate sovereignty on terrestrial powers would ultimately end in hegemonic ruin. No human institution could resist the siren call for national uniformity and hegemony.

History aside, there were deeper theological reasons why Kuyper could not bestow ultimate sovereignty on these mortal powers. As a Christian pluralist, Kuyper held that Jesus Christ alone was the true and ultimate sovereign. His sovereignty alone knew no bounds. For, he famously declared, "there is not a square inch in the whole domain of human existence over which Christ, who is sovereign over all, does not cry: 'Mine!'"[6] To seize Christ's sovereign authority and hand it over to a state, a people, or a church would, in essence, be an act of blasphemy.

It is important to note that Kuyper's Christological sovereignty did not make him a theocrat. Naming Christ as sovereign is something altogether different from naming Christians as sovereign. Kuyper insisted that no Chris-

---

6. Abraham Kuyper, "Sphere Sovereignty," in *Centennial Reader*, 488. Additional references to this work are given parenthetically in the text.

tian leader, movement, or institution could claim Christ's sovereignty for themselves. Kuyper set the standards for ultimate sovereignty so high that no church could claim Christ's crown. The following, he argued

> is required for wielding absolute sovereignty over any object: (1) that I have this object completely in my possession; (2) that I have made it with my own hands as I saw fit; (3) that calling the necessary raw materials into being depends on my omnipotence; and (4) that it is up to me to set the laws that will govern its action and regulate its relation to other objects.[7]

Kuyper declared that Jesus Christ alone could claim this level of sovereignty over the diverse peoples and faiths of the Netherlands. It goes without saying that the Christian church came up short in all four of these requirements for sovereignty.

Before we explore the pluralistic implications of Kuyper's perspective, I want to briefly examine his criticism of the two dominant theories of sovereignty that he was up against in Europe at the time. The first vision of sovereignty, popular then in Germany, rendered ultimate sovereignty to the nation-state. The second theory, popular in France, rendered ultimate sovereignty to the people. In his evaluation, Kuyper systematically demonstrates how, when either the nation-state or the people are declared sovereign, deep pluralism suffers.

Turning first to Germany, Kuyper warned that the nineteenth-century cocktail of German nationalism, romanticism, and pantheism had bestowed a dangerous level of sovereignty upon the German nation-state (*Lectures*, 88). The German people had come to believe that the spirit of the German *Volk* and the Spirit of God were one and the same. Kuyper warned that as God, culture, and state fused, the nation-state would begin to be seen as the ultimate sovereign, a "mysterious being, with a hidden *ego*; with a state-consciousness, slowly developing . . . with an increasingly potent state-*will*" (*Lectures*, 88). Soon enough, Kuyper warned, "everything must bow before this will . . . this state-apotheosis" (*Lectures*, 89). Kuyper predicted that once the *Volk* nation-state was vested with this level of ultimate sovereignty, deep diversity and pluralism would soon be crushed. Minority rights would increasingly be defined and controlled by the nation-state to the point where there would be

---

7. Abraham Kuyper, *Our Program*, trans. Harry Van Dyke (Bellingham, WA: Lexham Press, 2015), 17. Additional references to this work are given parenthetically in the text.

no other right, but the immanent right, which is written down in the law. The law is right, not because its contents are in harmony with the eternal principles of right, but because it *is law.* If on the morrow [the *Volk*-state] fixes the very opposite, this also must be right. . . . [Justice] becomes the ever-changing will of the state, which, having no one above itself, actually becomes *God,* and has to decide how our life and our existence shall be. (*Lectures,* 89)

Under this nationalistic pantheism, independent German churches were losing and would continue to lose their autonomy and authority. Eventually, Kuyper warned, these churches would be assimilated into the German national whole. He argued that such an all-embracing and immanent theory of sovereignty could never cultivate a free and diverse public square. It would, by its very nature, assimilate diverse communities into and under its nationalist *Volk*-centered grip.

This was not a speculative fear, Kuyper warned; one could witness Germany's nationalist grip tightening in the daily news. One could see the "apotheosis" of the German nation-state in

the cool determination with which leading jurists in Germany are forging the shackles by which the church must be chained. . . . [Y]ou see where the [pantheistic] erasure of boundaries is taking us, and you are no longer surprised when another [German] jurist, Professor Zorn, dares to write that the church of Christ is nothing more than a religious association and that the current relationship between state and church "rests on the principle of state sovereignty, to which the church too is subordinate."[8]

If the German *Volk*-state could not protect deep pluralism and religious freedom, the French model of popular sovereignty was no better. It is true that Kuyper frequently expressed sympathy with the French Revolution's opposition to the *Ancien Régime* of royal and clerical oppression. He also expressed a common desire to protect the democratic rights and liberties of the people. Nevertheless, Kuyper deeply differed with the French Revolution on the question of whether or not the democratic will of the people ought to be rendered ultimate sovereignty.

The French people, like the German *Volk*-state, would, according to Kuyper, inevitably abuse their sovereignty. Drunk on their ultimate author-

---

8. Kuyper, "The Blurring of the Boundaries," in *Centennial Reader,* 390.

ity the people would marginalize religious minorities who did not fit into their—now divine—will. He warned that the majority would begin to "view itself as supreme" placing itself squarely "in the seat of God" (*Our Program*, 23). In this fateful act, the majority would begin to "dominate" (*Our Program*, 23) minorities justifying their decisions with nothing more than "I do these things at my own pleasure" (*Our Program*, 23). Kuyper knew that if pluralism depended solely on the will of the majority, it could be cast aside when the majority happened to find that pluralism inconvenient or undesirable.

Declaring the people divinely sovereign, Kuyper warned, would create a political culture in which "man grovels before his fellowmen" pleading for rights that were given to him by God (*Lectures*, 88). Kuyper insisted that people are free not because the people declared it to be so out of their own magnanimous generosity, but because Jesus Christ had commanded that they be free. No citizen should have to grovel for the rights, respect, and value that is already his or hers in Christ. Kuyper loathed the French practice of "tinseling over this self-abasement" (*Lectures*, 88). In the end, he concluded, "Authority over men cannot arise from men" nor can it arise "from a majority over against a minority, for history shows, almost on every page, that very often the *minority was right*" (*Lectures*, 82).

While Kuyper's warnings about the apotheosis of the French majority had already been confirmed in the violence of 1789, his warnings about the apotheosis of the German *Volk*-state would not find their ultimate fulfillment until the 1930s.

Deep pluralism and religious freedom required a sovereign who could resist all temptations to national uniformity and hegemony. Neither the people nor the nation-state could sustain its commitment to pluralism. Kuyper argued that deep pluralism demanded a sovereign that would yearn for deep freedom no matter what the cost to the sovereign's honor, prestige, progress, or power. Deep pluralism demanded a unique sort of sovereign power that could resist the hegemonic demons without becoming a demon itself.

Christological Sovereignty

A helpful way to approach Abraham Kuyper's Christological understanding of sovereignty is to divide his response into two parts—temporal and spatial. In terms of Christ's temporal sovereignty, Kuyper insisted that Christ alone was sovereign over the past, present, and future of nations, states, and religions. Christ alone ruled their histories. In terms of Christ's spatial sovereignty, Christ alone was sovereign over every social space in human life (families, schools, worship spaces, businesses, associations, and so on). The simple acceptance that Christ alone—and not the Christian—is sovereign over both time and space had deep and far-reaching public implications for Kuyper's constructive vision for Christian pluralism.

A great deal of the conflict over Islam in the Netherlands today is, in essence, a struggle over temporal sovereignty. The battle over who will control the nation's past, present, and future is a critical, though often ignored, aspect of the debate. The native Dutch claim that "we" are responsible for the nation's past glory, that we are responsible for the nation's present success, and that we, and we alone, should control the future identity of the nation. Likewise, Dutch natives fault Islam for their country's past failures, present difficulties, and any future calamities that may come. Speaking of Muslim citizens, many Dutch argue that "they" should not be part of "our" national past, present, or future. Geert Wilders's rhetoric is a perfect example. He ignores the past sins of Dutch colonialism. He ignores the present contributions of minorities to Dutch flourishing. He warns of a future disaster if "we" are not allowed to expel "them" from the future of "our" country.

The task of all pluralists—religious or secular—is to describe how these claims of temporal sovereignty can be avoided. Pluralists of all stripes must find a way to allow multiple voices and communities into the past, present, and future of a nation. Kuyper's Christological reply to the issue was, in many ways, quite simple. If Jesus Christ is sovereign over a nation's past origin, present development, and future end, then those who follow him may not claim total control over their nation's story. True Christian pluralists release the reigns of national history. They recognize that Christ and Christ alone guides the story of the nation, and that any past or future glory is not their own but is thanks to the providence of God.

In light of this, Kuyper argued, his pluralist movement needed to respect Christ's exclusive rights to temporal sovereignty by engaging their diverse neighbors with "persuasion to the exclusion of all coercion." For, one day "there will be coercion, when Christ descends in majesty. . . . He has a right to this. . . . But we do not. . . . Therefore, without any craftiness or secret intentions we accept our position of equality before the law along with those who disagree with us." Indeed, for a Christian pluralist who accepts Christ's exclusive claim to temporal sovereignty, it should "be considered inconceivable, even ridiculous, to discriminate against or offend anyone, whoever it may be."[9] Christ alone holds the keys to history.

9. Kuyper, "Maranatha," in *Centennial Reader*, 220–21.

It is important to note that, during the nineteenth century, Kuyper's liberal contemporaries were promising to establish a united Netherlands in the not-too-distant future. This future nation would be fully united around the ideals of modern liberalism. Kuyper argued that such promises of national unity were not only practically impossible, but that they were theologically blasphemous. Ideological dreams for future unity were, simply put, a sinful usurpation of Christ's temporal sovereignty. The eschatological unity of humanity would not be established by any state, nation, or church. Christ alone would build the final city where the nations would gather. "At present," Kuyper insisted, that final city of ultimate unity

> is hidden. Here, on earth, it is only, as it were, a silhouette that can be dimly discerned. In the Future, *this new Jerusalem* shall descend from God, out of heaven, but at present it withdraws its beams from our sight in the mysteries of the invisible. And therefore the true sanctuary is now *above*. (*Lectures*, 60)

This future city of human unity rests above, beyond the grasp of terrestrial states, churches, and cultures. Any effort to preempt Christ's unifying work, any effort to establish an immanent universal sanctuary on earth was completely out of bounds for those who recognized Christ's temporal sovereignty. While humanity was united in the past (the Garden of Eden) and would again be united in the future (the new Jerusalem), at present the unity of humanity could only be "dimly discerned" (*Lectures*, 60).

Along with the pluralistic implications of Christ's temporal sovereignty, Abraham Kuyper fully explored Christ's spatial sovereignty. For Kuyper, Christ alone was sovereign over every social space in a pluralistic nation. Under Christ's all-encompassing spatial sovereignty, no state, church, business, ideology, or association could claim ultimate sovereignty for itself. The totality of what we call society belonged to Christ alone. Kuyper's theoretical work on this subject is more popularly known as sphere sovereignty.

How exactly did this commitment to Christ's exclusive spatial sovereignty impact Kuyper's approach to Christian pluralism? To start, Kuyper insisted that all social spaces or spheres received both their right to exist and their freedom to flourish directly from Christ himself. In other words, the diverse schools, families, universities, newspapers, art galleries, and religious communities do not receive their dignity and purpose as a gift from the government; they receive it as an exclusive gift from Christ.

Therefore, Kuyper concludes, a state "does not *confer* but *acknowledges*"

("Sphere Sovereignty," 468) the divine rights of different religions and communities. Under Christ's spatial sovereignty, religious communities "do not derive the law of their life from the superiority of the state" but from Christ alone (*Lectures*, 90). Christ alone will be the ultimate judge of their community. Christ alone will judge their religious practices and organizations. Christ alone will determine their value. Christ alone will decide their fate. For if Christ is truly sovereign over all social spaces and cultural activities,

> Neither the life of science nor of art, nor of agriculture, nor of industry, nor of commerce, nor of navigation, nor of the family, nor of human relationship may be coerced to suit itself to the grace of the government. The state may never become an octopus, which stifles the whole of life. . . . [I]t has to honor and maintain every form of life which grows independently in its own sacred autonomy. (*Lectures*, 96–97)

Many today might think it strange to include agriculture, science, and art in a discussion of religious diversity and freedom. Many assume religious freedom implies little more than the liberty to hold a set of private beliefs or rituals. Religion, it is said, has nothing to with public lives led in agriculture, science, or art. Not so for Abraham Kuyper—and not so for contemporary Muslims in the Netherlands. Nineteenth-century Kuyper and twenty-first century Muslims recognize that faith is irretrievably public and unavoidably wrapped up in the cultural work of agriculture, science, and art. Recent Dutch-Islamic conflicts over the slaughter of sheep, the use of modern medicine, and the freedom of artistic expression bear this reality out. Early on, Kuyper argued that if a faith was going to be truly free, it not only demanded a free worship space, but it demanded free cultural spaces, as well. If the faiths of humanity were going to be truly free, they had to be allowed to spill out into public and cultural life, as well. Under Christ's spatial sovereignty, Kuyper argued, disparate faith communities could not be impeded from developing their own faith-based schools, universities, health centers, farms, art practices, families, newspapers, and political parties.

Christ's exclusive claim to spatial sovereignty deeply informed the Christian's life in a pluralistic society in two important ways. First, it greatly limited the Christian's ability to claim sovereignty over non-Christian organizations and practices. Second, it politically motivated Christians to construct laws that would guard against government overreach into religio-cultural practices and institutions. Christians had to support these laws if they wanted to honor Christ's spatial sovereignty. More than simply force the deconstruction of uniformity, Christian pluralists needed to be a constructive force cultivating a generous public square in which all faiths could embody and express their convictions freely.

Under this Christological canopy of both temporal and spatial sovereignty, states were understood to be stewards and not sovereigns. States were expected to demonstrate a humble and even "pious respect" for the "sacred autonomy" of faith-based institutions and practices. Kuyper argued that before a state "crosses the boundary" into a faith community, it recognizes that it is walking on holy ground and "respectfully 'takes the shoes off from its feet'" ("Sphere Sovereignty," 477). For the state must "reverence the innate law of life" in each religious community and it must not demean, modify, or disrupt that community's unique attempt to follow its own conscience.

However, Kuyper was not an anarchist or multicultural libertarian. There were legal limits to his pluralism and the state could, and indeed should, enforce those limits. Kuyper outlined how, why, and when a state should invade the sacred autonomy of a distinct religion or culture. To understand that, we turn to Kuyper's description of the pluralistic state.

The Pluralistic State

[S]in alone has necessitated the institution of governments.
ABRAHAM KUYPER (*Lectures*, 82)

Kuyper insisted that, from the beginning of creation, God had always desired the cultural development of the arts, sciences, agriculture, education, and more. God desired cultural organizations to grow, flourish, and diversify. While these various cultural organizations and practices were all distorted by human sinfulness, Kuyper insisted that they all reflected God's original design for human culture-making. There was, however, one importance exception. Abraham Kuyper did not believe that the cultural practices of politics and statecraft were a part of God's original intentions for humanity. Rather, Kuyper saw politics as an inherently coercive activity that was never intended by God.

> For, indeed, without sin there would have been neither magistrate nor state-order. . . . Neither bar of justice nor police, nor army, nor navy, is conceivable in a world without sin . . . all control and assertion of the power of the magistrate would disappear, were life to develop itself, normally and without hindrance, from its own organic impulse. Who

binds up, where nothing is broken? Who uses crutches, where the limbs are sound? (*Lectures*, 80)

Instead, Kuyper considered the state to be a lamentable but necessary restraint on human violence, injustice, and oppression. Kuyper saw the state as a temporary gift of God, graciously given to restrain and sustain a feral and violent human race. Kuyper argued that the "glory of God" demanded that humanity's violent "horrors be bridled, that order return to this chaos, and that a compulsory force, from without, assert itself to make human society a possibility" (*Lectures*, 81). Kuyper insisted that this coercive governmental force was not a natural aspect of human life but a "mechanical" and "unnatural" imposition on organic human society. Thus, while Kuyper certainly gave thanks for the state, any apotheosis of its existence was out of the question.

Because the state was merely a temporary and limited restraint on human injustice, Kuyper believed that its coercive purview over religious communities needed to be extremely limited. In all, Kuyper outlined only two situations in which the state was permitted to invade the sacred autonomy of religious institutions and practices.

The first situation calling for state intervention was one in which one ideological community was intruding upon the affairs of another. In such a situation, the state had a responsibility to "compel mutual regard for the boundary lines" of each community in question (*Lectures*, 97). The state would never force either community to accept or embrace the convictions or practices of the other—that was not its task. Its task was simply that of promoting public justice between the communities in question. The state was neither competent nor called to serve as the nation's moral teacher, cultural civilizer, or philosophical arbitrator. The state's task was simply to compel the offending community to recognize the rights and sovereignty of their neighboring communities. The state's obligation to protect ideological communities from attack extended beyond simply guarding their private beliefs and practices. Because faith was deeply public, cultural, and communal, Kuyper demanded that the state protect a faith's particular cultural practices and institutions as well. If a particular faith established a school, political party, newspaper, charity, or the like, those religious-cultural institutions would need to be protected from undue harm as well.

The second instance in which state intervention was required was in the defense of what Kuyper called "weak ones" living within faith communities. The "weak ones," Kuyper warned, were always vulnerable to "the abuse of power of the rest" (*Lectures*, 97). For, because of sin, an individual's "life can be suppressed by the group . . . [and] the state must protect the individual from the tyranny of his own circle" ("Sphere Sovereignty," 468). The state must ensure that "anyone may withdraw from an association" (*Our Program*, 158). Furthermore, the state must see to it that "he is not molested for his withdrawal by those who stay behind" (*Our Program*, 158).

While these were the only two circumstances under which Kuyper's pluralistic state might intervene, both of them leave much to our own imagination and interpretation. What, after all, constitutes a clash of faith communities? What constitutes an attack? What are the exact boundaries between religious communities, and how do we interpret when they have been breached? Interpreted broadly enough, the pluralist state could outlaw all forms of interfaith criticism, debate, or missionary activity. Furthermore, what constitutes the abuse of an individual within a faith community? Interpreted broadly enough, the parental practice of compelling one's children to attend a religious school could be interpreted as something that demands the state's intervention. Moreover, in times of national crisis and danger, what is to stop the pluralistic state from dramatically expanding its reach and becoming the octopus that Kuyper so feared?

Kuyper recognized that states, in their sinfulness, were "always inclined" to expand their executive mandate. Given free rein, states would always try to "invade social life, to subject it and to mechanically arrange it" (*Lectures*, 93–94). The critical question, therefore, was how the state's natural inclination to dominate could be curtailed. Here we arrive at a principal question stated in the introduction. How will the pluralistic state avoid the hegemonic temptation? Rather than a single check on state expansion, Kuyper outlined a whole series of legal, political, and cultural brakes designed to stop the slide of a pluralistic state into hegemony.

The first brake was a legal one. Kuyper supported the construction of a pluralistic constitution, the rule of law, and the establishment of democratic representation (*Lectures*, 97–99). Kuyper's pluralist movement spent a great deal of time and effort in the late nineteenth century attempting to amend the constitutional, legal, and electoral system of the Netherlands to safeguard the principles of pluralism.

Kuyper was particularly concerned with the legal protections for faith-based schools, associations, and institutions. His answer to the question of government aid for these institutions is a more complicated one. In his early years, Kuyper was adamantly against any provision of state funds for Christian institutions. For it "cannot be said enough: money creates power for the one who gives over the one who receives" ("Sphere Sovereignty," 478). He insisted that the state was not responsible for funding the institutions of civil society; it was only responsible for protecting their freedom. Funding of free associations would bring a vast network of government regulations, expectations, discipline, and finally direction. While this was Kuyper's early perspective, it would not last.

Kuyper and those who followed in his wake progressively made three political arguments regarding state funding of civil organizations. First, the state has a responsibility to ensure that all people have access to social services (such as education, health care, and welfare). Second, they argued, none of these social services is religiously neutral. All of these activities (education, charity, health care) are shot through with faith-based assumptions about the mind, body, work, and human flourishing. Third, they argued, because these services all necessarily involve faith-based assumptions, the state could claim singular ideological control over how those services should be provided. Using these three arguments, Kuyper's pluralists would conclude that it was not for the state to favor one form of education, health care, or charity over another. They came to this conclusion for the simple reason that different faith communities had very different perspectives on the meaning and purpose of such social services as education, health care, and charity.

The pluralists went on to argue that the state could not establish its own neutral schools, hospitals, newspapers, and so on. These social services could never attain perfect secularity or impartiality. In the words of Kuyper, these hospitals and schools could never keep their creeds unwritten or their thrones empty. Every system of education made faith-based assumptions about the purpose of learning. Every hospital made faith-based assumptions about the meaning of health and the purpose of the human body. Every charity made assumptions about human dignity, work, and the way in which the poor should be treated. The state could not be unbiased in the design or execution of these social services, for it would always favor one ideology over another. The challenge was clear. Christian pluralists had to find a way for the state to justly and equally fund the social services provided by a variety of religious communities without impinging on their unique faith identities.

For an example, consider the social service that was the most important to the Christian pluralists of the nineteenth century—public education. Kuyper and the Christian pluralists argued that the state should provide equal funding to all schools, regardless of their faith orientations. The pluralists argued that state funds should come with some basic limits and expectations. For example, the state could expect that subjects like math, reading, and writing be taught. That said, the state could not dictate the philosophical spirit in which those subjects would be taught. The basics of this pluralistic model of church-state partnership would soon be extended to the Dutch systems of health care, charity, arts, media, and more. The basic principal was that the free association—not the coercive state—would direct and provide social services.

If the state believed that individuals were being oppressed within a particular organization, the initial responsibility for stopping this injustice was placed on the institution itself. The state would instruct the community to develop its own procedures for protecting individuals from abuse. If the community ultimately refused or failed to protect their members then, and only then, could the state intervene.

After a decades-long fight with liberal nationalists, Kuyper and the pluralists were able to successfully enshrine these principles of pluralism into the constitution. These provisions guaranteed the freedom and equal funding for social services provided by all faith communities. If constitutional reform was the first brake on the hegemonic growth of the state, the second was democratic representation. As I mentioned earlier, Abraham Kuyper fundamentally agreed with his contemporary liberals that democratic reforms were important (*Lectures*, 97). Democratic representation was, in Kuyper's mind, one critical method by which the state's power could be limited and religious freedom defended.

That said, while liberals based their theories of democratic representation solely on the French theory of popular sovereignty and on an individualistic ontology (one individual, one vote), Kuyper wanted to balance the French individualism with a more communitarian approach to democratic representation. While Kuyper never fully developed his theory of communal representation, his argument was essentially this: the pluralistic state must acknowledge the voices—not simply of individuals—but of whole communities as well (*Lectures*, 98). At one point, Kuyper even proposed the formation of a third house of parliament, which would represent the various organizations and institutions of Dutch civil society. Kuyper's arguments for corporate representation stemmed from his conviction that the state does not simply govern autonomous individuals; it governs networks of communities, associations, and institutions as well. Finally, if the state is called to do justice not simply to individuals but to communities as well, it seems to follow that the state must find an effective way to hear communal grievances as well. In short, complex communal justice requires complex communal representation.

Abraham Kuyper concluded that while these legal and political brakes on state power were important, they were ultimately insufficient on their own. Deep pluralism, if it would stand, would need more than legal and political structures. Left alone, these structures were all vulnerable to being usurped by the cultural temptations of hegemony and uniformity. Constitutions could be amended, laws could be changed, state funding could be unfairly distributed, voters could band together to exclude minorities. Simply put, if a culture decided that it no longer desired pluralism, all the political structures in the world could not stop a slide back into coercive hegemony.

The Pluralistic Culture

Contrary to what is sometimes claimed, the constitution does not radiate out a life-giving energy. That energy begins with the people themselves and radiates out from the spirit by which they live.

SAVORNIN LOHMAN[10]

When it comes to Islam, Dutch people today will listen to you when you make the old pluralist argument. They will understand what you are saying—the difference is, they no longer feel a desire for that pluralism in their bones.

JAMES KENNEDY[11]

If a political culture no longer feels a desire for pluralism in its bones, if it can no longer come up with reasons to defend difference, no measure of constitutional brakes will be able to stop a nation's slide into coercive uniformity and hegemony. A pluralistic state cannot resist a culture that consistently demands ideological hegemony and assimilation.

Abraham Kuyper argued that it was inevitable that "public opinion" would "exert influence on the conscience of those in government" (*Our Program*, 40). He insisted that the "spirit of a nation and the spirit of its government . . . are not hermetically sealed from one another: they interpenetrate" (*Our Program*, 40). States are influenced by the political spirits at work within their borders.[12] If a political culture takes on a spiritual posture of fear, revenge, anxiety, aggression, or apathy, its pluralistic structures will not long stand. For,

---

10. Savornin Lohman was an early collegue of Abraham Kuyper in the Christian pluralist movement. Lohman made this statement in his pamplet *Onze Constitutie* (Utrecht: Kemink, 1901), 50.

11. James Kennedy, interview with the author, Amsterdam, NL, November 24, 2011.

12. Abraham Kuyper, *De Gemeene Gratie*, vol. 3 (Leiden: Donner, 1902–1905), 182.

In any successful attack on freedom, the state can only be an accomplice. The chief culprit is the citizen who forgets his duty, wastes away his strength in the sleep of sin and sensual pleasure, and so loses the power of his own initiative. Among a nation healthy at its core . . . no state can subvert the principles of justice without meeting the people's strong moral resistance under God. ("Sphere Sovereignty," 473)

According to Kuyper, healthy and sustainable political cultures contain the following attributes: First, they expect their states to behave like humble servants and stewards of a diverse public square. The government is expected to exist alongside and not above the many cultural and religious spheres of national life. Strong political cultures will expect the state to humbly protect a just public square in which a wide variety of faith-based communities can flourish (*Lectures*, 93–94). States will be expected to safeguard a safe contest of ideas and ways of life between worldviews and their institutions.

Second, a healthy political culture will see its governmental leaders as fundamentally mortal and finite. "The persons in government," Kuyper insists, must "remain for us perfectly ordinary people who in themselves have not the least to say, not even over the least of the subjects, and who in their own littleness are on the same level as the day-laborer and the beggar" (*Our Program*, 48). State officials must be seen as no closer to ultimate truth or ultimate justice than any other citizen. Officials are not qualified to direct or judge the conscience of an individual or an institution. Healthy political cultures expect their leaders to be the guardians of faith communities—not their directors.

Third, pluralistic cultures will not pressure their states to artificially prop up or favor one particular faith or its institutions. Kuyper insisted that the beliefs, practices, and institutions of various ideologies and religions must rise and fall by the strength of their own character and integrity. The state could not get into the business of picking winners and losers for its own social or political ends, no matter how benevolent. In a parliamentary speech, Kuyper asked what he believed to be a foundational question for pluralism: "Is there only *one* motor, that of the state, whose power must set all the wheels [of society] going . . . or does each life sphere possess its own motor which we call free initiative? I believe the second."[13] A political culture that looks to the state to artificially prop up one specific religious community is already well on its way down the road to ideological hegemony.

13. Kuyper quoted in Wendy Fish Naylor, "Abraham Kuyper and the Emergence of Neo-Calvinist Pluralism in the Dutch School Struggle," PhD diss., (University of Chicago, 2006), 141–42.

Fourth, when circumstances dictate and the state is finally forced to intervene in the internal life of a religious community, Kuyper argues that a truly pluralistic culture will never ask the state to assume a "salvific" posture.[14] Instead, a healthy political culture will expect the state to intervene with a spirit of sadness, regret, and lamentation. According to Kuyper, state interventions in religious communities should be temporary, limited, and aim "only for the liberation" ("Sphere Sovereignty," 478) of the community in question. Pluralistic cultures never ask the state to turn religious institutions into a mere "branch of the civil service" ("Sphere Sovereignty," 478). Instead, truly pluralistic cultures see these faith communities as sovereign and sacred spaces of religious freedom.

Kuyper uses the image of a splint placed on a broken leg to illustrate for his readers the sort of intervention a healthy political culture desires from its government.[15] Kuyper's splint metaphor—though limited in its purchase—was meant to illustrate two key aspects of healthy state intervention. First, like a leg splint, government intervention should be a *temporary* response to a state of brokenness. The splint, by its very nature, aims at the future strength and independence of the leg. The mark of a good splint is that it will not always be necessary. Second, the splint acts as an *external* force for correction. The splint does not invade the leg, rearranging the muscles, arteries, and tendons to its liking. Likewise a healthy pluralistic culture will not ask the state to invade faith communities and reform them from the inside out. Invasive government interventions into the heart of religious communities ultimately weaken their spiritual, moral, and political integrity. For, Kuyper argued, sustainable civic "morality demands freedom to flourish."[16]

Fifth, a healthy and pluralistic culture will never allow a single ideology to dominate the state. Kuyper insisted that no Christian church should ever

> be given the right to decide what the divine ordinances for government are. To have an opinion is the church's right. . . . And on occasion nothing prevents the church from approaching the government with a petition or a complaint regarding political issues. But the church can never be given the authority in its own right to determine what should obtain for the state. . . . In a mixed community we do not desire a theocracy; rather, we oppose it with all our might. (*Our Program*, 35)

14. Kuyper, *Gemeene Gratie*, vol. 3, 285.
15. Kuyper, *Gemeene Gratie*, vol. 3, 100.
16. Kuyper, *Gemeene Gratie*, vol. 3, 182.

In conclusion, Abraham Kuyper desired a democratic culture with a deep and abiding desire for pluralism in its bones. He wanted a culture that would keep the state cognizant of its limits, fair in its decisions, respectful in its intervention, and always deeply aware that its very existence was mortal, temporal, and ultimately regrettable.

The question that naturally follows, of course, is how does one cultivate a healthy pluralistic culture? How will that culture sustain itself? How will it resist the temptations of uniformity and coercion? In Kuyper's words, how will a political culture become "healthy at its core" and capable of "strong moral resistance" against the forces of ideological hegemony?

At various times Abraham Kuyper lists affluence, apathy, sensual pleasure, laziness, godlessness, greed, selfishness, and state dependency among the parasitic forces that can drain the strength of a pluralistic culture. While the state was capable of limiting some of these destructive forces, it could not stop them all. Indeed, Kuyper argued, the state does not have a mandate to combat things like apathy and godlessness. Here we find ourselves facing a critical paradox that faces every pluralist movement. By its very nature, the pluralist state cannot support the one thing it desperately needs to survive—generative communities of civic conviction, charity, and action.

The Pluralistic Church

Despite the intolerance of many of their number, Calvinists created an extremely important condition for democracy and tolerance by defending the free church. . . . Ironically, this free church also brought about the destruction of their own theocratic ideal, and thus ultimately cleared the way for the separation of church and state.

JAN WILLEM SAP[17]

[The] comparatively small circle of the church will radiate influence upon civil life outside of the church.

ABRAHAM KUYPER[18]

17. Jan Willem Sap, *Paving the Way for Revolution: Calvinism and the Struggle for a Democratic Constitutional State* (Amsterdam: Free University Press, 2001), 100.
18. Kuyper, "Common Grace," in *Centennial Reader*, 189-90.

Abraham Kuyper's ecclesiology was, in many ways, very traditional. The church's ultimate purpose was not to be a political party, a social club, a financial charity, or a school of civility and manners—the church was the body of Christ, the disciples Jesus gathered and scattered throughout the world. The purpose of the church was to gather in worship, study the Scriptures, celebrate the sacraments, cultivate Christian community, and proclaim the gospel of Jesus Christ.

Would a local church limited to these fundamental tasks contribute in any way to a movement for Christian pluralism? Kuyper answered with a resounding "Yes!" Peppered throughout his speeches, articles, and texts are references to a wide variety of ways in which local churches could produce what we might call pluralistic byproducts. In essence, by pursuing their distinct mission, Kuyper believed, churches could function as a sort of production center of virtues, behaviors, practices, ideas, and institutions that contributed to a healthy political culture.

To clarify, it is in this sense that Kuyper's church was pluralistic. His churches were not pluralistic in the sense that they would count avowed Muslims, Buddhists, or atheists as members. They were exclusively run by and for members of the Christian faith. No, his churches were pluralistic in the sense that in serving Jesus Christ exclusively, they could serve the culture pluralistically. In other words, Kuyper believed that a pluralistic church dedicated to Jesus Christ alone could equip its members with a set of Christ-centered virtues, convictions, and practices inside the walls of the church that would have pluralistic consequences for their lives outside the walls of the church.

In fact, Abraham Kuyper regularly argued that the democratic implications of Christ's sovereignty were first discovered inside the internal political life of the church (*Lectures*, 63). For, if Christ alone was directly sovereign over a community of believers, this greatly weakened the ability of a single leader to claim exclusive authority over the community. Moreover, if Christ could directly meet with, speak to, and instruct a body of believers, this greatly limited a church leader's ability to claim exclusive access to Jesus—and therefore ultimate truth. Under such an ecclesiology, Kuyper argued, each member of the church stands as an equal participant under the sovereign rule of Christ. If Christ alone was the head, then no leader, council, document, or church law could claim a monopoly on the rule of the church. That level of ultimate authority belonged to Christ alone. In light of this Reformed doctrine, Kuyper argued that the Reformed church could not remain hierarchal, it had to became "democratic to its bones and marrow" (*Lectures*, 63). The church would still have leaders, but these leaders would be elected by the community, have restricted tasks, serve limited terms, and always lead under the sovereignty of Christ and in the service to the community.

Kuyper argued that early Reformed churches cultivated this democratic ethos internally within their own church politics and later brought those democratic convictions into the public square. But Kuyper argued that the democratic and pluralistic contributions of the church extended even further. He pointed to the fact that as the early Reformation spread across Europe, non-hierarchical networks and federations of Reformed churches began to take shape. Kuyper notes that as these federations of churches formed, no single church was allowed to "exercise any dominion over another." Because they were all "of equal rank . . . manifestations of one and the same body, [they could] only be united synodically, i.e., by way of confederation" (*Lectures*, 63). No leader of this federation could ever seek his own sovereign position but had to serve the sovereign churches that made up its body. Kuyper argued that these early ecclesial confederations would become "the pre-formation of state confederation" (*Lectures*, 171).

Members of these democratic churches and ecclesial confederations were, according to Kuyper, participating in political bodies that respected the freedom, equality, diversity, and unique responsibilities of individual participants. Churches knew that they were not under a church government; they were active participants in its construction. All church members were engaged in a communal and democratic practice of discerning the will of the sovereign Christ together.

Because early Reformed churches in Switzerland, Scotland, the United States, and the Netherlands had organized themselves into free and democratic confederations, Kuyper believed that their pluralistic governing structures made Reformed Christians uniquely open to political reforms that were democratic and pluralistic. After all, local churches engaged in the international Reformed movement were free to organize themselves according to local cultures, needs, and characteristics. For, Kuyper explained, if the local churches are

> united only in the way of confederation, then differences of climate and of nation, of historical past, and of disposition of mind [are allowed] to exercise a widely variegating influence, and multiformity in ecclesiastical matters must be the result. . . . [This] annihilates the *absolute* character of every visible church, and places them all side by side, as differing in degrees of purity, but always remaining in some way or other a manifestation of one holy and catholic Church of Christ in Heaven. I do not say that Calvinistic theologians have proclaimed this full consequence from the beginning. . . . But this does not in the

least detract from the great significance of the fact that by regarding their church, not as a hierarchy or institution, but as the gathering of individual confessors, they started for the life of the church, as well as for the life of the state, and civil society, from the principle not of compulsion, but of liberty. (*Lectures*, 63–64)

In short, there was no absolute church within the Reformed confederation. No single congregation was the platonic ideal into which all other churches needed to assimilate. Because Christ alone was the exclusive head of the churches, Christ alone sovereignly "places them all side by side." In this way, no Reformed church could command cultural or theological hegemony within the confederation of churches. According to Kuyper, this international diversity reflected the diverse unity that could only be found under the sovereignty of Christ. For, in Christ alone, diverse human beings could be gathered,

Not like a drop of water in a stream or a piece of gravel in a pit but like branches grafted into the one vine. . . . In the unity of the kingdom of God, diversity is not lost but all the more sharply defined. On the great day of Pentecost the Holy Spirit did not speak in one uniform language; instead, everyone heard the Spirit proclaiming the mighty works of God in his own tongue.[19]

Kuyper made his case for diversity by pointing to John Calvin's early insistence that, within the churches of the Reformation, "deviations in minor matters had to be tolerated" ("Calvinism: Source and Stronghold," 304–5). This tolerance was necessary because, and here Kuyper quotes Calvin directly, "there is none whose mind is not darkened by some cloud of ignorance" ("Calvinism: Source and Stronghold," 304–5). If churches knew God only in part and only through a glass darkly, any enforcement of a theological uniformity would be both unreasonable and unjust.

According to Kuyper, these early practices of diversity, tolerance, and forbearance within Reformed churches would eventually spill out into Reformed politics. He argued that early on, the members of the Reformation in France "extended" their internal habits of tolerance to

unarmed Catholics. Our Dutch Republic went even further and tolerated deviating forms of worship in private homes. In England it devel-

---

19. Kuyper, "Uniformity: The Curse of Modern Life," in *Centennial Reader*, 36.

oped further yet in the "Act of Toleration," until at last in America the logical conclusion is drawn of giving freedom to all forms of worship and each individual conscience. ("Calvinism: Source and Stronghold," 304–5)

For when "the ideal of freedom had established itself in the bosom of the church, it inevitably sought civil rights in the domain of the state" ("Calvinism: Source and Stronghold," 296). Internal practices of democracy and diversity made external practices of democracy and diversity more palatable. For our current "development of political liberty grew inescapably from the ideal of freedom of conscience, once grasped at its deepest root" ("Calvinism: Source and Stronghold," 296).

Kuyper's historical case for the Reformation's contributions to European democracy certainly deserves critical review. His love for romantic, hyperbolic, and sometimes Whiggish history is clear. That said, Abraham Kuyper's arguments for the political implications of internal church governance deserves our attention. In Kuyper's ecclesiology we find a tight religious community armed with the conviction that all of its members are equal, that they all must serve one another, that none should be allowed to dominate another, that their diversity is not a problem but an asset, and that none of them have a complete grasp of the whole truth. To be sure, no church in the Reformation consistently held to all of these ideals. That said, even an imperfect commitment to these ideals would have to contribute in some important ways to a healthy political culture.

Beyond participating in the internal democratic structures, practices, and polity of Reformed churches, Kuyper argued that Christians would also begin to see the need for religious tolerance simply by listening to good sermons. Take, for example, Kuyper's reflections on the theopolitical consequences of sermons on divine election or predestination. Imagine, if you will, a young woman sitting in a Reformed church pew who fully acknowledges that she has done nothing to deserve the love of God. Having accepted that she has been elected or chosen by God through no good work of her own, she must conclude that she has nothing to lord over her non-Christian neighbors. For Kuyper argues, the Reformers "never intended the doctrine" of election as an opportunity for self-promotion or "self-aggrandizement but only as a confession that all honor . . . belongs to God." Kuyper argues that a belief in predestination fundamentally "undermines any idea of religious persecution" ("Calvinism: Source and Stronghold," 310). If God alone is capable of spiritual transformation, all human efforts to force conversion are not only nonsensical, but they constitute a direct affront to the only one who can transform the human heart.

Beyond these comments, Kuyper was frustratingly brief and unsystematic in his explanation of frequent claims that local churches could contribute to the cause of democracy and pluralism. To remedy this deficiency, chapter seven will focus specifically on how participation in weekly worship can equip disciples with the sort of habits, virtues, and practices they will need to sustain their commitments to pluralism in the clash between Mecca and Amsterdam.

While Kuyper did not have a lot to say about how the gathered church would contribute to democracy and pluralism, he wrote extensively about how the scattered church active in the public square could do so. We now turn to his thoughts on the subject.

Institute and Organism

[The Church] must purify and ennoble the ideas in general circulation, elevate public opinion, introduce more solid principles, and so raise the view of life prevailing in the state, society, and the family.[20]

Kuyper consistently argued that the governance of the church and the governance of the state had to remain absolutely distinct. But did this separation of powers imply that the church should stay out of political discourse? Kuyper divided this age-old question and answered it with both a "yes" and a "no." In essence, Kuyper wanted to avoid two historical mistakes—the sectarian and the liberal. In Kuyper's mind, sectarian churches surrendered their public responsibility by pulling back from political discourse, while liberal churches surrendered their public distinctiveness by assimilating into political discourse.

First-time readers of Abraham Kuyper's public theology can quickly become confused and even frustrated by an internal tension within his work. At certain moments, Kuyper appears to advocate the political posture of Christian separation and distinctiveness in the world and at other moments he appears to advocate a political posture of Christian engagement and cooperation in the world. To understand this perceived tension requires an understanding of Abraham Kuyper's critical distinction between the church as institute and the church as organism.

In brief, the "church as institute" refers to Christians gathered institutionally in worship and community, while the "church as organism" refers to

---

20. Kuyper, "Common Grace," in *Centennial Reader*, 195.

Christians scattered organically throughout the world in their various public roles. According to Kuyper's schema, the gathered church institute was responsible for the internal institutional activities of the church (preaching, teaching, worship, sacraments, discipline, catechesis, and the communal life of the church). The scattered church organism was responsible for the external and organic activities of the church in the world (working, volunteering, evangelizing, serving the poor, raising families, voting, making art, doing research, starting businesses, and so on). If the church as institute was the body of Christ gathered institutionally on Sunday, the church as organism was the body of Christ scattered organically on Monday. In sum, Kuyper wanted the gathered church institute to be fiercely separate and distinct from the world, while he wanted the scattered church organism to be fiercely engaged within the life of the world.

While the two were deeply connected, Kuyper did not want the gathered institutional church to dominate or control the scattered organic church in the world. Kuyper therefore argued that church councils and pastors were not allowed to instruct Christian artists, scientists, or business owners on how they should paint, research, or run their businesses. Christian artists, scientists, and business leaders served Christ alone and they served him directly in their public lives. The scattered church looks to Christ, not their pastors, for immediate direction in their public lives. In other words, if the church gathered provides the theological framework for the Christian life, the church scattered is empowered and freed to apply that framework to their public callings.

In terms of politics, Kuyper argued that the gathered church institute should avoid all direct contact, cooperation, and interaction with the state. Moreover, the church as institute should not engage in overly political discourse or debate, nor should it instruct its members on how they should vote. Such activity, Kuyper argued, was not the competency of pastors, elders, or church boards—nor was it their calling or responsibility. That said, the church scattered, the church organism, was obligated to engage in political life. Kuyper argued that Christians were called by Christ to seek the public justice of their society. To accomplish this, Christians needed to organize themselves politically through the formation of Christian political parties, newspapers, unions, and advocacy organizations. In short, while Kuyper believed that the organic and scattered church was called to be deeply engaged in political life, Kuyper simply did not want the institutional church organizing that engagement.

The next question naturally follows: what is the proper relationship between the institute and organism, between the church gathered and the church scattered? While Kuyper clearly wanted to distinguish their roles, he did not want to separate them. In Kuyper's estimation both organism and institute needed each other. Without the institute, the scattered church would soon drift aimlessly into the world. Without the organism, the church as institute would have no connection or impact in the world. The organism needed to be connected to and formed by the institute. Likewise the church as institute need to encourage and honor the calling of the organism in the world. For those who gather for worship on Sunday must scatter for work on Monday. Sunday singers, Kuyper argued,

> are the same people who in their families act as parents and children, in their businesses as patrons and workers, in society as citizens and who, as such, make the powers of the kingdom felt in their domestic lives, in their education, in their businesses and in all contacts with people and also as citizens in society.[21]

According to Kuyper, both sides of the church were integral to its identity and mission. While they have distinct responsibilities and distinct authority, they must never separate.

In all of this, *Kuyper sought to avoid the sectarian and liberal mistakes by describing the church as both deeply distinct and deeply engaged in the life of the world.* In other words, the church must have walls that distinguish it from the world. Its walls must also have "wide open windows, and through these spacious windows the light of the Eternal has to radiate over the whole world. Here is a city, set upon a hill, which every man can see afar off. Here is a holy salt that penetrates in every direction, checking all corruption" (*Lectures*, 53).

From Two Cities to Three: Kuyper's Theology of Civil Society

Nicholas Wolterstorff argues that Abraham Kuyper's understanding of the relationship between the church and the world made him a curious sort of Augustinian. Wolterstorff explains that while Kuyper certainly affirmed Augustine's famous distinction between the two cities (the *civitas Dei* and the *civitas mundi*), Kuyper clearly adds a third city to the traditional Augustinian binary. Wolterstorff terms Kuyper's third city the *"civitas gentium."*

---

21. Kuyper, *Gemeene Gratie,* vol. 3, 421. Trans. in Gerard Dekker and George Harinck, "The Position of the Church Institute in Society: A Comparison between Bonhoeffer and Kuyper," *The Princeton Seminary Bulletin* 28, no. 1 (2007), 86–98.

In a fascinating reflection on Kuyper's work, Wolterstorff argues that throughout his life Abraham Kuyper tried to theologically envision a third space, a shared public square in which the "citizens of the *civitas Dei* participate along with the citizens of the *civitas mundi*."[22] Within this shared city, Kuyper argued, Christian citizens should stand alongside non-Christian citizens and "speak with a Christian voice, and act out of Christian conviction, within the structures, solidarities, and practices of our common humanity."[23]

Kuyper encouraged Christian citizens to neither withdraw into the city of God nor be absorbed into the city of the world.[24] Instead, within this third city, Christians and non-Christians alike should be able to express, develop, and advocate their distinct visions in free contestation and discourse. That said, Kuyper realized that if Christian citizens were going to speak and act as Christians in the public square, they would "need their own institutional base"[25] to "nourish and sustain such speaking and acting."[26] Secular schools and associations would never produce thoughtful Christian pluralists. The movement would need its own institutions to prepare its people to understand and advocate for deep pluralism within the common *civitas gentium*. In encouraging Christians to form their own institutions and schools, Abraham Kuyper was not advocating a retreat from the public square. Christian newspapers, schools, universities, and political parties were designed to prepare Christian citizens to thoughtfully engage the public square. For, he insisted, "living in a house of one's own by no means precludes [one from] going out onto the thoroughfares of life" ("Calvinism: Source and Stronghold," 398).

These separate institutions performed three critical functions for Kuyper's pluralist movement. First, as mentioned earlier, they equipped Christians to engage in the public square as Christians. If Christian pluralism wanted to have a discernable voice in the Netherlands, some measure of education and organization would be required. Kuyper insisted that autonomous and unorganized pluralists would never last in an exhausting battle of words with liberal institutions and culture. The ideas of Christian pluralism could not simply be argued by solitary individuals. These ideas had to be lived out, modeled, and advocated in community. This required formational communities like Chris-

---

22. Nicholas Wolterstorff, *Educating for Shalom: Essays in Christian Higher Education*, ed. Clarence Joldersma and Gloria Goris Stronks (Grand Rapids: Eerdmans, 2003), 278-89.

23. Wolterstorff, *Educating for Shalom*, 278.

24. See also Nicholas Wolterstorff, "Christian Political Reflection: Diognetian or Augustinian," *The Princeton Seminary Bulletin* 20, no. 2, (1999): 150-68.

25. Wolterstorff, *Educating for Shalom*, 278.

26. Wolterstorff, *Educating for Shalom*, 278.

tian churches, schools, universities, newspapers, and political parties. Kuyper here demonstrates an important recognition that deep pluralism requires more than ideas; it demands the production of alternative communities, institutions, and cultural practices that can challenge the vast cultural power of uniformity and hegemony.

This leads into the second function of Kuyper's Christian organizations. Simply by being separate and distinct from the liberal hegemony, Kuyper argued, these Christian institutions functioned as a countercultural resistance against the forces of modern liberal uniformity. The liberal nation-state wanted Christians to participate in their liberal institutions so that they might be absorbed into the modern liberal whole. Separate Christian institutions were a visual and political reminder to the entire nation that Christianity refused to assimilate. Their distinct presence and voice would remind the Netherlands that liberalism represented just one perspective among many. In this, Kuyper argued, liberals, who dream of national unity "must bear the sting of our setting ourselves apart."[27]

Third, separate Christian institutions also functioned as an act of resistance against Christian theocrats and nationalists who had not yet given up on the dream of a "Christian Netherlands." This group wanted Christians to participate in liberal institutions in an effort to redirect them in a more Christian direction. Kuyper not only disagreed with their aims, but he doubted that their individualistic strategy of cultural transformation would be successful. It was more likely that the liberal institutions they tried to transform would end up transforming them.

Kuyper's nineteenth-century dream of a church that was both distinct and engaged was not ultimately successful. Kuyper's followers would fail to hold onto both sides of his argument. The first group of followers excelled at being institutionally distinct from the world but failed to be publically engaged in it. This group enjoyed the ideological safety of Christian institutions so much that they decided to remain within their protective walls. An ever-expanding list of exclusively Christian clubs, associations, and unions in the Christian subculture made public engagement more and more rare. The institutional walls, originally constructed to protect against the world, soon walled them in.

---

27. Kuyper, "The Blurring of the Boundaries," in *Centennial Reader*, 398. This constructive and institutional strategy came from Kuyper's conviction that liberal hegemony could be "successfully countered only by the movement of an antithetical *life*. . . . Only thus can you regain your own base of operations. . . . Only thus can you fortify a line of defense. . . . [O]nly in this way is revived the holy comradeship, the confidence in your own cause, and the enthusiasm for the colors of your own glorious flag which redoubles the strength of any army."

The second group of Kuyper's followers took the opposite tack. They worked hard to become publically engaged, relevant, and influential but ultimately lost sight of their distinctiveness. The more their institutions sought to engage the world and the more they partnered with others and accepted government contracts, funding, and regulation, the more their ability to serve society as a distinctively Christian organization waned.

How might contemporary disciples effectively balance Kuyper's two-sided call to be both distinct and engaged in the clash between Mecca and Amsterdam? A return to Kuyper's original work is certainly a nice place to start, but his ideas and institutions are, on their own, fundamentally insufficient. In later chapters, I will argue that Christian pluralists need more than ideas and institutions; they need habits, virtues, and practices as well. There I will argue that it is not enough to be taught a belief in Christian pluralism; one needs to habituate, desire, and practice that belief as well.

Theological Resources for Commonness

With all of their resistance to the forces of ideological uniformity, pluralists of all stripes are frequently pressed to answer a simple question: Without some level of ideological commonness, how can different faiths and cultures ever dialogue, cooperate, or connect with one another? Don't we need some point of contact around which to organize a diverse society?

Such questions inevitably lead to what we might call the paradox of commonness. The paradox is essentially this: once a pluralist names some point of universal contact or consensus (something binding for all faiths, ideologies, and cultures), that point of consensus quickly becomes the root from which a new hegemonic regime can rise. Once the pluralist, in an effort to make connections across disparate communities, identifies a point of universal consensus, that pluralist falls prey to the paradox of commonness. While this paradox pushes on all pluralists—both religious and secular—pluralists in the Christian faith face additional questions. The primary question for them is how a Christian community with a distinct theological language and a distinct moral center can ever speak to, learn from, or cooperate with those with different philosophical languages and centers. Abraham Kuyper was deeply aware of these paradoxes and challenges and, while he did not fully solve them, in the rest of this section I want to briefly outline some of his more promising insights on the topic.

As I mentioned earlier, Abraham Kuyper insisted that humanity's sin had destroyed the race's ability to agree or coalesce around the one true faith or one moral system. Sin, in all its divisiveness, had opened up "an abyss in the universal human consciousness across which no bridge can be laid."[28] This philosophical and moral division continually inhibited humanity's unity in morality, theology, philosophy, economics, politics, the arts, and more. At no point could the human species, by its own efforts, bridge the gaping ideological divides it had opened up.

While Kuyper's diagnosis of human division and fragmentation certainly appears grim, he was not without hope. In God's infinite grace, humanity had not been left in a state of total ideological fragmentation, enmity, and agonism. Kuyper argued that God had graciously given the divided peoples of the earth something he called *gemeene gratie*.

A Common Grace

Kuyper's enduring hope for cooperation, connection, and contact across ideologies and cultures rested on *gemeene gratie* or common grace.[29] *Gemeene gratie* was his way of speaking about the mysterious and cosmic work of the Holy Spirit in all peoples, faiths, and cultures. According to Kuyper, no faith or culture had escaped the good and gracious gifts of the Holy Spirit. While *gemeene gratie* is a complex doctrine that would influence Kuyper's public theology on a wide range of issues, it had specific import for his approach to the question of pluralism and—more specifically—to his unique answer to the paradox of commonness.

Abraham Kuyper argued that the Holy Spirit's gift of common grace to all faiths and cultures performed three critical functions in a fragmented society. First, the Holy Spirit graciously restrains the selfish, violent, and hegemonic temptations active within every ideological community (*Lectures*, 123–24). Kuyper argued that without the restraining work of the Holy Spirit, no civic trust, peace, or cooperation could ever be established between diverse and battling faith communities.

Second, the Holy Spirit graciously pours the gifts of reason, morality, and virtue into every faith and culture within a divided nation. After all, if Christians alone received the divine gifts of reason and morality, non-Christians

28. Abraham Kuyper, *Principles of Sacred Theology*, trans. by John Hendrik De Vries (Grand Rapids: Eerdmans, 1954), 152.

29. See Abraham Kuyper's development of common grace in *Lectures on Calvinism*, 118–29 and *Gemeene Gratie*, vols. 1, 2, and 3 (Leiden: Donner, 1902–1905).

could only be the objects of Christian rule, education, and moral training. Instead, because of this pouring out of reason and morality on all faiths and cultures, Christians had to assume that their opponents had some God-given insights to contribute to public discourse as well.

Third, the Holy Spirit graciously develops the cultural artifacts, knowledge, and institutions of every faith and ideology. For Kuyper, the diverse global development of music, poetry, science, education, family, farming, and so on was a gracious gift from the Holy Spirit. God generously gave all people these gifts of culture. In short, for Abraham Kuyper, the Holy Spirit's work in the world is not limited to salvation of Christians; it goes beyond that, moving as a generous cultural force working for the flourishing and development of all faiths, people, and cultures. If this was true, Christian pluralists had to honor, respect, and give thanks for non-Christian artifacts, knowledge, and institutions. Kuyper believed that each of these three critical works of the Holy Spirit—restraining, pouring, and developing—enables sinful and divided ideologies (Christianity included) to achieve critical moments of connection and cooperation.

That said, a question remains, how will Kuyper's common grace avoid the paradox of commonness? In other words, how does common grace avoid becoming a universal point of connection that can turn into a weapon of ideological hegemony and uniformity? How do the connections formed by common grace avoid becoming ideological ties that bind and control?

The answer to this question is found in the level of ideological confidence one can place in a doctrine of common grace. While common grace provides hope that consensus can be found, it does not provide absolute and perfect certainty that it will be found. While Kuyper was extremely certain that the Holy Spirit was cosmically active in all faiths and cultures, bringing them together for moments of consensus and cooperation, Kuyper was never certain of what those moments of consensus would look like or how long they would last. Moreover, moments of consensus and cooperation were always just that, moments. Interfaith and intercultural moments of cooperation were always tenuous, temporary, and unpredictable. They were, with the help of the Holy Spirit, possible—but not always certain. A Christian pluralist's work for interfaith cooperation was driven by an uncontrollable and unforeseen hope in the mysterious work of the Holy Spirit, not by a certainty in some sort of identifiable and universal human morality.

Exclusively divine in its origin and execution, common grace could never be controlled or dictated by a single leader, state, church, or culture. Because Christians could not control or predict the work of the Holy Spirit, they could not define exactly what all faiths would have in common at any one moment. This is how Abraham Kuyper avoided the paradox of commonness. The doctrine would not allow Kuyper to set down a universal law or morality. He could not declare a divinely inspired political platform relevant for all times, places, and cultures. The knowledge that the Holy Spirit was blessing non-Christians would challenge Kuyper and his followers to remain open to unforeseen and unpredictable interfaith alliances and moments of consensus. These moments could not be controlled, predicted, or legislated.

A second question regarding common grace quickly emerges from those in theological circles. Why did Kuyper label this work of God in the lives of Muslims and Buddhists, liberals and atheists "grace"? Traditionally in Christian theology, human beings who experience grace are forever transformed by its power. But this is clearly not the case when non-Christians encounter this so-called common grace. These non-Christians continue to deny the existence of a Holy Spirit that is supposedly restraining, blessing, and developing their common life. They continue on as if nothing was happening. Kuyper's descriptions of *gemeene gratie* make it appear that he simply chose to use the word *grace* to communicate the undeserved and generous nature of the gift.

Common grace, in Kuyper's mind, is never transformative or salvific. Kuyper was simply attempting to demonstrate that it was only through the generous work of the Holy Spirit that any community (Christian or not) possessed any of the gifts of civic virtue, rationality, trust, and restraint. Common grace—while not salvific—was completely unmerited, completely unbound, and beyond human comprehension.

If a Christian understood that the Holy Spirit was active in the lives of non-Christians, this knowledge should have an enormously positive impact on how they interacted with non-Christian communities. Suddenly, non-Christian wisdom and insight are seen, not as threats, but as sacred gifts from God. Such gifts from God cannot, and indeed ought not, be ignored. For, Kuyper argued,

> Precious treasures have come down to us from the old heathen civilization. In Plato you find pages which you devour. Cicero fascinates you and bears you along by his noble tone and stirs up in you holy sentiments. And if you consider . . . [the] literary productions of professed infidels, how much there is which attracts you, with which you sympathize and which you admire. It is not exclusively the spark of genius or the splendor of talent, which excites your pleasure in the words and actions of unbelievers, but it is often their beauty of charac-

ter, their zeal, their devotion, their love, their candor, their faithfulness and their sense of honesty. Yea, we may not pass it over in silence . . . who among us has not himself been put to the blush occasionally by being confronted with what is called the "virtues of the heathen"? (*Lectures*, 121–22)

Here we find a humbling lesson for all Christian pluralists. Deep pluralism will ultimately stand or fall, not by the work pluralists, but by the work of the Holy Spirit. Moreover, sometimes democracy and pluralism will be upheld by the work of "virtuous heathens." In fact, these beautiful so-called infidels who have been blessed by the Holy Spirit with wisdom, patience, and courage may far outlast and outshine their Christian neighbors.

Strictly speaking, Christian pluralists will never achieve pluralism by their own strength, intelligence, or will. For, as Kuyper argued, "if God had not time and again poured vigor into those lifeless spheres, sometimes under pressure . . . the last distinct sphere would long since have broken down and nothing would remain of our freedom" ("Sphere Sovereignty," 474). If pluralism emerges, if the forces of hegemony are held at bay, if moments of interfaith cooperation occur, these things are ultimately thanks to the gracious work of the Holy Spirit. Kuyper insisted that, if left to themselves, sinful Christian pluralists would always stumble backward into theocratic hegemony. By its own power, Christianity goes back to Christendom.

After all, Kuyper notes, when one surveys the historical development of religious freedom in the Netherlands, one sees that it did not come from the selfless charity and generosity of Christians. The church learned the value of religious freedom only when God took it away from them. For, Kuyper states, their thirst for religious freedom was a painful gift which "came from above." The "Lord created a thirst for that as-yet-unknown freedom, not by a long course of philosophical development, nor by a refined civility, but by sheer *distress*, the *agony of defeat*" ("Calvinism: Source and Stronghold," 319). Dutch Christians did not discover religious freedom; they were rudely awakened to its necessity (*Lectures*, 28). Through an acute "fellowship in suffering" (*Lectures*, 28) under the Roman Catholics, early Protestants discovered the true value of tolerance. They did not

> *read* the chronicles of the martyrs, as we have. But they *heard* the screams of the tortured, the ghastly groanings of the strangled. Not black print but the ugly scaffold, painted red with blood, had shown them the image of a martyr . . . they wept and cried out: "Lord God!

Deliver thou us!" Then it came. Then the birthing hour of *freedom of conscience* struck.... It was God's plan.... *He* did it. ("Calvinism: Source and Stronghold," 319)

The human desire for religious freedom, democracy, and pluralism was not a Christian accomplishment; it was a gift from Christ—and a painful one at that.

In addition to humility, God's *gemeene gratie* provided early pluralists with a sense of hope that moments of contact and consensus in a diverse and fragmented nation could still be found. Protestants, Catholics, Liberals, and Socialists could have hope that they could work together and reach some contingent points of consensus. But, unlike traditional points of contact like a universal rationality and natural law, no mortal force could completely solidify or control what these "points of contact" would be for all times and places. There was hope for consensus even if it would always be temporary and contingent.

In common grace, Kuyper attempted to avoid two Christian tendencies that would ultimately prove fatal to Christian pluralism. The first tendency imagines that God is active only within the Christian church. This tendency holds that God gives nothing good, true, or beautiful to other faith communities—they are morally, aesthetically, and intellectually empty. From this perspective, interfaith dialogue is hopeless, naïve, and potentially dangerous. We might call this the sectarian Christian tendency. The second tendency that Kuyper wanted to avoid imagined that God's goodness, truth, and beauty were distributed equally across all faiths and cultures. In this tendency, nothing is special, distinctive, or authoritative about the word and work of God in the Christian church. From this perspective, the Holy Spirit speaks everywhere equally. Here interfaith dialogue is equal to Scripture in discerning God's will and work in the world. We might call this the liberal Christian tendency.

Kuyper was looking to avoid both the sectarian and the liberal tendencies. He was not willing to give up on his orthodox Christian conviction that God had revealed himself in a unique, authoritative, and salvific way in Jesus Christ. He was also not willing to give up his conviction that God was graciously involved in the lives of those who were not yet a part of Jesus Christ or his church.

In summation, all of this was Kuyper's way of holding together two fundamental beliefs. First, God's special grace was at work in the exclusive saving work of Jesus Christ. And second, God's common grace was at work in the universal blessing of the Holy Spirit. Special grace transforms, common grace enriches. Special grace is exclusive, common grace is universal. Collectively, both common and special grace mysteriously serve the will and glory of triune God in the world.

Equipped with common grace, Abraham Kuyper believed, pluralists could engage in interfaith dialogue with the hope that at some time, and in some way, momentary points of understanding, connection, and partnership might occur. Convinced of common grace, pluralists could know that their expectations for interfaith cooperation were not built on their own efforts or on a false hope but on a gracious gift from above. Common grace enables pluralists, when accused of political naïveté, to shrug their shoulders and press on in hope.

A Common Humanity

Common grace was not the only resource for commonness and connection that Kuyper would appeal to in his theological case for pluralism. His second resource was one of theological anthropology. Kuyper argued that humanity, though deeply divided in terms of faith and culture, had a common historical origin. By virtue of their common ancestry, every human being was "organically united with the whole race." He argued that, despite our differences, "Together we form *one humanity*, not only with those who are living now, but also with all the generations behind us and with all those who shall come after us—pulverized into millions though we may be. All the human race is from *one blood*" (*Lectures*, 79).

Kuyper's distinction between those inside or outside the church was not, in any way, an ontological distinction. All people from all times, cultures, and faiths were created in the image of God. Because of this common origin, all people had equal value. Moreover, there was nothing a person could do to destroy or remove the created *Imago*. No amount of evil, injustice, or violence could strip human beings of the divine image they bore. All humanity shared in the same ontological value and beauty of the *Imago Dei*. While humanity's sin had broken its ideological unity, its ontological unity remained intact.

While Kuyper's theological arguments for a common humanity may appear straightforward, these statements have not always been self-evident for the Dutch people in Kuyper's day or our own. Consider, for example, the language used to describe Muslim immigrants on Amsterdam's streets today. Horrible names are commonly exchanged including *geitenneuker* (goat-fucker) and *kut Marrokkanen* (Moroccan cunt). On the Muslim side, it is not unheard of for local mosques to demonize Dutch culture as being wholly evil and outside of Allah's care. The temptation to demonize, "foreignize," and turn neighbors into aliens presses on all people—both the religious and the secular.

To combat this temptation to "otherize" one's neighbor, Kuyper insisted that all faiths, nations, and cultures collectively shared in God's image. But more than that, Kuyper insisted that only when all cultures, races, and eras were brought together at the end of time would they fully reflect the full complexity and beauty of the *Imago Dei*. Excluding one piece of humanity, one culture, or one race made God's *Imago* and God's glory incomplete.

Kuyper argued that humanity had been specifically created to progressively diversify and develop so that in the eschaton humanity could fully reflect the complex and kaleidoscopic beauty of God's own image. The "image of God," he argued, was "certainly much too rich a concept to be realized *in one single person*."[30] "Do we not come closer to the truth by saying that the bearer of the full multifaceted image of God is not the individual person but *our entire human race*?"[31] For the *Imago* "comes into its own only when we extend it to our entire race down through the ages, and in the combination of the talents bestowed upon all the various persons. It is not so that merely one individual brain, or one individual genius, or one individual talent [bears the *Imago*] . . . but all of them together."[32]

In conclusion, Christian pluralists are closer to reflecting the image of God—indeed closer to God himself—when they engage in relationship with diverse nationalities, cultures, and faiths. For while it is true that Cain killed Abel, Kuyper insists the declaration "you are all brothers" has not "lost its validity for us."[33]

A Common Creation

Abraham Kuyper was convinced that, though the world had fallen into sin and social fragmentation, God had graciously maintained a modicum of order and stability in social life. Humanity, in other words, did not live in a world of total moral confusion and division. By God's providence, all faiths and cultures inhabited a common world, a common created space that had been preserved with a common and stable set of laws, structures, boundaries, and

---

30. Kuyper, "Common Grace," in *Centennial Reader*, 177.
31. Kuyper, "Common Grace," in *Centennial Reader*, 177.
32. Abraham Kuyper, *Wisdom and Wonder: Common Grace in Science and Art*, trans. Nelson D. Kloosterman (Grand Rapids: Christian's Library Press, 2011), 42.
33. Kuyper, "Uniformity: The Curse of the Modern Life," in *Centennial Reader*, 34.

norms. Kuyper argued that because all faiths and cultures inhabited the same creation, they all intuitively felt the same creational limits, laws, and patterns guiding their collective lives. In other words, while the world's faiths and cultures would always disagree about the exact specifics of these divinely given laws and norms, they would all intuitively sense and desire some measure of justice, beauty, family, peace, relationships, and flourishing. These common moral desires and longings, Kuyper argued, were imprinted into nature at creation. Because of sin, humanity's direct and perfect knowledge of these was distorted and darkened. No priest, politician, or scientist had access to these creational laws.

And yet, through the Holy Spirit's work of common grace, creational laws and norms endure and occasionally make themselves known. Humanity is not left in a state of total moral confusion or fragmentation. Though our many moral disagreements will continue unabated, those disagreements will not be total. The creational and moral stability of the human race enables us to at least partially discern the need for justice, charity, and solidarity in our societies. In other words, when a socialist advocates for economic justice, when a conservative advocates for tradition, when a liberal advocates for liberty, and when a Muslim advocates for submission, all their moral longings (though imperfect) reflect a real interaction with the divinely given norms and laws imprinted in creation. Their moral desires for solidarity, tradition, freedom, and submission are not mere human constructions—they emerge from divinely created origins.

Moreover, while there are deep moral differences between faiths and cultures, by virtue of the common creation they all share, those moral differences are not total. For example, while cultures take diverse political, economic, artistic, educational, and familial turns, all cultures seem curiously interested in somewhat common moral ends. They all seem doggedly interested in some form of political justice, economic fairness, artistic creativity, educational exploration, and familial integrity. Because of sin, these cultures and faith will consistently disagree about the specific definition of justice, fairness, integrity, and so on. That said, because they all share the same created life, they will all experience moments when their desires intersect with those of other faiths and other cultures.

Kuyper's work on this topic of creational commonness can be extremely helpful for contemporary Christian pluralists hoping to avoid the extremes of either total cultural relativism or total cultural universalism. After all, both positions render deep and lasting dialogue across cultures and faiths difficult if not impossible. Total cultural relativism denies the possibility of cross-cultural consensus or cooperation. Total cultural universalism imposes one cultural understanding of law, order, morality, or rationality on all other cultures, declaring that one cultural position universal. Both relativism and universalism label deep and authentic cross-cultural dialogue at best naïve and at worst dangerous.

Abraham Kuyper's discussion of a humble yet hopeful approach to interfaith dialogue and cooperation points to a third way beyond the dead ends of relativism and universalism. With a common grace, a common humanity, and a common creation, Kuyper's pluralists can engage their non-Christian interlocutors with a real hope that moments of moral consensus and cooperation can be found. That said, these pluralists will not expect too much from these moments of moral consensus and cooperation. Because of their doctrine of sin, they will recognize that moments of agreement will always be temporary and partial. In this way, Christians can engage the public square with both a humble realism about humanity's deep divisions and a hopeful optimism about their common humanity, creation, and grace.

A Trinitarian Path through Mecca and Amsterdam

While Kuyper and his movement were not without their faults and blind spots, their theological insights and political activism have the potential to inspire a twenty-first century imagination for Christian pluralism. Equipped with Abraham Kuyper's robust Christological pluralism, followers of Jesus walking amidst Mecca and Amsterdam can begin the process of not only deconstructing hegemony (secular and religious), but they can also begin to construct new ways of defending the rights and dignity of different faiths and cultures.

One could, in fact, choose to organize Abraham Kuyper's case for pluralism around the Trinitarian base that lies at the foundation of his theology. First, in a pluralistic culture, God the Son is both temporally and spatially sovereign over all faiths and cultures. God the Son declares all faiths and cultures free, and he alone sits in sovereign judgment over their public lives. Second, in a pluralistic culture, God the Holy Spirit is at work in all faiths and cultures through the generous gift of common grace. All faiths and cultures have been blessed with some measure of goodness, virtue, and knowledge by the Holy Spirit. Third, in a pluralistic culture, God the Father is the common creator and father of all people. All are brothers and sisters under his reign. Furthermore, God the Father has placed all his children together in a common creation that is arranged with a common set of norms, patterns, and laws that they can all sense.

Drawing on Abraham Kuyper's Trinitarian pluralism, contemporary Christians will be better equipped to resist today's xenophobic cries for Islamic assimilation. They will know that God the Son is sovereign over the history, culture, and politics of their nation. When they see Muslim schools, families, mosques, and associations erected in their neighborhoods, Christian pluralists can respect these institutions and know that Jesus Christ alone is sovereign over their institutional life. When Christians hear Islamic music, smell Islamic food, and see Islamic clothing in the streets, they can know that God the Holy Spirit has blessed their Muslim neighbors with the gifts of cultural beauty, creativity, and development. Tasting that food and hearing that music, Christians can give thanks to the Holy Spirit for those cultural goods. Demanding that their Muslim neighbors alter their clothing, practices, or institutions will be seen as tantamount to denying the good cultural gifts that they Holy Spirit gave them. Finally, when Christians listen to Muslims speak about the need for sexual, economic, or familial ethics, they can give thanks to God the Father for creating in all people a common desire for sexual, economic, and familial integrity. While Christians and Muslims may very well disagree strongly on moral and political issues, Christians can always know that deep down we all share a common creational order and that all of us are haunted by a common set of creational laws written deep within our hearts.

Beyond this Trinitarian base, Christian pluralists find in Kuyper a robust vision for the life of the church in a pluralistic culture. The church played a critical role in strengthening and sustaining Kuyper's early pluralist movement. The same can be true today. In their local churches, Christian pluralists have an opportunity to participate in a democratically formative space. Within the walls of the church every member and every gift can be—and should be—considered equal and valuable. Leaders in the church are elevated not to dominate, but to serve. Within the global church, cultural diversity can be celebrated and unity can be sought, not in a single culture, but in Christ alone. Within the walls of the church, the pluralist can be reminded of the radical freedom, justice, diversity, and unity that can be found in Christ alone.

Moreover, in light of Kuyper's emphasis on the power and importance of cultural institutions, contemporary Christian pluralists must recognize the critical importance of coming together to model, practice, and advocate pluralism collectively. Rightly structured, their institutions can equip Christians to go out into public life to embody a different way of living between Mecca and Amsterdam.

Following Kuyper's lead, Christian pluralists will not simply be peacemakers; they will be distinct and active contestants in the public square. They will put forward their ideas and institutions and put them up against the ideas and institutions of others. They will not run away from but will fully engage with the public square, the *civitas gentium*, the third city of our common humanity. As they engage in these debates and dialogues in the public square, they will not superficially smooth over the deep differences that divide different faiths and cultures. They will honor the distinct beliefs, practices, and institutions of their Muslim and liberal neighbors, not by ignoring them, but by engaging them in a thoughtful contest of ideas and practices.

Finally, however deep the difference, Christian pluralists will continue to pursue moments of commonness, connection, and cooperation. They will continue to place their hope, not in themselves, but in the Holy Spirit's work of common grace in the lives of their Muslim and liberal neighbors. Through common grace, Christians will be able to affirm a liberal's desire to protect the individual rights of women, a multiculturalist's desire to protect the cultural rights of diverse cultures, and a Muslim's desire to submit to Allah. The Christian pluralist will even give a qualified thanks for the right-wing nationalist's desire for a strong and healthy national community. It goes without saying that Christian pluralists will differ with all of these voices on the exact nature of individual rights, cultural diversity, divine submission, and national community. That said, in the light of common grace, Christian pluralists will be equipped to engage those differences with a humble hope that moments of commonness can be found.

In conclusion, as Christians walk pass veiled women walking the streets of Amsterdam, they need not frame their veiled neighbors as foreign aliens, political ideologues, oppressed wives, religious zealots, uncivilized barbarians, or poor people in need of aid. Christians pluralists can see these women as sacred creatures created in the image of God—loved by the sovereign creator of heaven and earth. They can understand that the past, present, and future of these veiled women's lives are governed and understood by Christ and his sovereign rule. These pluralists can know that the Holy Spirit has been mysteriously active in the lives of these women since the day they were born, restraining their sin and generously blessing them with gifts of justice, beauty, virtue, morality, generosity, and reason. These Christians can recognize that each of these women bears a sacred and powerful *sensus divinitatus*. They will not be surprised or scandalized when these women seek to publically express their faith through their habits of clothing, the structures of their family, the teachings in their schools, their needs for health care, and their opinions on politics. Any ideology, state, or nation that demands that these Muslim women alter their cultural practices, institutional affiliations, or intellectual beliefs to fit the national consensus will be seen by our Christian pluralists as guilty of usurping Christ's claim to exclusive sovereignty over them. Christ, and Christ alone, has the authority to direct the faith these women embody and proclaim in the public square. Any governmental interference in their practices, institutions, or beliefs will have to be enacted as an absolute last resort executed by a just state with care, humility, regret, and a singular desire for the future freedom of these women and their faith.

Finally, these pluralists walking by these Muslim women will feel a deep desire to know them. While they will certainly disagree with their neighbors on important theological, cultural, and political matters, these pluralists will want to discover the good gifts the Holy Spirit has given these women. These pluralists will want to be enriched by the divine gifts these Muslim women received, and they will want to faithfully give thanks to the One who blessed them.

Beyond Kuyper

Abraham Kuyper's theopolitical vision ignited an international movement of Christian activists, scholars, and institutions that crisscrossed the globe throughout the twentieth century. Today, advocates of Kuyperian pluralism can be found in Brazil, Canada, Nigeria, South Africa, the United Kingdom, South Korea, the United States, and beyond. Indeed, it is difficult to find a tradition of political theology in all of Christendom that has thought as long and as hard about pluralism as the heirs of Abraham Kuyper.

That being said, Kuyper and his movement were not without their weaknesses and blind spots. While not exhaustive, this brief interlude will highlight three areas—Christology, worship, and action—in which Abraham Kuyper and his followers stand in need of either addition or correction. The final three chapters will be dedicated to pushing beyond Kuyper in these three areas toward a fuller and richer vision for Christian pluralism.

Pluralism and Christology

The first and most pressing shortcoming of Abraham Kuyper's approach is the relatively narrow Christological lens he applies to the issue of pluralism. When discussing pluralism, Kuyper speaks of Jesus Christ almost exclusively as a sovereign king who demands public justice for all faiths. In limiting his Christological vocabulary to terms like sovereignty, authority, and freedom, Kuyper's vision of political discipleship is dramatically limited to the language of power, rights, and freedom.

Two primary problems come with a political theology that focuses exclusively on Christ's crown—his authority and sovereignty. First, this theology fails to recognize that Jesus Christ is much more than a sovereign king demanding justice and liberty. And second, it fails to see that following Jesus requires more than simply a thirst for justice and liberty. Jesus is depicted in the Gospels, not only as a king, but also as a prophet, a servant, a friend, healer, reconciler, liberator, advocate for the weak, teacher, priest, and dinner host. It follows, therefore, that those who follow this more complex picture of Christ are called to live public lives—not simply of justice and liberty—but lives of reconciliation, friendship, vulnerability, service, healing, liberation, hospitality, and grace.

Kuyper's failure to explore these aspects of Christ's life and teaching in his discussions of politics and pluralism greatly limit his public Christology. Followers of Christ are called to more than justice; they are also called to heal, listen, care, reconcile, forgive, and welcome. His defenders will, no doubt, argue that Kuyper was well aware of these other aspects of Christ's life. They will point to Kuyper's devotions, sermons, and biblical studies in which the other aspects of Christ's life are explored. While this cannot be denied, neither Kuyper, nor his immediate followers, demonstrated a desire to apply these diverse Christological images to their public lives or philosophies. Christ the compassionate, the hospitable, the gracious, and the crucified was relegated to the private and personal life of the Kuyperian.

In an effort to remedy this deficiency, the chapter on "Pluralism and Christ" explores how a more robust public Christology might inform the future of Christian pluralism.

Pluralism and Worship

The second deficiency in the pluralism of Abraham Kuyper is the lack of attention he gives to character formation. In short, my question for Abraham Kuyper is this: how will pluralists become the sort of people who not only understand pluralism in their minds but actually embody pluralism in their lives? It is one thing to have pluralistic ideas; it is another thing entirely to embody those ideas in one's life amidst the cacophony and chaos of Mecca and Amsterdam. The question that Kuyper and his followers ignored was how one connects pluralistic beliefs to pluralistic behavior. In short, how might a Christian cultivate a character of deep pluralism?

Historically speaking, Christian character has been developed by participating in the communal life and worship of the church. While Kuyper believed the church could develop a system of democratic ideas, he never explored how the church could actually develop a democratic character. To remedy this deficiency, the chapter on "Pluralism and Worship" explores a wide variety of ways in which Christian rituals, stories, images, prayers, and songs can actually cultivate in worshippers a pluralistic character.

This chapter comes out of the deep conviction that while Kuyper's ideas and institutions are important, they will not long stand if the people who inhabit them do not possess characters of integrity. Periods of anxiety and crisis demand deep and abiding characters that can withstand the voices of fear, anger, and retribution. When skyscrapers fall, when mosques and churches burn, when shouts for ideological uniformity and hegemony come, a Christian pluralism that is long on ideas and institutions and short on character will go up in smoke.

Pluralism and Action

The final area of addition and emendation is aimed not at Abraham Kuyper, but at his followers. If one surveys their legacy in the twentieth century, one discovers a long list of political activists, scholars, and leaders. Their primary ambition was political and juridical reform—the construction of a governmental system of pluralistic legal structures. Their implicit assumption was that, once a just legal and constitutional structure is established, all of the social and cultural challenges of pluralism will take care of themselves.

The enormous blind spot in this vision was perfectly captured by a Kuyperian legal philosopher I met during my time at the Vrije Universiteit in Amsterdam. The scholar was trying to explain to me how a just, free, and democratic nation like the Netherlands was being torn apart over the issue of Islamic immigration. He told me, in a moment of humility, that

> if you had asked me thirty years ago, "Can Dutch society handle a significant influx of Muslim immigrants?" I would have replied with a very confident "Yes." I would have explained to you that our pluralistic governing structures were perfectly suited to make space for new religious communities like Islam. Nothing else was needed—now I am not so sure.

Islamic immigration and the cultural upheavals that followed clearly demonstrate that diverse societies like the Netherlands require more than pluralistic constitutions—they require a citizenry that actually desires and enacts pluralism in their daily lives and work.

Abraham Kuyper himself insisted that a healthy political culture depended on Christians who were deeply engaged in a wide variety of social spheres—not just politics and law. Through the manifold callings of Christians as parents and neighbors, teachers and artists, writers and doctors, entrepreneurs and evangelists, Christian citizens can act as pluralistic salt, light, and leaven in a diverse nation. In the end, as Kuyper himself argued, the hope of democracy rests, not in the state, but in the lives of *de kleine luyden* (the little people). Unfortunately for us, Kuyper never explicitly connected the vocations of the "little people" to his political theories of pluralism. Likewise his followers—all too focused on legal and political reform—largely ignored the democratic importance of *de kleine luyden*.

Addressing this oversight, the chapter on "Pluralism and Action" explores how everyday citizens active in health care, education, the church, the neighborhood, and the home act as pluralistic salt, light, and leaven in the clash between Mecca and Amsterdam. This closing chapter does not provide a single answer to the challenge of Mecca and Amsterdam. Instead, it highlights a mosaic of smaller answers. Standing alone, each *kleine* answer to Mecca and Amsterdam appears incomplete and insufficient. However, when brought together, these small and disparate acts of justice, hospitality, and grace function as a potent cultural force for civic tolerance, peace, and democracy.

PART THREE

Christian Pluralism: A Future

CHAPTER SIX

Pluralism and Christ

> Despite being the targets of policies, headscarf-wearing women
> were mainly talked about or talked for—both by advocates and
> by opponents of restrictive legislation.
>
> DOUTJE LETTINGA[1]

In her book *Framing the Hijab,* political scientist Doutje Lettinga compares
how recent public debates over the Muslim headscarf have been framed in
the Netherlands, France, and Germany.[2] Lettinga identifies and outlines eight
frames through which these nations interpreted and debated the public display
of the Muslim hijab. These eight interpretive frames for the headscarves would
dramatically impact the governmental restrictions that would soon come.

The first frame applied to the hijab was that of public secularity. Here the
hijab was framed as a religious symbol, which potentially violates or endangers
the secularity of the European public square. When worn by police officers,
judges, teachers, and other state employees, the hijab allegedly compromises
the secular neutrality of the state and its officers. Extended beyond employees
of the state, the secularity frame has even been applied to those who receive
state services and funds. Schoolgirls in France, for example, have been banned
from wearing the hijab in government-run schools. As secularity's domain ex-

---

1. Doutje Lettinga, *Framing the Hijab: The Governance of Intersecting Religious, Ethnic,
and Gender Differences in France, the Netherlands, and Germany* (Ridderkerk, NL: Ridderprint,
2011), 242.

2. Lettinga, 42–44.

pands, so too do the restrictions on the headscarf. Bans on the hijab have been proposed across Europe for public buses, trams, and even sidewalks. Some have even proposed that the private home and the explicitly religious building should be the only place where women are permitted to wear the hijab.

The second European frame applied to the headscarf is that of free expression. Here, the hijab is framed as an individual's personal expression of religious conviction. Interpreted in this light, it should be protected under Western free-speech laws. This frame argues that—however reviled the hijab might be—it must be protected by the state. That said, two things naturally follow from the use of this frame. One, Muslim women must show their piety and submission to Allah using the foreign paradigms of individual liberty, personal expression, and free speech. Two, consistent application of free expression requires that those who publically criticize and even mock these women must be free to express their beliefs, as well.

The third European frame for the headscarf discussions is that of Christian Occidentalism. Here, the woman's hijab is interpreted as a foreign symbol of an oriental religious power that runs counter to Europe's Judeo-Christian history and identity. The presence of a veiled Muslim woman is seen as a scandalous public reminder that Europe's Judeo-Christian culture is slipping away. Seen through this frame, the presence of the headscarf demands governmental action to discourage the influence of the Islamic orient on behalf of the Judeo-Christian Occident. Laws against the hijab are necessary, it is argued, to protect the very cultural foundations of Europe.

The fourth frame depicts the woman's hijab as a scandalous symbol of racial and cultural segregation—even apartheid—in Europe. Headscarves, it is argued, are a visual reminder that these citizens have failed to successfully integrate (read: assimilate) into European culture. Rhetorically framed as intrinsically divisive, the sight of a woman's hijab signals that European states must work harder to integrate/assimilate Muslim women.

The fifth frame for the scarf is that of political Islam. Here the hijab is cast, not as a symbol of religious devotion, but as a symbol of political ideology, subversion, and even violence. The hijab, it is argued, represents a radical, theocratic, and violent political movement that is fundamentally antithetical to European democracy. This rhetorical frame argues that European states have a responsibility to legislate against the hijab in the interest of defending democracy and political stability.

The sixth is the security frame. Promoters of this frame argue that the veil constitutes a clear and present danger to public safety in Europe. A woman's veil, they argue, might be used by terrorists to conceal their identity during a terrorist attack. Through the security frame, the state is obligated, for reasons of public safety, to expose women's faces to the public gaze.

The seventh frame is that of oppression. Here, the hijab is a symbol of religious and sexual oppression. The assumption of this rhetorical frame is that no woman would freely choose to wear a headscarf, so therefore, our Muslim neighbors must have been forced or tricked into wearing them. When the hijab is seen through the rhetorical frame of oppression, European states are not only justified, but they are positively compelled to liberate these women from their oppressive religion.

The eighth and final frame argues that women who wear the headscarf are vulnerable to discrimination in Europe. The hijab, it is argued, slows the empowerment process that will lead to their successful integration. European states must take action to protect these women with an array of antidiscriminatory laws, hiring quotas, awareness programs, and benefits. It is believed that through these state-based efforts to protect Muslim women, empowerment—and therefore integration—will move along more smoothly.

According to Doutje Lettinga, these eight major frames have been available to Dutch, German, and French citizens since the beginning of the twenty-first century. Note that while Muslim women are the objects of considerable debate, they are rarely—if ever—invited to actually speak for themselves. Journalists, activists, and politicians speak with confidence about the desires, motives, and needs of Muslim women with little apparent interest in actually listening to them.

It is also striking how narrowly each of the eight frames casts the supposed problem of the hijab. In each frame, the hijab is understood to symbolize one thing and one thing only. These small pieces of cloth are either a danger to secularism, a form of free speech, a foreign cultural invasion, a marker of apartheid, a radical political banner, a security threat, a tool of oppression, or a discrimination danger. Depending on the political and rhetorical needs of the day, Doutje Lettinga demonstrates, politicians in France, Germany, and the Netherlands will use any combination of these frames to do one thing— marginalize, "foreignize," and problematize Muslim women.

A Ninth Frame

How are European Christians framing their Muslims neighbors? So far, there is no clear consensus. One can find disparate evidence of Christians following the logic of nearly every one of the eight frames that Lettinga describes.

Despite their diverse responses, there is one common factor that seems to hold across the entire spectrum of European Christianity—the absence of Christ.

If one makes the rather bold theological assumption that Christianity should have something to do with Christ, what explains the lack of a Christocentric response to the hijab? Christ's absence from Christian politics is not a uniquely European problem. Christians in my own country of the United States are notorious for regularly excluding their namesake from their politics.[3] Some American Christians find the first-century carpenter too removed from modern life to have any relevance. Others find him too weak or gracious for the strength our current political climate demands. Many find Jesus helpful for private issues of the heart but irrelevant for the public issues of the real world. Finally, others fear that Jesus is a divisive and overly religious figure—someone unwelcome in purely secular discourse.

But rather than speculate on the many reasons for Christ's absence in this debate about the hijab, let's explore what fruit his actual inclusion might bring. In other words, what would it mean for Christian citizens in the West to see the Muslim women who pass them on the street through a ninth frame, the frame of Jesus Christ?

The immediate problem with describing Jesus Christ as a frame is, of course, that he is much more than an epistemological lens through which Christians view the world. For those who call Jesus Lord, he is not simply a way of viewing others; he is a flesh-and-blood way of living with others as well. Moreover, a Muslim woman is not simply a foreign object to be framed by Christ; she is a human being who must be engaged, befriended, and loved in and through Christ, as well.

As we saw in the last chapter, Kuyper's Christology offered his followers a useful and imaginative Christ-centered approach to political pluralism. That said, Kuyper's political Christology fell short in two critical ways. First, as we pointed out in the last Interlude, Jesus is infinitely more than a sovereign king who demands justice and freedom. Jesus is also a servant, prophet, friend, liberator, healer, and priest. Second, Kuyper's royal Christology cannot respond to the deep complexity and mystery of the conflict between Mecca and Amsterdam. The conflict between them demands more than Christ's justice; it also requires Christ's forgiveness, reconciliation, humility, struggle, hospitality, and vulnerability.

---

3. See the blistering critiques of this American tendency in John Howard Yoder, *The Politics of Jesus* (Grand Rapids: Eerdmans, 1972), 1–20.

This chapter attempts to enrich Kuyper's Christological approach to pluralism with a broader and more diverse range of Christological images. In bringing these more diverse images of Christ's life and work together, I hope to construct a more complex Christ-centered approach to life between Mecca and Amsterdam.

In an effort to construct this ninth frame, this chapter will draw on the rich and imaginative Christologies of three theologians who followed in Kuyper's wake: Herman Bavinck, Klaas Schilder, and Hans Boersma. My intention in this chapter is not to summarize the work of these three theologians, nor is it to explore the many ways in which they either agree or disagree with each other. Instead, this chapter will accomplish two primary goals. First, it will highlight a few of the most promising Christological images in the work of these three theologians. Second, it will explore how those images can inform a more robust Christ-centered frame for the challenges and opportunities of life amidst Mecca and Amsterdam.

Herman Bavinck: The Kaleidoscopic Christ

Nothing in Christ is excluded in the demand to follow him . . . every word and deed of Jesus is useful for our instruction and ought to be taken to heart.

HERMAN BAVINCK[4]

Herman Bavinck (1854–1921) was a colleague of Abraham Kuyper and a fellow foot soldier in the Dutch movement for Christian pluralism. While his theological corpus is expansive and rich, I will focus my attention on his career-long interest in a simple question: how does one follow Jesus in the modern world?

Herman Bavinck's vision of *de navolging van Christus* (the following of Christ) is outlined in two magisterial essays composed at the beginning and end of his theological career. In both pieces, Bavinck insists that Christians are obligated to follow the whole Christ in the whole of their lives.[5] This convic-

---

4. "De navolging van Christus," *De vrije kerk* 12 (1886): 331–32.

5. Herman Bavinck, "De navolging van Christus," *De vrije kerk* 11 (1885): 101–13, 203–12, and 13; (1886): 321–33 and *De navolging van Christus en het moderne leven* (Kampen: Kok, 1918). An excellent analysis of these works can be found in John Bolt's "The Imitation of Christ Theme in the Cultural-Ethical Ideal of Herman Bavinck" (PhD diss., University of St. Michael's College, Toronto, 1982). I will be drawing on both of Bavinck's essays throughout the chapter. For

tion made Herman Bavinck somewhat of a theological outlier in nineteenth-century Christology. At this time, it was common for modernistic theologians in Europe to label many of the teachings of Jesus as outdated, irrelevant, or merely thematic for modern Christian life. In light of this, the modern theologian's task in Europe was that of rescuing a few stories, teachings, or themes in Christ's life that could be distilled into something more palatable to the modern context and European sensibilities. In opposition to these limited Christologies, Bavinck set about his task.

According to Herman Bavinck, holistic and Christ-centered discipleship meant that no aspect of Christ's life or work could be excluded or ignored—the whole Christ for the whole of life. Nothing about Jesus could be left out, smoothed over, and limited in its application. Christ's relevance could no longer be relegated to one's private life. Whether in politics, science, or the arts, true disciples must "walk in all these areas [of modern life] as a child of God and a follower of Christ." Bavinck admits that such a totalistic understanding of following Christ will neither be easy, clear, or smooth, and yet, he insists, "it is precisely this that is required of us" (*De Navolging* II, 144). Grounded in this unwavering conviction, Bavinck set out to describe a more holistic picture of Christ, along with a more holistic vision of what it meant to follow him in the modern world.

It is important to note from the outset that Herman Bavinck recognized that Christian discipleship is not a fixed destination but a dynamic and unfolding journey. Bavinck refused to turn his Christ-centered ethic into a rigid system of static rules holding for all times and places. Bavinck argued that disciples of Christ would need to continually discern and imagine new ways to follow Christ's example in a wide variety of dynamic contexts.[6]

Did Bavinck believe that disciples were therefore completely free to determine for themselves how they should follow Christ in their contexts? Not at all. Bavinck insisted that disciples would always need to wrestle with the scriptural stories of the whole and concrete Christ. Moreover, their individual

---

clarity's sake I will label them "De Navolging" I and *De Navolging* II in parenthetical citations. My thanks to John Bolt for sharing his personal translations of these two pieces. I have made some adjustments, but on the whole they represent his work, not mine.

6. "Naturally the application will vary depending upon circumstances. Although all are subject to one and the same moral law the duties under that law vary considerably. It is different for the civil authorities than for subjects, for parents than for children, for the rich than for the poor, and it will be different in times of prosperity than in times of poverty, in days of health than in days of illness. Thus while the virtues to which the imitation of Christ calls us are the same, circumstances may modify the application" (Bavinck, *De Navolging* II, 142–43).

discernment of the Scriptures could not happen in a state of personal isolation. Disciples had to discern the depth and breadth of Christ's call on their lives within the communal fellowship and discipline of the church.

Bavinck's first essay on following Jesus in the modern world began with an overview and critique of five models for imitating Christ—three models were historical and two were modern. On the historical side, Bavinck outlined three models of Christological imitation that were prominent in the stories of the ancient and medieval church. He called these models the martyr, the monk, and the mystic. While appreciative of all three, Bavinck concluded that each model was ultimately insufficient for two specific reasons. First, each focused too narrowly on a single aspect of Christ's life and work. In turn, each model made its singular aspect the dominant ethical norm for all Christian discipleship. In doing this, the full breadth of Christ's life and work was reduced. The second problem with these three models was that they each produced an unnecessary hierarchy between ordinary and extraordinary disciples (that is, martyrs, monks, and mystics). These three models communicate that ordinary Christians who, for a variety of reasons, do not fully imitate Christ through either martyrdom, monasticism, or mysticism are somehow lesser or failing in their discipleship of Jesus. Bavinck lamented that within each of the three models, discipleship becomes the calling of the few and an unrealistic ideal for the rest. Convinced that the whole of the church must follow the whole Christ, Bavinck is forced to go beyond the narrow images of Christ-followers as either martyrs, monks, or mystics.

Bavinck then considers two modern visions of following Jesus. He labels these models the literalist and the rationalist. The literalist, he argues, attempts to rigidly mimic and reproduce the exact words and actions of Jesus in the modern world. Bavinck believed that this literalist model represented a tragically wooden and overly brittle reading of the Christian life. He concludes that the literalist ultimately lacks the theological wisdom, creativity, and imagination necessary to faithfully apply the life and teachings of a first-century Jew to the dynamic and complex reality of the modern world.

If the literalist lacked creativity, the rationalist lacked courage. The rationalist, Bavinck argued, finds the life and teachings of Jesus to be too radical, too demanding, and too extreme for modern European sensibilities. The rationalist concludes that modern Christianity must smooth out Christ's rougher edges. The theologian's task is to domesticate Jesus and turn him into a modern sage of moderate Christian values. Having distilled a few universal themes and values, such as kindness, service, or integrity, from the historical Jesus, then and only then can Jesus serve as an example for the modern European.

Bavinck could not bear the modern domestication of Jesus. He demanded that Christian discipleship take the whole, concrete, and sometimes rough reality of Jesus Christ seriously.

In surveying these five models, Herman Bavinck finally concluded that if contemporary Christians were going to follow the whole Christ, they would require a more complex Christological ethic. For, he concluded, the "work of Christ is so multifaceted that it cannot be captured in a single word nor summarized in a single formula." Disciples require not one but multiple images of Christ "to give us a deep impression and a clear sense of the riches and many-sidedness of the mediator's work."[7] Jesus was not simply a savior; he was a teacher, liberator, friend, and healer. He was at one and the same time our prophet, our priest, and our king. Bavinck believed that these multiples aspects of Christ's life and work would "supplement one another and enrich our knowledge" of Christ and what it means to follow him (*Reformed Dogmatics*, vol. 3, 384). For Christ came to earth not simply to save souls, teach morality, or liberate the poor—he came for the complex work of restoring the whole of his world to himself. In this sense, the redemptive "benefits that accrue to us from the reconciliation of God-in-Christ are too numerous to mention. . . . [They are] juridical . . . mystical . . . ethical . . . moral . . . economic . . . physical. . . . In a word, the whole enterprise of re-creation, the complete restoration of the world and humanity . . . is the fruit of Christ's work" (*Reformed Dogmatics*, vol. 3, 451–52).

Bavinck's desire to explore the complex richness of Christ's life and work was not a new or ground-breaking practice for a Reformed theologian. Commenting on John Calvin, Stephen Edmondson notes that the early reformer himself cobbled

> together a kaleidoscopic Christological mosaic from stones not necessarily cut to fit. [John Calvin] wants to depict Christ as fountain, brother, criminal, and king as Christ exhibited these realities in the varied details of his life. This eclecticism is essential to Calvin's thinking, for it represents simply the fullness of Christ's history. . . . To commit oneself to [Calvin's kaleidoscopic Christ] is to commit oneself to a broad, diverse, detailed reality that threatens at all times to exceed one's grasp.[8]

7. Herman Bavinck, *Reformed Dogmatics*, vol. 3, ed. John Bolt, trans. John Vriend (Grand Rapids: Baker Academic, 2003–2008), 383. Additional references to this work are given parenthetically in the text.

8. Stephen Edmondson, *Calvin's Christology* (Cambridge: Cambridge University Press, 2004), 224.

When one surveys the complexity of the conflict between Islam and the West, between Mecca and Amsterdam, when one considers the dynamism, depth, and speed of the ethical questions involved, it becomes exceedingly clear that following Christ in such a multifaceted crisis will require a multi-faceted Christology.

Herman Bavinck offers three critical Christological insights for the Christian life between Mecca and Amsterdam. First, the present conflict will require the work of all Christians in a variety of political, cultural, and ministerial callings. Christian pluralism requires not simply a few extraordinary martyrs, mystics, and monks—it requires the whole body of Christ. Second, unlike the rigid literalists and the moderating rationalists, Mecca and Amsterdam demand disciples who wish to follow Christ with both creativity and courage. Third and finally, the kaleidoscopic challenge of Mecca and Amsterdam requires a kaleidoscopic Christ—a simplistic understanding of Christ's life and work will not suffice. Christians need the whole Christ: the teacher, healer, judge, prophet, priest, and king. With this more multifaceted vision of Christian discipleship, we turn now to a diverse collection of Christological images that will help us develop a more complex understanding of Christian discipleship amidst Mecca and Amsterdam.

Klaas Schilder: The Slave-King

Islam is coming to take over! It is coming to bind the West—to restrict, rule, and control us. Such cries are common in discussions about Islamic immigration in North America and Europe. Islam, it is argued, is an ideology of power and control. Such an ideology deserves—and can only understand—a like-minded response of both power and control.

In the 1930s, a Dutch pastor and theologian by the name of Klaas Schilder produced a powerful series of meditations on the trial, suffering, and crucifixion of Jesus.[9] Over three separate volumes, Schilder painted a vivid, impactful, and shockingly raw picture of Christ's final days on earth. Readers of his meditations are invited to stand and watch as Jesus, the sovereign king of the universe, is arrested and accused, beaten and broken, stripped and speared. Schilder's raw and challenging theological reflections on Christ's

---

9. Klaas Schilder, *Christ in His Sufferings*, trans. Henry Zylstra (Grand Rapids: Eerdmans, 1938); *Christ on Trial,* trans. Henry Zylstra (Grand Rapids: Eerdmans, 1939); *Christ Crucified*, trans. Henry Zylstra (Grand Rapids: Eerdmans, 1940).

final days invite the reader to ponder the meaning of a life lived in the shadow of Golgotha. Rather than summarize the whole of Schilder's passion trilogy, I want to highlight two specific meditations that bear striking relevance to our current question of Christian ethics between Mecca and Amsterdam.[10] These two meditations highlight some unique images of Christ that are rarely found in Abraham Kuyper's depictions of Christ's kingship—namely Christ's slavery and his nakedness. To be brief, while Kuyper explores the political consequences of Christ's crown, Schilder explores the political consequences of Christ's cross.

Schilder's first meditation focuses on Christ as a slave-king. Here he reflects theologically on the binding of Christ in the garden of Gethsemane. Schilder argues forcefully that in Christ's infamous healing of a slave, he reveals his true royal and sovereign calling to be the "liberator of slaves in the form of a slave." On the night he was betrayed, Jesus and his disciples went to pray in the garden of Gethsemane. As darkness fell, Roman soldiers and officials from the high priest came to arrest Jesus. A skirmish broke out during the course of the arrest. Peter drew his sword and struck the ear of the high priest's slave named Malchus. Amidst the chaos and cacophony of his own arrest, Jesus rebuked Peter's aggressive attack and healed the slave who had come to bind him.

This brief and oft-ignored episode in Christ's passion narrative is the subject of a detailed and haunting theological reflection from Klaas Schilder. The theologian was convinced that in this, Christ's final miracle on earth, readers are witness to the "culmination and close" of Christ's "prophetic teaching and self-revelation."[11] In this brief exchange between the slave and the slave-king, "All the issues of the Gospel" are "laid bare" ("Christ's Last Wonder," 431). For here, Christ reveals his true royal calling to be the "liberator of slaves in the form of a slave" ("Christ's Last Wonder," 415).

From the beginning of Israel's history, the people were commanded by God to celebrate a day of Jubilee. Every fifty years all slaves were to be liberated, all debts forgiven, and all land returned to its original owner. While the divine command to celebrate the Jubilee was received, it is important to note that kings of Israel never actually obeyed God's command, that is, Schilder argues, until this exchange in the garden between the slave and the slave-king. Schilder proposes that the royal line of David was restored in Christ's sovereign healing

---

10. "Christ Disrobed," in *Christ Crucified*: 167–87 and "Christ's Last Wonder in the State of Humiliation: The Liberator of Slaves in the Form of a Slave," in *Christ in His Sufferings*: 415–34.

11. Schilder, "Christ's Last Wonder," 421. Additional references to this work are given parenthetically in the text.

of Malchus ("Christ's Last Wonder," 415). For, there in the garden, while the "police scream and yell . . . Christ devotes subtle attention to doing full justice to one of God's slaves. In this He is reverently obedient to the law of the year of Jubilee, to the law of the right of slaves" ("Christ's Last Wonder," 415). Jesus here embodies the sort of kingship and sovereignty God demands—a power that liberates and heals. Schilder imagines Jesus, as he is being arrested, bending over and whispering in his Malchus's newly-healed ear, "Am I not He who is willing to deliver you from the bonds of death and from the yoke of everlasting slavery? Listen, my son; listen, Malchus: I am the priest who would become a slave in order to convert servants into lords" ("Christ's Last Wonder," 427).

While previous kings of Israel ignored the Jubilee, Jesus fulfilled God's call to liberate the enslaved—even while he himself was being violently bound. Schilder insists that this brief encounter "vividly presents" the paradoxical nature of Christ's sovereign reign over "both the world and His church" ("Christ's Last Wonder," 431). In Christ's act of sacrificial healing and liberation, the royal line of David, "broken as it was, is restored to continuity" ("Christ's Last Wonder," 431). Christ's sovereign act reveals that the liberation of the oppressed is a critical marker of any Christ-centered execution of sovereignty and power. Schilder argues that in this small act, Jesus reveals that David's royal line of kings did not fall because "the chariots of war were sent against him by the mighty powers of Babylon and Cain"; but rather, David fell because of "his stumbling over the lives of slaves" ("Christ's Last Wonder," 430). For a true king of Israel would honor the Jubilee command. A true king "is merciful, tender, just, and He ever sees the Father and the slave."

Schilder argues that the small and humble scale of Christ's final miracle reveals something important, as well. Christ's sovereign healing and power will not always take the cosmic and revolutionary scale the world so often expects or demands. The royal power of Christ's sovereign is often limited, humble, partial, and seemingly small. Christ's healing is not always "a piece of fireworks; it is a fire which gives warmth and a light, which points out and discovers the way" ("Christ's Last Wonder," 425). For the God who stopped to heal Malchus "does not know what small wounds are; and he does not know what insignificant people are" ("Christ's Last Wonder," 420).

While the fate of the cosmos hangs in the balance, while God's only son is being arrested, Schilder marvels, Christ stops and gives his full attention to wounds of a "little one" like Malchus. This is instructive. In times of seemingly cosmic-level crisis and chaos, Christ's humble attention to small wounds appears "foolish and offensive to the flesh" ("Christ's Last Wonder," 424). What scandal that the final miracle of God on earth is disclosed just "to a slave"

("Christ's Last Wonder," 427). What scandal that a slave is the last mortal to hear the "roaring turbulence of the waters of God's justice and grace, the thunder of the coming judgment and the present plea of grace" ("Christ's Last Wonder," 431–32).

Schilder observes that this brief encounter in the garden makes it abundantly clear that Christ's royal liberation and healing are a gift graciously given—not earned. The slave neither said nor did anything to deserve Christ's healing touch. Moreover, Malchus's aggression deserved a violent response from both Peter and Jesus. Instead, the sovereign king reached out a vulnerable hand to his attacker, a hand that would soon be pierced, and he healed the one who came to break him. He liberated the one who came to bind.

This healing of Malchus had to happen, Schilder concludes. Jesus knew that the "wind of the kingdom of heaven," was going to pass through the garden that night. It was going to "brush past" Malchus. Jesus knew that slave, without new ears, would not be able to hear "whence it comes nor whither it goes." Deafened by the violence and control of imperial Rome, the slave would not be able to hear Christ's call to freedom—not until his ears were healed. The aggressor could not recognize the rushing sound of heaven's wind until he "actually begins to *hear*" ("Christ's Last Wonder," 419).

Klaas Schilder: The Naked King

In debates over Mecca and Amsterdam, it is common to portray Islam as uniquely violent and the West as uniquely peaceful. Citizens in the West robe themselves with the labels of rationality, peace, and freedom while they robe their Muslim neighbors with the labels of irrationality, violence, and tyranny. The rhetorical game is to make one's Muslim neighbor completely other. Robed in all that is right and good, the West is free to take its sovereign throne above Islam.

Schilder's second meditation is entitled "Christ Disrobed." In this extremely raw reflection, Schilder explores a rather unwelcome question: What is the theological significance of the Christ's disrobing on the cross? What does it mean that the sovereign king of the world allowed himself to be stripped naked?

Schilder's primary readers were Dutch Calvinists—a rather reserved and reverent lot. For readers who highly respected the honor and dignity of their Lord, Schilder's exploration of Christ's nakedness would be nothing short of traumatizing. Schilder acknowledges this fact when he asks his readers, "if the majesty of Christ is so overwhelming that we would not dare approach Him by way of untying the laves of His sandals, how could we dare to approach him in order to see his complete disrobing?"[12] Excruciating as it might be, Schilder demands that his readers stand watch as their "great Clothier is being stripped naked" ("Christ Disrobed," 183). "We want to avert our eyes, but we may not. We *must* look on." For Jesus "made this plundering of His clothes a sign for all ensuing generations" ("Christ Disrobed," 168). For, in his disrobing, "the Naked Christ speaks" ("Christ Disrobed," 186). Those who claim to be disciples must stand, look, and listen to "what the Spirit has to say to the churches about the naked Christ who was crucified amidst the bandits" ("Christ Disrobed," 168).

God's body was stripped, mocked, and spit upon on. This fact, Schilder argues, confronts casual Christians with the truly scandalous nature of the cross and what it means to carry one. When Jesus is stripped naked, exposed for all to see, the world mocks him. The naked king exposed before the world is not beheld as beautiful, wise, or powerful—he is mocked as ugly, weak, and pathetic. Those who gaze at his nakedness either pity or mock the disgraced criminal and failed revolutionary who claimed to be king. For, Schilder writes,

> the offense and the foolishness of the cross was intensified and aggravated by the spectacle of the naked Christ. . . . We have here a naked God, a naked Messiah, hanging on the cross. Is it any wonder that even today we can find on the walls of certain old barracks of antiquity [Roman] caricatures in which the Savior of the Christians was represented by this or that soldier as a crucified donkey? ("Christ Disrobed," 175)

Those following the naked king should not expect praise or acceptance from the world, Schilder insists. The vicious mocking and derision the naked king received on the cross is closer to the mark. After all, Schilder notes, Jesus, in his Sermon on the Mount, himself predicted that his followers would have to "endure three requisitions. . . . Injury of the body, impairment of property, and infringement of liberty" ("Christ Disrobed," 184). Here on the cross, "Christ himself was completely faithful to His own threefold demand" ("Christ Disrobed," 184). In succession he allowed himself to be bound, beaten, and robbed. In this degrading moment, the true cost of following such a king is fully ex-

12. Schilder, "Christ Disrobed," 169. Additional references to this work are given parenthetically in the text.

posed—stripped bare. His nakedness represents an opportunity for onlookers to behold and consider the cost of following him.

At this point, Schilder makes a dramatic and unexpected pivot. While Christ was indeed stripped bare on the cross, Schilder argues that in fact humanity is "really the one who was disrobed on Golgotha" ("Christ Disrobed," 186). For, as we "look carefully upon His naked death, upon His essential nakedness" ("Christ Disrobed," 187), we see that in our stripping of Christ, our own sinful aggression and violence is being stripped bare. His nakedness exposes our own. We see on the cross that it is "*We*" who "have robbed God" and in God's naked exhibition all "souls are being discovered" ("Christ Disrobed," 169).

Schilder argues that the stripping of Jesus lays bare humanity's pretensions of morality, tolerance, and intelligence. Christ's nakedness exposes our acts of benevolence as a thin and tattered cloth feebly covering our deeper desires for domination and oppression. In the shadow of Christ's nakedness, Schilder declares that I must look at myself and finally admit "to those who ask about it: I am the soldier who removed His clothes" ("Christ Disrobed," 187). Moreover, in allowing me to disrobe him, Schilder declares that he now sees what truly happened—Christ "has taken all my clothes from me, and has put me, naked and cold, on display before the universe" ("Christ Disrobed," 187). For in his disrobing we are fully exposed. We see ourselves for who we truly are—violent, fearful, and selfish. Beholding the naked king, we see our true nature in all its nakedness. Our pretentions of love, tolerance, and peace are laid bare.

While Schilder's view of human nature is dark indeed, he does not leave his readers naked and shivering in a state of total despair. In fact, it is here at the lowest point of the meditation that Schilder points to a deep hope. This hope is grounded—not in the goodness of humanity—but in the goodness of God. "Nevertheless," Schilder declares, "blessed be his hand. He did no gambling" with humanity's clothes. While Christ "was in His rights," to leave humanity cold, naked, shivering, and alone, "He acted justly and mercifully." By Christ's grace a warm "cloak has been prepared for me," a garment "of righteousness" ("Christ Disrobed," 187). For in "His loss we gain"—in his nakedness we are clothed ("Christ Disrobed," 174).

Following the Naked Slave-King between Mecca and Amsterdam

Schilder's two meditations evoke a wide range of Christological insights for Christians walking amidst Mecca and Amsterdam. While Abraham Kuyper was correct in his assessment of Christ as a sovereign and almighty king, Schilder's two meditations offer needed insights into the person of Jesus Christ and the shape of Christ's sovereign reign. The following brief reflections on the political implications of the naked slave-king are only a start.

First, in his healing of Malchus, Christ's royal concern for the poor, the outcast, and the oppressed is marked out as a central characteristic of his divine sovereignty and justice. More than that, Christ's sovereign act of liberation and healing is directed, not toward a friend who comes in peace, but toward an enemy who comes to bind. As noted earlier, it is not uncommon to hear cries that Islam has come to bind the West and that Muslims know nothing of freedom, tolerance, and peace. Such claims are, of course, highly debatable. That said, even if these claims were true, the supposed violence of Islam does not negate the normativity of Christ's peaceful response to Malchus. Christ healed, not simply when he was safe and secure, but also when he was being bound and led to his death. Disciples who follow the healer of Malchus are called to stretch out their hands even toward those who would come to bind them. The chaotic cacophony of Gethsemane, Mecca, and Amsterdam is complex, challenging, and sometimes frightful—this crisis, however, does not negate the command.

Moving on, those who follow the healer of the slave will often be called to respond to the enormity of Mecca and Amsterdam in ways considered small and insignificant in the eyes of the world. Nurses, teachers, and shopkeepers, people who interact with Muslims in the everyday and mundane activities of life, all of them follow a king who "does not know small wounds" or "insignificant people" ("Christ's Last Wonder," 420). Amidst this clash of civilizations, humble disciples are called to engage in small acts of tender care for their Muslim neighbors—and enemies.

Third, following a king who turns "slaves into lords" directly impacts how disciples frame the potential futures of their Muslim neighbors. Rather than framing new Muslim immigrants as future recipients of government aid, education, and care, disciples need to frame them as potential lords. Christ approached the wounded slave as a sacred creature made in the image of God, someone created for lordship. Jesus saw in Malchus not a weak slave, but a powerful lord who was created to fill, steward, and rule the earth. In the same way, framing Muslim immigrants as nothing more than helpless or passive recipients of Western generosity, surveillance, and education needs to be taken off the table. Disciples of the slave-king will not stand to see immigrants languish as passive clients of the state. Muslims were not created to be the objects of cultural assimilation campaigns. They were created to be the makers of culture themselves.

Will my Muslim neighbors convert? Will they ever join my church? How do I know if they are saved? It is instructive that Malchus's ultimate fate is never explored in the biblical account. Readers are not told whether he ultimately joined the Jesus movement. The focus of the narrative is on Christ's initial act of healing—not on Malchus's secondary response. Likewise, Christian pluralists must be more concerned with faithful initial acts of healing and liberation toward Islam. The secondary response of their Muslim neighbors is, biblically speaking, not their responsibility. Knowing the ultimate fate of either Malchus or Islam is not our primary concern.

Fourth, disciples of a naked Christ who choose to walk vulnerably alongside their Muslim neighbors should expect to be mocked and misunderstood by the watching world. The accusations that they are soft on terrorism and are comingling with criminals should come as no surprise to those who follow the one who was "crucified amidst the bandits" ("Christ Disrobed," 168).

Fifth, Christian pluralists look at themselves and recognize their own tendencies toward cultural and political hegemony. Their inherent aggression and violence has been exposed by the naked Christ. In the shadow of the cross, they too have heard their own voices cry out for violence and vengeance. Christian pluralists walking between Mecca and Amsterdam will carry a deep recognition of their own naked aggression and selfishness. They will know that there is no potential for violence in Islam which is not also present in them. They will know that, while they might clothe themselves with the veneer of Western tolerance and multiculturalism, all citizens, themselves included, are capable of the violence exposed at Golgotha.

Finally, Christian pluralists will remember that when they were naked, cold, and shivering in their own violence and aggression, the naked king took pity on them and clothed them with grace and peace. When they were intolerant, he was tolerant. Furthermore, such Christians will know that their robes of righteousness that warm and protect them were graciously given—not earned. Without their great Clothier, they would still be alone shivering in naked violence and aggression. If Christian pluralists ever prove capable of any love or any tolerance for their Muslim neighbors, it is thanks to clothes they never could have made.

Hans Boersma: The Hospitable King

> Into this world, this demented inn, in which there is absolutely
> no room for Him at all, Christ has come uninvited. . . . His place
> is with those others for whom there is no room. . . . He is myste-
> riously present in those for whom there seems to be nothing but
> the world at its worst.
>
> THOMAS MERTON[13]

> [God] stretched out His hands on the Cross, that He might em-
> brace the ends of the world; for this Golgotha is the very center
> of the earth.
>
> CYRIL OF JERUSALEM[14]

In the fragmented and fractured West the ancient concept of hospitality has
made a resurgence in political discourses about Islamic immigration and integration. But what, exactly, is meant by the term *hospitality*? When Western
politicians ask their citizens to show hospitality to Muslim immigrants and
asylum-seekers, it is only natural to request a definition. What is hospitality?
What are its demands? What are its limits? And why, exactly, is the West obligated to show hospitality to Islam? To continue this chapter's theme of refram-
ing Islam through Christology, how might a Christ-centered understanding
of hospitality frame a Christian's response to Islam?

Hans Boersma is a contemporary theologian whose recent work explores
the theme of hospitality in the atoning work of Christ on the cross. Atonement
studies are historically concerned with two primary questions. First, what
work has the cross of Christ actually accomplished? And second, what is the
significance of that atoning work for the Christian life? Responses to these
questions have historically fallen into one of three lines of argument. The first
line argues that the cross functions as a moral example or model of the sort of
non-violent and sacrificial life a follower of Jesus should lead. The second line
argues that the cross was the moment in which the moral debts of humanity
were paid. The third and final line insists that the cross was the site of Christ's
victory over the spiritual and political powers of this world. The diversity of in-

13. Thomas Merton, *Raids on the Unspeakable* (New York: New Directions, 1964), 72,
73, 75.

14. Cyril of Jerusalem, "Catechetical Lectures" in Nicene and Post-Nicene Fathers, Second
Series, trans. Edward Hamilton Gifford, ed. Phillip Schaff and Henry Ware (Peabody, MA:
Hendrickson, 1994), 7:89.

terpretations and positions is no accident. It reflects the diversity of metaphors, images, and messages attributed to the cross in the Scriptures themselves.

Hans Boersma's theological contribution to these interpretations of the cross is the unifying theme of hospitality. In the end, Boersma concludes that the cross should be understood, first and foremost, as an act of hospitality. Moreover, Boersma regards "hospitality as the soil in which the various models of the atonement can take root and flourish."[15] He argues that at its very core the cross represents an opening up of God's very self to a world that has closed itself off from the divine embrace. In other words, the cross makes space in a world that regards itself as full.

Boersma sees hospitality, not only as the essential calling of Christ, but as the essential calling of the Christian, as well. For him, "Christ's death and resurrection constitute the ultimate expression of God's hospitality and form the matrix for an understanding of all God's actions and as such the normative paradigm for human actions" (*Violence, Hospitality, and the Cross*, 26). Moreover, Boersma concludes that disciples of the hospitable One must actually embody his hospitality in their ecclesial and public lives.

While Boersma has his differences with his own Reformed tradition (which we will explore later), he continues to defend some critical aspects of its perspective on the atonement. One of the most prominent points of agreement between Boersma and the tradition is their mutual affirmation and defense of the wrath of God against sin, violence, and injustice. While many modern theologians have attempted to remove any vestige of divine wrath from the cross, Boersma praises the Reformers for recognizing that divine wrath is a necessary aspect of God's hospitality (*Violence, Hospitality, and the Cross*, 92). The violence of the world is not simply endured on the cross—it is punished, in and through Christ's body. For Boersma and the Reformers argue that violence demands justice, aggression demands punishment, and sin demands death. If God truly loves the world, the violence that actively despoils and destroys it must, by necessity, summon God's wrath. Boersma argues that the Reformed tradition's frank recognition of God's wrath is to be preserved and praised.

Beyond this, Boersma also affirms the Reformers for rightly arguing that Christian love and hospitality require the maintenance of limits and boundaries. Walls need not necessarily separate—they can, in fact, cultivate connection. Bounded communities—social spaces with insiders and outsiders—such

---

15. Hans Boersma, *Violence, Hospitality, and the Cross: Reappropriating the Atonement Tradition* (Grand Rapids: Baker Academic, 2006), 18. Additional references to this work are given parenthetically in the text.

as families, associations, institutions, nations, and states are, in one sense, a gracious gift of divine hospitality. Each of these bounded communities provides a dedicated space in which a finite number of human beings can experience the safety, solidarity, and intimacy of community. Describing these bounded communities as merely exclusive fails to recognize their capacity for hospitality.

Moreover, Boersma argues, these bounded communities provide an opportunity for insiders to reflect Christ's hospitality by periodically opening their spaces to outsiders. To illustrate the point, take my family, for example. In order for my family to reflect divine hospitality, it must open itself up to outsiders—it must welcome them in. That said, my family can practice that hospitality only if it is allowed to maintain some level of distinction between insiders and outsiders. Some boundary between what is family and what is world is crucial. If my family was perpetually open for all to come and go as they please, if I made no distinction between my wife and my neighbor, if I treated my children and neighbor's children the same, two things would happen. First, my family would lose its integrity and sense of self when no distinction between family and world is maintained. Second, in losing its integrity, my family would lose its internal capacity to offer hospitality to outsiders in the future.

Let's move our analogy of hospitality from the family to the state. All states require borders if they hope to develop any sense of safety and solidarity among their citizens. Without borders, without a distinction between insiders and outsiders, hospitality quickly becomes impossible. States, as we will discuss later, must also reflect in some way God's divine hospitality. That said, a state's hospitality to outsiders must not destroy its communal integrity and its ability to show hospitality in the future. Finite states, like finite families, must recognize their boundaries and limits. It is certainly true that sometimes the walls of the family and the state are too high; it is true that sometimes doors are closed when they need to be open. That said, those walls and doors remain necessary—they make the ensuing hospitality possible.

The need for communal limits is not only a matter of practical common sense, argue Boersma and the Reformers, but communal limits are also a matter of theological command. Both argue that God has created human beings and their communities as finite, limited, and bounded spaces. Thus to deny the finite limits of a community's hospitality is not only to deny the law of common sense; it is to deny the law of God, as well.

Both Boersma and the Reformers argue that the world is not only finite, but it is also fallen. Boersma praises the Reformers for their recognition of humanity's fall into violence and aggression. Moreover, he praises them for understanding that, in a fallen world, sometimes social boundaries of communities need to be protected with the use of force. In a violent world, state coercion is required if families, schools, communities, and states are to have integrity and remain hospitable in the future. Violent behavior cannot go unpunished. Lawless societies must be made lawful. In this sense, Boersma argues, the Reformers are to be praised because they have "taken these limitations and boundaries extremely seriously" (*Violence, Hospitality, and the Cross*, 75).

In its desire to protect distinct communities from violence and disorder, the Reformed tradition has developed a brilliant and effective political theology based on the necessity of public justice, law, order, and punishment. Throughout the centuries, Reformed political leaders and theorists have insisted that finite and fallen communities require a set of enforced boundaries if they are to live together in peace. Thus, while a utopian "politics of *absolute* hospitality and absolute nonviolence may seem appealing," the Reformers knew that a society without boundaries would be "a recipe for . . . the worst kind of violence" (*Violence, Hospitality, and the Cross*, 178; emphasis mine). In short, they knew that a society without limits would not be a dream, but a nightmare.

In the end, Boersma concludes that the Reformed tradition's emphasis on law and order, boundary and punishment was cultivated through its highly juridical understanding of the cross. According to this juridical approach, the cross was a place where unlawfulness was punished, order was restored, and debts were repaid. On the cross, the limits and boundaries of the law were satisfied.

Toward a Reformed Hospitality

> John Calvin's Geneva, Oliver Cromwell's England, and Hendrik
> Verwoerd's South Africa all suffered the effects of a theology that,
> in many respects, was less than hospitable.
> HANS BOERSMA, *Violence, Hospitality, and the Cross*, 239

While Hans Boersma is appreciative of the Reformed tradition's juridical contributions to his understanding of the atonement and Christian hospitality, he is not uncritical. Though the Reformers were certainly correct that "God's hospitality requires violence" and that "his love necessitates wrath," Boersma repeatedly insists that violence and wrath are not among God's essential attributes. In his origin, essence, and end, God is love. God is "not wrath; he is a

God of hospitality, not a God of violence. Hospitality bespeaks the very essence of God, while violence is merely one of the ways to safeguard or ensure the future of his hospitality" (*Violence, Hospitality, and the Cross*, 49). The danger for the Reformers is this: in their eagerness to defend divine wrath, they allow this penultimate work of God to overshadow God's ultimate work—the work of hospitality.

Boersma reminds his readers that John Calvin himself evinced a clear and enduring "desire to hold on to the hospitality of God" (*Violence, Hospitality, and the Cross*, 68). For in Calvin there is "no rationale" given for God's beautiful work of the cross "beyond his generous hospitality" (*Violence, Hospitality, and the Cross*, 55). God freely elects, saves, and welcomes people into the divine embrace because God is, at God's core, hospitable. Reading Calvin's reflections on the cross, one does not encounter a God of intrinsic wrath but one of everlasting love. The violence and judgment God displays on the cross is not an enduring posture; Calvin sees it as a temporary task. According to Calvin, the cross restores God's everlasting covenant of hospitality through a temporary work of violence and wrath. The ultimate work of the cross, according to Calvin is not wrath—it's love.

That said, Boersma worries that a lingering danger hovers throughout John Calvin's work on the atonement. Calvin, he explains, unwittingly allows a problematic "tension" to develop "between the forceful and even violent character" of God and the "hospitable" character of God (*Violence, Hospitality, and the Cross*, 68). In short, Calvin's depiction of the cross sometimes begins to reflect a work that is equal parts divine wrath and divine mercy, equal parts divine judgment and divine hospitality.

While Calvin successfully maintained this tension, Boersma fears that many of his "successors eliminated it all together" (*Violence, Hospitality, and the Cross*, 68). Unfortunately, "in later Calvinism the violence of God's absolute will overshadows the hospitality of his revealed will" (*Violence, Hospitality, and the Cross*, 56). The heirs of Calvin extended the momentary judgment of the cross "into the realm of eternity, thereby locating the violence of divine exclusion at the very core of God's character" (*Violence, Hospitality, and the Cross*, 75). In such a picture, the "hospitality of God is constantly in danger of being overshadowed" (*Violence, Hospitality, and the Cross*, 61). The wrath of God comes to define the very essence of God. Judgment—not hospitality—gradually becomes God's telos. The political result of this overly juridical approach to the atonement was a Reformed theopolitical imagination that demanded justice and lost sight of hospitality, that demanded political order and lost sight of political love.

Cruciform Hospitality between Mecca and Amsterdam

How might a Christ-centered understanding of hospitality be publically embodied amidst Mecca and Amsterdam? The task of the theologian is, once again, not to lay down a set of universal prescriptions, but to develop what we might call a hospitable imagination. Christian hospitality will look different in different times and places. Teachers, lawyers, shop owners, politicians, managers, nurses, and architects will need to develop their own hospitable imaginations for their specific callings amidst Mecca and Amsterdam. The Christian act of making space for Islam will look different in every sphere of society. Christian hospitality will need to be creatively imagined in the home, neighborhood, business, school, and state.

While I cannot, and should not, proclaim what Christian hospitality toward Islam looks like in all times and places, I can say with great confidence that the hospitality of the cross is normative for every aspect of public life. To reappropriate Abraham Kuyper's famous phrase, there is not "a square inch" in the entire public square where Christ's model of hospitality does not have relevance and normativity. Christ made space for humanity on the cross, and the proper human response to that hospitality is to make it one's own. One's personal experience of divine hospitality must overflow into the social, economic, cultural, and even political lives of those who live amidst Mecca and Amsterdam. Because Christ opened his nail-pierced hands to friend and foe alike, his disciples must reflect that posture in all of their interactions with Islam.

Furthermore, Christian disciples must make hospitality, not justice, the primary frame through which they understand their public and political obligations toward Islam. This does not mean that justice and order have lost their importance. The state remains responsible for establishing law, order, and public justice. In a sinful world of terrorism and extremism, the coercive tasks of the state remain necessary. In this sense, the juridical task of Abraham Kuyper's pluralistic state remains fundamentally unaltered. However, in the light of the cross, Kuyperian discussions of plural justice must now be placed within the larger frame of plural hospitality. For now, the state does not execute justice for the sake of justice. No. Public justice must now be executed to protect a greater goal—public hospitality. Justice divorced from hospitality ceases to be justice (*Violence, Hospitality, and the Cross*, 255). For, as Boersma argues, "just as penal elements do not have a final say with regard to the atonement, so also public justice cannot rely on legal categories alone" (*Violence, Hospitality, and the Cross*, 239).

The word *hospitality* must not be misunderstood. The hospitality of the cross is neither soft nor permissive. It does not appease, it is not naïve about worldly violence, nor is it incapable of defending itself. The state's defense of hospitality within its borders requires regulation, coercion, and even occasional acts of war. Hospitable families, schools, neighborhoods, churches, and mosques can never flourish when disorder and violence are allowed to run rampant. Terrorism must be punished and justice must be executed if hospitality is to endure. Likewise, the state has a divinely given responsibility to protect its boundaries and acknowledge its limits. In a finite and fallen world, one cannot ask a state to open wide its doors and let individuals come and go as they please. The long-term hospitality of the state depends on the integrity of its laws and borders.

In this sense, disciples of the hospitable king can and should be involved in the maintenance of state limits, laws, and boundaries. Followers of Jesus can therefore be called to serve the state through the police, military, and counterterrorism forces. Disciples who participate in these activities should never do so out of an ultimate desire to inflict revenge, gain advantage, or even to establish public justice. The ultimate goal of their service must be the restoration of public hospitality through the provision of a safe and just public square.

Finally, Christian hospitality amidst Mecca and Amsterdam cannot be sustained in individualistic isolation. Boersma argues that God's hospitality must be celebrated, remembered, and practiced in community. Without the encouragement of the community, individuals can quickly become swept up in the violent narratives of Mecca and Amsterdam. The church itself, Boersma insists, must become a generative space of hospitality (*Violence, Hospitality, and the Cross*, 238). For if "the Church is the continuation of Christ's presence in the world, the redemptive hospitality of the atonement continues in and through the Church" (*Violence, Hospitality, and the Cross*, 20).

Finally, the Reformers were right to insist that the atonement is the work of Christ—not Christians. Likewise, Christians are not the original authors of hospitality—Christ is. Left to their own devices, Christians would never open their doors; they would close them. On their own they would do nothing but build higher and higher walls around their homes, neighborhoods, schools, and states. If any hospitality is going to be lived out by Christians amidst the violence and hatred of Mecca and Amsterdam, it will be the work of Christ—not of Christianity. The only reason Christians could ever make space for a Muslim is because Christ first made space for them.

The Complex King

We have now met Christ the sovereign and Christ the slave, the liberator and the healer, the naked and the hospitable. We have also seen that Christ's life is not limited to the sphere of the heart, but that it is deeply public. He calls his disciples to be agents of hospitality in politics and economics, the arts and sciences, in nature and the city, the family and the church.

While this complex image of Christ and his work is inspiring, it is also overwhelming. After all, how can a single Christian ever hope to follow such a multifaceted Christ and engage in such a multifaceted mission? Which images of Christ do we follow? Which spheres of life do we engage for Christ? Following the complex Christ between Mecca and Amsterdam is far from simple. Feelings of inadequacy and paralysis quickly sweep in. Overwhelmed by the complexity of Christ's call, we are tempted to select a single image of Christ and declare it the exclusive governor of the Christian life. Some select Christ's call to fight for justice, others to serve vulnerably, punish evil, show hospitality, defend diversity, or liberate the oppressed. But whenever the Christian life is directed by a single Christological image or command, it inevitably becomes myopic in its scope and fails to grasp the multifaceted work of redemption and the fullness of life that is found in Jesus Christ.

This section will explore how disciples might begin to bring these disparate images of Christ and his work together and, in doing so, construct a ninth way of framing their Muslim neighbor and her headscarf. Here we will see how this ninth frame or this Christological lens can avoid the ideological reductionism of the world's eight frames by focusing on the complex person and multifaceted work of Jesus Christ.

I have found the reflections of Herman Bavinck to be particularly helpful in bringing these kaleidoscopic images of Christ together. His theological and ethical work is shot through with an absolute rejection of all narrow and simplistic understandings of sin, redemption, and the Christian life. According to Bavinck, the destructive influence of sin in the world is both extremely pervasive and complex. Like a virus, sin and violence have spread to politics and business, religion and culture, art and science. In order to meet this multifaceted need for healing and restoration, Bavinck argues, Christ's redemptive calling to serve as a prophet, priest, and king becomes

> so multifaceted that it cannot be captured in a single word nor summarized in a single formula. . . . [A]ll of them together help to give us a deep impression and a clear sense of the riches and many-sidedness

of the mediator's work. . . . [They] supplement one another and enrich our knowledge. . . . What matters above all, now, is not to neglect any of them but to unite them into a single whole and to trace the unity that underlies them in scriptures." (*Reformed Dogmatics*, vol. 3, 383–85)

The fruits of Christ's sacrifice are not restricted to any one area of life; they are not limited, as so many people think nowadays, to the religious-ethical life, to the heart, the inner chamber, or the church, but are extended to the entire world. For however powerful sin may be . . . [t]he grace of God and the free gift through grace are superabundant. (*Reformed Dogmatics*, vol. 3, 451)

Therefore Christ has also a message for home and society, for art and science. The word of God which comes to us in Christ is a word of liberation and restoration for the whole man, for his understanding and his will, for his body and his soul.[16]

In his *Reformed Dogmatics*, Herman Bavinck creatively reappropriates the medieval concept of the *munus triplex* to speak about the complexity of Christ's life and work. The *munus triplex* was historically used to describe the three distinct offices or callings given to Jesus Christ by God. Jesus was simultaneously charged to function as "the highest prophet, the only priest, [and] the true king" (*Reformed Dogmatics*, vol. 3, 345). His threefold anointing meant that he was called by God to teach the world (as a prophet), to reconcile the world (as a priest) and to lead the world (as a king) (*Reformed Dogmatics*, vol. 3, 367–68). Jesus was therefore responsible for the threefold work of proclaiming truth, healing division, and establishing justice. All three offices were essential to who Christ was and to what Christ accomplished. Moreover, Bavinck insists, all three callings are "essential to the completeness of our salvation" (*Reformed Dogmatics*, vol. 3, 367–68). Reducing Jesus to either a prophet, a priest, or a king not only reduces his calling, but it reduces his call on a disciple's life, as well.

Note that, historically speaking, the three offices were not meant to rigidly limit the richness of Christ's person. They functioned, rather, as a heuristic device through which medieval Christians could grapple with the complexity of Christ's significance for the world and their lives. In a similar manner, Her-

---

16. Herman Bavinck, "Common Grace," trans. R. C. Van Leeuwen, *Calvin Theological Journal* 24, no. 1 (1989): 62.

man Bavinck never limited Christ to being *simply* a prophet, priest, and king. He regularly spoke of Jesus as a friend, healer, fountain, creator, liberator, and teacher, as well.

Bavinck adds that Jesus is not sometimes a king, sometimes a priest, and sometimes a prophet. "Christ is everywhere and always simultaneously a prophet, priest, and king. . . . He is always these things in conjunction, never the one without the other" (*Reformed Dogmatics*, vol. 3, 368). For, "no single activity of Christ can be exclusively restricted to one office" (*Reformed Dogmatics*, vol. 3, 366). Christ's crucifixion functions simultaneously as "a confession and an example," a "sacrifice and a demonstration of his power" (*Reformed Dogmatics*, vol. 3, 367). For, "it is not possible to separate" the three callings of Christ or, for that matter, the Christian (*Reformed Dogmatics*, vol. 3, 367).

Moreover, Bavinck insists that these three callings do not exist in tension with one another. Instead, they participate in and actively inform the execution of the others. Christ's priestly healing and prophetic proclamation impact the administration of his kingship, power, and sovereignty. In this, Christ the King "rules not by the sword but by his Word and spirit." Likewise, in his prophecy his "word is power" and in his priesthood he "conquers by suffering, and is all-powerful by his love" (*Reformed Dogmatics*, vol. 3, 368).

> It is, accordingly, an atomistic approach, which detaches certain specific activities from the life of Jesus and assigns some to his prophetic and others to his priestly or royal office. Christ is the same yesterday, today, and forever. He does not just perform prophetic, priestly, and kingly activities but is himself, in his whole person, prophet, priest, and king. And everything he is, says, and does manifests that threefold dignity. . . . [H]e bears all three offices at the same time and consistently exercises all three at once both before and after his incarnation, in both the state of humiliation and that of exaltation. (*Reformed Dogmatics*, vol. 3, 367)

Bavinck argues that the *munus triplex* combines the rich character of Christ's "wisdom, righteousness, and redemption; truth, love, and power" (*Reformed Dogmatics*, vol. 3, 367–68). These three callings enrich each other. The reconciliation found in Christ's priestly cross informs the justice found in his kingly crown. Both works have public relevance and normativity. The healing cross does not rest in tension with the just crown. The two are both essential to who Christ is and what it means to follow him. Similarly, Christ's mercy is not opposed to Christ's justice and the "cross of Christ is the most powerful proof of this" (*De Navolging* II, 140). For, in "the cross mercy and justice are reconciled" (*De Navolging* II, 140). The cross "is at the same time a revelation of the highest love and of strict justice, simultaneously a fulfillment of law and gospel" (*De Navolging* II, 132).

On the cross, the prophetic, priestly, and kingly aspects of Christ are unified and displayed in their fullness. They do not overshadow or absorb one another. On the cross, Christ is weak and strong, slave and king, stripped and sovereign. The wholeness of the cross must be held together, Bavinck insists. "Then it was suffering; now it is entering into glory. Then it was descent to the nethermost parts of the earth; now it is ascent on high. But the two are equally necessary to the work of salvation. In both states it is the same Christ, the same Mediator, the same Prophet, Priest, and King" (*Reformed Dogmatics*, vol. 3, 475).

In view of this threefold calling, Christians living amidst Mecca and Amsterdam cannot reduce their callings to either the prophetic deconstruction of hegemony, the priestly reconciliation of diverse faiths and cultures, or the kingly establishment of plural justice. Disciples of the whole *munus triplex* will continue to seek Abraham Kuyper's "public justice." That said, they will do so not simply as kings but as servants and sufferers, liberators and healers. They will execute justice in ways that are informed by the priest's healing and the prophet's proclamation.

In light of this, disciples amidst Mecca and Amsterdam will be called to approach the state from three different directions. Some members of the church will be called to prophetically criticize the state from the outside, others will be called to establish royal justice from the inside, and still others will be called to serve as priests of healing and reconciliation throughout the political culture. The royal, prophetic, and priestly callings of the body of Christ will not be held in tension nor will they be ranked in a hierarchy of importance. Instead, all three callings of grace, truth, and justice will be understood to be part of the complex and multifaceted mission of Christ. For, as Bavinck argues,

> Christ—even now—is prophet, priest, and king; and by his Word and Spirit he persuasively impacts the entire world. Because of him there radiates from everyone who believes in him a renewing and sanctifying influence upon the family, society, state, occupation, business, art, science, and so forth.[17]

17. Bavinck, *Reformed Dogmatics*, vol. 4, ed. John Bolt, trans. John Vriend (Grand Rapids: Baker Academic, 2003–2008), 371.

Complex Discipleship between Mecca and Amsterdam

At the beginning of the chapter I described eight distinct frames Europeans apply to Muslim women and their headscarves. Each of these frames shapes the way in which Europeans understand and respond to their Muslim neighbors. I went on to argue that Christ should constitute an alternative frame for those who call him Lord. Having surveyed a wide range of Christological images in this chapter, I now want to briefly explore how these images might contribute to that ninth frame.

We will begin with Abraham Kuyper's royal image of Christ as a king. Framing these Muslim women with Kuyper's royal Christ, the Christian would begin to view the women as the sovereign possessors of divinely given authority and power. Their clothing, families, cultures, schools, and organizations would be seen by Christian onlookers as possessing a sacred freedom given to them by Christ. Citizens and states that impinge upon the sacred freedom and sovereignty of these Muslim women will be seen as trampling, not simply on the sovereignty of these women, but on the sovereignty of the king who gave it to them.

Christians who take up Klaas Schilder's images of Christ would frame these Muslim women in a very different way. According to Schilder's frame, these Muslim women would be seen as the sacred objects of Christ's sacrificial love. In vulnerability and humility, Christ came to liberate and heal, convict and clothe these women with his very self. Whether these women are friends or foes does not alter the disciples' calling to humbly seek the liberation and healing of these women. Framed by the One who does not know "small wounds" or "insignificant people" ("Christ's Last Wonder," 420), these women and their wounds will be taken seriously. These Christians do not know and do not control the ultimate decisions the women make; they are called simply to the ministry of healing and reconciliation. Framed by the disrobed and naked Christ, these Muslim women will never be seen as uniquely violent. Christians who use this frame will see no aggression or violence in the Muslim that they do not also see in themselves, for on the cross the disrobed king has exposed the naked aggression and violence of Christians and Muslims alike.

Framed by the Christology of Hans Boersma, these women will be seen as a calling to a life of Christ-centered hospitality. When these women are framed by the hospitable One, Christians will work to make space for them in the nation's laws, schools, businesses, neighborhoods, and even their own homes. When these women are framed by the hospitality of the cross, there can be no other response.

From Kuyper, Schilder, Boersma, and Bavinck these Christological images constitute the beginnings of a more complex ninth frame that far surpasses the other eight frames in its sensitivity to the complex reality of who these women are, what they are owed, and where they are going.

That said, as stated earlier, Jesus is more than a frame to those who call him Lord. He is more than a lens through which a person can peer at a Muslim neighbor. Christ's incarnation demands that Christians step through the frame and actually live their lives alongside their Muslim neighbors. In other words, Christians are called not simply to look at these Muslim women through a Christ-shaped frame, but they are called to walk alongside them with a Christ-shaped life, as well.

Followers of a complex Christ will walk with their Muslim neighbors in a complex variety of ways, and each of their unique callings will reflect a different facet of Christ's complex mission. Christ's hospitality will be embodied in the Christian teacher who intentionally makes space for students who don the hijab. Christ's justice will be embodied in the Christian lawyer who defends the rights of Muslim schools and organizations. Christ's healing will be embodied in the Christian doctor who shows sensitivity to the cultural needs of a Muslim woman under his care. Christ's truth will be demonstrated in the activist who prophetically criticizes both secular and religious attempts to demonize and control Islam. Christ's nakedness will be revealed in Christian politicians who openly confess past acts of anti-Islamic bigotry and discrimination. Christ's liberation will be shown in the Christian manager of a grocery store who empowers young Muslims with the honor and dignity of work. Christ's friendship will be embodied in a Christian family who welcomes their Muslim neighbors over for a meal.

This is a book of Christian ethics, not evangelism. That said, I believe that this is as good a time as any to make one humble comment on the topic of evangelism. A Christian's witness lives and dies with a Christian's ethics. When Christians fail to ethically embody Christ's healing, justice, nakedness, and hospitality with their Muslim neighbors, their attempts to proclaim Christ's good news to them will fall on deaf ears.

The vast majority of these Christological acts of hospitality, friendship, and healing will be small in scale and short on public notoriety. But, as Bavinck reminded the Christian pluralists of his own day, "What we need in these momentous times is not in the first place something extraordinary but the faithful fulfilling of the various earthly vocations to which the Lord calls his people."[18]

18. Bavinck, "Common Grace," 63.

Conclusion: Beyond Paralysis

This much is clear, if people accept the call to follow Jesus amidst Mecca and Amsterdam they will be quickly flooded and overwhelmed by two realities. First, the conflict between Mecca and Amsterdam will overwhelm them with its complexity and its size. Any one issue or question within the conflict is more than enough for a lifetime. One could dedicate one's whole life to anti-racism, women's rights, and antiterrorism activities and never actually solve any of the issues. Second, if Christians are not already overwhelmed by the size of the challenge, they will certainly be overwhelmed by the scope of Christ's call. The depth and complexity of the call to follow Jesus quickly convinces disciples of both their finitude and their falleness. If the complexity of Mecca and Amsterdam does not overwhelm the Christian, Christ's call amidst the two cities will. Despair, apathy, and paralysis will quickly follow.

Reflecting on the call to follow Jesus in the modern world, Herman Bavinck was acutely aware of this danger. He argued that if we see Christ as our "moral example" we will be certain "to experience judgment on our own conscience." For, if Jesus is only our "example then he comes to judge us and not to save us" ("De Navolging" I, 326–27). No mortal could ever bear the full weight of Christ's cross. No one could pay the full cost of discipleship. The weight is too much—the cost too high.

Herein lies the critical pivot in Bavinck's understanding of Christian discipleship. "Only when we know and experience Jesus as our *Redeemer*, as the one whose suffering covers our guilt and whose Spirit fulfills the law of God in us, only then do we dare to look at him and consider him our example" ("De Navolging" I, 326–27; emphasis mine).

On her own, a disciple could never follow Christ's example in the chaos and complexity of Mecca and Amsterdam. Bavinck insists that she must first understand her need for a "mystical union" or "living communion with Christ." This intimate friendship and indwelling with Jesus is "the primary element of the imitation of Christ" ("De Navolging" I, 328). Bavinck laments that all too often the gospel is believed to be a moral and ethical "burden too heavy to bear. . . . The gospel is not law but good news! It came not to judge but to save. . . . [I]t has welled up from God's free, generous, and rich love. It does not kill but makes alive."[19]

For Bavinck, the initiating work of Christ's grace must be at "the beginning, the middle, and the end" of the entire Christian life (*Reformed Dogmat-*

---

19. Bavinck, "Common Grace," 62.

ics, vol. 3, 579). Christian ethics and the *imitatio Christi* flow out of Christ's redemptive grace. A deeper union and communion with Christ is not the work of the disciple—it is a gracious "work of God" (*Reformed Dogmatics*, vol. 3, 579). Discipleship comes out of the grace of Christ. "It is of him, and through him, and therefore also leads to him and serves to glorify him" (*Reformed Dogmatics*, vol. 3, 579).

Christian disciples attempting to follow Jesus amidst Mecca and Amsterdam can know that Christ does not simply walk in front of them as a distant moral ideal; he walks alongside them, as well. The paralysis one feels, the sense of being overwhelmed by the size and complexity of the issue is birthed from the mistaken notion that the Christian—and not Christ—must somehow save Mecca and Amsterdam.

CHAPTER SEVEN

Pluralism and Worship

The first time I spoke about Muslims in one of my sermons a man stood up and walked out of the service. One of the elders brought him back in and told him to sit down. After the service I asked the elder what went wrong. He told me that the man had recently had a conflict with a Moroccan colleague at work. The man said he came to worship to forget his problems with Islam. He complained that worship should be a place where he could forget about Muslims.

REV. CEES RENTIER[1]

[I]t is good to sing in the congregation with mouth and heart. We are unable to compute the profit and edification which will arise from this, except after having experimented.

JOHN CALVIN[2]

In their work *Rethinking Pluralism: Ritual, Experience, and Ambiguity,* Adam Seligman and Robert Weller argued that modern liberalism has fundamentally failed to grasp the deep complexity and ambiguity of life in a pluralistic

---

1. Reverend Cees Rentier, interview by author, Amersfoort, the Netherlands, March 21, 2012.

2. John Calvin, "Articles Concerning the Organization of the Church and Worship at Geneva Proposed by the Ministers at the Council January 16, 1537," in *Calvin: Theological Treatises,* trans. and ed. J. K. S. Reid (Philadelphia: Westminster Press, 1954), 53.

world.[3] Drawing on the tradition of American pragmatism, the authors argue that modern liberals suffer from a fatal overconfidence in their ability to fully grasp and manage every aspect of life in a pluralistic culture. Seligman and Weller provide a name for this modern liberal behavior; they call it "notation." Through this process of notation, modern liberals commit themselves to the universalizing mission of solving pluralism through a sophisticated system of laws, labels, boundaries, and government programs. In other words, through notation the modern liberal hopes to categorize and control an infinitely plural and complex world.

Seligman and Weller argue that this strategy of notation inhibits the liberal's ability to respond to diverse faiths and cultures in four critical ways. First, notation fails to humbly grasp the infinite complexity and contingency of life in a pluralistic society. Second, notation fails to equip liberal citizens to accept the mysteries, risks, and ambiguities of diversity. Third, notation fails to provide liberals with resources for social bonding across the categories, labels, and government programs they create. Fourth, notation fails to cultivate a sense of empathy, solidarity, or affection across the laws and systems these citizens construct. In the end, Seligman and Weller conclude that if citizens are going to accept the complexity of life in a globalizing world, if they are going to cultivate a sense of connection and affection, they will need something more than liberal notation. It is here that the authors turn toward a new idea—that is actually quite old.

Seligman and Weller submit that what liberalism really needs is something they call "ritual and shared experience." In short, the authors argue that as diverse citizens participate in a wide variety of rituals, traditions, and shared experiences, they begin, ever so slowly, to imagine and practice a life together. Through common rituals and shared experiences the boundaries and labels of modern notation begin to fall away.

Well-versed in the rituals of ancient Israel and ancient China, these two scholars explore a number of ways in which these premodern civilizations used both ritual and shared experience to navigate the challenges of deep religious and cultural difference. Rituals helped these ancient societies navigate the complex challenge of difference without the use of liberal notation. It was ritual that empowered them to balance order and openness, justice and mercy. It was ritual that helped them avoid the extremes of a rigid exclusivism and a rootless relativism.

---

3. Adam Seligman and Robert Weller, *Rethinking Pluralism: Ritual, Experience, and Ambiguity* (Oxford: Oxford University Press, 2012).

From here, Seligman and Weller shift their attention to the rituals and shared experiences of contemporary life. The authors point to the everyday experience of sharing common grocery stores, buses, concerts, stadiums, and workplaces. They argue that, while seemingly insignificant, these shared spaces, experiences, and rituals can function as aesthetic and kinesthetic connectors for citizens who feel divided.

Rather than engage in intractable debates over questions of ultimate truth and justice, Seligman and Weller encourage diverse citizens to cheer for a common football team, share a seat on the train, and serve one another in a restaurant. Through these rituals and practices, the authors believe, citizens might begin to cultivate a common sense of identity and solidarity with their neighbors—almost by accident. While the deep ideological differences will remain, the authors argue, ritual and shared experience can be a way of surviving and even thriving amidst the ambiguity and contingency of life in a diverse city.

William Connolly, another philosopher influenced by pragmatism, presents a like-minded case in his book *Pluralism*.[4] Like Seligman and Weller, Connolly argues that the infinite complexity and contingency of pluralism can never be fully grasped by the modern mind or controlled by the modern state. Connolly concludes that diverse cities do not have a need for citizens with a single philosophical answer or political solution to their deep differences. Instead, diverse societies need citizens who are capable of engaging the world's fractal, complex, and contingent mysteries with openness and empathy. As citizens ponder the ambiguity and contingency of the diverse people around them, Connolly believes, they might just come to recognize the ambiguity and contingency of their own identities, stories, and beliefs. Citizens will begin to recognize that the life of the world—and even their own lives—extends beyond their grasp and control.

But how, exactly, do citizens begin to wrestle the deep contingency and ambiguity of life? How do they open themselves up to the fractal and complex nature of the world, the complexity of time and space, and the contingency of history and their own identity? What opens them up to this reality?

William Connolly points to the importance of aesthetic practices. To illustrate his point, he reflects on his recent visit to a movie theater. The cinema had decided to rescreen *The Maltese Falcon*, a classic 1941 film. The screening attracts a diverse and disconnected group of citizens who share a common

---

4. William Connolly, *Pluralism* (Durham, NC: Duke University Press, 2005). Additional references to this work are given parenthetically in the text.

desire to relive and memorialize a common experience from their past. With the audience settled into their seats, the film begins. As the story goes, the audience members begin to collectively remember their favorite moments in the film. Each of them starts to enter into the story. As they experience the twists and turns of the story, they are offered a unique opportunity to imagine "how a slight twist here or there could have turned [their own] experience in a different direction." Within the aesthetic world of the film, the modern liberal audience is able to relax their need to control and define their lives and the world around them. In the theater and through the story, they begin to simply "dwell in the experience of becoming" (*Pluralism*, 165). Entering into a character's life, story, and beliefs, individual viewers are able to set aside (if only for a moment) their own lives for the sake of another. By dwelling in the contingency of the characters and their lives, Connolly believe that you (the viewer) can begin the process of "recoiling back modestly upon the self-certainty of your own judgment" (*Pluralism*, 168).

Connolly argues that shared aesthetic experiences can break citizens from the iron logic of modern liberalism and the need to grasp and control a fractal world. But films like *The Maltese Falcon* can do more than simply teach a viewer modesty and empathy; they can provide fleeting but critical experiences of encouragement and hope. Connolly argues that dwelling in the life of the film, your life can be

> "warmed," "set in motion," "revivified," and "uplifted" as you dwell in [its] duration. . . . Dwelling in duration affects the sensibilities with which we act. And it can prime us to do more work yet upon them. . . . [It] can enliven life . . . it can expand the connections you pursue with others across cultural distance as you glimpse some forks in your own past. . . . *Running the [aesthetic] experiment is the best way to test the claims.* (*Pluralism*, 166; emphasis mine)

In other words, the cinematic "experience of belonging to time can enliven the feeling for life and deepen appreciation of diversity at the same time" (*Pluralism*, 168). Connolly's aesthetic

> wager is that those who run such experiments—through reading, testimony, and meditation, in concerts, theaters, temples, and other ritual settings—emerge better prepared to respond with presumptive receptivity and courage in a world that moves faster than heretofore and more often issues in surprising forks in time. We also become better

equipped to combat on their own turf those who seek to roll the world back to a putative condition of deep unity. (*Pluralism*, 169)

Opening oneself up to the deep differences of the world is a risky endeavor—Connolly admits as much. However, he argues, it is only through this process of opening up that citizens will discover ways to hold together. Connolly's sentiments are captured nicely in the following statement from Maurice Merleau-Ponty: "The human world is an open and unfinished system and the same radical contingency which threatens it with discord also rescues it from the inevitability of disorder and prevents us from despairing of it."[5]

Philosopher Jeffrey Stout has also joined the chorus of pragmatists calling for rituals and practices to renew pluralistic and democratic cultures. In his book *Democracy and Tradition,* Stout repeatedly presses on America's need for citizens to continually engage in communal practices and democratic discourse.[6] One American ritual that is particularly important to Stout is the regular practice of "giving and receiving" reasons with one's neighbors. Even if citizens do not philosophically agree on the origin, essence, or end of human life, Stout believes that the continuous ritual of giving and receiving reasons has the potential to bind diverse interlocutors together in a powerful and formative way. Stout argues that a culture of democratic virtues can be cultivated through the rituals and practices of neighbors holding each other accountable. Beyond mere democratic discourse, Stout also suggests that citizens engage in "a loose and ever-changing collection of social practices that includes such activities as quilting, baseball, and jazz."[7] These everyday common practices, he argues, will play a crucial role in building solidarity across differences.

In recent years, Stout has become increasingly interested in the ability of sports to bind individuals together and cultivate the democratic virtues and habits that are so critical to life in diverse cultures. In a newspaper interview, Stout reflected on the ability of sports to offer new insight into classic political debates such as the eternal tension between individual expression and communal solidarity. The game of soccer, he argues, is "somewhere in the middle of that spectrum and that's what's good about it. A soccer team without individual expression loses, and so does a soccer team without community."[8] Moreover, in

---

5. Maurice Merleau-Ponty, *Humanism and Terror: An Essay on the Communist Problem,* trans. John O'Neill (Boston: Beacon Press, 1969), 188.

6. Jeffrey Stout, *Democracy and Tradition* (Princeton, NJ: Princeton University Press, 2005).

7. Stout, *Democracy and Tradition*, 303.

8. Jeffrey Stout interview Douglass Todd, Sports teach the classical virtues – but soccer

playing soccer citizens are forced to learn how to make decisions that are both quick and wise in dynamic situations. Soccer coaches cannot predict, control, or dictate every decision that will come the player's way. Coaches must equip their players to make good decisions in the moment. In this sense, soccer can teach a citizen something that the liberal state cannot: the ability to navigate challenging and dynamic situations with wisdom and calm.

Stout also reflects at length on the democratic dynamics of his own deeply diverse neighborhood in New Jersey. He asks himself how such a diverse collection of people will ever hold themselves together. He is curious in what sense he can consider his neighborhood a community if its members do not hold any "ultimate truths" in common. In the end, Stout points to the common practices of the neighborhood. For,

> what we have going for us as a community, are valued social practices and the forms of excellence they involve. We care about soccer, about how the pizzas and tortillas are made, and about having our voices heard in town hall. We want to hold each other responsible for commitments and actions, so we talk about them. We debate the merits of center forwards, anchovies, and school board candidates.[9]

In the end, Stout claims, "it would be foolish" to think these practices and neighborhood conversations will encompass the "whole of politics, but it should count for something." Here Stout refers to a correspondent from Sweden whose government makes it "their business to foster common activities" in a political effort to help democracy "survive the increasing awareness of ethnicity and race."[10] Stout argues that while advocates of democracy and pluralism do not know all that will come from these common neighborhood practices, sports, and rituals, we know enough to "experiment boldly and prudently with this end in view."[11]

Surveying the work of pragmatists like Stout, Connolly, Seligman, and Weller, what can we take away from their insights? One thing is clear: All four theorists of democratic life believe that democracy requires more than democratic ideas and institutions—it requires democratic rituals and experiences as well. But more than that, they all seem convinced that democracy requires a

---

does better than football http://vancouversun.com/news/staff-blogs/sports-teach-the-classical-virtues-but-soccer-does-better-than-football

9. Stout, *Democracy and Tradition*, 302.

10. Stout, *Democracy and Tradition*, 302.

11. Stout, *Democracy and Tradition*, 302.

group of citizens with certain affections or "habits of the heart," as sociologist Robert Bellah would call them.

Each of these theorists appears convinced that democratic states are incapable of cultivating the habits of the heart that they need to maintain democratic ideas and institutions. Instead, the theorists look to neighborhoods and theaters, sports fields and neighborhood pubs. They look for democratic salvation in stories, films, songs, exercise, and conversation.

But can these everyday practices truly provide citizens with the thick and durable levels of modesty, empathy, and solidarity they need to live together in diverse cities? Can a visit to the grocery store, a soccer game, or a movie theater hold a nation together when skyscrapers are falling and missiles are launching? Stout, Seligman, Weller, and Connolly never suggest that any one of these daily rituals will solve the challenges of democratic life. Difference, discomfort, and even clashes will continue.

In the pages that follow, I provide a uniquely Christian reflection on these post-Christian attempts to cultivate democratic habits and affections. I share the pragmatists' dissatisfaction with liberal notation and government action. I share their belief that citizens need more than ideas and institutions. I agree that citizens need democratic sensibilities, dispositions, and—dare I say—virtues. I agree that habits of the heart are not cultivated through philosophical argument or political force. I even share their cautious hope that public rituals and shared experiences like going to the movies together will contribute to democratic culture and deep pluralism. That said, for me as a uniquely Christian theorist, my most prized ritual and shared experience is Christian worship.

In this chapter, I show that the Christian church has always known what liberals and pragmatists are just now discovering—the habits of the heart are shaped more by ritual and shared experience than by ideas and institutions. Historically speaking, Sunday morning worship has always been the most critical space for Christian formation. It is here that Christians engage in a series of rituals and shared practices that guide, encourage, humble, and form them. The by-product of healthy Christian worship is the formation of the Christian heart. The aim of this chapter is simple: to explore how the rituals and shared experiences of Christian worship can form a citizen with the habits, virtues, and affections she will need to contribute to fight for Christian pluralism.

The initial similarities between a Friday night at Connolly's movie theater and a Sunday morning at Christian church are quite striking. Both are communal experiences. Both engage my body and my senses. Both experiences can ask me to set my personal story and beliefs aside and introduce me to an alternative set of stories, characters, and beliefs. Both experiences can confront me with the limits of human understanding and control over time and space. Both rituals can teach, encourage, humble, and challenge me. Both can help me imagine a different way of living in the future. That said, while the initial similarities are striking, a number of critical differences will emerge as we delve into what Christian worship means and what it means to be a Christian worshipper.

As I mentioned in the second interlude, this chapter was ignited by my sense of dissatisfaction with Abraham Kuyper and his followers who focused almost exclusively on the construction of pluralistic ideas and institutions to the exclusion of pluralistic affections and virtues.[12] This chapter represents an attempt to remedy that oversight by exploring how worship can cultivate the habits, virtues, and character needed to sustain a Christian life amidst Mecca and Amsterdam.

When Pluralists Sing

Across the centuries, Christians have maintained that the Holy Spirit accomplishes a variety of good works in and through the act of Christian worship. On any given Sunday morning, the Holy Spirit calls and convicts, encourages and restores, listens and teaches, trains and commissions. The Spirit accomplishes these many works through an equally wide variety of practices and mediums. In worship, a disciple encounters the Holy Spirit through images and stories, prayers and songs, standing and bowing, rituals and sacraments. Through these liturgical mediums, worshippers cannot only learn about the many works of the Holy Spirit, but they are also invited to practice and participate in those many works themselves.

In the last chapter, we considered the complexity of Christ's work in the world. We observed his hospitality, grace, vulnerability, sovereignty, and love.

---

12. To formulate this argument, I will need to go beyond the work of Abraham Kuyper and his immediate kin. While they obviously provided an impressive set of intellectual and institutional structures for pluralism, they failed to describe a liturgical foundation for the movement. Nineteenth-century pluralists like Kuyper did not ignore worship. (See K. W. de Jong, *Achtergronden en ontwikkeingen in de eredienst van de Gereformeerde Kerken in Nederland* [Baarn: Ten Have, 1996].) They dutifully attended worship every week (twice on a Sunday and sometimes during the week as well). Kuyper wrote extensively on nearly every conceivable aspect of worship. (See Abraham Kuyper's *Onze Eeredienst*, now published as *Our Worship*, trans. and ed. Harry Boonstra [Grand Rapids: Eerdmans, 2009].) Moreover, Kuyper spent his entire career, nearly fifty years, composing weekly devotionals for his movement's periodical *De Heraut*. Kuyper clearly argued that piety mattered a great deal.

In the sanctuary, the worshipper not only witnesses the whole work of Christ but also is invited to actually participate in the whole work of Christ. She can sing songs of Christ's hospitality, she can hear stories of Christ's justice, she can taste the cup of Christ's grace, she can feel Christ's love in the physical embrace of her neighbor. In worship, the pluralist can be led to pray for her Muslim neighbors, she can confess her sins against her secular neighbors, she can offer up the mysteries, challenges, and struggles of life amidst Mecca and Amsterdam to the whole Christ in prayer.

If the Christian pluralist has experienced some deep frustration with her Muslim neighbor, a psalm of lament can provide her with words of holy sorrow and anger. Likewise, if she has encountered some great beauty or goodness from her Muslim neighbor, a psalm of praise can provide her with words of gratitude. Bending her knees in confession, she can feel her own brokenness and pride as it rises through her bones. Grasping hands with her neighbor in prayer, she is reminded that she is not an isolated individual amidst the waves of Mecca and Amsterdam—she is a part of a body. Through weekly participation in these simple practices, the pluralist can begin not only to understand the idea of Christ's hospitality, grace, and humility, but she can begin—ever so slowly—to make those aspects of Christ's character a part of her own.

Clarification

Before I make my case about the formative potential of worship, a number of clarifying remarks are in order. First, to say that worship has formative potential is to acknowledge that it might it be otherwise. Worship can, and often does, fail to make any impact on the worshipper at all. Worship can become a dead ritual encouraging cultural apathy and political indifference. Worship can be privatized. Its formative power can be neutered by poor planning and leadership, as well as inane forms of sappy sentimentality.

Worse than impotence, worship can also deform worshippers into political monsters. Worship can reinforce and even strengthen the forces of nationalism, hate, and the desire for Christian hegemony and uniformity. James K. A. Smith in particular has wrestled with the uncomfortable and undeniable fact that Christian liturgies have been perverted to support everything from the African slave trade, to American racism, to the genocide in Rwanda.[13]

---

13. James K. A. Smith, *Awaiting the King: Reforming Public Theology* (Grand Rapids: Baker Academic, 2017), see chapter "Contested Formations: Our 'Godfather' Problem."

In light of this fact, this chapter does not claim that worship automatically leads to a pluralistic heart—or a pluralistic culture. The claim, rather, is that, when worship is rightly practiced and blessed by the Holy Spirit, it has the potential to cultivate Christian pluralists who not only understand but practice Christ's hospitality, justice, and grace.

Second, debates about worship often myopically focus on questions of musical style. Such debates often produce more heat than light. The arguments below are applicable to many different styles of worship. They assume that a wide variety of liturgical practices are capable of equipping Christian pluralists. In fact, the next chapter will highlight two worshipping communities, one traditional and the other contemporary, who have each embodied rich hospitality for their Muslim neighbors.

Third, I am not suggesting revolutionary reimagining of Christian worship. There is no need for a new hymnbook full of pluralistic songs, prayers, and rituals that explicitly mention Muslims or tolerance. Many of the oldest songs and rituals of the church communicate Christ's hospitality, justice, and grace quite plainly. The true deficiency, rather, is the congregation's inattentiveness to the pluralistic implications of their old songs. Below is a brief illustration of the point.

During the 1970s, Richard Mouw, a Christian ethicist and philosopher, was asked to give a sermon to a conservative, white church in America concerning the connection between Jesus and racial politics.[14] Before he preached, he was told that this conservative church did not believe that Jesus had anything to say about race or politics. Mouw's sermonic assignment appeared doomed from the start. What would he say?

Mouw found that two old hymns did the work for him. Before he got up to preach, the congregation sang two songs. One was entitled "O, Worship the King" and this led into the Sunday school classic that begins, "Jesus loves the little children, all the children of the world, red and yellow, black and white." When it was finally Mouw's turn to preach, his sermon was all but finished. All he needed to do was point out what the congregation had already sung—Jesus is a king and he loves black kids. In short, if the congregation truly meant what they had just sung, they would need to wrestle with the fact the Jesus had both political authority and multiracial affection. Mouw stresses that the liturgical task in challenging political times, "is not so much for us to begin saying new things; rather, it is to begin to reflect and act on the commitments we have made in [our expressions] of piety, the hymns and prayers with which we

---

14. Richard Mouw, *Called to Holy Worldliness* (Minneapolis: Fortress Press, 1980), 6–8.

are already familiar."[15] In other words, what should we the church do in the emerging age of fear and reactionary politics? We should sing old hymns and wrestle with their subversive political implications.

Fourth, while this chapter explores how worship can contribute to pluralism, we must be clear that worship is an end in and of itself. The glory of God is its own justification. Our primary purpose for going to worship is to praise God, not to morally better ourselves. The moral side-effects of worship—the ways in which worship makes us more humble or hospitable—are a secondary by-product focusing one's primary attention on the humility and hospitality of the worshipped One. Simply put, if the worshipper is focused primarily on herself and the betterment of her moral nature, she will not be able to see or receive the moral nature of the One she is worshipping.

Finally, this chapter is meant to be introductory, not exhaustive. The burgeoning academic discussions between liturgical and political theology are vast and increasingly complex. I cannot hope to summarize their fullness here. Those interested in further exploration should consult the works listed in the footnotes.

Worship and Public Life

Throughout the nineteenth century, thousands of Protestants from the Netherlands immigrated to the United States. In 1876, these immigrants founded Calvin College in western Michigan.[16] As the decades rolled on, the college began to do more than simply preserve the Dutch Protestant faith—they began to push the tradition forward.

One significant area of theological development has been the college's interest in the connection between worship and public life. Professors Nicholas Wolterstorff, Richard Mouw, John Witvliet, and James K. A. Smith in particular have been important players in this growing discussion. This chapter draws heavily on their work and seeks to creatively apply it specifically to the emerging questions of Christian pluralism and politics amidst Mecca and Amsterdam.[17]

15. Mouw, *Called to Holy Worldliness*, 8.

16. James D. Bratt, *Dutch Calvinism in Modern America: A History of a Conservative Subculture* (Grand Rapids: Eerdmans, 1984).

17. A few brief notes on these scholars should be made from the outset. First, though each of them would call Dutch Calvinism his liturgical home, they are all clearly indebted to numerous non-Dutch and non-Calvinist resources as well. The fingerprints of Alexander

During the 1960s and '70s, the United States was deeply embroiled in fierce political debate over race relations and civil rights. The question of how churches would respond to the issue was heated. Most churches insisted that the gospel had nothing to say on public issues like racial politics. In a 1978 article entitled "Baptismal Politics," philosopher Richard Mouw decided that he needed to challenge the churches, not with philosophy, but with liturgy. He wrote:

> A few weeks ago our congregation issued another declaration on race relations. We do this kind of thing regularly these days. As far as I can tell, there is never a dissenting voice. The entire congregation just speaks out in unison and commits itself to the cause of race relations.
>
> Here is how the most recent declaration occurred. Darryl was brought by his mother to the front of the church to be baptized. At a certain point in the ceremony, the minister asked these questions of the congregation: "Do you, the people of the Lord, promise to receive this child in love, pray for him, help care for his instruction in the faith, and encourage and sustain him in the fellowship of believers?" And we all answered: "We do, God helping us."
>
> Darryl is black. And so the congregation's response had significant and far-reaching implications. For a predominately white congregation to promise to receive Darryl in love, to pray for him, to watch over his instruction in the faith, to sustain him in Christian fellowship, was a

---

Schmemann, the Eastern Orthodox father of the liturgical theology movement, can be found throughout the work of all four of these Reformed scholars. Beyond Schmemann one finds ecumenical references to a wide variety of non-Calvinist and non-Dutch resources including Walter Bruggemann, William Cavanaugh, Marva Dawn, Peter Leithart, Henri Nouwen, Eugene Peterson, Don Saliers, Stanley Hauerwas, Charles Taylor, Vatican II, John Howard Yoder, Graham Ward, and N. T. Wright. Second, each of these scholars approaches the question of worship and public life asking his own distinct questions from a different field of research. Nicholas Wolterstorff is an analytical philosopher whose interests in worship surround the issues of lament, justice, art, and aesthetics. James K. A. Smith is a continental philosopher interested in how worship shapes an individual's desires, character, and imagination. Specializing in ethics, Richard Mouw is interested in how worship can impact the way Christians approach moral issues in the public square. John Witvliet is a church musician and liturgical theologian interested in the historical development of Reformed worship and, more specifically, the relationship between theological doctrines and worship practices. This chapter will not explore the subtle and minor differences in their backgrounds, interests, or work. Instead, it will explore how aspects of their research can contribute to the chapter's governing question: how can worship inform Christian pluralism between Mecca and Amsterdam?

profound commitment on his behalf—with important implications not only for this congregation, but also for the traditionally Dutch-ethnic denomination of which it is a part, and for the entire church of Jesus Christ.

To love Darryl will require that we try to look at the world from his point of view, to make his hopes and fears our very own. To assume an obligation for his Christian instruction and nurture is to commit ourselves to attempting to understand what the gospel means for him, with his tradition and history. It means that from here on in we will have to keep Darryl in mind when we plan our sermons, write our liturgies, plot out our educational programs. All of this will involve us in change, in patterns of "contextualization" that are different from those which have characterized our lives in the past. We are also going to have to pay close attention to what others are saying to and about Darryl. If American society tries to treat him like a second-class citizen, we will have to protest on his behalf, since he is our brother in a holy nation of kings and priests. If he is ever the object of a cruel joke or a vicious slur, we will have to consider this to be an affront to the very body of Christ. If someone ever complains that he is not "one of our own kind," we will have to respond with the insistence that, through the blood of Jesus, we are Darryl's "kind."

Some Christians have been known to ask whether the church can legitimately become involved in politics, or more specifically whether the church's proper task has anything to do with such things as race relations. These questions assume that these are areas in which the church is not yet involved. They treat these matters as if they were still options for the Christian community. But this is not the case. On the day that my denomination baptized its first black child, on that day the denomination got involved in race relations. To make the covenantal promises on behalf of a black child is to commit ourselves to "the black struggle."

The baptism of a child from an oppressed race or class is, for the Reformed community, a profoundly political act. And it is an act engaged in before the living God. Once that commitment has been made, there is no turning back. Questions which we might have wished to have been "whether" questions have now become "how" questions. It is a good thing that after we say, "We do," we remember to add, "God helping us."[18]

18. Richard Mouw, "Baptismal Politics," *The Reformed Journal* 28, no. 7 (1978), 2–3.

Throughout their reflections on worship and public life, Wolterstorff, Mouw, Witvliet, and Smith consistently make a twofold argument. First, they insist that worship must inform the issues of public life. Second, they insist that the issues of public life must be addressed in worship. They each argue without reservation that if a separation is allowed to occur between Sunday and Monday, a breakdown in both the spiritual and political integrity of the Christian will soon follow. Sunday and Monday must become reacquainted.

Nicholas Wolterstorff sums up the urgency of the issue when he compares the function of Sunday morning worship to that of the human heart. For, Wolterstorff notes, any healthy human heart has a systolic and a diastolic function; it draws the blood in from all over the body, it renews the blood with life-giving oxygen, and then it sends blood out to give life to every artery throughout the body. In a similar way, worship draws a Christian's public life into the sanctuary only to send the Christian back out into the world renewed with the oxygen of the gospel. This cardiac rhythm of six days out in the world and one day in the sanctuary is critical to the spiritual and political health of the Christian citizen.[19] Drawn into the heart of worship, the public disciple

> carries her daily life along with her . . . to present that life to God. . . . She thanks God for what she has found good in her life and that of others, she laments to God for what she has found painful in her life and that of others, she confesses to God what she and others have done wrong, and she praises God for God's incomparable majesty.[20]

Walking amidst the challenges of Mecca and Amsterdam, Christian pluralists experience powerful moments of joy and fear, confusion and anger, gratefulness and guilt. The sanctuary must be a place where those experiences can find a listening ear, a guiding voice, and a comforting touch. Wolterstorff argues that in gathering for worship "we carry with us the thanksgivings, regrets, and laments of daily life." Likewise, in dispersing from worship we "carry into daily life the guidance and strength, the courage and hope, that we have received."[21]

All four scholars believe that, while worship and public life are distinct

---

19. Nicholas Wolterstorff, *Until Justice and Peace Embrace* (Grand Rapids: Eerdmans, 1983), 147.

20. Nicholas Wolterstorff, "Imitating God: Doing Justice as a Condition of Authentic Worship," *Reformed Worship* 68 (2003).

21. Nicholas Wolterstorff, "The Theological Significance of Going to Church and Leaving," in *Hearing the Call: Liturgy, Justice, Church, and World*, ed. Mark R. Gornik and Gregory Thompson (Grand Rapids: Eerdmans, 2011), 240.

callings in the Christian life, they must never be separated from one another. In making this argument the scholars hope to correct two fatal errors.

The first error posits a strict separation between worship and public life. Here worship's relevance is limited both temporally (to Sunday morning) and spatially (to the sanctuary). Worship is reduced to an individual's private, emotional, and spiritual experience—something that has no relevance or impact on public life. Conversely, one's public life is not welcome in the sanctuary. Sunday morning prayers and songs become acts of spiritual pretense—deaf to the political cries in the street. The challenges, questions, and frustrations of life amidst Mecca and Amsterdam are excluded from the activities of sanctuary. All four scholars, each in his own unique way, decry this fierce separation as absolutely fatal to the integrity of both worship and public life. For, in the words of Wolterstorff, if worship is allowed to detach itself from the public call to justice, it becomes "a malformation so serious as to anger God."[22]

The second error dissolves all distinctions between worship and public life. This error begins with a statement that sounds promising. It is argued that "all of life is worship" and that God can be encountered and glorified anywhere. While these scholars agree in part, they insist that a Christian's week is not liturgically "flat." They insist that the Sabbath is—and ought to be—a distinct and mountainous peak in the week of a Christian citizen. Climbing the Sunday mountain, the Christian can have a better view of the week that has past and the week that is to come. For, as James K. A. Smith argues, "If all of life is going to be worship, the sanctuary is the place where we learn how."[23]

A Liturgical Dance amidst Mecca and Amsterdam

Are these arguments about the deep connection between worship and public life a radically new idea for the Christian faith? All four scholars reply with a firm and collective "no." Citing the early church Reformers and even the early church and Scripture itself, they point to a long tradition of arguing that Christian integrity depends upon the deep connection and conversation between worship and public life.

John Witvliet has done a great deal of work tracing the ways in which the early Reformation movement stressed these connections. He argues that songbooks in the earliest days of the movement were routinely taken out of

---

22. Wolterstorff, "Justice as Condition of Authentic Liturgy," in *Hearing the Call*, 53.
23. James K. A. Smith, "Sanctification for Ordinary Life," *Reformed Worship* 103:19.

the sanctuary and into the streets and fields. Early Lutherans and Calvinists brought their worship books into their homes, shops, and marketplaces, singing Psalms with their children and their fellow workers.[24] After the Bible itself, the Psalter was the most common text found in homes of the early Reformation.

Witvliet adds that John Calvin himself frequently "described public worship as a school of faith" (*Worship Seeking Understanding*, 143). Calvin insisted that Sunday morning had to contribute to the public formation and sanctification of Christian disciples. The reformer frequently referred to songs and rituals as critical "'props,' 'stimulants,' and 'exercises'" in the faith (*Worship Seeking Understanding*, 144). Worship was an act of receiving "nourishment, the giving and receiving and tasting of spiritual food" (*Worship Seeking Understanding*, 141). Through worship, Christians could be "trained" for public lives of "godliness" (*Worship Seeking Understanding*, 143).

In the centuries following Calvin, forms of Reformed worship became quite diverse. The Reformation took a unique shape in each nation and culture it entered. That said, regardless of context, Reformed worship tended to organize itself around a few common principles. I want to briefly explore three common pillars of Reformed worship and ask a simple question: how might this approach to worship inform life amidst Mecca and Amsterdam?

The first pillar for Reformed worship is theocentricism. God alone is the center, the primary subject, object, purpose, and agent in worship. Witvliet explains that for Reformers like Calvin, the "first move" in worship is "God's move toward humanity" and the second is the people's responsive move toward God. The people do not approach and discover God in worship, they are approached and discovered by God in worship. Worshippers do not summon God to worship, they are summoned by God to worship. As Witvliet explains, "God descends" to us in worship first "that we might ascend" to God second (*Worship Seeking Understanding*, 133–34).

Theocentric worship, therefore, is marked by a consistent pattern and practice of God's primary action and the people's secondary reaction. In the dance of worship, God takes the first step and the people take the second. God acts, the people react. God leads, the people follow. The posture of the dance partner in the second position is that of waiting, open reception, and response.

What are the public implications of a theocentric approach to worship amidst Mecca and Amsterdam? First, over time theocentric worshippers be-

24. John Witvliet, *Worship Seeking Understanding* (Grand Rapids: Baker, 2003), 229. Additional references to this work are given parenthetically in the text.

come practiced in assuming a posture of waiting, open reception, and response. On a weekly basis, they are learning to anticipate, await, and rely on something other than their own ego. Their sense of identity, security, and power comes, not from within, but from without.

Walking amidst Mecca and Amsterdam, the primary posture of a theocentric worshipper is that of patient reception and humble response rather than inpatient grasping and prideful initiative. To put it simply, liturgical postures of patience and humility should lead—if they are meaningful at all—to public postures of patience and humility. If they do not, something has gone wrong (and we will get into this issue later).

John Witvliet notes that theocentric worship, "is one of the few activities" in self-centered Western cultures "that has as its intrinsic purpose to 'decenter' the human actor." Western schools serve the students, businesses the customers, theaters the audience, and governments the people. But in worship, worshippers are not the purpose—their fulfillment and actualization are not the end. Instead, in the sanctuary the participant experiences "what it feels like *not* to be the center of the universe."[25] In the sanctuary the autonomous individual encounters a deeply countercultural rite—the practice of decentering.

Practicing this decentering ritual on a weekly basis, the Christian pluralist should, over time, be well trained in making space for something outside herself. She should be practiced in holding her own desires, interests, and agenda with a loose grasp. Those who see her walking amidst Mecca and Amsterdam should notice that she is curiously interested in and open to the public interests, questions, and desires of others. More than that, she is curiously open to having her public life informed by those outside herself. Such a worshipper will know that she is not responsible for controlling her nation's story, for in worship she found that she is not in control of her own. Recognizing the finitude of her knowledge and power does not make her feel exposed or vulnerable—it does not fill her with a desire to "take her country back." Her sense of finitude gives her peace. The sovereign task of ruling the world is not hers, for she met the true ruler on Sunday.

But won't this theocentric posture of reception lead to an overly passive approach to politics and social responsibility? In their firm "no," liturgical scholars like John Witvliet point to a second pillar of worship after the Refor-

---

25. John Witvliet, "The Cumulative Power of Transformation in Public Worship," in *Worship That Changes Lives: Multidisciplinary and Congregational Perspectives on Spiritual Transformation,* ed. Alexis D. Abernathy (Grand Rapids: Baker Academic, 2008), 50. Emphasis mine. Additional references to this work are given parenthetically in the text.

mation—active lay participation. While God is the sole initiator of worship, those in the second position have a responsibility to actively respond to God's initiation. From the very beginnings of the Reformation movement, its leaders insisted that worship is the action and work of all of the people, not an exclusive practice performed on their behalf. Instead of outsourcing worship practices to special priests, musicians, artists, and choirs, the Reformers insisted that worship be the active response of the people with their own hearts and voices. Not passive recipients, the people were an active priesthood.

Nicholas Wolterstorff echoes this insistence on active participation when he argues that worship must be understood as "*action*." Sunday morning is "a sequence of actions—actions on the part of God addressed to the people interwoven with actions on the part of the people addressed to God."[26] Both God and the people take action in the liturgical dance. God does not passively hear the praises and laments of the people nor do the people passively receive the commands and grace of God. The covenant between God and the people is enacted; it is memorialized and renewed in a dynamic dance between two active partners.

What is the public significance of participatory worship for life amidst Mecca and Amsterdam? The connection is straightforward. As an active participant, the disciple is trained to recognize that when God acts a response must be given. Therefore, when a Christian receives some blessing, forgiveness, or grace from God, an active response is required. When a pastor declares that the congregation is forgiven, the congregation does not shrug its shoulders and move on. It must actively go into the city and forgive others just as they have been forgiven. Nicholas Wolterstorff does not mince words here; he insists that if a disciple experiences God's justice in the sanctuary and does not actively respond with justice in her public life, her worship will make God "nauseous." Wolterstorff could not be clearer on this point: songs of justice that do not lead to lives of justice constitute "a malformation so serious as to anger God."[27] In both the sanctuary and the square Christians must actively respond to the justice and mercy of God. If they do not, both their worship and their politics become abominations.

Let's take John Calvin's treatment the Lord's Supper as a quick illustration of the point. Before a disciple comes forward and takes the bread and wine

26. Wolterstorff, "The Theological Significance of Going to Church and Leaving and the Architectural Expression of That Significance," in *Hearing the Call*, 240.

27. Wolterstorff, "Justice as Condition of Authentic Liturgy," in *Hearing the Call*, 53.

in the sanctuary, he is instructed to investigate his life—private and public. According to Calvin,

> Paul enjoins that a man examine himself before eating of this bread or drinking from this cup [1 Cor. 11:28]. By this (as I interpret it), he meant that each man descend into himself, and ponder with himself . . . whether he aspires to the imitation of Christ with the zeal of innocence and holiness.[28]

The body and blood being offered in the sanctuary pose serious questions to a Christian's public life in the square. Will you, oh Christian, honor the table of the Hospitable, Just, and Gracious One as you walk amidst Mecca and Amsterdam? Will you allow that body and that blood to nourish and guide you in the public square? If not, you defame this table by privatizing and spiritualizing its political implications.

While the table commands humility and self-reflection, it brings nourishment and encouragement as well. In consuming Christ's body and blood, the participant is actively reminded that she walks amidst Mecca and Amsterdam in the strength of another. After the table, she never walks alone. In the sanctuary and the square, Christ's body and blood are a part of her. Through the unifying power of the Holy Spirit, Christ is actively making his hospitality, justice, and grace hers.

If the first two pillars induct the pluralist into God's life and work, the third pillar inducts them into God's timing and story as well. In other words, one's identity is not the only thing that is decentered in a worship service; one's sense of timing and history is decentered as well. For the sanctuary represents more than simply a counter-space; it represents a counter time as well.

Moving through the liturgy, worshippers are invited to enter into God's story, an alternative story about the origin and end of the world. Worshippers are reminded that God is not only sovereign over space, but that God is sovereign over time as well. While battles rage between religions, races, and cultures concerning ultimate control over a nation's past and future, the sanctuary reminds its inhabitants that their individual stories must find their places within a larger story.

Reflecting on the story-telling character of Reformed worship, John Wit-

---

28. John Calvin, *The Institutes of the Christian Religion*, ed. John T. McNeill and trans. Ford Lewis Battles, The Library of Christian Classics (Philadelphia: Westminster Press, 1960 [1559]), 4.17.40.

vliet explains that "Nearly every major work on the meaning and purpose of liturgy written by a prominent Reformed theologian has emphasized the memorializing function of liturgy, the way it recounts divine action in the past in ways that anticipate divine action in the future" (*Worship Seeking Understanding*, 31). Worship, in other words, orients our story of God's past, present, and future actions. James K. A. Smith adds that as the story of God is sung, pronounced, and prayed, "the Spirit recruits us into the story of God."[29] No longer spectators to the story, worshippers "begin to see [themselves] as characters within it."[30]

Voices on the streets of Mecca and Amsterdam declare with a sense of temporal finality, "The time for patience and tolerance is over!" "We have had enough!" "Time is up!" The sanctuary asks its inhabitants a simple question, "What time is it?" or—better yet—"*Whose* time is it?" Within its walls, worshippers practice, ever so clumsily, releasing their sense of timing to God's. They begin to recognize that their stories and the stories of their neighbors are not theirs to control. Moreover, they begin to see that their neighbor's stories do not belong in the hands of state, religion, or culture. Instead, the diverse stories of those walking amidst Mecca and Amsterdam will find their fulfillment in the sovereign story of God alone. God alone knows what time it is, and God alone knows when the time is up. In the sanctuary, worshippers try on the knowledge that God's story and God's timing will continually exceed their understanding and grasp. The true concern of a worshipper who inhabits God's time is not "When will my patience run out?" but "When will God's?"

Worship that is all three of these things—theocentric, participatory, and temporal—constitutes a potent and formative practice for life amidst Mecca and Amsterdam. In theocentric worship one practices making space for others by decentering one's self. In participatory worship one practices a posture of active response to the justice, hospitality, and grace of God. And finally, in temporal worship, one's sense of timing and history is humbled.

Homo Adorans

Like many Reformed theologians before him, James K. A. Smith has found a great deal of theological and political insight in the work of Augustine. Smith's

---

29. Smith, "Sanctification for Ordinary Life," 19.

30. James K. A. Smith, *Desiring the Kingdom: Worship, Worldview, and Cultural Formation* (Grand Rapids: Baker Academic, 2009), 196.

recent books, *Desiring the Kingdom, Imagining the Kingdom,* and *Awaiting the King* constitute a rich Augustinian articulation of what we might call a liturgical approach to anthropology. While I will not fully capture the significance of Smith's trilogy, I want to briefly reflect on two of his most critical anthropological claims.

Smith's first claim, simply put, is that human beings are driven more by their desires than their thoughts. Smith's work is aimed at countering the anthropological assumptions of modernity, which assume that human beings are guided primarily by their thoughts, reasons, and observations—their minds. In contrast, Smith asserts that human beings are guided primarily by their deepest yearnings, desires, and loves—their hearts. Here Smith is following Augustine's anthropological argument that human beings are, at their very bottom, lovers. Put another way, the human mind is downstream from the human heart. If modernity begins its anthropology with a thinking brain, Smith begins his with a yearning heart—or better yet, a hungry gut.

> Rather than being pushed by beliefs, we are pulled by a *telos* that we desire. It's not so much that we're intellectually convinced and then muster the willpower to pursue what we ought; rather, at a precognitive level, we are attracted to a vision of the good life that has been painted for us in stories and myths, images and icons. . . . Those visions of the good life begin to seep into the fiber of our (everyday, noncognitive) being (i.e., our hearts) and thus govern and shape our decisions, actions, and habits.[31]

If we take Smith at his word for a moment, if we grant that human beings are driven primarily by the deep yearnings of the heart, then the next question quickly follows: what determines or directs the desires of the heart? Smith asserts that the desires of the heart are guided slowly and over time by daily habits, practices, and surroundings of the body. He argues that the everyday life of the body shapes our hearts and minds. The images we see, the stories we hear, the postures we assume, the spaces we enter, the habits we practice, and the company we keep all shape the way in which our hearts desire and our minds think. Through these corporeal practices, the heart is trained to desire certain things. In the service of these desires, the mind is slowly, but powerfully, trained to recognize some things as good, true, just, reasonable, beautiful, and desirable and other things as false, unjust, irrational, ugly, un-

---

31. Smith, *Desiring the Kingdom,* 54.

civilized, and loathsome. "Our bodies," Smith argues, "are students even when we don't realize it."[32]

> [W]hat appear to be "micropractices" have macro effects: what might appear to be inconsequential microhabits are, in fact, disciplinary formations that begin to reconfigure our relation to the wider world—indeed, they begin to make that world.[33]

> My longings are not simply "chosen" by me; they are not self-generated "decisions." I don't wake up on a Monday morning and say, "From now on, I am going to long for X." We don't choose desires; they are birthed in us. They are formed in us as habits, as *habitus*. And as Merleau-Ponty helped us to see, the acquisition of such habits is ultimately a rearrangement of our corporeal schema. . . . In short, the way to the imagination is through the body.[34]

Moderns would like to believe that they are driven by their thoughts and reason. Smith makes an exhaustive case that moderns are, in fact, deeply ritualistic and liturgical creatures who are shaped by the modern world they have constructed. Modern life, he argues, is shot through with rituals, liturgies, and practices that reinforce modern desires and thinking. A modern citizen's ideas about human flourishing, the good, true, and beautiful are not rationally deduced. Instead, they are gathered from a collection of news stories, trips to the mall, commercials, vacations, films, celebrity gossip magazines, and the ritualistic repetition of modern mantras like "believe in yourself." Indeed, if Kuyper exposed modern liberals as "the most stubborn of dogmatists,"[35] Smith exposes them as the most stubborn of liturgists.[36]

---

32. Smith, *Imagining the Kingdom*, 97.

33. Smith, *Imagining the Kingdom*, 143.

34. Smith, *Imagining the Kingdom*, 125.

35. Abraham Kuyper, "Modernism: A Fata Morgana in the Christian Domain," in *Abraham Kuyper: A Centennial Reader* (Grand Rapids: Eerdmans, 1998), 115.

36. Smith takes the simple example of weekly participation in a shopping mall to illustrate his argument. The rituals of the secular shopping mall, he argues, bear a striking resemblance to the rituals of religious communities. In the mall, he argues, modern shoppers encounter icons of beauty, the creeds of consumption, the narratives of success, and the cathartic and redemptive practices of expenditure. Smith insists that weekly participation in a mall, while not immediately, will slowly discipline and transform a shopper into a consumer through a wide range of images, narratives, and practices. The shopper will never encounter a didactic or intellectual argument for capitalism in the mall. The mall, quite frankly, is not concerned

These two anthropological claims are much more complex and nuanced than I have explained here. Smith spends many pages developing, nuancing, and supporting them through a careful philosophical dialogue with the likes of Charles Taylor, Martin Heidegger, Maurice Merleau-Ponty, and Pierre Bourdieu. While I cannot explore the full depths of his arguments, I can test their explanatory power on the current conflict between Mecca and Amsterdam.

Imagine, for a moment, how these two competing anthropologies would describe the current crisis of Mecca and Amsterdam. The modern anthropology would diagnose the clash as an issue of ignorance—a lack of awareness and understanding. Mecca does not understand Amsterdam and vice versa. To alleviate this ignorance, moderns prescribe increases in research, education, and public awareness campaigns. This strategy is perfectly captured in a recent sociological article with the subtitle "Combating Myth through Progressive Education." The author argues that the "real threat facing humanity is not Islam but ignorance, myths, and stereotypes, and, as such, it is only through progressive education that effective change, stimulating debate, intelligent discussion, and critical thinking can be attained."[37] The solution to Mecca and Amsterdam is the modern liberal educator.

An Augustinian anthropology like Smith's would certainly agree that knowledge matters. That said, an Augustinian approach would press modernity's single-minded approach with a number of simple questions. How long will rational thinking endure when a mosque is burning? How long will critical thinking survive when a bus has been bombed? What impact will awareness have when Mecca and Amsterdam no longer desire one another's presence? In other words, can knowledge withstand the cacophony of Mecca and Amsterdam's sights, sounds, stories, and experiences that push citizens toward violence and hegemony?

Take, for example, an individual Dutch citizen who has been educated in both the basic tenets of Islam and the importance of liberal tolerance. Now imagine she is confronted night after night with news reports of violent Muslims around the world and in her own city. Imagine that her afternoon reading time is consistently interrupted by her local mosque's call to prayer. Imagine further that the strange smell of roasted goat and lamb drifts into her Am-

---

with the mind; it wants the heart. Once the desires are set, the mall "knows" the mind will obediently follow. See Smith, *Desiring the Kingdom*, 23–27.

37. Anas Al-Shaikh-Ali, "Islamophobic Discourse Masquerading as Art and Literature: Combating Myth through Progressive Education," in *Islamophobia: The Challenge of Pluralism in the Twenty-First Century,* John L. Esposito and Ibrahim Kalin, eds. (Oxford: Oxford University Press, 2011), 169.

sterdam home every evening. Imagine that that her coworkers tell racist jokes about immigrants every day over lunch. Imagine that her brother repeatedly recalls the story of how he was robbed on the streets of Rotterdam by a group of Moroccan boys. Imagine that she loses her job to a young Turkish woman.

How sustainable will her liberal education on Islam be? How long will her essay on Locke's view of tolerance last? Will her ideas endure these experiences amidst Mecca and Amsterdam? If, day after day, these are the only images, sights, sounds, jokes, and habits that she participates in, won't her ability to resist hegemony be compromised? Won't her mentality, at some point, begin to shift? Consider the words of Haffid Bouazza:

> In the Netherlands there has been much public discussion concerning the need to eliminate the word "foreigner." . . . The assumption seems to be that a change in designation also engenders a change in mentality. If only things were that easy.[38]

From Sermons to Senses: Liturgies for Christian Pluralists

If the ideas of modernity are not enough to cultivate deep affection amidst the cacophony of Mecca and Amsterdam, what is? Apply the question to Christianity. How might churches equip their people to resist not only the ideas of hegemony and hatred, but also the multisensory practices of hegemony and hatred? Smith's work leads us to conclude that it is best to combat practices with counter-practices, stories with counter-stories, habits with counter-habits. What the church needs amidst this conflict is an argument against hatred and hegemony that is not so much theological but sensual, habitual, aesthetic, and narrative-based. In short, the church needs to cultivate a liturgical argument against hegemony and for plurality.

Are churches capable of developing multisensory counter-liturgies? Much to Smith's consternation, his own Reformed churches have focused their energy almost exclusively on the development of the Christian mind. Appropriating the modernistic anthropologies of the world, the church focuses its liturgical energy on didactic information-oriented sermons. This is ironic, Smith wryly observes. After all, Reformed theologians like Abraham Kuyper have consistently praised the complexity and multifaceted nature of the hu-

---

38. Hafid Bouazza, "Islam in Europe," in *Dromen van Europa*, ed. Bas Heijne (Amsterdam: Bert Bakker, 2004), 59.

man person. Why is it, Smith asks, that when they lead worship these same theologians treat their people like nothing more than "brains-on-a-stick"?[39]

Here we arrive at our first conclusion: if churches are going to counter the destructive practices and liturgies of Mecca and Amsterdam, their worship services will need to engage more than their people's brains. Churches will need to explore the sonic, aesthetic, kinesthetic power of song and story, image and taste, smell and design, posture and embrace. In the next section I explore a variety of multisensory worship practices through which disciples can be formed for life amidst Mecca and Amsterdam.

Mediums of Liturgical Formation

While liturgical formation is sometimes immediate and direct (sermonic exhortation), more often than not worship's formative work is slow, subtle, and complex. John Witvliet argues that "worship forms us not only through the explicit messages that are communicated, but also in a quiet, more subterranean way, through the bodily gestures, sensory perceptions, and language it invites us into" ("Cumulative Power of Transformation," 48–49). The worship experience

> exposes us to and gives us practice in ways of talking, seeing, and gesturing that provide the categories in which we think, talk, and gesture about our faith. It helps us experience emotions that may be new to us, emotions we would never have felt or cultivated on our own. It not only speaks about virtue but also forms us to become virtuous over time. Worship is a powerfully forming and transforming force. . . . [P]articipation [in it] quietly but powerfully sculpts our souls. ("Cumulative Power of Transformation," 52)

One way in which worship forms its practitioners is through the visual medium. One's mind immediately turns, of course, to gazing at stained glass windows, murals, and grand paintings and reflecting on their visual messages. It is obviously clear how these images can powerfully communicate Christ's justice, hospitality, and grace. That said, artwork is not the only form of visual communication that churches have at their disposal.

---

39. James K. A. Smith, "Teaching a Calvinist to Dance," *Christianity Today* 52, no. 5 (2008): 42.

Consider, for example, the simple act of watching as people of different ages, races, abilities, cultures, callings, and classes file into a sanctuary and sit together as one. This powerful image can itself serve as a potent illustration of what it means to be a part of a diverse community. No one amidst this motley collection of disparate members will ever fully understand how they all came together. None of them can claim to understand the community's complete origin, essence, and end. They sit together acknowledging a common need for one another and for Christ. Gathered together, Witvliet argues, worshippers "are called to be aware not only of God's presence, but of each other."[40] The very sight of these people is a visual reminder that worship is not a personal spiritual experience for the autonomous individual; it is a "first-person-plural activity." Diverse and divided as we are, we stand as one.

James K. A. Smith adds that as the worshipper looks across the sanctuary he receives a visual reminder that many of his neighbors are not there. Their physical absence reminds him of a deep divide that exists within his city.[41] His city is not "one" in a very important sense. The separateness of this worship gathering visually communicates to him the deep abyss that exists between the church and the world. Smith notes that

> There is a certain hint of scandal here, of a reality that cuts against the grain of our late-modern liberal sensibilities: for as we are making our way to worship, not everyone is coming. . . . [T]he neighbors and strangers we pass on the way remind us that God's peculiar people is also a *chosen* people.[42]

However much Christians might yearn for unity with their Muslim and liberal neighbors, the visual grappling with their physical separation on Sunday morning reminds them that a deep unity will not come until Christ's return.

Continuing our exploration of the visual, Nicholas Wolterstorff argues that the architectural design of a worship space can impact how the worshipper visualizes her relationship to God, other worshippers, and the world outside.[43]

---

40. John Witvliet, "Teaching Worship as a Christian Practice," in *For Life Abundant: Practical Theology, Theological Education, and Christian Ministry*, ed. Dorothy C. Bass and Craig Dykstra (Grand Rapids: Eerdmans, 2008), 121.

41. Smith, *Desiring the Kingdom*, 161.

42. Smith, *Desiring the Kingdom*, 161.

43. See Wolterstorff, "Thinking about Church Architecture," in *Hearing the Call*, 245–53 and "The Theological Significance of Going to Church and Leaving and the Architectural Expression of That Significance," in *Hearing the Call*, 228–40.

A worship space can make her feel isolated or connected, independent or dependent, complete or incomplete, small or big. Different spaces can make her feel like a part of an audience, a class, a family, or an informal gathering of friends. The building's very structure and design can train her to relate to the outside world primarily as a stranger, a ruler, a servant, or a soldier.

Abraham Kuyper himself recognized the power of the visual in the sanctuary when he made a sustained argument concerning the placement, size, and design of the communion table. Kuyper insisted that, if possible, the table should allow worshippers to physically encircle the table and share the meal together. He claimed that worshippers needed to look across the table with their eyes and physically see a wide range of individuals sharing in the body and blood of Christ with them. For, he argued, it "is not until individual believers gather together around one table and eat of the same bread and drink from the same cup that they enjoy the unity of the mystical body of the Lord."[44]

While John Calvin is commonly described as being anti-visual when it comes to the sanctuary, Witvliet insists that this label has largely been misapplied. To make his case, he cites Calvin's arguments that the display of bread and wine are a visual gift from God that "direct and almost lead men by the hand to Christ . . . [and] show him forth to be known" (*Worship Seeking Understanding*, 141). These images, Calvin insists, win the viewers' "attention by their propriety, arouse the mind by their luster, and by their lively similitude so represent what is said that it enters more effectively into the heart" (*Worship Seeking Understanding*, 133).

Applying the power of the visual to the conflict between Mecca and Amsterdam, consider the formative power of the following images. Imagine the sight of a Middle Eastern child being taken forward for baptism. Imagine a largely white congregation standing as one, pledging allegiance to that child. Imagine photos of Muslim immigrants flashing across a screen as a congregation confesses their sins of fear and anger against their neighbors. Imagine a colorful quilt being held before a congregation while a women's group describes their cooperative sewing work with Muslim women in the neighborhood. Imagine the sight of Christians from Africa, Asia, Europe, and the Americas sitting around a common table sharing a single cup. Imagine the flags of multiple nations being paraded through the sanctuary as the congregation prays for Christ's peace.

Beyond the power of the visual, Witvliet and Smith also explore the role that bodily movements and postures can play in the training of the heart and mind. Through disciplining "our bodies to move in certain ways," Witvliet ar-

44. Kuyper, *Our Worship*, 269.

gues, "worship is forming in us deep bodily patterns that shape our souls, our relationships, and our patterns of thinking, feeling, and being" ("Cumulative Power of Transformation," 45).

> Some churches form us to raise our hands as an act of exuberance. Others teach us to kneel as an act of humility. Others teach us to reach out beyond our comfort zones to greet strangers in our midst. . . . What is especially significant to see is that those bodily patterns form in us new capacities for attentiveness, humility, courage, and gratitude. ("Cumulative Power of Transformation," 45)

> [In] every tradition, worship forms our bodies in certain gestures, postures, and movements. In so doing, worship traditions inscribe on our bodies certain modes of relating to God and to each other. We are formed with certain capacities and certain deficiencies that, in part, define how we perceive God, how we express our faith, and how we live out our calling. ("Cumulative Power of Transformation," 46)

Smith adds that, from the beginnings of Christian worship, the church knew that bodily

> gestures are not just something we do but they also do something to us—that kneeling for confession is a kind of cosmological act that inscribes in us a comportment to God and neighbor, a way of being-in-the-world that sinks into our bones and becomes sedimented into the core of our being through the crackle of our old knees. The postures of our bodies spill out beyond the sanctuary and become postures of existential comportment to the world.[45]

Imagine a seated congregation confessing their failure to show hospitality to Muslims—now imagine that they are on their knees. Imagine a congregation praying for the ethnic tensions in their neighborhood—now imagine that they are physically walking the streets while they pray. Imagine a pastor encouraging a congregation to love their Muslim neighbors—now imagine congregation members holding hands in a physical display of their common commitment, support, and solidarity. Employing the body is particularly uncomfortable for many Western Christians for the simple reason that their dis-

---

45. Smith, *Imagining the Kingdom*, 167.

embodied ideas about faith demand less than their embodied actions of faith. The anxious discomfort a Westerner feels when she commits her whole body to a liturgical act tells us something about that action's power and implications.

Music is a powerful sonic medium for liturgical formation. From its very beginnings, the church has approached God with melodies of praise, confession, lament, and hope. Witvliet explains that singing has a unique kinesthetic ability to inscribe into the heart, mind, and body "a new way of thinking, praying, or even living" (*Worship Seeking Understanding*, 276). In moments of mental confusion, emotional distress, and bodily anxiety "when words fail us," when we have no response to give, "music gives us something to say. It gives us a way of expressing our lament and our hope."[46] Witvliet argues that through years of singing, a worshipper stores up a rich spiritual and emotional vocabulary that will help her express praise in times of joy, confession in times of guilt, and lament in times of frustration. For as we sing, Witvliet concludes, we rehearse the songs we will desperately need to "hum to ourselves in moments of deep despair" (*Worship Seeking Understanding*, 276).

Worshippers walking amidst Mecca and Amsterdam will need to have these songs written deeply into their hearts and bodies. They will experience real moments of frustration and fear, confusion and despair. The church's melodies of lament, confession, prayer, and praise will need to be at the ready. If they are not, the worshippers will be empty-handed when controversies arise and skyscrapers fall.

The final medium of formation we will discuss is that of language and metaphor. Witvliet makes the case that the linguistic imagery found within Scripture, sermon, song, and psalm can act as a powerful medium of liturgical formation.

> As with every other cultural experience, participation in communal worship gives us a language to say things that we would not have come up with on our own. We know that a breathtaking sunset evokes a response, but it is the church that teaches us to say, "Praise God from whom all blessings flow." We cannot sleep after watching yet another dismal news documentary about hunger, and it is the church that teaches us to say, "Lord, have mercy." The church gives us practice in saying things that form in us new capacities for relating to God and to each other. ("Cumulative Power of Transformation," 47)

46. John Witvliet, "We Are What We Sing: Searching for a Balanced Diet," *Reformed Worship*, June (2001).

[Language theorists] suggest that our language not only reflects our thoughts but also shapes our thoughts. Language creates new modes of relating to other people. It evokes and awakens new emotions—emotions we might not have had if we were not given the words to name them and form them in us. To use a phrase from Thomas G. Long, worship is "God's language school." . . . [W]e live most faithfully when we let those speech patterns, and the deeper relational capacities they inform, become our daily, spontaneous responses to God, the world, and those around us. ("Cumulative Power of Transformation," 48)

Through these metaphors, images, bodily gestures, songs, and stories, Christian worship can induct its participants into a new way of seeing and living in the world. The God of the incarnation meets fleshly disciples through poured wine and broken bread, bent knees and raised hands, bright bells and haunting chords, stone crosses and wooden tables.

Liturgical Training for Death

[D]etailed visions of what constitutes a healthy public order will not accomplish the whole job for us. We need those very personal resources for living out our lives in the midst of the tragedy of existence.

RICHARD MOUW[47]

At crucial moments of choice, most of the business of choosing is already over.

IRIS MURDOCH[48]

On November 2, 2004, Theo van Gogh was brutally murdered on the streets of Amsterdam by Mohammed Bouyeri. Soon after, sweeping through the city and the nation was a pervasive and palpable sense of sadness and confusion, fear and rage. Soon enough, mosques and churches alike were under attack. Both Amsterdam and New York were attacked on a Tuesday. Five days later, Christians (and many non-Christians) would gather for worship. Some gath-

---

47. Richard Mouw, "Public Discipleship and Spiritual Formation," *Catalyst* 38, no. 2 (2012).

48. Iris Murdoch, *The Sovereignty of Good* (New York: Schoeken Books, 1971), 37.

ered looking for hope and comfort, others to mourn and lament, still others to demanded God's swift revenge. In these moments of crisis, wise and thoughtful liturgical planning is critical. People need to have liturgical space to bring the questions, anger, and sadness to God.

That said, this section will argue that the true power of worship lies in its ability to prepare worshippers for tragedies and crisis before they come. While worship can be reactive, it works better when it is understood as preparatory. When one considers how slowly worship works, one begins to realize that five days after an attack is, in many ways, years too late.

To illustrate my point, imagine that after the attack in New York one hundred American churches gathered to sing this hymn entitled, "O God of Every Nation."[49]

> O God of every nation,
> of every race and land,
> redeem the whole creation
> with your almighty hand;
> where hate and fear divide us
> and bitter threats are hurled,
> in love and mercy guide us
> and heal our strife-torn world.
>
> From search for wealth and power
> and scorn of truth and right,
> from trust in bombs that shower
> destruction through the night,
> from pride of race and nation
> and blindness to your way,
> deliver every nation,
> eternal God, we pray!
>
> Lord, strengthen all who labor
> that we may find release
> from fear of rattling saber,
> from dread of war's increase;

49. Words: William Watkins Reid Jr., "O God of Every Nation," in *Worship and Rejoice* (Holland, MI: Hope Publishing, 2001), no. 626. © 1958, Ren. 1986 The Hymn Society (Admin. Hope Publishing Company, Carol Stream, IL 60188). All rights reserved. Used by permission.

when hope and courage falter,
your still small voice be heard;
with faith that none can alter,
your servants undergird.

Keep bright in us the vision
of days when war shall cease,
when hatred and division
give way to love and peace,
till dawns the morning glorious
when truth and justice reign
and Christ shall rule victorious
o'er all the world's domain.

Now, imagine that fifty of the one hundred churches singing the hymn had never sung this song—or anything like it—ever before. Imagine that the other fifty churches had been singing songs like this for decades. It is not difficult to imagine that the two groups would respond differently to the song. The group of churches who have never sung about political issues of war, peace, forgiveness, race, and so on would find the song confusing and even potentially frustrating. The second group of churches, who had been singing lyrics like these for years, would find these lines to be a welcome comfort, reminder, and challenge. Having ingested these rhythms, words, and commands over decades, these churches made these songs a part of who they were. In short, they were prepared.

A worshipper's response to falling skyscrapers and murdered countrymen will be determined much more by the three thousand songs he sang before the trauma than the three songs he sings after. John Witvliet therefore encourages worship leaders to

> Plan and lead the liturgy in your community as if your life and death depended on it. The services you plan and lead have by the Spirit's power, the ability to form in people the kind of realism, hope, and solidarity necessary to approach death well. . . . No saccharine substitute will suffice. (*Worship Seeking Understanding*, 300)

Training in Humility

Earlier in this chapter, I stated that the philosopher William Connolly asserts that a pluralistic society requires citizens who are capable of humbly engaging a diverse nation's complexity, mystery, and contingency. These citizens need a sense of modesty about their own knowledge, power, and self. They need to be able to recognize "how a slight twist here or there could have turned [their] experience in a different direction" (*Pluralism*, 165). They need to be able to recoil "back modestly upon the self-certainty of [their] own judgment" (*Pluralism*, 168). Connolly hopes that aesthetic experiences like going to a movie theater might instill this sense of modesty.

Modesty is a nice word. But Christians have historically used heavier words to describe what they wrestle with during periods of self-examination. Christian descriptions of the self include weighty words like blind, broken, depraved, evil, weak, selfish, and feeble. The Christian virtue of humility goes beyond Connolly's sense of modesty. Christian pluralists confess that they are not simply contingent—they are bent, broken, and deformed.

Good worship reminds pluralists every week that they stand in need of exterior transformation, restoration, and completion. While this weekly reminder of one's brokenness and finitude can be achieved through many liturgical mediums, this section examines how it is practiced through three acts of prayer—prayers for illumination, of confession, and of intercession.

The prayer for illumination invites the Holy Spirit to guide the interpretation of Scripture during worship. Here, the pastor and congregation collectively declare their cognitive inability to fully grasp the Scriptures on their own. They admit that Scripture is not something they create, command, or control. Instead, it is a gift they can only receive. In this prayer they collectively admit that they interpret Scripture "through a glass darkly." They collectively declare that they are not enlightened—that they need the light of another. In this simple prayer, Smith declares, we the worshippers "are training ourselves in a stance of reception and dependence, of epistemic humility. This position recognizes that in order to see things for what they really are . . . we are dependent on a teacher outside of ourselves (1 John 2:27)."[50]

If the prayer for illumination trains worshippers in epistemic humility, the prayer of confession trains them in moral humility. Here they engage in a weekly rehearsal of their individual and corporate failures. They are asked to consider and admit to their own hypocrisy, selfishness, aggression, and

50. Smith, *Desiring the Kingdom*, 194.

laziness. This rehearsal can establish in a congregation a sense that they are united by their moral failures, not their moral excellence. They have gathered in hope of receiving divine grace, not divine justice.

Mouw argues that this rather jarring and uncomfortable moment of confession is critical in the cultivation of moral and civic humility.

> The formation of positive moral character does not always proceed smoothly, because we are sinners who are prone to self-deception. The process must include transforming moments when we are forced to look directly at our own depravity. Often, we need to be shocked into an awareness of the motives that really shape our thoughts and actions and to respond to these revelations by pleading for the mercy that will allow us to repair our ways. All of this must happen in contexts where the basic issues of sin and grace are openly displayed in the worshipping life of a Christian community. And unless that community explicitly attends to the need to be morally formed—better yet, *transformed*—for our lives as citizens, little good can be expected of Christian involvement in the crucial issues of public life.[51]

As a species, human beings are capable of remarkable feats of moral self-deception. In light of this, the church has historically prescribed a weekly return to the prayer of confession as a critical resource in the fight for humility.

The final prayer is not concerned with reminding the worshipper of her own epistemic or moral limits. In fact, it is not concerned with her at all. In the intercessory prayer worshippers are directed to pray—not for themselves—but for others. Self-forgetfulness is a central element in any intercessory prayer. Here, the healthy pray for the sick and the sick for the healthy, the black worshipper prays for the white, and the white worshipper for the black. Men pray for women, and women for men. Finally, as one body, the congregation prays for those who are not present. They pray for neighbors and nations, friends and enemies. Smith explains that "in intercessory prayer, we are called outside of ourselves. . . . [We pray] for our neighborhoods; for municipal and government leaders; for the poor and those in prison; for those suffering persecution, exploitation, or the effects of natural disasters; even for our enemies."[52] Abraham Kuyper adds that the practice of intercessory prayer was prescribed by Christ himself. For when Jesus saw that rich and poor "had lost their unity" as brothers

---

51. Richard Mouw, "A Spirituality for Public Life," *Theology Today* 61 (2005), 482.
52. Smith, *Desiring the Kingdom*, 193-94.

and sisters, he commanded that they pray the same prayer to together. For "in every Lord's Prayer . . . the poor prays *for the rich* that God may give him his bread, and the rich prays it *for the poor*. Nowhere is there an *I* or *my* but always *we* and *us*."[53] In the intercessory prayer the worshippers practice taking on the hopes and fears, needs and feelings of others. While their efforts are clumsy and imperfect, they practice placing the needs of others before their own.

These three prayers have the potential to decenter and humble the pluralists who pray them. According to Witvliet, these "prayers are not only acts of expression but also acts of 'alignment' or submission which challenge us as worshippers to speak words that we are still 'growing into.'"[54] "Left on our own, there are all sorts of things we would never choose to say to God."[55] These prayers remind worshippers in powerful and vivid ways of their own finitude, brokenness, and need for God's primary action in our lives and world. Richard Mouw (a Dutch Calvinist) closes his discussion of prayer and its public power with a reference from Henri Nouwen (a Dutch Catholic). Nouwen writes

> Prayer is the only real way to clean my heart and to create new space. I am discovering how important that inner space is. When it is there it seems that I can receive many concerns of others. . . . I can pray for many others and feel a very intimate relationship with them. There even seems to be room for the thousands of suffering people in prisons and in the deserts of North Africa. Sometimes I feel as if my heart expands from my parents traveling in Indonesia to my friends in Los Angeles and from the Chilean prisons to the parishes in Brooklyn. Now I know that it is not I who pray but the Spirit of God who prays in me. . . . He himself prays in me and touches the whole world with his love right here and now.[56]

As I emerge from my time with God, Nouwen remarks, the world's questions about whether or not prayer has any public relevance "seem dull and very unintelligent."[57]

---

53. Abraham Kuyper, *Christianity and the Class Struggle*, trans. Dirk Jellema (Grand Rapids: Piet Hein Publishers, 1950), 27 and n. 10.

54. John Witvliet, "Words to Grow Into: The Psalms as Formative Speech," in *Forgotten Songs: Reclaiming the Psalms for Christian Worship*, Ray Van Neste and C. Richard Wells, eds. (Nashville, TN: B&H Publishing, 2012), 8.

55. Witvliet, "Words to Grow Into," in *Forgotten Songs*, 9.

56. Henri J. M. Nouwen, *The Genesee Diary* (Garden City, NY: Doubleday, 1976), 7. Quoted in Richard Mouw, "A Spirituality for Public Life," 482.

57. Nouwen, *Genesee Diary*, 7.

Training in Lament and Hope

Gestures will be misunderstood, offense will be taken, vulnerability will be felt, hearts and even bodies will be broken—such is life amidst Mecca and Amsterdam. In the skirmishes between Islam and the West, Christian citizens will experience real anger and fear, real discomfort and confusion, not to mention real physical danger. To ignore this reality, to cover the real challenges of diversity with a thin veneer of political correctness not only deepens the wounds, but it heightens the inevitable backlash. The radical shift in Dutch political culture from the politically correct gag orders of the 1990s to the aggressive and cathartic nationalist outbursts in the 2000s is a perfect example of how destructive a regime of denial can be.

In globalizing cities like New York and Amsterdam, where difference is deep, close, and fast, citizens require spaces where they can give voice to their confusion, frustration, fear, and anger. In 2011, right-wing nationalists in the Netherlands, under leadership of Geert Wilders, created such a space for their real (and imagined) quarrels with Eastern European immigrants. They developed a website where citizens could post their complaints about immigrants who had annoyed or wronged them in some way.[58] While the deep human need for lamentation is clear, not all spaces of lament are created equal. Rather than releasing the emotional pressure of the people and leading to national reconciliation, Wilders's website only doubled the tension between natives and foreigners.

Within the sanctuary, Christian pluralists have at their disposal a wide array of liturgical resources for lamentation and petition. Biblical texts, songs, prayers, and rituals of lament are all available to them. These resources can provide powerful opportunities to express their raw experiences of anger, confusion, doubt, and lament on the underside of pluralism.

Take, for example, the Hebrew Psalms. The God of the Psalms is well versed in and fully capable of receiving the most extreme expressions of human rage, despair, and lament. According to Witvliet, this God wants people to bring their laments "right into the sanctuary." In the Psalms we experience "the value of direct discourse." Our pale subjunctives and indirect speech ("We would want to ask you why this might be happening") are transformed to bold

---

58. The website asks visitors, "Are you having trouble with a Central and Eastern European? Or did you lose your job because of a Pole, Bulgarian, Romanian or other Central and Eastern European? If so, we would like to hear about it. The Party for Freedom provides this website as platform to report your complaints. We will take these complaints to the Minister of Social Affairs and Employment." See http://www.meldpuntmiddenenoosteuropeanen.nl/.

and honest address ("How long, oh Lord? Will you forget me forever?") (*Worship Seeking Understanding*, 44). The direct and sometimes brutal honesty of the Psalms about the cruelties of life "comforts the bereaved and expresses solidarity with the wronged" (*Worship Seeking Understanding*, 44). The Psalmist repeatedly demonstrates that "questions and protestations are not illegitimate in the life of prayer." A pluralist's words to God can "feature question marks" and even "exclamation points" (*Worship Seeking Understanding*, 44). The powerful lyrics of the Psalms do not deny the pluralist's raw experiences of rage and anger, doubt and despair. The Psalmist himself regularly uses dramatic words like "enemy," "darkness," "pit," "blood," "repulsive," "valley," and "death." Compare, for a moment, the vivid imagery of the Psalmist to the politically correct niceties of the multiculturalist. Ask yourself which vocabulary is more capable of capturing the raw experience of life on the streets of Mecca and Amsterdam.

In reading and singing the Psalms together, worshippers can also be inducted into a new vocabulary of reconciliation. After expressing their anger and confusion, they can begin to find new patterns of hope. Walking through the Psalms, worshippers are not only honest about where they are, but they see where they need to go. In the words of Athanasius, the Psalms act

> like a picture, in which you see yourself portrayed and, seeing, may understand and consequently form yourself upon the pattern given. . . . [I]n the Psalter . . . you learn about yourself. You find depicted in it all the movements of your soul, all its changes, its ups and downs, its failures and recoveries. . . . [The Psalms are] given us to serve both as a reminder of our changes in condition and as a pattern and model for the amendment of our lives.[59]

Unlike Geert Wilders's website, the Psalms are not a nihilistic cry of rage into a bottomless Internet abyss. Instead of encouraging an endless cycle of anger and resentment, the Psalms move the worshipper into self-examination and transformation.

Wolterstorff argues that God is ready to listen to our suffering and anger because God actually experiences that suffering and anger with us. "Instead of explaining our suffering" to us, our "God shares it."[60] The God of the cross is "the God who suffers." Wolterstorff continues on with this fascinating re-

---

59. Quoted in Witvliet, *The Biblical Psalms in Christian Worship* (Grand Rapids: Eerdmans, 2007), 7-8.

60. Nicholas Wolterstorff, *Lament for a Son* (Grand Rapids: Eerdmans, 1987), 81.

flection: "It is said of God that no one can behold his face and live. I always thought this meant that no one could see his splendor and live. A friend said perhaps it meant that no one could see his sorrow and live." Then again, Wolterstorff wonders, "perhaps his sorrow is splendor."[61]

Those who follow a God of death and resurrection must cultivate liturgical spaces for both lament and praise, doubt and hope, anger and thanks. To ask "How long, oh Lord?" is not to deny God's power; it is to follow Christ's very own example. After all, Jesus himself cried out, "My God, my God, why have you forsaken me?" The laments of the Christian pluralist implicitly acknowledge the depth of Christ's death and the power of his resurrection. In this sense, Witvliet argues, Sunday worship has to be both "a weekly rehearsal of honest realism and heavenly hope." Worship must be a bifocal. It must act as a "lens through which to view a world that is rooted in Jesus' death *and* resurrection." Its songs, prayers, stories, and rituals must hold "the Christlike pattern of dying and rising before us . . . [training] us to be always dying and rising" (*Worship Seeking Understanding*, 299; emphasis mine). Christian pluralists who sing of both Christ's suffering and his resurrection are intimately aware of both deep hardship and deep hope. Worship does not deny the challenges of life; it does not attempt to cover up the reality of death. Worship is, however, "all about putting death in its place" (*Worship Seeking Understanding*, 299).

The Liturgical Deformation of Citizens

[B]ad liturgy eventually leads to bad ethics. You begin by singing some sappy, sentimental hymn, then you pray some pointless prayer, and the next thing you know you have murdered your best friend.[62]

I have listed a wide variety ways in which worship can form disciples for pluralism. However, the opposite is also a possibility. Worship can just as well form disciples against pluralism. Worship can become twisted and perverted in such a way that it actually promotes violence, hatred, and hegemony. Obviously, the most straightforward way in which this can happen is through blatant liturgical support for a hateful and hegemonic state or ideology. Sermons

---

61. Wolterstorff, *Lament for a Son*, 81.

62. Stanley Hauerwas, *The Truth about God: The Ten Commandments in Christian Life* (Nashville, TN: Abingdon Press, 1999), 89.

can speak exclusively about the goodness of insiders and the evils of outsiders. Songs can ask God to bless a single religion, culture, or nation. Prayers can be offered to aggressively take back the nation. James K. A. Smith explores the overt perversion of Christian worship for violent ends at great length in his recent work *Awaiting the King: Reforming Public Theology*.[63]

While blatant and overt calls for anti-Muslim violence and Western cultural uniformity are rare in American churches, there is a wide variety of more subtle ways in which worship can and does misdirect and deform Christian disciples. In the following section, I will briefly explore a few slow and subtle ways in which the liturgical deformation of citizens can occur.

Oversimplification is the first way in which worship can fall short of our stated ideal. When the rich complexity of worship is reduced to a single, monolithic ritual, emotion, theme, or medium, worship's rich and formative power can become deeply compromised. Witvliet argues that excellent worship leaders understand themselves to be "spiritual dieticians" responsible for providing a complex diet of diverse and healthy spiritual nourishment (*Worship Seeking Understanding*, 232). Just as the body cannot live on a single kind of food, so also the spirit cannot live solely on one aspect of worship.

Worship that is nothing but praise or lament, confession or petition, judgment or grace will be too narrow to respond to the complex life in a diverse city. The complexity of Mecca and Amsterdam demands a multifaceted worship life that engages a diversity of human emotions, issues, and realities. It must engage the life of the heart, the head, and the hand. It must engage personal, cultural, and political life. Worship cannot become reduced to a single theological theme, such as liberation, suffering, grace, or justice. Worship cannot become reduced to a single medium—the sermon or the sacrament, images or songs, raised hands or bowed heads.

The complex experience of life in a pluralistic society must be met with complex liturgies of joy and regret, thanks and frustration, encouragement and exhortation, lament and mystery. For all of the ups and downs of life, Wolterstorff argues, worshippers desperately require "trumpets, ashes, and tears—all three."[64] Simplistic worship will ultimately lead to simplistic pluralists.

While good worship will engage a complex range of emotions, there is one emotion that can have no place in the worship of a pluralist—sentimentality. Life in diverse cities will not be comfortable, smooth, or easy. Worship

---

63. James K. A. Smith, *Awaiting the King: Reforming Public Theology* (Grand Rapids: Baker, 2017).

64. Wolterstorff, "Trumpets, Ashes, and Tears," in *Hearing the Call*, 28.

must take the struggles and challenges of life amidst Mecca and Amsterdam seriously, but sentimental and kitschy worship cannot do this. Rather than engaging the hard questions and realities of life, sentimental worship covers them up with platitudes. Rather than providing a space for real lament, sentimental worship enforces a thin veneer of happiness. Rather than engaging the fullness of Scripture with all its rough edges, sentimental worship only selects uplifting messages of personal empowerment. Rather than introducing a God of fierce wrath against injustice and even fiercer love, sentimental worship introduces a god of niceness who resembles a kind but woefully out-of-touch grandfather. Such a god is deaf to the real cries and struggles of raw life amidst Mecca and Amsterdam.

John Witvliet worries that this liturgical "disease of sentimentality" can have a crippling effect on the formative power of worship. Returning to his food metaphor, Witvliet worries that "If we feed our souls a steady diet of musical candy," we will have "little spiritual protein to sustain us" during periods of real crisis.[65] The immediate presence of violence, danger, and fear amidst Mecca and Amsterdam cannot be painted over or denied with three happy songs. "No saccharine substitute will suffice," Witvliet warns (*Worship Seeking Understanding*, 300). A worship experience of "candy-coated happiness and bliss" can neither humble, convict, nor empower a citizen walking amidst Mecca and Amsterdam. Reducing the church to a spiritual sort of entertainment space with nothing but funny stories, colorful light shows, and motivational speeches will render the formative potential of worship impotent.

Finally, even if worship is thoughtfully designed and executed, formation can still fail. The spiritual food that is prepared will nourish a worshipper only if she actually sits down and eats. True formation requires more than presence; it requires participation. Worshippers must be an attentive, open, and active participants in worship ("Cumulative Power of Transformation," 53). Worshippers must understand the meaning of the practices they are engaging in. If they are not attentive, if they are not open, if they do not join the liturgical dance, the best worship in the world will fall on deaf ears, a hard heart, and a dull brain. The worshipper has a responsibility to open herself to worship's disruptive and formative power.

---

65. John Witvliet, "We Are What We Sing: Searching for a Balanced Diet," *Reformed Worship* 60 (2001).

Conclusion: Nourishing Christian Pluralists

Liturgical shortcomings can be found in every church and in every worship style. Filled with broken people, imperfect churches will always sing songs that bear the marks of the singers' own sinfulness. Will their shortcomings render their worship useless and inert? Without intervention, yes, it most certainly will.

Thankfully, Scripture ensures worshippers that when two or three are gathered in Christ's name his justice, hospitality, and grace will make itself present among them. As I have stated from the outset, the primary agent in worship is not the pluralist—it is God. Through the Holy Spirit's invasion into the sanctuary, the imperfect sermons, songs, and practices of disciples can become powerful avenues for spiritual and political nourishment. The liturgical formation of the pluralist is primarily the work of God—not the pluralist. Without an intimate encounter with Love himself, all the individuals, ideas, and institutions of Christian pluralism will be nothing more than "a resounding gong or clanging cymbal" (1 Cor. 13:1).

At the beginning of this chapter we asked a simple question: is there any meaningful political difference between the pragmatist's movie theater and the Christian's sanctuary? Is there is any difference between the formative effects of Christian worship and the formative effects of soccer games, concerts, movies, neighborhood cafes, city council meetings, and parades?

In the end, I suspect that the difference can be found in the following passage from the pragmatist Jeffrey Stout. Here he argues that the spirit of democracy will be self-actualized and self-nourished by the streams of solidarity located within the human spirit itself. These streams of democratic solidarity, Stout insists, "are in us and of us." We, the people, are responsible for nourishing ourselves "as we engage in our democratic practices."[66]

Those who enter the Christian sanctuary speak of a thirst they cannot quench, and they speak of a stream that they do not control. Raising Christ's cup, they drink from a spring that does not come from within but from without. Their stream flows as well, not with water, but with blood.

---

66. Stout, *Democracy and Tradition*, 308.

CHAPTER EIGHT

Pluralism and Action

[T]he smallness of the seed need not disturb us.

ABRAHAM KUYPER[1]

"What should I do?" "How should I respond?" "What is the answer?" These are predictable questions when one comes to the end of a book like this, and books like this typically end with a predictable answer—political activism and engagement. Here is where authors like me urge you to vote, protest, organize, legislate, and litigate. Here is where I urge Christian churches and organizations to call their politicians and sign declarations defending Muslim rights and dignity. While I certainly believe that such macro-level political activism is critical and necessary, this is not how I want to end this book.

Instead, I suggest that we think about a movement of pluralism, justice, and hospitality as something more than simply political activism—it is a way of life. I want to suggest that raising children, worshiping in church, going to work, volunteering in schools, taking in a refugee, inviting neighbors over for coffee can all be potent actions for pluralism. My desire here is not to demean the importance of overtly political action but to honor and raise up the thousands of small ways in which a healthy political culture can be protected and cultivated.

Abraham Kuyper himself believed that the ordinary and everyday life and work of common people were critical to the endurance of democracy. He consistently argued that a lasting culture of freedom depended on the humble

---

1. Abraham Kuyper, *Lectures on Calvinism* (Grand Rapids: Eerdmans, 1931), 195.

faithfulness and integrity of the *kleine luyden* (the little people). Constitutions would not last long if the everyday spirit of the people no longer desired or embodied their rights and freedoms in their daily lives. For Kuyper insisted that the "spirit of a nation and the spirit of its government . . . are not hermetically sealed. . . .They interpenetrate."[2]

Kuyper's chief political strategy was to urge common citizens to make "godliness" their "primary weapon in the struggle for independence."[3] For, he argued, if we hope to "undermine" tyranny, we must each work in our own everyday lives to establish "a solid foundation on which all national life can rest. To that end we can all work together, each in his own family, each of us in his own heart. For the national spirit does not descend from the air but arises from the spirit of the home."[4] According to Kuyper, even the smallest Dutch citizens and organizations needed to act as salt, light, and leaven in the struggle for independence. Parents and lawyers, teachers and journalists, writers and doctors, entrepreneurs and evangelists all contributed to the political culture, in their own ways. The future of democracy rested, not so much in the structures of the state, as in the small, ordinary acts of faithfulness of *de kleine luyden*.

That said, neither Abraham Kuyper nor his followers ever actually explained why or how the everyday lives of "little pluralists" were so important to democracy. As I mentioned in the second interlude, Kuyper largely focused his attention on macro-level political activism. The everyday micro-level encounters between different faith communities received little, if any, attention from Abraham Kuyper or those who followed in his line.

In this section's closing chapter I hope to remedy this oversight. Here I explore a simple question. What might the "micro-practices" of Christian pluralism and hospitality look like? I do this by recounting the actual stories of citizens modeling Christ's justice, hospitality, and grace amidst Mecca and Amsterdam. Active in the fields of health care, education, politics, the church, neighborhood, and home, they provide us with micro-theologies of Christian pluralism amidst the cultural tension.

Standing alone, their micro-practices appear insignificant, ineffective, and incomplete. Many of them don't seem bothered by the possibility that they are not effectively changing the world. When interviewed, many did not seem concerned at all with being effective on a national scale. None of them dreamed

2. Abraham Kuyper, *Our Program* (Bellingham, WA: Lexham Press, 2015), 40.

3. Abraham Kuyper, "Uniformity: The Curse of Modern Life," in *Abraham Kuyper: A Centennial Reader*, ed. James Bratt (Grand Rapids: Eerdmans, 1998), 43.

4. Kuyper, "Uniformity," 42.

of changing the Netherlands or converting all Muslims to Christianity. They simply believed that God had called them to follow Christ in a specific way alongside their Muslim neighbors.

This book does not have a single solution. The loose ends are not all tied up. That decision is intentional. The goal of this final chapter is not to provide a final conclusive answer to the many challenges of Mecca and Amsterdam. No one should attempt such a thing.

Instead, the goal of this final chapter is to illuminate a mosaic of Christian answers (notice the plural). These pluriform answers are being articulated in and through a variety of different careers and social spheres. Each of these answers is partial, incomplete, and imperfect. None of the people I interviewed faithfully reflect every aspect of Christ. Many of them have no idea what pluralism means or who Abraham Kuyper was. Many of them have never read about political philosophy or considered the contours of a pluralistic legal order. Being finite and fallen, these citizens have all experienced failure and disappointment. In fact, their humility made my interviews particularly difficult and sometimes frustrating. When I pressed them to explain why they were showing hospitality to their Muslim neighbors, most of them could do little more than shrug their shoulders at me, look at the ground, and say, "What else was I supposed to do? Jesus commanded me to love my Muslim neighbors." A number of them seemed to speak as if they had little choice in the matter—they had to show hospitality.

In sharing their stories I am not trying to romanticize these individuals as morally superior. Nor do I want my readers to mindlessly mimic their exact actions. Christian hospitality, justice, and grace must and will look different in different contexts. My hope, rather, is that through these stories readers might begin to cultivate their own redemptive imagination for their own unique lives and callings amidst this conflict. In this sense, what is required is not a single answer to Mecca and Amsterdam, but many smaller answers.

Sewing in the Abyss

Rotterdam is home to one of the largest Islamic populations in Europe. Some of Europe's fiercest debates over Islam take place in this city. White Rotterdammers complain that their city has been overrun with fundamentalism, unemployment, and crime. Many Muslim Rotterdammers complain of employment discrimination, media demonization, political marginalization, and religious bigotry. Trust is low and tensions are high.

In this urban fray a small group of conservative Christian women has decided to make its mark.[5] They do not protest. They do not run for office. They do not call for national dialogues, laws, or programs. They sew.

Every month, for more than a decade, these women have faithfully gathered in a heavily Muslim section of Rotterdam to stitch, knit, and talk. And every month they invite their Muslim neighbors to join them. As the Muslim and Christian women gather together, measuring and cutting, folding and seaming, they begin to talk. Working together on a new set of djellabas they discuss the weather, their work, their families, and anything else that comes to mind. Over piles of blankets, shirts, and pants, the religious and cultural barriers begin to crack and bonds begin to form. Ever so slowly, in fits and in starts, these women begin to see their own hopes, struggles, and humanity in the supposedly foreign women stitching across from them.

The Christian women begin to realize that Islam is not what they see on the news. The Muslim women begin to realize that Christianity is not what they see in the Rotterdam red-light district. They discover a mutual concern for morality, character, and family. They worry together about their children. They share mutual concerns about the deep secularity and the over-sexualization of women in the Netherlands. "We share a common frustration with Dutch culture," they report.

As the Muslim women share their stories of immigration, Christian listening turns to Christian empathy. The Christian women begin to hear how the Dutch have ignored, abused, and excluded their new neighbors. "We don't like that!" one of them announces to me. "We want to make them feel at home!" Another adds, "When you get to know them, you get to see that they are not that different from you and me. They are just as human as you and me. They like it when you visit them in their homes. They like to show us hospitality, too. They like to have us over for tea." Achieving what no government program could, this little sewing group is producing a rare social phenomenon in Dutch civil society—inter-ethnic, interfaith friendship and affection.

This sewing group was originally designed in the 1980s to serve as a group for interreligious dialogue, but the effort completely failed. In retrospect, the women report that theological dialogues and intellectual debates with complete strangers was not something either group of women was interested in.

5. Interviews by the author, Rotterdam, May 23, 2012. My thanks to Annemarie Krijger and Maarten de Vries for their guidance and cooperation. I also drew from Annemarie Krijgers' internal organizational report "*Gastvrijheid en betrokkenheid: Verslag van het vrouwenwerk in 'Het Kompas'*" provided October 12, 2012.

Sewing proved to be a brilliant kinesthetic way to break boundaries and build relationships. Dialogue would come later. Sewing provides a safe, simple, and engaging topic for women of different faiths and ethnicities to discuss. It keeps hands and minds busy during awkward silences. When a question is uncomfortable, or simply does not have an answer, the simple act of inquiring about a new color or pattern provides conversational relief. Moreover, some Muslim participants speak little or no Dutch. Sewing provides a way for them to encounter Christian women without being forced to give a long religious defense in a language they have not yet mastered.

When I asked why the Muslim women feel drawn to the club, I was told that they initially come "because they like to sew." However, the women say with a smile, it is the *gezelligheid* that keeps them coming back. *Gezelligheid* is the most beautiful word in the Dutch language. This is not up for debate. The Dutch are fond of declaring that English has no word for it—and they are right. The best approximation an English-speaker can make is that *gezelligheid* is a description of a communal sense of coziness, conviviality, trust, joy, and connection. *Gezelligheid* is exactly what these women have built together. As they sew in a stark and stale old building in inner city Rotterdam, their conversations and relationships fill the space with a warm sense of trust, connection, and community. Yes, "they come for the sewing and they stay for the *gezelligheid*."

When I finally asked the sewing group what their ultimate goal was, the Christian women stated unapologetically that their hope was to share the story of Jesus. "But," they hastened to add, "that is a very long road." It is not one that should be rushed or forced. "Only God saves people!" one of them declared to me. We need "to make them feel at home because a lot of them feel unhappy here in the Netherlands. They want to go home." Another adds that, "God alone sows the seeds of conversion in a person's soul. God alone makes the seeds of faith grow." We simply need "to remove the stones from their garden." The many stones of misunderstanding, mistrust, and enmity need to be rooted up through care and conversation. Sewing djellabas together, the women hope that God will sow seeds.

Academic Hospitality

I tell every student who comes to study theology at the Free University you are all welcome here whether you are Christian, Jewish, Muslim, liberal, Atheist, or something else. We will not ask you to hide, change, or apologize for your faith. However, in our program, you will have to learn about and listen to the beliefs of those around you. If you are not willing to do that you can go somewhere else.

MARTIEN BRINKMAN[6]

The Free University of Amsterdam was established in 1880 by Abraham Kuyper and his movement of Christian pluralists. Its founding mission was to educate young Christian leaders to serve in the churches, schools, and organizations of the new movement. The university was called "free" to indicate that within its walls, Christian scholars and students would be free to explore God's world without the interference of the liberal state or the Christian church.

Abraham Kuyper insisted that no professor (be he religious or secular) could pretend to be neutral. All professors would unavoidably allow their ideological commitments to influence their teaching and research. This, he argued, was the great and destructive myth of modern education. If the modern dream of academic objectivity was impossible, Kuyper insisted, a pluriformity of educational communities should be cultivated to embody and explore the plausibility of their own worldviews. In other words, Christian scholars required a free academic space to conduct their research in conversation with their own Christian commitments. In 1880, Kuyper promised that his *Vrije Universiteit* would be exactly that.[7]

That said, Kuyper's dream for a university dedicated to Christian scholarship and study would not last. While free from the church and state, the university would not be free from the culture. The cultural waves of secularization that swept over the Netherlands in the 1960s crashed into the university as well. Today the university no longer places Christianity at the center of its research or teaching.

While many Christians have greatly lamented this loss, they can take some pride in the fact that the university still bears witness to at least one of Kuyper's key principles—academic neutrality is a myth. The Free University's awareness that every student and every scholar will bring a particular worldview into his or her research is still alive and well.

This principle is clearly at work in the recent reforms of the school's theology department. While most religion departments are filled with so-called

6. Martien Brinkman, interview by the author, Amsterdam, September 6, 2011.
7. For a fine and comprehensive history of the Free University see Arie Van Deursen's *The Distinctive Character of the Free University in Amsterdam, 1880-2005: A Commemorative History* (Grand Rapids: Eerdmans, 2008).

neutral scholars of religion, the Free University has purposefully recruited scholars who consciously research and teach out of particular faith traditions. Today the Free University is actively recruiting Muslims to teach Islam, Christians to teach Christianity, Jews to teach Judaism, and so on. The department is by no means perfect, but, on the whole, this effort represents a unique and creative attempt to model what we might call academic pluralism—or better yet—academic hospitality.

Students from a wide variety of religious traditions are required to take courses with faculty and students who both do and do not share their own particular convictions. For example, a Pentecostal student will take a certain amount of courses in Pentecostalism from a Pentecostal professor. That same student will also be required to take courses on Islam, Catholicism, Calvinism, and so on with professors and students from those specific traditions. Students, therefore, are able to both develop their own faith and be challenged by other faiths as well. At no time are students asked to deny or ignore their faith in some sort of charade of neutral learning. Nor are students ever forced to use the tired, modern mantra that all faiths—however conflicting—are equally true. Students will, however, be required to honor other faiths by studying them carefully with academic attention, accuracy, and civility.

In 2005, as a result of its unique reputation for academic pluralism and hospitality, the Free University was awarded a grant from the Dutch government to begin the first accredited training program for imams in the Netherlands. The university hired a group of Muslim scholars and began to recruit students. I asked Martien Brinkman, a Christian theology professor and former chair of the department, why Muslim students preferred the Free University to other secular universities in the Netherlands. He explained that their university "respects religion's power and authority, it treats faith as something that is both alive and public, not dead and private." "While our Muslim students are required to study the Koran with intellectual and critical rigor, they are never asked to give up their conviction that its pages are sacred, true, or authoritative for their daily lives." The department "accepts Muslim students for who they are." He continued,

> Because we take faith seriously, students are not allowed to simply express their religious opinions and then walk away. They have to respect the texts and traditions they are studying and wrestle with them. We are a university, not a debating club. We are an academic community who reads carefully and reflects thoughtfully together. We take these subjects seriously.

Henk Vroom, a philosopher of religion at the Free University, explains that at the Free University we "do not treat 'religion' as one systematic whole of which Islam is merely a part."[8] "Islam," he explains, "must be allowed its own unique particularity." Brinkman concurs,

> Muslim students appreciate that we don't treat Islam as if it is the same as all the others. We *presuppose* a real difference and then we talk about it. Muslim students do not appreciate so-called neutral Dutch scholars explaining to them that their faith has a lot in common with other faiths. Such statements are often imperialistic. The neutral religion scholar is always the one who names what we all have in common.

Moreover, Brinkman adds, "My Muslim students prefer to be around students who take their own faith, whatever it is, seriously. I have seen Muslim students get angry when they hear Christian students apologizing for or dismissing biblical teachings which do not square with modernity (for example, the virgin birth)." I quickly asked him, "Why would Muslims care about a Christian's belief in the virgin birth?" "Because," Brinkman explained, "the Muslim students know what comes next. They know that soon enough, they will be asked to join Christians in apologizing for their own scriptures or beliefs that don't square with modernity." In other words, "My Muslims students feel safer around Christians willing to hold their ground against modernity."

Henk Vroom adds that interfaith education is becoming increasingly critical for religious leaders across Western Europe. He explains that religious leaders are routinely being forced to "explain their religion and develop their religion in exchange with others."[9] A pluralistic context requires a generation of religious leaders equipped with what Vroom calls a "tough theology." Cultivating such a theology will require

> an academic environment: a university setting in which Muslim scholars . . . not [neutral] Islamologists—study their own tradition and dialogue with people from other areas of expertise and other worldview traditions. I like religious studies, but it is not enough. Universities should study and teach theologies and train leaders of Buddhists, Hin-

8. Henk Vroom, interview by the author, Amsterdam, April 25, 2012.
9. Henk Vroom, "What Policies towards Islam?" Paper presented at the European Ideas Network and Centre for European Studies, Brussels, February 9, 2011.

dus, Humanists, Islam, churches: not in isolation but authentically in their tradition and in dialogue with one another.[10]

If Muslim leaders are going to sustain and develop Islam under multiple points of Western pressure, free academic spaces like the Free University will be crucial in that project. Vroom shows no interest in controlling the research of his Islamic colleagues. He does, however, want to cultivate an academic environment in which that research can be done in direct conversation with others.

In the 1970s and 1980s, the Free University (VU) theology department was dominated by liberal Protestant theologians, many of whom considered traditional religion to be an outdated relic of the past. Some doubted the existence of God altogether. Today, the VU's theology department is filled with a wide variety of believing theologians who take their specific traditions seriously. Today, the department is beginning to be filled with devout Evangelical, Pentecostal, Reformed, Jewish, Baptist, Mennonite, Catholic, and Muslim scholars who openly confess and critically explore their distinct faiths. Their creative and living approaches to theological analysis make the modernistic methods they replaced look like the true relics. No longer expected to hide their convictions or melt into a liberal whole, these scholars are now truly free to deepen and develop their own convictions in critical academic conversation with others. Abraham Kuyper should not be too upset.

A Training in Hospitality

During the liberal revolution of the 1960s and 1970s, many churches in the Netherlands abandoned Christian orthodoxy in an effort to chase liberal culture. One of the consequences of this action was the growing acceptance in these churches of the liberal mantra that all religions are equally valid and they all lead to the same God. The natural end of this development was the growing suspicion that evangelistic efforts toward Islam were not only unnecessary but that they were unethical as well.

In 1977, a small group of evangelical Christians took issue with this development. Together they established *Evangelie & Moslims*, a new organization with the goal of "*bouwen aan respect, met passie voor waarheid*" ("Building respect, with a passion for truth").[11] Like their liberal brothers and sisters,

10. Vroom, "What Policies towards Islam?"
11. Evangelie and Moslims' website can be found at this address http://www.evangelie

Evangelie & Moslims wanted to show respect and tolerance to their new Muslim neighbors. They wanted to build a relationship. The difference, in short, was the issue of difference. E&M insisted that a respectful relationship between Christianity and Islam did not require a denial of deep difference. Islam and Christianity were different. Respect and hospitality did not require an abolition of that difference—it required a civil discussion of those differences. The ultimate goal of E&M was, without apology, to share a different story about the origin, essence, and end of the world. They wanted to tell the story of Jesus. For them, nothing is more foundational to the faith than sharing that story. They could not, and would not, give that up.

While they are committed to evangelism, E&M shares the story of Jesus in a very different way from many American evangelicals. They do not hold large evangelism rallies. They do not sponsor large advertisements aimed at Islam on national television. They do not try to convert Muslims through forceful speeches or debates. They have no interest in asking the Dutch government to lure or force Muslims into their churches. They do not send out professional missionaries to Islamic neighborhoods. They do not offer social services in exchange for Bible studies.

Cees Rentier, E&M's director, explains to me that their first goal is to raise awareness in local churches about the Islamic faith and the lived experience of Muslims.[12] From there, E&M trains these churches to be civil and gracious in their interactions with their Muslim neighbors. Through courses, DVDs, sermons, articles, retreats, Sunday schools, mobile phone apps, and Twitter, *Evangelie & Moslims* will use any method available to equip Christians to lovingly engage with their Muslim neighbors. "We do not send missionaries," Rentier explains, "we send local churches—regular people." In this E&M seeks to constitute "a movement of Christians who want to build respectful relationships with Muslims as fellow citizens." "In word and in deed," they seek "to demonstrate that Jesus Christ is worthy to be worshipped and served as Savior and Lord."[13] E&M encourages Christians to consider "the example of Jesus," who met with those, not at the center of society, but on the margins.

Cees Rentier regularly invites his Muslim friends to help him lead training

---

-moslims.nl/. (The website was originally accessed on December 18, 2012.) For an updated document about the vision and work of the organization see Evangelie & Moslims, *Hoop om te delen met passie en respect: Visie op het omgaan met moslims vanuit de christelijke gemeente*, Amersfoort, 2013. This document can be accessed online at http://issuu.com/evangelie-mos lims/docs/visienota_evangelie-moslims_2013?e=7893994/259 5810.

12. Cees Rentier, interview by author, Amersfoort, March 21, 2012.

13. E&M website.

sessions for groups of Christians. In front of the class he engages his Muslim friends in an open, civil, and gracious dialogue. In doing this he hopes to demonstrate that Muslims can be engaged in ways that are not marked with either fear, apology, anger, or recrimination. "There is little need for us to spend time pointing out the dark sides of Islam," Rentier notes. "The government does that enough already. The task of the church is to share the love of Jesus." He continues,

> Rather than attack the anti-Islamic rhetoric of someone like Geert Wilders, I try to demonstrate an alternative way of speaking about and speaking with Muslims. I try to demonstrate that while there are differences between Christianity and Islam, we do not need to engage those differences with anger.

Rentier notes that while his initial goal was simply to give churches more information about Islam "my goal has now become giving Christians the right attitude about Islam. Teaching was easy," he says. "Changing attitudes is much more of a struggle." E&M seeks, in a variety of ways, to equip Dutch churches to become more hospitable to other ethnicities, cultures, and languages. Rentier adds that, as an organization,

> We try to help former Muslims who have come to Jesus. We help them to find a local church and support them. We visit them. Rather than help them start separate immigrant churches, we try to help them join and survive in Dutch churches. It is a blessing for those Dutch churches to add color and diversity. They need to learn that the global church is not ethnically homogenous. It should be a house of worship for all the nations.

When asked if certain styles of Christian worship had proved more attractive to Muslims, Rentier responded with a hearty "No." "What is really important is that there is a group of people in the church who really cares about other cultures and will treat the former Muslims carefully and thoughtfully. The style of music does not matter."

Speaking about the relationship between his work and his own Calvinism, Rentier said that,

> My Reformed theology gives me a patience and a peace about my work with Muslims. When I realize that God alone finds and saves the people

I talk to, I can rest in His providence. Islam is not my "project." I don't have a big strategy or goal with Muslims. My concern is to be faithful to Jesus and his story. God is in control of history. God is in control of the Netherlands. . . . I suppose Calvinism frees me from an optimistic belief that I will be a success. God meets Muslims. I am not above my Muslim neighbors, I am next to them.

While *Evangelie & Moslims* is clear about the deep differences between Christianity and Islam they also note that

Christians in the Netherlands have a lot in common with Muslims, especially compared to the empty secular culture around us. We both want to align our lives to God's commandments. We both share similar values such as respect for authority, for parents, and for creation. We both want the rhythm, direction, and vision of our lives to emerge out of our convictions. Cultural differences or social problems sometimes make it difficult to recognize these similarities. That said, in a country where religion is hardly allowed a public role at all, sometimes it feels as if our Muslim neighbors are our distant relatives.[14]

Evangelie & Moslims also lists a number of ways in which Dutch citizens are being challenged by their Muslim neighbors. They can no longer take their general Christian heritage for granted. They can no longer leave it unexamined. Islam challenges Dutch citizens to make a clear decision: Christianity, Islam, or secularism. E&M argues that this challenge can ultimately prove fruitful for the mission of the church in the Netherlands. The presence of devoted and outspoken young Muslims "challenge[s] us to justify our own faith."[15] The simple presence of Islam confronts moderate Christians with a series of blunt questions about the way they are living their lives. "Are you so devoted in your beliefs that you pray five times a day?" the website asks. "Would you fast every year for a month solid? These Muslims hold up a mirror to our faith and we Christians must dare to look at ourselves honestly. We cannot escape it."[16]

In his book, *Europa, Het Mekka van de Islam?* Rentier adds a few additional reasons why his fellow Christians should be thankful for the challenges that Islam brings and the questions it raises.

14. E&M website.
15. E&M website.
16. E&M website.

The clash between orthodox Islam and the secular West offers a new opportunity for Christians. . . . [T]he intellectual arrogance of liberal secular humanists in Europe is now being openly challenged. There now enters a realization that, if we are going to live together in peace, religious people can no longer be dismissed as backward fundamentalists—they have to take us seriously. This offers new opportunities for the gospel to be spoken aloud in public life.[17]

While the Dutch "often talk about postmodernism being the dominant intellectual current," Rentier insists that Islam's arrival has revealed that the Dutch are "at the very most, late-moderns."[18]

There is, in many cases, still the unspoken assumption that the Western rational man is the culmination of human development, he alone is able to comprehend every expression of culture and faith throughout the centuries. He alone is able to test and examine them according to his own criteria. This attitude is demeaning to Muslims and Christians alike.[19]

Finally, Rentier argues, the arrival of immigrants in the Netherlands has blessed the Dutch people by exposing them to the "richness and variety" of God's creation. For, in the first and last books of the Bible, God praises the diversity and multiplicity of cultures that flourish on his earth. For,

the diversity of people is willed by God and is not in itself a consequence of sin. Every culture, of course, has been touched by sin and the power of evil. That said, what one culture has lost in terms of values, knowledge and skills, the others have properly preserved and developed. [Dutch Christians] must therefore see their diverse society as an opportunity for enrichment. By meeting the other nations, we can receive and learn things that we have lost in our own history. It is, therefore, very unchristian to ask newcomers to fully adjust to our customs. Nor should we close our borders, because then the identity of our nation would not be challenged by others. To make one historical

---

17. Cees Rentier, *Europa, het Mekka van de Islam? Evangelisch perspectief op het samenleven met moslims* (Amsterdam: Buijten & Schipperheijn, 2007), 13.

18. Rentier, *Europa*, 43.

19. Rentier, *Europa*, 43.

period absolute is contrary to God's providence. God's involvement in our history is not aimed at the preservation of the [Dutch] past but the coming kingdom of God.[20]

The Micro-Politics of Food

Eating is very important, always eat.

Serge de Boer[21]

Only thirty-two percent of the people living in Amsterdam's *Nieuw-West* neighborhood are indigenous, white, Dutch citizens. The remaining sixty-eight percent have arrived from Africa, Asia, the Middle East, and the Caribbean. Half of the neighborhood adheres to some version of Islam. Like many urban neighborhoods in Europe, *Nieuw-West* struggles with higher rates of crime, violence, poverty, unemployment, poor schools, and interethnic tension than surrounding neighborhoods.

In the last twenty years, more than ten Catholic and Protestant churches in the neighborhood have closed their doors. *De Bron,* a very traditional Reformed church, was quickly on its way to joining them. Fearing the worst, the members of *De Bron* decided that something dramatic needed to be done. Concluding that their church was too old and set in its ways to effectively connect with their new neighbors, *De Bron* supported a group of energetic young Christians who wanted to invest in the neighborhood and plant a new multicultural church.

Newly graduated from the Free University, Serge de Boer and four other Christians moved into the neighborhood. They called their small gathering *Oase voor Nieuw-West* (Oasis for New West). *Oase* invited Cees Rentier and *Evangelie & Moslims* to come and teach them how to live and interact with their Muslim neighbors. De Boer recalls that they received three significant lessons from Rentier and E&M. First, they learned the importance of listening to Muslims' stories. Second, they learned the importance of finding ways to show them honor and respect. And third, they learned the importance of making space for Muslims to share their gifts and culture.

The members of *Oase* began visiting their neighbors and frequenting their

20. Rentier, *Europa,* 9.
21. Serge De Boer, interview by author, Amsterdam, April 3, 2012.

local public market. They would engage young immigrants in conversation and would invite them to come to *Oase* for dinner. They usually responded, "No." Discouraged, *Oase* soon made a critical discovery that would change their posture toward the community. Rather than offering to cook a meal for the people, Oase began to ask the people if they would be willing to cook for them. The response was fascinating. They discovered that

> When the people come to cook for *Oase* they are often cooking for a large group of their fellow neighbors. For them that is a real honor. They work hard to bring good food from their own culture and share it with others. God has given their culture something beautiful and the mealtime gives us all a chance to celebrate that. In every culture there are good and bad things but when you eat together you share in the good things that God has done in a person's culture.
>
> We have a woman here from the Caribbean who came to cook a meal for the community. She worked hard for six hours straight to prepare a traditional meal from her culture. She was so proud. When we cook and eat together, we not only learn about a person's culture— we taste it.

Reflecting on the critical shift that occurred, de Boer notes, "I don't think they liked being treated like just another client for Dutch people to care for. They don't want to be served by a community, they want to be a part of a community."

So far, *Oase* has invited cooks from the Antilles, Italy, India, Morocco, Indonesia, Iraq, Egypt, Surinam, Turkey, Senegal, the Dominican Republic, and more. "Share your food and your story" could very well serve as a motto for *Oase*. "When we eat together," Serge found, "we are much more relaxed, open, and willing to talk to those around us."

The people enjoyed cooking and eating together so much that the group began to eat together every week. Soon enough they moved the communal meal to Sundays and folded it into the worship service. Gradually, they moved from having a single cook at the meal to having a potluck-style meal in which every person contributes a unique dish from her or his culture to the common meal. "When you eat together," de Boer explains, "you are doing something you normally only do at home—we try to make people feel at home here. When Jesus is the host of the meal, all cultures can be welcome at the table."

The centerpiece of a Sunday in traditional Dutch churches is the sermon. For more modern churches, it is the praise songs. While sermons and songs are certainly important to *Oase*, their community has made the meal the center of their life.

Moreover, at the close of a typical church service in the Netherlands, members traditionally share a small cup of coffee, a cookie, and a brief chat before they disperse to their individual homes. Such a model of church does not appeal to the multicultural residents of *Nieuw-West*. Many come from cultures where eating together is a crucial element in community-building and peace-making. Many of them are estranged from their families. They are looking, quite simply, for a new one.

Oase is a weekly experiment in Christian hospitality and pluralism. The church is always trying new things. Sometimes they succeed and sometimes they fail. When something doesn't work, they try something else. They have hosted language courses for the neighborhood. They have helped new arrivals find everything from a job to a second-hand couch. They hold sports camps for children. They visit local mosques for tea and conversation. De Boer has sat and read portions of the Koran and the Bible with the local imams. They have tried gathering in culturally specific small groups during the week, while on Sundays they all come together for a multicultural worship service. Sunday worship sometimes includes songs in Dutch, English, Spanish, and Arabic. "We usually pronounce everything wrong," de Boer laughs, "but we try."

Healing: The Micro-Politics of Medicine

> My work in the clinic is just bits and pieces. Hopefully God will make it effective.
>
> Dr. Cornelie Scheeres

Joanne Smit and Dr. Cornelie Scheeres are both active members of *Oase*.[22] Smit loves eating with her neighbors. Compared to more traditional churches, which strike her as a little cool and distant, the intimate conversations over a meal are "refreshing" and "*gezellig*." "I like that you can make mistakes at *Oase*," she adds, "you can try things there, you can grow and learn." Scheeres has lived and worked in *Nieuw-West* for nearly two decades and was delighted

---

22. Dr. Cornelie Scheeres, interview by the author, Amsterdam, April 24, 2012; Joanne Smit, interview by the author, Amsterdam, May 22, 2012. Dr. Scheeres prefers to be called "Cornelie" and Joanne has asked me to alter her last name to "Smit" because of her missionary work in Middle Eastern countries.

to find a church that wanted to invest in the neighborhood. "I felt lonely for a long time here," she says, "I am so happy to find other Christians who want to serve as salt and light in the neighborhood."

Both of these women serve as medical professionals in dense urban neighborhoods that are heavily Islamic. Providing medical care to Muslims presents a number of unique challenges for medical professionals who are accustomed to caring for Dutch liberals. While it is certainly true that a body is a body and sickness is sickness, Muslim bodies bring with them a different belief system and set of cultural practices about life, death, and sickness. These deep differences demand a level of medical flexibility and sensitivity that can be challenging. For doctors and nurses used to dealing with a single paradigm of health and wellness, life and death, Muslim patients bring a host of new questions and issues.

Joanne works as a district nurse in *Amsterdam-Oost*. District nurses are responsible for visiting and providing basic medical care to patients in their homes. Joanne's day-to-day tasks vary widely. She is never entirely certain what she will find when she walks into a home. Some days she gives baths and injections. Some days she visits patients with dementia. She makes sure that people are healing properly from injuries, illnesses, and surgeries. And sometimes she is simply responsible for administering palliative care for those who are near the end of their lives.

Joanne believes that the home is an intimate space and the body is a sacred thing. Every time she enters a home, she says a prayer and asks that the Holy Spirit would guide her words and actions. No matter what, she says, "I enter knowing that Jesus is with me. I know that the only thing I can do is give the love He has given me. I know Jesus comes with me into their home." Joanne insists "that care, not evangelism, comes first. I do my best to care for them and love them like Jesus does. If there is an appropriate opening to talk about God, I will take it, but my first responsibility is to care for them and show them God's love."

Joanne tells the story of serving in the home of a 46-year-old Turkish man who was dying of cancer. It was clear that the end was near, but he was insistent on receiving more medical opinions and procedures. Joanne recalls that "it was hard for him to accept that he was going to die." He refused to hear her words of comfort. He refused to respond to her acts of care. "If one door is closed on me," Joanne explains, "I try to go around it and give love elsewhere in the home. His wife and children were obviously very sad to be losing their husband and father. I tried my best to provide them with care during that difficult time."

When asked about the meaning of hospitality, Joanne replies, "Well, most Muslims are very hospitable. So I can learn from them, actually! As I am a guest in their house, they are often hospitable toward me! They don't serve with Jesus in their hearts, but they often serve well!"

It was striking how often Joanne interrupted during the interview to declare, "they are human beings just like us!" "They get hurt and sick just like us." "They want to live and they are afraid to die. Just like us." In a culture where Muslims are so commonly described as the other, almost as if they are different species, Joanne was convinced that their common humanity was something that had to be declared loud and clear.

Dr. Cornelie Scheeres serves as a doctor in a small clinic in the multicultural neighborhood of *Osdorp*. As a young medical student in the 1980s, she became acquainted with Muslim immigrants living in Amsterdam. Upon her graduation, she volunteered for eight years at a hospital in Yemen. When she returned to Amsterdam in the 1990s, she found that her old neighborhood of *Osdorp* had completely changed. The immigrants had moved in and the Dutch had left.

Rather than retreat to the suburbs with her countrymen, Dr. Scheeres went to work in a local clinic serving her new neighbors. "It is not always so easy," Scheeres remembers. "Muslims in Amsterdam tend to be much more on guard than those I worked with in Yemen. They seem to be more defensive here in the Netherlands."

Many of the Muslim women she cares for experience depression. "They stay in their homes all day and are very overweight. When they talk about their troubles, I just try to ask them questions." Occasionally, Muslim women refuse care from her colleague, a male doctor.

Many of her patients are engaged in unhealthy and dangerous lifestyles. Cornelie expresses periodic frustration and sadness with their unwillingness to change their habits. Like Joanne, Cornelie has also struggled with the common Islamic desire to live as long as possible, no matter the cost to the patient, the family, or the state. "It is not easy to talk to them about death," she says. "Living longer is so important to them."

While her Muslim patients present many unique challenges, Cornelie also expresses great appreciation for their presence. She appreciates their more communal approach to periods of sickness and death. "When one of them has died," she says, family members and friends "will just come and sit with those who are grieving. They won't say anything. They will just sit there! I think that is very beautiful." Cornelie recalls that, "My Dutch patients will not have many visitors when they are sick or dying. We Dutch don't know what to say, so we stay away. Of course," she adds, "when an entire Muslim family enters a hospitable room that can be difficult for the hospital staff to manage. But all the same," she says, "I think it is a nice difference from the Dutch."

Cornelie explains that she "mostly tries to be a Christian witness without words. I try to simply encourage them to talk about their experiences, and troubles. I ask them if their faith is helping them." Furthermore, she notes,

> I try to make Christ's approach to healing a model for my own work with Muslim patients. Christ treated so many people with an eye for their uniqueness. Jesus did not treat people all the same. There is so much more that I need to learn about him. I want to look at the way Jesus treats people so that I can do the same.

Through this work,

> I have come to learn that we white Europeans are not the only thing. I have learned about God's love for the variety of people that God has created. I have learned that there are many good and beautiful things in other cultures. Even if I don't understand them all the time, I know that God loves them and that I need to love them.
>
> Having Muslims here has challenged Christians like myself to not be so shy about our faith. I have seen Muslims stand up for their faith in public, many of them very young. They say, "This is our belief and we will stand for it." I tend to be shy. Their courage has encouraged me to speak about my own faith a little bit more.

The Micro-Politics of Coffee

Sint-Joriskerk is one of the most traditional Reformed churches in Amersfoort. The congregation sings only Psalms, and they do it in the oldest style possible. The preachers use words that no one uses today. It is, on the whole, a terribly boring service. However, in *Sint-Joriskerk* there is a small group of Christians who are very faithful to Muslims and other asylum-seekers living in Amersfoort. They show them hospitality and invite them into their homes regularly. Some of the immigrants are even being baptized. You should go talk to them.

ANONYMOUS AMERSFOORT RESIDENT

> I think that Muslim immigration has been God's joke on the Dutch people—and on the Dutch church.
>
> RITA HUNINK, *Sint-Joriskerk* member

Islam was not a question *Sint-Joriskerk* was ever looking to answer. That was, of course, until the Islamic question came right up and knocked on the church's front door. A snow-white community of conservative Calvinists, *Sint-Joriskerk* was not sure what do when Shawky Hafez, a drug-addicted Muslim from Egypt, rapped on their door and announced, "I want to know about Jesus. Can you help me?"

In response, Rita and Gert Hunink, along with a few other church members, began inviting Shawky into their homes for coffee.[23] As his visits became more regular, Shawky and the small group of Calvinists grew closer. The Hunink family walked alongside Shawky as he worked through numerous challenges with addiction, unemployment, housing, and faith.

Soon after Shawky's arrival, a couple more asylum-seekers joined their little group. Every week, Jonathan from Yemen and Ishmael from Somalia[24] would join Shawky in the Huninks' home to play games and enjoy cake, coffee, and conversation. They would discuss the weather, the eccentricities of Dutch culture, the challenges of immigration, and the love of Jesus. Their numbers continued to grow.

Each new arrival brought with them a new set of challenges, questions, and blessings. As the group grew and the conversations deepened, things became more complicated for the Hunink family, not less. Jonathan could not return to Yemen because of the threat of a Fatwa over his conversion to Christianity. Jonathan's son is currently missing in Yemen and is feared dead. Meanwhile, Ishmael was in need of a place to stay and has now lived in the homes of two different church families. "We also had a young man from Eritrea come to our home," Rita recalls. "He had been a child soldier back home and was terribly traumatized from the experience. As a result, he had a terrible alcohol problem." Gert adds, "All we do" with these difficult stories "is try to listen, try to discern God's will, and try to be obedient. Sometimes this obedience brings us sorrows, but mostly it enriches our lives."

Sundays have a set rhythm for traditional churches like *Sint-Joriskerk*.

---

23. Rita and Gert Hunink, interview by the author, Amersfoort, April 26, 2012. A second interview took place on May 6, 2012. This interview included Jonathan and Ishmael, as well as Shawky.

24. Their names have been changed for security concerns.

Families go to church in the morning, they disperse to their individual homes, and in the evening they return to church for an additional service. Because of this rhythm, Sunday afternoons were always a sacred family time for the Hunink household. However, when the family discovered that many immigrants went home every Sunday morning to a cold and sterile asylum center, they realized that their definition of family needed to expand.

While opening one's home to strangers may be a common practice in some cultures, it is very rare in the Netherlands. Living in a cramped country, Hollanders treasure the sacred privacy of their homes. Shawky recalls, "I lived in the Netherlands for eighteen years before I was invited into a Dutch home—the Huninks were the first to open their door."

Through this experience, Rita began to recognize that immigrants coming to *Sint-Joriskerk* were not looking for a good sermon, exciting music, or even financial help—they were looking for a home, for a family. They didn't want a visit from another government worker; they wanted a relationship with a brother or sister.

Word of the strange hospitality of *Sint-Joriskerk* quickly spread through the asylum center and the group soon outgrew the Hunink home. The asylum-seekers spilled into more church homes, and more and more members of the church began to open their doors. As the little group continued to grow, the church decided to begin a special weekly gathering to share with their new guests. They called their group Mosaic (Gert explains, "We chose the name because we want our members to retain their culture; we are not a melting-pot church"). Mosaic meets every Wednesday in a church building to play games, talk, and welcome new immigrants and asylum-seekers to the Amersfoort area. "It is not immediately about evangelism," Gert insists, "but when people ask us why we do these things, we simply tell them that we have experienced God's love and hospitality and we want to share that with others. Echoing the sewing group of Rotterdam, Gert explains, "Some come for the food, some for the gospel, and others for *gezelligheid*. We don't tell them to go to church; we are just interested in them and their lives." Reflecting on how the whole effort began, Gert shrugs his shoulders and says, "It just grew out of the ground."

Sint-Joriskerk's new-found openness to immigrants has not led to the destruction of the church's high doctrinal standards or its liturgical forms. If anything, it has reminded the church of what it means to be a Calvinistic community. When Shawky Hawfez announced that he wanted to be baptized, he was told that he would first need to take the proper classes and answer a number of questions about the content and sincerity of his faith. Shawky took the (very long) process seriously and, with the help of Rita, Gert, and other church members, he soon became a member of *Sint-Joriskerk*, participating in the sacraments of baptism and communion. *Sint-Joriskerk* and Shawky were both honored and renewed through the very old, traditional process.

All, of course, is not roses. A few members of *Sint-Joriskerk* remain very critical of Islam, and some are less than thrilled with the new immigrants in their congregation. Some complain that immigrants arrive late to worship. Others don't like hearing the noise of the new English and Arabic translations going on during Dutch sermons.

That said, the critics' numbers are dwindling, and many others report that they have come to appreciate the new arrivals. Some members argue that their children need to learn about the diversity of the global church. They need to see that the church is not an old, dead, white institution. They need to see that it is a global and relevant community.

Still others have found a great benefit in having non-Western perspectives present in their Bible study groups. Middle Eastern members, they argue, better understand the cultural context of the biblical stories. The Bible is full of refugees, exiles, immigrants, and new converts. "When they join us," Gert argues, "we can read these stories with new eyes."

Finally, the hospitality of *Sint-Joriskerk* has, not surprisingly, spilled into the real lives of the overtly political. Gert Hunink currently serves on the Amersfoort city council. He is an active leader in the *ChristenUnie* (Christian Union). As a national political party, the *ChristenUnie* is being pulled in multiple directions on the issue of Islamic immigration. In the past few years, some of their constituents have left their party in favor of more right-wing, anti-Islamic parties. As a result, the *ChristenUnie* has felt an increasing pressure to take a more aggressive stance toward Islam.

Gert Hunnink insists that fear is not an acceptable guide for Christian political action. Being in Christ, disciples have no right to fear Islam. "The only thing we *can* be afraid of is a weak church that does not faithfully reflect our savior's love and hospitality," says Gert. Furthermore, he argues, "Muslims coming to the Netherlands should never have to fear Christian oppression. If they are going to fear anything, Muslims should fear that Christians will be so loving to them that they will feel the strong temptation to convert!"

Drawing on his lived experience with Shawky, Jonathan, and Ishmael, Gert Hunink, along with his colleague Stephen Haak, has recently argued that any political party working under the title "Christian" must evaluate its policies on immigrants in the light of both Christ's hospitality and the multiple commands to care for foreigners in the Old Testament.[25] This, they insist, must be the model for immigration policy in the *ChristenUnie* party.

In a letter sent to their national party, both Hunink and Haak argue repeatedly that the people's demand for security and peace will not come from anti-Islamic rhetoric or more government programs. Instead, the work of security and peace must begin with micro-level acts of Christian hospitality. Families, schools, churches, institutions, and leaders within the *ChristenUnie* movement need to model Christ's hospitality through an open engagement with Muslim individuals and institutions in their local communities.

By taking this initiative, the *ChristenUnie* could accomplish two critical goals. First, their party could quietly begin to build a critical trust between Christianity and Islam. And second, by actually listening to immigrants, the *ChristenUnie*'s voters could make better political decisions. More than that, once Christians build thick relationships with Muslims, the hyperbolic caricatures of the right will be recognized as such.

Both Hunink and Haak openly discuss the deep religious and political differences between Christianity and Islam. They do not romanticize or smooth over the rough spots. They insist that there should be debate, disagreement, and even criticism between Islam and Christianity. Of course, they want the *ChristenUnie* party to fight for law and order, borders and boundaries. Security concerns are legitimate.

That said, they caution that, if there is going to be lasting security, law, and order, they need to be built—first and foremost—on the hospitality of Christ. Haak and Hunink understand that any political platform founded on a word like *hospitality* is at risk of being dismissed by most citizens as naïve, cowardly, and weak. To these charges the two men offer a simple retort: amidst the cities of Mecca and Amsterdam, cities so bereft of trust, vulnerability, and friendship, few things are more desperately needed than an open door and a cup of coffee.

---

25. Stephen Haak and Geert Hunink, "*Veiligheid door gastvrijheid,*" proposal submitted to the *ChristenUnie*, March 18, 2010.

PART 4

Islam and Christian Pluralism in America

CHAPTER NINE

Islam and Christianity in America

American Christians' views about Islam usually divulge more about American Christians than about any actual Muslims.

THOMAS KIDD[1]

In 2008, a mosque in the small town of Columbia, Tennessee, was broken into, vandalized, and set aflame. The arsonists were eventually captured. When asked to give a rationale for their attack, they cited the Bible. They insisted that the mosque had to be burned because the worship of Allah was against the law of God.[2] In the days and weeks following the attack, many local churches were silent about this act of Christian terrorism.

While a sad moment for the Christian faith, it would not be the defining moment. Upon hearing the news of the attack, one pastor "collected money during a service at the church and provided Muslims with a set of keys to his church so that they could worship there. He set aside a room for them to use for meetings and prayers and even offered to remove any Christian symbols that might offend them."[3]

This brief episode in a small Tennessee town captures the decidedly mixed nature of Christian responses to Islam in American history. In truth, the his-

---

1. Thomas S. Kidd, *American Christians and Islam: Evangelical Culture and Muslims from the Colonial Period to the Age of Terrorism* (Princeton, NJ: Princeton University Press, 2009), xii. Additional references to this work are given parenthetically in the text.

2. Akbar Ahmed, *Journey into America: The Challenge of Islam* (Washington, DC: Brookings Press, 2010), 138.

3. Ahmed, *Journey into America*, 138.

tory of Muslim-Christian relations in America is a disorganized, inconsistent, and confused mixture of both hostility and hospitality, judgment and justice, diatribes and dialogue.[4]

If we narrow our historical survey to *evangelical* interactions with Islam in America, the historical picture becomes less mixed and more dark. In fact, if we judge an individual simply by demographics, I—this book's author—am from the last demographic you would expect to write a book defending Muslim rights and dignity. Pick your category: white, male, evangelical, conservative, suburban—I am not from the demographic segment who is expected to speak out on behalf of Islam. But here I am.

In 2016, more than 80 percent of my demographic kin voted for Donald Trump—a candidate who regularly demonized Muslims, repeatedly called for a ban on Islamic immigration, and continually stoked the nation's darkest existential fears and prejudices about the Muslim foreigner. A recent poll showed that 76 percent of white, evangelical Republicans approved of Trump's recent travel ban against Muslims. Sixty-nine percent of them say that they are "very concerned" about domestic Islamic extremism. Compare this number to less than a third of religious "nones" in America who report in the same poll that they are "very concerned" about these matters.[5] Another study revealed that evangelicals "are more likely than any other Christian group to have low respect for Muslims."[6] Yes, as a white, evangelical male, I am the type of person who should be writing this book. I am a statistical rarity in the fight for Muslim rights, but—as we will soon see—I am not alone.

While humble, a small but growing movement of evangelicals in the United States is beginning to go beyond the politics of fear when it comes to Islam. Consider, for example, the following acts of local Christian churches— many of whom would describe themselves as evangelical:

4. Peter Makari's words here are important, for the overall picture and history of Muslim-Christian relationships in America is extremely complex: "In a society as complex and diverse as the United States, it would be dangerous to attempt to understand Muslim–Christian relations as simply positive or negative or even to characterize trends in dialogue and relationships as polarized." Peter Makari, "Muslim-Christian Relations in the United States," in *The Oxford Handbook of American Islam,* Jane I. Smith and Yvonne Yazbeck Haddad, eds. (Oxford: Oxford University Press, 2015), 361.

5. Gregory A. Smith, "Most white evangelicals approve of Trump travel prohibition and express concerns about extremism," Pew Research Center, accessed February 27, 2017, http:// www.pewresearch.org/fact-tank/2017/02/27/most-white-evangelicals-approve-of-trump-travel -prohibition-and-express-concerns-about-extremism/.

6. Jong Hyun Jung, "Islamophobia? Religion, Contact with Muslims, and the Respect for Islam," *Review of Religious Research,* 54, no. 1 (March 2012): 122.

- In Idaho, Cole Community Church hosts a "peace feast" with a local mosque. During these feasts Muslims and Christians break bread together, share their faith experiences, and build friendships and understanding.
- In Texas, a local mosque was destroyed in a fire. Christian and Jewish communities offered both support and space to the displaced Muslims. Children from a local Catholic school visited and presented a tree to be planted at the site of their new mosque.
- In Georgia, Smoke Rise Baptist Church rallied local support for a Muslim man whose convenience store was ransacked and robbed.
- In California, First Covenant Church received an award from a local mosque for sponsoring and hosting more than one hundred Muslim refugees. The church supports these refugees by finding and furnishing homes and by offering them English classes, after-school tutoring, driving lessons, job training for adults, and soccer for children.
- In Arizona, a group of churches formed a physical barrier between a local mosque and an inflammatory "Draw Mohammed Contest." This highly offensive and threatening rally was organized by a group of armed motorcyclists wearing t-shirts that read "Fuck Islam." The Christians stood in the gap.
- In Texas, Northwood Church, a conservative Baptist community, has engaged in regular dialogues with local Muslims. Their pastor advocates honest and candid conversations about the real differences between the two faiths. While friendly, these dialogues never hide the fact that both sides would honestly love to convert the other. "I tell my Muslim friends that I hope to baptize them one day," the pastor declares. "They tell me I would make a great imam."
- In Tennessee, Christ Community Church responded to terrorist attacks in Paris with a collective prayer the following Sunday:

Father, we offer our prayer, not in self-righteous judgment, but as your weary children. . . . [F]ree us from all bitterness and a lust for revenge. Vengeance belongs to you, not to us. Make us warriors of peace and agents of hope. . . .

Grant us wisdom to know what loving mercy, doing justice, and walking humbly with you looks like in Paris and in our own communities. Replace our frets and fears with faith and trust, and our rage and wrath with patience and courage. So very Amen we pray, in Jesus' triumphant and grace-full name.

These relatively isolated acts do not suddenly erase a long historical pattern of Islamophobia among American evangelicals, but these moments do represent a hopeful window opening on an alternative future. In the same way, the final section of this book is designed to explore exactly this—*a generative future for evangelical engagement with Islam in the United States.*

It should be noted that I have limited my focus here to the evangelical strain of American Christianity. I do this, not out of a desire to exclude other Christian traditions, but for three important reasons. First, the strictures of space make it impossible to survey all American denominations and their unique responses to Islam. Second, by all measures, American evangelicals had a particularly problematic relationship with Muslims. I therefore believe that this tradition stands in particularly urgent need of attention. Third, with some reservations, I still call this tradition home. Because evangelicalism is my theological home, I feel a sense of calling to theologically serve, challenge, and push the tradition forward to its best self. For Christian readers outside the evangelical tradition, my hope is that you will find many of the reflections useful and relevant to your own stories and contexts.

By way of summary, a generative future for evangelicals on this issue of Islam depends on the tradition wrestling with three key elements. The three final chapters of this book are designed to cover each of them in turn. First, they must begin with an honest assessment of the historical challenges Muslims have faced in America up to this point. Second, they must recognize the agency Muslim Americans have already assumed for themselves in overcoming these historical challenges. Finally, only after these two realities have been understood, can they begin to chart a faithful Christian response to their Muslim neighbors. With that said, we begin this first chapter by examining an American past—and present—filled with significant challenges for Islam.

Islam in America: Before 9/11

While the fact may be surprising to many, Muslims have been a part of the American story from the very beginning. In his recent book, Thomas Kidd, an American historian, charts the arrival of Islam all the way back to the colonial period (*American Christians and Islam*). In fact, an examination of nineteenth-century history reveals that most of America's first Muslim immigrants did not sneak into the United States; slave traders captured them in Africa and brought them to America against their will.

While Muslims have been participants in America's story from the nation's very inception, Islam's cultural footprint has been relatively small and largely ignored for most of American history. Historically speaking, Americans have been much more focused on the distinct religious and cultural identities of the Native Americans, Jews, Catholics, Mormons, and later, on African, Asian, and Latino American communities. For much of the twentieth century, Muslim immigrants were largely ignored as the foreign threats of Nazism and communism dominated the nation's political imagination. While this pattern of ignoring American Muslims would shift at the end of the twentieth century, for much of American history, Muslim immigration was not a matter of significant conversation.

During the 1970s and 1980s, the Muslim population in America began to grow dramatically. At this time Europe was opening its doors to mostly rural and uneducated Muslims to serve in their service and industry sectors. The United States, however, more exclusively welcomed a select group of highly educated and highly skilled Muslim professionals to serve in their science, technology, and international business sectors.[7] Whether one considers the social status indicators of wealth, employment, or education, Muslims living in America today are significantly more privileged and powerful than those in Europe.[8] It is therefore important to note that the differences in the debates over Islam in Europe and North America are thanks, in part, to the significant differences of socioeconomic power and privilege possessed by European versus American Muslims.[9]

7. "Unlike the United Kingdom and Western European countries, America has enjoyed the influx of a middle-class professional movement of educated Muslims from the Middle East, Indonesia, and India as the predominant immigrant profile," according to John H. Morgan, "Disentangling Religion and Culture: Americanizing Islam as the Price of Assimilation," *International Journal of Islamic Thought* 4 (2013): 29.

8. Consider, for example, that "A 2009 study found that 70 percent of Muslims in the United States were employed—a percentage higher than the American average of 64 percent—whereas that was true of only 53 percent in Germany, 45 percent in France, and a miserable 38 percent in the United Kingdom. Remarkably, though perhaps not surprisingly in view of its less generous welfare state, Muslims in the United States were actually more likely to be employed there than in any Muslim-majority country. Moreover, reflecting their higher class background, 31 percent of non-employed Muslims in the United States are full-time students, as compared with only 10 percent of the overall population." Christian Joppke and John Torpey, *Legal Integration of Islam: A Transatlantic Comparison* (Cambridge, MA: Harvard University Press, 2013), 129.

9. "The North American posture is strongly facilitated by a more fortunate profile of Muslim immigrants in the United States and Canada, resulting from a selective immigration policy that prizes skills and wealth over other criteria. If the United States were faced with a

During the 1980s in the United States, Muslim immigration rates continued to rise. By 1990, there were 871,000 foreign-born immigrants from Muslim countries; by 2000, that number had grown to 1,717,000.[10] The exact number of Muslims living in America today is a matter of significant debate. Estimates range from two to four million—roughly one to two percent of the American population.[11]

To say that "Islam in America" is a diverse phenomenon would be a significant understatement. While most European countries have historically drawn Muslim immigrants from two or three specific countries (often their old colonies), the United States has drawn a wide diversity of Muslims from every Islamic country in North and East Africa, the Middle East, Central and South Eastern Asia. Kambiz GhaneaBassiri remarks that in many ways the vast diversity of American Muslims represent "a microcosm of the world's Muslim population."[12] Moreover, because of the vast diversity of American Islam, "no one narrative can capture the varying experiences of American Muslims. . . . [T]here is no single American Muslim experience."[13]

For the most part, these diverse Muslim communities flourished in the United States throughout the 1970s and 1980s. Muslim Americans benefited from an American economy that was free, an education system that allowed their children to flourish, a dominant Protestant culture that largely ignored

---

sizeable Muslim underclass leaning toward a strict practice of their religion, we suspect that the easygoing stance would quickly yield to more serious self-examination—of the sort that followed the publicization of the plans to build a mosque near Ground Zero." Joppke and Torpey, *Legal Integration of Islam*, 160.

10. Kambiz GhaneaBassiri, *A History of Islam in America: From the New World to the New World Order* (Cambridge: Cambridge University Press, 2010), 348.

11. "The census has not collected data on religious affiliation since 1936, which means that any figures on the number of Muslims in America are necessarily estimates. The current estimates are between 2 and 7 million based on sources ranging from Muslim to nonpartisan and conservative non-governmental organizations. At the lower end of the scale are figures by the Pew Forum on Religious and Public Life, a nonpartisan polling research center, which sets the number of Muslims in 2010 at 2.6 million, or 0.8 percent of the US population. At the higher end are figures produced by those with more vested interests, namely some Muslim associations and conservative groups (CAIR, 2012; Elver 2012; Johnson 2011). All of these estimates are based on surveys and polling conducted by these various organizations. The largest three racial/ethnic groups represented among Muslims in America are South Asians, Arabs, and African Americans." Randa B. Serhan, "Muslim Immigration to America," in Smith and Haddad, *The Oxford Handbook of American Islam*, 31.

12. GhaneaBassiri, *A History of Islam in America*, 2.

13. GhaneaBassiri, *A History of Islam in America*, 2–3.

them, and a generous set of constitutional protections that ensured a great deal of religious freedom.[14]

Before the 1990s, the few moments of notable tension over Islam's presence in America were largely limited to debates over an African American movement known as the Nation of Islam. And yet, even in these brief moments of tension, the nation's discomfort with this movement largely focused on the group's African race rather than its Muslim religion. Thus, with the important exception of African American Muslims, a significant portion of American Muslims felt relatively safe and at home in America during the 1970s and 1980s.[15] In fact, before 1990, few American citizens ever thought about or even discussed the small but growing population of Muslims within their borders. Islam was a distant and exotic faith, something that a missionary would travel thousands of miles to engage. It was not something that would move in next door.

While September 11, 2001, certainly looms large in the history of American Islam, the fall of the Soviet Union in 1991 is another critical moment in the community's story. GhaneaBassiri remarks that every nation needs an enemy, some sort of national "other" over against which that nation can shape and define its own national identity. From 1945 to 1991 the Soviet Union served as this "other" for the United States of America. With the fall of communism in 1991, GhaneaBassiri argues, a new "other" was needed; America needed a new "clashing" partner. He points here to a critical shift in the American political imagination away from communism and toward Islam.[16] In short, before 1990 Americans had to be on a vigilant watch for subversive communist cells; after 1990, they needed to be on the lookout for subversive Muslim cells.

In the 1990s, America's more apocalyptic and dispensationalist pastors played a role in the shift away from communism and toward Islam. A survey of their books reveals that "the Muslims" gradually took the place of "the Russians" as the villain in their eschatological visions. According to Thomas

---

14. Joppke and Torpey, *Legal Integration of Islam*, 124.

15. "In sum, Muslim Americans are substantially integrated into the American economic and political order. Yet that picture must be qualified by the extent to which African American Muslims feel as though they are irremediably outsiders. But this is really a matter of race, not religion; sadly and remarkably, native blacks in American life continue to look more like immigrants in European societies with respect to the degree of their incorporation into the society and their view of their own situation. It may well be that the kind of Islam that most needs integrating into American life is that associated with its 'indigenous' adherents, but that will require attention to the disabilities suffered by black Americans rather than those faced by Muslims per se." Joppke and Torpey, *Legal Integration of Islam*, 136.

16. GhaneaBassiri, *A History of Islam in America*, 328–30.

Kidd, dispensational theologies of the cosmic clash between Islam and Israel would "set the stage for an explosion of new Christian literature on Islam after the terrorist attacks on September 11, 2001." Indeed, this dispensational literature "tended to paint Muslims, especially Arab Muslims, as being on the wrong side of the global eschatological conflict" (*American Christians and Islam*, 142–43). Grayson Robertson echoes these sentiments when he writes that while "Islam has consistently represented one of many antagonists to Christianity in the minds of dispensationalists, the fall of Communism in 1989 cleared the way for Islam to once again become the primary eschatological enemy of Christianity."[17]

While the 1991 conflict in the Persian Gulf was an important first clash between America and Islam *internationally* speaking, one of the first *domestic* examples of this growing tension can be found in the aftermath of the 1995 Oklahoma City bombing. In the landmark report *A Rush to Judgment*, more than two hundred incidents of harassment and hate crimes were recorded against Muslims in America in the days immediately following the bombing.[18] Coincidentally, there were no recorded attacks against Roman Catholic churches, priests, or nuns after it was revealed that the bomber had, in fact, been raised a Roman Catholic.

Islam in America: After 9/11

The true character of an individual or nation is best judged under duress.

AKBAR AHMED[19]

September 11 was not a turning point; it was a dramatic amplification of an already existing American fear and suspicion of Muslims buried within the nation's psyche.[20] When the World Trade Center towers fell in New York City, a hailstorm of American grief, fear, and anger came crashing down on the Muslim American community. The events of 9/11 poured gasoline on the al-

---

17. Grayson R. Robertson, "Confronting the 'Axis of Evil': Christian Dispensationalism, Politics and American Society Post-9/11," *Journal of Muslim Minority Affairs*, 34 (2014), no. 2: 112.

18. GhaneaBassiri, *A History of Islam in America*, 344.

19. Ahmed, *Journey into America*, 139.

20. "The events of 9/11, however, did not mark a new epoch in the history of Islam in America; rather they amplified processes and tendencies that had already begun in the late 1980s." GhaneaBassiri, *A History of Islam in America*, 328–29.

ready existing flames of American fear and suspicion. Soon a brush fire of discrimination, harassment, surveillance, interrogation, and incarceration would spread across the country. Akbar Ahmed recalls that

> On September 11, 2001, Muslim immigrants from the Middle East and South Asia who had been attracted to and invited in by pluralist America, woke to find they had tumbled from their comfortable positions in the professional middle class. These Muslims had not studied enough history to know that this was but another side of American society. From the time of the earliest settlers, Americans have reacted with ferocity to any threat [real or imagined].[21]

The Council on American-Islamic Relations (CAIR) documented "more than 1,717 acts of discrimination against Muslims in the year after the attacks, particularly in the workplace and airports."[22] There were "more than 700 violent crimes against Arab Americans in the weeks after 9/11."[23] According to Jocelyne Cesari, "nearly 1,200 resident aliens of Muslim origin were arrested in America after 9/11."[24]

It is particularly distressing to note that at this time most of the harassment and discrimination complaints were directed toward official agents of the American government.[25] The widespread governmental pattern of discrimination and interrogation would only grow in the coming months.[26] By November 2001

21. Ahmed, *Journey into America*, 97.

22. Jocelyne Cesari, *When Islam and Democracy Meet: Muslims in Europe and in the United States* (New York: Palgrave Macmillan, 2004), 38.

23. Charles Kimball, "The War on Terror and Its Effects on American Muslims," in Smith and Haddad, *The Oxford Handbook of American Islam*, 501.

24. Cesari, *When Islam and Democracy Meet*, 38.

25. "Of all the institutional settings tracked by this report, the largest number of complaints involved profiling incidents at airports or those at the hands of government agencies, especially the INS, FBI, and local law enforcement authorities." Amir Hussain, "(Re)presenting: Muslims on North American Television," *Contemporary Islam* 4 (2010): 73.

26. Charles Kimball writes, "Not surprisingly, men and women whose name or appearance seemed to be Islamic were subjected to additional screening at airports within the United States and on flights bound for the United States. As one American Imam told a university audience in 2011, 'I always get the VIP treatment at airports. TSA [Transportation Security Administration] officials provide special services for me as a "Very Islamic Person"!' This type of special attention along with periodic congressional hearings on the dangers posed by Islamic extremists fueled an ongoing controversy about 'profiling' particular racial or religious groups." Kimball, "The War on Terror," in Smith and Haddad, *The Oxford Handbook of American Islam*, 495.

Attorney General John Ashcroft announced that the government would conduct investigations of nearly 5,000 foreign Muslims living on American soil. By the end of 2002, more than 3,000 additional investigations had been announced. According to official sources, only around twenty people from the first group were arrested and accused, and those for reasons other than terrorist activities.[27]

At this time, new interrogation activities were "coupled with other new policies, such as the government's ability to designate anyone, including American citizens, as 'enemy combatants' and to imprison them indefinitely."[28]

Ahmed notes that with "9/11 now firmly entrenched in the American psyche, a chasm of fear [soon separated] the American and Muslim communities."[29] In a 2002 poll of American Arabs and Muslims, 66 percent of them "reported being worried about their future in this country. . . . 81 percent thought they were being profiled."[30] One quarter of American Muslims reported being the victims of discrimination.[31] Reflecting on these and other studies, Peter Gottshalk concludes "that experiences of discrimination have continued to rise even a decade after 9/11, with a quarter of [Muslim] respondents in 2011 saying that their mosque has been the target of controversy or hostility."[32]

In the aftermath of 9/11, the dramatic increases in governmental interrogations, surveillance, and restrictions were supported by large segments of the American public. "A Gallup poll in the summer of 2006 of more than 1,000 Americans showed that 39 percent were in favor of requiring Muslims in the United States, including American citizens, to carry special identification."[33] The same poll "found that 39 percent of Americans believed Muslims were not loyal to the United States, and a full third said that Muslims living in the United States were sympathetic to al-Qaeda."[34] The increasing sense of distrust and division on both sides of the divide would lead Jocelyne Cesari to conclude

27. Cesari, *When Islam and Democracy Meet*, 38.

28. Kimball, "The War on Terror," in Smith and Haddad, *The Oxford Handbook of American Islam*, 494.

29. Ahmed, *Journey into America*, 98.

30. GhaneaBassiri, *A History of Islam in America*, 364.

31. Liyakat Takim, "The Ground Zero Mosque Controversy: Implications for American Islam," *Religions* 2, (2011) 135.

32. Peter Gottschalk, "Islamophobia and Anti-Muslim Sentiment in the United States," in Smith and Haddad, *The Oxford Handbook of American Islam*, 516.

33. Takim, "The Ground Zero Mosque Controversy," 135.

34. Joppke and Torpey, *Legal Integration of Islam*, 123.

that the long believed "gap" between the "American and European experiences in matters of Islam" was now "shrinking."[35]

From 2001 to 2006, American discourse concerning domestic Islam largely focused on the issues of terrorism, surveillance, and security. In 2006, the discourse began to expand in its scope to include American concerns about the cultural, sexual, educational, organizational, and legal integration of Islam. Islamophobia went from a narrow to a broad national concern. Muslim immigrants were no longer simply a security threat; they were a cultural threat as well. The American conversation about Islam was sounding more and more European.

By 2006, American pundits were increasingly importing European discourses about the coming "Islamization of the West." It was at this point that stories of the so-called Dutch experience with Islam began to show up in American thinking.[36] The growing American fear over domestic Muslims led to a series of political efforts to block the advance of "Islamization." One tangible example of this can be found in the growing popularity of Shari'a bans. Across the country, states "from Georgia to Missouri to New Mexico" began "considering bans on the possible implementation of the Shari'a, or Islamic law in their states."[37] These legal movements were, in many ways, quite perplexing, since America has a long history of delegating legal authority to Jewish, Catholic, and Protestant courts and tribunals for limited private disputes.[38]

---

35. Cesari, *When Islam and Democracy Meet*, 32.

36. Consider the following: Bruce Bawer, *While Europe Slept: How Radical Islam Is Destroying the West from Within* (New York: Broadway Books, 2006); Craig S. Smith, "In Mourning Slain Filmmaker, Dutch Confront Limitations of Their Tolerance," *New York Times*, November 11, 2004; William Pfaff, "Europe Pays the Price for Cultural Naïveté," *International Herald Tribune*, November 11, 2004; Andrew Stuttaford, "How Enlightenment Dies," *National Review*, November 12, 2004; Suzanne Fields, "The Menace of Multiculturalism: Amnesia Renders the West Unable to Defend Itself," *Washington Times*, September 15, 2005; Theodore Dalrymple, "A Wiser Holland: The Dutch, Mugged by Reality, Toughen Up on Radical Islam," *National Review*, January 30, 2006; Robert Carle, "Demise of Dutch Multiculturalism," *Society*, March/April 2006; Bruce Bawer, *Surrender: Appeasing Islam, Sacrificing Freedom* (New York: Anchor, 2010); Mark Steyn, *America Alone: The End of the World as We Know It* (Washington, DC: Regnery, 2006); Bridgette Gabriel, *They Must Be Stopped: Why We Must Defeat Radical Islam and How We Can Do It* (New York: St. Martin's Press, 2008); Abigail R. Esman, *Radical State: How Jihad Is Winning over Democracy in the West* (Santa Barbara, CA: Praeger, 2010); Bruce Bawer, "Paradise Lost in the Netherlands," *Christian Science Monitor*, May 19, 2006; Rod Dreher, "Murder in Holland: Pim Fortuyn, Martyr," *National Review*, May 7, 2002; H. E. Baber, *The Multicultural Mystique: The Liberal Case against Diversity* (Amherst, NY: Prometheus, 2008).

37. Takim, "The Ground Zero Mosque Controversy," 138.

38. "Across the United States, religious courts operate on a routine, everyday basis. . . . The

The growing Islamophobia inspired large segments of America to abandon this long-standing American tradition of limited deference to religious courts.

Another important development in post-9/11 America was the enormous role of the national media in shaping America's perception of Islam. Small Muslim communities were powerless to withstand the immense waves of 24-hour-news stories portraying their faith as inherently dangerous, violent, and disloyal to America. A hoard of conservative pundits led the media charge. Bill O'Reilly compared the Koran to Hitler's *Mein Kampf*.[39] Michelle Malkin openly considered internment camps for Muslims.[40] Michelle Bachmann speculated there was "a conspiracy by the Muslim Brotherhood to infiltrate the top reaches of the US government."[41] Glenn Beck, interviewing the first Muslim member of Congress, demanded "prove to me you are not working with our enemies."[42]

Reflecting on the immense cultural power of the American media, Andrew Shryock notes that, "Whatever their social position, Arabs and Muslims in the United States must contend with a mass mediated realm of endlessly updated imagery and knowledge about them that is highly unfavorable, at times hostile. . . ."[43] With American Muslims under high levels of media scrutiny and pressure from all sides, it is easy to see why Salam Al-Marayati would conclude that,

> Although the vast majority of American Muslims do not live in economically depressed physical ghettos, many live in a psychological ghetto caused by the lack of acceptance they feel from their neighbors and colleagues, especially in the post– Sept. 11 era. This psychological ghetto may prove the largest challenge in the war on terrorism.[44]

Roman Catholic Church alone has nearly 200 diocesan tribunals that handle a variety of cases, including an estimated 15,000 to 20,000 marriage annulments each year. In addition, many Orthodox Jews use rabbinical courts to obtain religious divorces, resolve business conflicts and settle other disputes with fellow Jews. Similarly, many Muslims appeal to Islamic authorities to resolve marital disputes and other disagreements with fellow Muslims." Kimball, "The War on Terror," in Smith and Haddad, *The Oxford Handbook of American Islam*, 497.

39. Ahmed, *Journey into America*, 7.

40. Ahmed, *Journey into America*, 118.

41. Cesari, "Islamic Organizations in the United States," in Smith and Haddad, *The Oxford Handbook of American Islam*, 80.

42. Ahmed, *Journey into America*, 59.

43. Andrew Shryock, "On Discipline and Inclusion," in *Being and Belonging: Muslims in the United States Since 9/11*, ed. Katherine Pratt Ewing (New York: Russell Sage, 2008), 203.

44. Salam Al-Marayati, "America's Muslim Ghettos," *Washington Post*, August 15, 2005.

The destructive and demonizing rhetoric of American pundits on the national level would inevitably have an impact at the local level. Small American towns began to imagine themselves to be a part of a worldwide clash of civilizations. Protesting a local mosque became a patriotic duty—a battle for civilization itself.

> One of the more heated confrontations centered in Murfreesboro, Tennessee, the home of Middle Tennessee State University. Having outgrown their small mosque in the town of 100,000, located thirty-five miles south of Nashville, the Muslim community bought fifteen acres of land south of town and developed plans to build a new Islamic center that would include the mosque, a school, a gym, and a swimming pool. Hostile opposition was visible, vocal, and active in a city that has at least 140 churches and one mosque. After construction began, a fire started by arson at the construction site destroyed a bulldozer and damaged three other vehicles. A sign announcing the new building project was vandalized with the message, "Not welcome." Over 500 people marched to protest the construction, some wearing T-shirts bearing the word Infidel, while others carried placards reading "Stop TN Homegrown Terrorism."[45]

Reflecting on the decade-long growth of Islamophobia in the United States, Charles Kimball asks and answers his own question.

> Is America Islamophobic? More than a decade after the terrorist attacks of 9/11, this much is clear: A substantial and vocal segment of the wider population has been gripped by fear of having an Islamic center nearby and profoundly worried that Muslims constitute a threatening monolithic entity committed to world domination and imposing Islamic law on everyone. Precisely how American Muslims, who make up only 1 to 2 percent of the population, will be able to accomplish these presumed goals is never clearly explained.[46]

---

http://www.washingtonpost.com/wp-dyn/content/article/2005/08/14/AR2005081401038.html (accessed June 15, 2017).

45. Kimball, "The War on Terror," in Smith and Haddad, *The Oxford Handbook of American Islam*, 496.

46. Kimball, "The War on Terror," in Smith and Haddad, *The Oxford Handbook of American Islam*, 498.

It is important to note that the term *Islamophobia* is, in many ways, too narrow to describe what is happening in post-9/11 American culture. A 2012 mosque attack in Virginia captures the complex religious, racial, sexual, and cultural aspects of the growing problem in America. Describing the attack, Gottshalk reports that

> among the graffiti obscenities and the images of genitalia on the mosque walls were slurs against "Irakis" and racial epithets usually reserved for Arabs and African Americans, all apparently meant to underline the spray-painted proclamation "This is America, bitches." This interweaving of racial, ethnic, gendered, and nationalist prejudice demonstrates the multidimensionality of many Islamophobic and anti-Muslim expressions.[47]

Leaders of the Christian right followed this growing movement of Islamophobia in America. Franklin Graham called Islam a "very evil and wicked religion"; Jerry Falwell called Mohammed a "terrorist," while Jerry Vines claimed he was a "demon-possessed pedophile" and he claimed that Islam teaches the destruction of all non-Muslims (*American Christians and Islam*, 145). Randall Price asked "Is the United States waging a war with Islam?" He answered, "if it isn't, it should be!" (*American Christians and Islam*, 145). Most notoriously, a church in Gainesville, Florida, planned to commemorate the ninth anniversary of the September 11 attacks by hosting a Qur'an-burning ceremony. Pastor Terry Jones told CNN, "We believe that Islam is of the devil, that it is causing billions of people to go to hell, it is a deceptive religion, it is a violent religion and that is proven many, many times."[48]

Thomas Kidd remarks that leaders of the Christian right successfully cultivated "a sense of political futility" in American Christians, a firm belief that "violent conflict between Muslims, Jews, and Christians was inevitable. Ironically, this fatalist belief in predestined conflict mirrors a similar rhetorical tactic by Muslim jihadists" (*American Christians and Islam*, 15). In the end, the efforts of the Christian right were successful: evangelicals now hold "by far the most negative estimation of Islam among those surveyed" (*American Christians and Islam*, 162).

---

47. Gottschalk, "Islamophobia and Anti-Muslim Sentiment," in Smith and Haddad, *The Oxford Handbook of American Islam*, 509.

48. Takim, "The Ground Zero Mosque Controversy," 137.

Kidd remarks that before 9/11, there had been a diversity of competing evangelical views about Islam. Before 9/11, evangelical discourses on Islam "revolved around several key themes: the desire to see Muslims convert to Christianity, the fascination with missionary work among Muslims, the mixing of political policy and theology as it relates to the Muslim world (and Israel), and the insertion of Islam into eschatological schemes" (*American Christians and Islam*, 165). Before 9/11, many evangelical missionaries resisted the aggressive political theology of right-wing dispensationalists. They found their views of Islam "embarrassing, and feared they would obstruct evangelism" (*American Christians and Islam*, xvii). Unfortunately, the missionaries lost ground after 9/11 and the previously diverse evangelical perspectives on Islam narrowed to a very sharp point. After 9/11, missionary protests on behalf of Muslims were largely ignored as more and more evangelicals "indulged the temptation to essentialize Muslims, terrorism, the Middle East conflict, and the Iraq war into an inevitable spiritual clash hurtling towards Judgment. In doing so," Kidd sadly concludes, the Christian right "unwittingly aped the rhetoric of the Muslim jihadists they demonize" (*American Christians and Islam*, 163).

While terribly brief, this historical survey of the Muslim experience in America makes one conclusion painfully clear. The fear and hatred of Donald Trump's 2016 campaign was not novel—nor was it created ex nihilo by the candidate himself. The seeds of Islamophobia and clash rhetoric were planted in American hearts long before the political rise of Donald Trump. The fear and animosity within American hearts is political, theological, emotional, racial, and cultural. Removing Donald Trump from office will not remove the sickness that lies at the heart of America. Donald Trump is not the instigator of American Islamophobia—he is its most recent convert.

With this brief historical survey of Islam in America completed, we return again to our guiding questions: How might evangelicals resist and reverse the politics of fear? How might they write a new chapter in this darkening story of Islam in America? What should American evangelicals do to help their Muslim neighbors? Surprisingly enough, the first step is not to do anything more than recognize what Muslim Americans are already doing for themselves. The next chapter will examine exactly this. Once we have understood how Muslims are standing up for themselves, then, and only then, can evangelicals understand how they might stand alongside them.

CHAPTER TEN

Muslim Spaces in America

Before they take action against the politics of fear, American evangelicals need to recognize how Muslim citizens are already taking action and agency for themselves in the American public square. Muslims have long been and currently are actively participating in the American story. Zayn Kassam, a scholar of Islam, wisely reminds us that amidst all the noisy headlines and cacophony of the American media, everyday Muslim Americans are actively "weaving their own threads of hope, despair, creativity, and belonging into the tapestry of American life."[1]

How exactly are Muslims engaging American culture? How are they adding their voice to the American project? In every way imaginable. Muslim Americans are voting, working, studying, shopping, going to hospitals, doing research, building families, moving into neighborhoods, traveling, dating, going to concerts, watching TV, and starting businesses.

While we could explore all of these diverse cultural activities, I want to zero in on one particularly critical aspect of Muslim engagement in American life—the creation of what I call "Muslim spaces." Zayn Kassam, Kambiz GhaneaBassiri, and many other sociologists and scholars of religion are beginning to uncover the extremely important role of Muslim communities, organizations, and institutions in the formation and empowerment of everyday Muslim citizens.

---

1. Zayn Kassam, "The Challenges of Migration and the Construction of Religious Identities: The Case of Muslims in America," in *Intersections of Religion and Migration: Issues at the Global Crossroads,* ed. Jennifer B. Saunders, Elena Fiddian-Qasmiyeh, and Susanna Snyder (New York: Palgrave Macmillan, 2016), 111.

In this section, I want to encourage American evangelicals, and any other reader, to observe and appreciate the critically important role of Muslim families, schools, mosques, charities, organizations, media, and institutions in the lives of their Muslim neighbors. In doing this, I hope to actively combat the destructive myth that when Muslims gather in uniquely Muslim spaces they are necessarily dangerous or suspect. Rather than viewing such a gathering as a cell of terrorists, American Christians need to see these Muslim spaces as critically important arenas of Muslim formation and empowerment.

Observing this critical development in Muslim American life, GhaneaBassiri notes that the everyday "processes of institution and community-building play a much more significant role in shaping Muslims' lives than we have thus far acknowledged."[2] While Muslim ideas and beliefs matter, he insists that the much more crucial factor in Muslim citizenship is the construction of Muslim spaces in which Muslims can grow, deepen, and amplify their public voice. GhaneaBassiri argues that Muslims are "shaped more concretely by the institutions and communal relations they have formed" than by the abstract beliefs and dogmas they hold in theory.[3] Andrew Shryock echoes these sentiments when he argues that observers of American Islam must focus on "zones of communal discipline, where citizenship is crafted and tested. . . . These zones (schools, houses of worship, community centers, markets, the political arena, the press) are important and worthy of our full attention."[4]

Consider, for example, a displaced and isolated Muslim immigrant who has recently arrived in the United States. Scholars of migration and religion are increasingly discovering the absolutely critical role of mosques and Muslim community centers in supporting the individual migrant through the harrowing immigration process. Reflecting on their research, scholars note that faith communities like mosques serve "as a powerful guiding, coping, protective, and mediating force." Moreover, these spaces "help us understand how migrants fortify and psychologically prepare for the journey, how they experience their journeys, and how they are received and then adjust in a new land."[5] Again, Kassam notes:

---

2. Kambiz GhaneaBassiri, *A History of Islam in America: From the New World to the New World Order* (Cambridge: Cambridge University Press, 2010), 380.

3. GhaneaBassiri, *A History of Islam in America*, 380.

4. Andrew Shryock, "On Discipline and Inclusion," in *Being and Belonging: Muslims in the United States Since 9/11*, ed. Katherine Pratt Ewing (New York: Russell Sage, 2008), 206.

5. Holly Straut Eppsteiner and Jacqueline Hagan, "Religion as Psychological, Spiritual, and Social Support in the Migration Undertaking," in Saunders, Fiddian-Qasmiyeh, and Snyder, *Intersections of Religion and Migration*, 50.

For many migrants, their religious identity and affiliation provides a sense of community and ready-made networks among people of the same religious tradition in the host country, while their faith imparts a source of strength and hope that they will overcome the challenges of resettlement as they integrate into their new home.[6]

While the forces of Islamophobic politics and media attempt to preemptively define what it means to be Muslim, these mosques allow Muslim individuals the necessary space to define for themselves the true nature of Islamic identity and citizenship in America.

Once the immigrants' Muslim identity is formed, mosques and other Muslim organizations equip them with the necessary support and social capital to counter and contest the prevailing national narratives that demonize them. Here consider the observations of Islamic anthropologist Louis Cristillo:

Facing a growing sense of disconnectedness because of widespread racialized prejudices in the post-9/11 era, the neighborhood mosque, like other faith-based community associations, helps people find ways to pool resources, receive and distribute aid, hold meetings, learn about public issues, and recruit members for committees and projects.

Cristillo continues, "Muslim diaspora communities are thus reinventing the mosque, creating space to cultivate experiences, civic values, and personal networks easily transferable to other forms of local civic and political engagement."[7]

These Muslim spaces offer more than simply an internal function of formation. They also often have an exterior bridging function. According to Kassam,

Islamic civil organizations have . . . sought to educate the broader American populace on issues pertaining to Muslims. In addition to responsiveness, North American Muslim civic organizations are also generating Muslim discourses and engaging in practices that could be

6. Kassam, "The Challenges of Migration," in Saunders, Fiddian-Qasmiyeh, and Snyder, *Intersections of Religion and Migration*, 111.

7. Louis Cristillo, "The Case for the Muslim School as a Civil Society Actor," in *Educating the Muslims of America*, Yvonne Y. Haddad, Farid Senzai, and Jane I. Smith, eds. (Oxford: Oxford University Press, 2009), 73. Additional references to this work are given parenthetically in the text.

termed forms of reconstruction of Muslim identities and contributing to playing an energetic role in civil society.[8]

Jocelyne Cesari, a global observer of Islam, extremism, and security issues, argues that these Muslim spaces do more than simply empower and connect citizens; they also help them put down roots and feel more at home. More than a matter of justice, Cesari insists, the creation of Muslim spaces is a matter of national security as well. For, "One of the most common denominators of these young people attracted to jihadist movements and causes is not their socioeconomic level, but rather their displaced status." Surveying young men most vulnerable to extremism, Cesari notes that "these men's trajectories all point to a kind of nomadism, a permanent mobility in the countries and cultures of the West."[9] Muslim Americans most vulnerable to the temptations of extremism and terror are not the poor but the disconnected.

The irony here is painfully clear. American citizens are consistently fearful of the perceived dangers of Muslim spaces despite the fact that these communities and institutions are actually critical to national security. Muslim spaces connect nomadic and displaced young Muslims to community, faith, jobs, social capital, and communal discipline, and yet these same Muslim spaces are the constant subject of American interrogation, infiltration, surveillance, protest, and demonization.

Beyond the social significance of the mosque and the local community center, Louis Cristillo's research uncovers the tremendous civic importance of the local Muslim school. While fearful Americans may see these Muslim schools as terrorist training grounds, Cristillo's research reveals that "participation in the founding and life of a Muslim school produces overlapping social networks to bring individuals and groups into greater involvement in American civic life and participatory democracy" ("Case for the Muslim School," 69).

Rather than being exclusive spaces of Muslim seclusion, Cristillo notes "that the Muslim school creates a transitional space for immigrant Muslims to test the waters of associational life outside the private domain of the family or the limited sphere of the workplace" ("Case for the Muslim School," 79). Studying the three largest Muslim schools in New York City, Cristillo observes that each of them has

8. Kassam, "The Challenges of Migration," in Saunders, Fiddian-Qasmiyeh, and Snyder, *Intersections of Religion and Migration*, 103.

9. Jocelyne Cesari, *When Islam and Democracy Meet: Muslims in Europe and in the United States* (New York: Palgrave Macmillan, 2004), 102.

a student government, with class representatives and officers who campaign and debate to win office. A variety of student academic and service organizations provide structures in which youth and their faculty sponsors become engaged in discourse and debate on major social and public issues of the day. . . . From the above discussion, it is clear that the Muslim school is serving as a pathway for students . . . to cultivate social trust, leadership skills, and community values commonly associated with citizenship and civic engagement. ("Case for the Muslim School," 78–79)

The civic and social impact of Muslim schools is not limited to the children. Cristillo also points out the dramatic effect they can have on the Muslim women who serve as teachers. According to Cristillo, the school is

a valuable mechanism by which women may gain workplace knowledge and skills, network with others outside the circle of family and kin, and develop social capital in ways that promote greater public and civic engagement. A good example of this is a female principal of a Muslim elementary school in Queens who rallied her school to join a coalition of local neighborhood associations and a public elementary school. At issue was the flow of two-way traffic on a narrow street that was putting schoolchildren at risk. With this formidable community partnership behind her, this Pakistani-born principal successfully lobbied the local community board to change the road to a safer one-way traffic pattern. ("Case for the Muslim School," 76)

Cristillo's research locates "the Muslim school in a nexus of people and institutions—the mosque, the professional and business sector, the family, and the state." In doing this he directly challenges "the Islamophobic assumptions in public discourse that have fueled the widespread misconception that attendance at a Muslim school isolates American-born youth in a real or imagined ethno-religious ghetto" ("Case for the Muslim School," 80).

Kassam notes that smaller communal spaces often feed into national Muslim organizations that can serve as critically important platforms for national Islamic discourse and advocacy. Kassam writes,

Well-established [Muslim] organizations . . . not only . . . foster in-group solidarity, but also . . . build alliances with other faith groups through a common set of values. . . . [T]hey have identified and denounced people and instances evincing Islamophobia or Islamic fundamentalism. They have also worked to socialize young Muslims . . . [and] enlarge their social capital as leaders, innovators, and upstanding citizens.[10]

The integrity of these Muslim institutions and community is absolutely critical. For as Akbar Ahmed remarks, "It was not just individual Muslims who faced the wrath of American predator identity after 9/11. Muslim organizations and charities across the land were also subjected to special scrutiny and investigation."[11]

While these institutions were the subject of scrutiny, GhaneaBassiri remarks, these institutions also "played a fundamental role in helping American Muslims weather the backlash of 9/11."[12] Consider, for example, the post-9/11 impact of Muslim associations in the greater Detroit area. This region of Michigan is historically home to some of the strongest Muslim families, schools, mosques, institutions, and organizations in America. "Within a week of September 11, more than 4,000 Arabs from Detroit called to volunteer their services to the FBI and CIA as translators."[13] A group of sociologists wanted to understand why Detroit Muslims behaved in this way. Here is what they found:

> Overall, our data suggest that Arab Detroit weathered the post 9/11 backlash with fewer scars than the Arab American community nationwide and that Arab Detroiters, relative their counterparts elsewhere, are more confident about their future in the United States and more assertive of their rights as citizens.[14]
>
> What accounts for these differences? The answer lies in Arab Detroit's unparalleled amalgam of successful institutions, politically incorporated individuals, economic clout, and concentrated populations. . . . [F]indings suggest that participation in ethnic associations correlates

10. Kassam, "The Challenges of Migration" in Saunders, Fiddian-Qasmiyeh, and Snyder, *Intersections of Religion and Migration*, 104.

11. Akbar Ahmed, *Journey into America: The Challenge of Islam* (Washington, DC: Brookings Press, 2010), 149.

12. GhaneaBassiri, *A History of Islam in America*, 362.

13. Sally Howell and Amaney Jamal, "Detroit Exceptionalism and the Limits of Political Incorporation" in *Being and Belonging: Muslims in the United States since 9/11*, ed. Katherine Pratt Ewing (New York: Russell Sage, 2008), 67.

14. Howell and Jamal, "Detroit Exceptionalism" in Ewing, *Being and Belonging*, 58.

directly to greater empowerment among Arab Detroiters. . . . These organizations act as gateways to a larger world.[15]

Sociologists have also explored the importance of Muslim organizations in amplifying Islamic voices in American media, entertainment, and the arts. Andrew Shryock remarks that because "Muslim Americans are easily associated with enemy aliens" in the media, they are increasingly organizing themselves to change this. Focusing their efforts on Hollywood, Muslim organizations are committing themselves to "altering this image, guarding against its reproductions."[16] Kassam adds that Muslim organizations have also begun "applauding positive portrayals of Muslims in Hollywood, within the larger context of an ongoing attempt to critique the depiction of Muslims as terrorists in widely watched television series and blockbusters." More than that, Muslim institutions are now actively working to advance "Muslim American perspectives in the entertainment industry" and "to nurture creative talent and connect aspiring Muslim filmmakers, writers and actors with Hollywood professionals." Their approach is "proactive in that it seeks, continuously, to build capacity within American civil society and among Muslim Americans to address issues of Islamophobia, national security, foreign policy, religious freedom, women's empowerment, civil rights, and immigration."[17] Amir Hussein concludes that

> Until Muslims become more involved in television and film, we will leave the telling of our own stories to others. As such, while we can and should protest against inaccurate descriptions, we also cannot expect others to tell our stories in the ways that we would like them to be told. We, as Muslims, must help in the construction of an America where our stories are told for what they are, part of the nation's fabric.[18]

While this survey has been brief, we have now explored one the most important ways in which Muslim Americans are proactively responding to their difficult history in the United States—through the creation of uniquely Muslim spaces. We have seen how these spaces play a critical role in protect-

15. Howell and Jamal, "Detroit Exceptionalism," in Ewing, *Being and Belonging*, 58.
16. Howell and Jamal, "Detroit Exceptionalism," in Ewing, *Being and Belonging*, 203.
17. Kassam, "The Challenges of Migration," in Saunders, Fiddian-Qasmiyeh, and Snyder, *Intersections of Religion and Migration*, 106.
18. Amir Hussain, "(Re)presenting: Muslims on North American Television," *Contemporary Islam* 4 (2010): 74.

ing, nurturing, maturing, and extending their Islamic vision of the good life in America. While we must move on to the final chapter, I encourage readers to investigate these resources and stories in more depth. Understanding how Muslims Americans are standing up for themselves, we can now explore what it might mean for American Christians to stand up alongside them.

CHAPTER ELEVEN

American Evangelicals and Islam: The Pluralist Option

This final chapter briefly and informally explores ten ways in which American evangelicals might take action and apply the insights of Christian pluralism in their own context. These ten reflections draw from the major theological and political lessons explored throughout this book. It is my opinion that if evangelicals are going to become a generative force for Muslim rights and deep pluralism in America, they will need to make these ten moves—among others.

1. Avoid the Rhetoric of the Right and the Left

The first lesson American evangelicals can learn from the European experience with Islam is to avoid listening to right- and left-wing rhetoric when it comes to Muslim immigration and the politics of difference. In the opening chapters, we explored in great detail how both of these political voices framed the debate over Islam in narrow and counter-productive ways. Both paradigms were found to be simplistic, myopic, and ultimately destructive.

The left-wing voice in the Netherlands framed the conflict with words like openness and generosity, tolerance and diversity, inclusion and multi-culturalism. For this voice, the political goal was inclusiveness and an open door. In reaction to this voice, a second, right-wing voice arose in the Netherlands to frame the debate with words like law and order, safety and security, nation and culture. For this voice, the political goal was a restrictive and high wall. And so the majority of Dutch discussions about Islam over the past four decades have been dominated by a desire for either "open doors" or "high walls."

If the Dutch story has taught us anything, it is this: myopic political visions that seek either high walls or open doors as political ends in and of themselves are not only destabilizing, they are also dangerous.

As you will recall from the first two chapters, the politics of open doors ruled the Netherlands during the 1980s and 1990s to disastrous effect. The left's generous but flawed policies failed the country in a variety of ways. First, they failed to provide a sufficient plan for how they would sufficiently prepare Muslim immigrants to thrive in a very different culture and a very challenging marketplace. Second, advocates of open doors did not wrestle with the many cultural challenges and questions these newcomers would present to the Dutch people or their neighborhoods, schools, organizations, and cities. As newcomers failed to thrive and as their rates of poverty, unemployment, crime, and domestic abuse rose, so too did the racial and cultural tensions. Third, the left instituted a harmful gag-order of political correctness on Dutch political discourse. Citizens who questioned the generous open-door policies or criticized Islam in any way were quickly branded with the deadly labels of "racist" and "bigot." Fourth, Dutch citizens were not prepared to show the sort of deep vulnerability, hospitality, and love that immigrants and asylum-seekers need. Many of the Dutch treated the religious conservatism of the newcomers with sarcasm, jokes, patronizing re-education programs, and a sense of modern superiority. The individualistic spiritualities of Amsterdam did not provide Dutch citizens with a thick enough moral life for the challenges of deep—and sometimes dangerous—difference. Finally, while Dutch advocates of the open door liked the idea of diversity, they were not prepared for the raw and challenging reality of living next door to people with convictions about gender, sexuality, religion, politics, and morality that differed significantly from their own. As the saying goes, liberals want a diverse society of citizens who look different—but think the same—as they do. Deep diversity, it turns out, was much easier for the left to espouse in theory than it was for them to embody in practice.

Predictably, the failures of the left's open-door policies led to a fierce political backlash. Dutch political culture took a hard and fast turn to the right. Today, Dutch politicians rarely dare to mention the word *multiculturalism*. Moreover, across the political spectrum, politicians regularly advocate for higher levels of immigrant scrutiny and restriction, higher language requirements, and higher expectations for the cultural assimilation of Islam into the secular Dutch whole. The political discussion today is now dominated by the rhetoric of high walls—not open doors. As a result of this shift, large swaths of Dutch citizens now see Islam as fundamentally incompatible with Dutch society. They embrace the narrative of a clash of civilizations, believing that one side must ultimately win out. Needless to say, this hard right-wing turn from open doors to higher walls has done nothing but worsen the already growing tensions between Mecca and Amsterdam.

American evangelicals are now being drawn into a similar false choice. The left offers American citizens vague talk about diversity and acceptance, political correctness, identity politics, and simplistic chants of "Let them in! Let them in!" Meanwhile, the American right responds to the issue by parroting European clash rhetoric, casting this historical moment as an absolute confrontation between two completely opposing worldviews—which only one side can win.

In the end, the story of the Netherlands is an object lesson for American evangelicals in the failure of an exclusive focus on either open doors or high walls. When differences are deep, fast, and close, simplistic approaches to complex and dynamic differences fall apart. American evangelicals must find ways to avoid these faulty and ultimately fatal approaches to the politics of difference.

2. Defend Muslim Spaces

American evangelicals commonly look at Muslim spaces (Islamic families, charities, mosques, schools, and organizations) with great suspicion. They imagine these gatherings to be subversive and diabolical. Like many Americans, they worry that Muslim spaces encourage segregation, extremism, and violence. The research in the preceding chapter demonstrates these assumptions to be seriously flawed.

The true driving force of Islamic extremism and terrorism in the West is not Islamic community—but Islamic individualism. As Cesari stated earlier, terrorists are most commonly produced—not through poverty—but through a sense of fragmentation and displacement. When an individual Muslim is disconnected from communal ties of a healthy family, school, mosque, and culture, that person is most vulnerable to join the more cosmic and violent forms of Internet-based Islamic extremism. If American evangelicals are determined to fear something, they should not fear the gathering of Muslims, but their scattering.

Reflecting on the production of extremism in the Netherlands, Sam Cherribi points to a variety of social and political pressure points that fracture and destroy Muslim families and communities. When combined, these external

forces quickly become a "pulverizing machine that destroys the individual who happens to be Muslim and reconstitutes him or her as someone who is only a part of a larger, alienated, monolithic entity, in this case the 'Muslim threat.'"[1]

As it was demonstrated earlier, Muslim families, schools, mosques, and organizations in the United States all play a critical role in the communal formation and empowerment of Muslim American citizens. Finally, these communities have an important bridging function in that they give Muslim Americans the ability to connect and have conversations with outside institutions, religions, and governments.

As an important aside, note that while these spaces connect Muslims to each other and American society, evangelicals should never ask these spaces to serve as an American assimilation factory. A Muslim space, be it a family, mosque, or school, should never be judged by its ability to turn an individual Muslim into a modern, democratic capitalist. This is emphatically *not* its purpose.

Instead, American evangelicals should praise the fact that these Muslim spaces produce distinctly *Muslim* citizens with their own distinct visions of the good. These distinctly Muslim visions will, at times, conflict in the public square with Christian, Hindu, Buddhist, conservative, and liberal visions. And this is a *good* thing, which evangelicals should celebrate. For, if evangelicals want the freedom to voice their own distinct visions in America, they must fight for the Muslim's right to do so as well. As Abraham Kuyper declared to his Christian pluralists more than a century ago, "That freedom which we want for ourselves we must not withhold from others!"[2]

3. Embrace Cultural Marginalization

American evangelicals are a moral and political minority in the United States. Their cultural and political power is receding with each passing year. Many of them have yet to accept this fact. Wounded veterans of old culture wars, older American evangelicals are well trained in fighting for their own religious rights and privileges, but they have little experience fighting for the rights and privileges of other faiths. This will need to change. For the time being, many

---

1. Sam Cherribi, *In the House of War: Dutch Islam Observed* (Oxford: Oxford University Press, 2010), 5.

2. Abraham Kuyper, *Pro Rege of het koningschap van Christus* (Kampen: Kok, 1912), 3:181–82.

evangelicals still long to "take America back" and "claim America for Jesus." The path forward for American evangelicals must include an acceptance of their minority status in a pluralistic culture.

Critical theorist Nancy Fraser argues that lasting democracy depends, not on an enforced moral or cultural consensus, but on a generative conflict between diverse subcultures. She argues that the common belief that democracy requires a homogenous set of national values and beliefs is wrongheaded. Democracy requires a "multiplicity of publics" challenging one another's conception of the good.[3] Fraser argues that diverse moral communities and countercultures each serve a critical democratic function. Moreover, Fraser warns that if the majority community goes unchecked by these minority "counterpublics," the majority will inevitably grow in its destructive hegemony and pursue even more aggressive cultural uniformity.

The path forward for American evangelicals must include a reimagining of what it means to be a moral minority who agitates for the rights of other moral minorities—including Islam. At this point, evangelicals might learn from the insightful questions asked by Gert-Jan Segers, a pluralist parliamentary leader in the Dutch Christian Union. He asked his fellow Dutch evangelicals, "Can we be peacemakers? Can we make a constructive contribution to this great social dispute even if our contribution is from the margins of society?"[4]

As soon as evangelicals lay down their dreams of American cultural domination, they can pick up the more humble—and, frankly, more interesting—dream of American pluralism, justice, and respectful contestation.

4. Build Institutions

In order to constitute a minority counter-culture for Christian pluralism, evangelicals will need to do more than write a series of books like this. Abraham Kuyper and his movement for Christian pluralism demonstrate that good ideas go nowhere without strong institutions. Vibrant Christian organizations, universities, and media outlets perfect, empower, and extend the ideas of Christian pluralism into the public square. Evangelicals will need a rich collection of schools, organizations, and journals dedicated to the ideals of

---

3. Nancy Fraser, *Justice Interruptus: Critical Reflections on the "Postsocialist" Condition* (New York: Routledge, 1997), 85.

4. Gert-Jan Segers, *Voorwaarden voor vrede: de komst van de islam, de integratie van mosliims en de identiteit van Nederland* (Amsterdam: Buijten and Schipperheijn Motief, 2009), 107.

Christian pluralism. While American evangelicals are well known for their organizing skills, many of their current institutions were initially designed for a period of cultural dominance, not a period of cultural pluralism and partnership. In this new age, evangelical colleges, universities, and seminaries will still need to form strong leaders with strong evangelical convictions. That said, their students will also need to be well prepared to build cultural bridges, collaborations, and conversations, as well.

Evangelical contestations with other moral communities will continue—they may well proliferate. That said, evangelical students will need to be prepared to handle these contestations with grace, civility, and creativity. If the evangelical curriculums of the past were designed for cultural dominance, those of the future will need to be designed for cultural conversation and constructive contestation.

Evangelical political organizations will also need to be radically reconceived. First and foremost, they will need to detach themselves from their unhealthy alliance to the Republican Party. This perverted political alliance has drawn evangelical leaders and institutions deeper and deeper into a party that has become increasingly nativist and Islamophobic. In this new age, many evangelical activists will still feel called to serve faithfully within the Democratic and Republican Parties. That said, evangelical activists *must* cultivate a more provisional and contingent connection to these parties and the ideologies they represent. When it comes to the political issue of Islam, evangelicals must come to support Christian political organizations and think tanks who not only resist the demonization of Islam, but who positively advocate for Muslim rights, freedoms, and dignity.

Surveying the current landscape of evangelical political organizations, I see one tangible bright spot in the Center for Public Justice in Washington, DC. This bipartisan, Christian think tank is uniquely committed to the pluralistic approach to justice issues that we have been discussing throughout this book. While many evangelical organizations advocate for the religious rights of Christians, CPJ is unique in that it advocates for the public rights and freedoms of all faith communities—including Islam. CPJ does not engage in this work because it believes that all faiths are somehow equally true—whatever this bromide means. Instead, CPJ advocates for the universal rights of all religions because of their exclusive commitment to Christ, who commands justice for all.

Across the United States, numerous peacemaking and dialogue organizations are being developed that evangelicals can support and join. Peace Catalyst is dedicated to catalyzing peace, understanding, and reconciliation between Christians and Muslims. Peace Catalyst provides hands-on training and seminars for Christian leaders, churches, and organizations interested in peacemaking activities and engagement with their Muslim neighbors.[5]

American evangelicals can join countless other institutional and organizational efforts. In terms of regular reading material, the *Evangelical Interfaith Dialogue Journal* contains excellent reflections from scholars and practitioners on the front lines of interfaith engagement. Another area of potential engagement is refugee resettlement. Some of the largest organizations resettling Muslim refugees in the United States are actually run by Christian churches. Their numbers include Lutheran Immigration and Refugee Services, Episcopal Migration Services, World Relief, and the US Conference of Catholic Bishops. Finally, beyond formal institutions, numerous organic conversations and organizations are springing up throughout North America. For example, two women in California—one Muslim, the other Christian—recently launched an online conversation entitled "Miss Understanding" to report on their growing friendship.

5. Find Muslim Cobelligerents

One of the most critical lessons American evangelicals can learn from Abraham Kuyper and the early Christian pluralist movement is the need for cobelligerents. Kuyper's movement was relatively small in the Netherlands (roughly 15 percent of the population), yet the pluralists won monumental constitutional reforms through their cobelligerence with Roman Catholics. As we saw, Dutch Protestants and Catholics had a long history of contention, distrust, and even hatred. However, they found that they had a number of common political concerns and ultimately they decided to work together. Rather than fighting alone to secure their own rights and freedoms, imagine what could be achieved if evangelicals invited American Muslims, Jews, Catholics, Hindus, and Buddhists for a discussion about how their communities could advance their common concerns for religious freedom and the flourishing of all.

While cobelligerence with other faiths could certainly increase the political influence of evangelicalism, that is not my primary concern. For decades now, evangelicals have cultivated a terrible public reputation for being politically selfish and cynical. The optics of evangelicals standing side by side with

---

5. My thanks to Cory Willson and Matthew Krabill, the editors of the *Evangelical Interfaith Dialogue Journal*, both of whom provided me with numerous helpful suggestions of churches and organizations of note.

Muslims, Jews, Catholics, Mormons, Buddhists, and Hindus is far superior to the optics of evangelicals standing alone, demanding more freedom for themselves. The added bonus, of course, is that this is the right thing to do.

Furthermore, while American evangelicals may not recognize it, they have a lot in common with their Muslim neighbors. Both sides care deeply about the spiritual integrity of their worship, families, schools, and community. Both sides are concerned about the over-sexualization of their children and culture. Both are annoyed when liberals explain to them that all religions are basically the same. Both are tired of being labeled culturally backward, ignorant, and regressive. Both desire to freely embody their visions of the good life in the public square. While evangelicals and Muslims are different in a variety of ways, there are more than enough opportunities for their occasional cooperation and cobelligerence in American life.

Beyond increased influence and a better public image, cobelligerence has one final benefit for evangelicals—(trans)formation. When evangelicals engage in dialogue and collaboration with Muslims, they might actually learn something from their interlocutors. Evangelicals might slowly come to know, respect, and even enjoy their Muslim neighbors.

While deep differences will—and should—remain between Muslims and evangelicals, through dialogue and cobelligerence these two interlocutors might begin to imagine a contested but generative political life together.

6. Deconstruct Christian Nationalism

Kuyper was able to convince his movement of nineteenth-century Christian pluralists that Christian nationalism would be detrimental to both Christianity and the nation. American evangelicals should listen. Kuyper insisted that the Dutch church should never attempt to coercively unite the pluriform faiths of the Netherlands under its own roof. The church, he argued, is, by definition, "antithetical to the unity dream. . . . This is its essential character, its very nature."[6] The church is, and ought to be, a distinct moral community within the nation. American evangelicals who long to "claim America for Christ" would do well to heed his warnings about the detrimental effects of Christian nationalism.

6. Abraham Kuyper, "Calvinism: Source and Stronghold of Our Constitutional Liberties" in *Abraham Kuyper: A Centennial Reader*, ed. James Bratt (Grand Rapids: Eerdmans, 1998), 390.

In chapter three we explored Kuyper's indentification of two distinct ways in which churches have historically attempted to solve the problem of religious diversity. The first was through force and aggression. Here the church tried to unite the nation through the violent assimilation of minority faiths. The second method was by watering down the church—thinning the church out so that it could unite the diverse faiths of the nation. The first solution violently dissolves the nation into the church; the second disolves the church into the nation.

While these two modes of Christian nationalism appear quite different, Kuyper argued that they rest upon the same fatal mistakes. They both assume that the religious diversity of a nation is a solvable problem, and they both assume that it is the church's responsibility to solve it. In order to solve religious difference, the church must either surrender its peaceableness (and become violent) or the church must surrender its principled distinctiveness (and become watered-down). For Kuyper, if the church forcefully assimilated outsiders or allowed itself to be assimilated into another community, it would suffer a fundamental "loss of its character."[7] In light of this, when American evangelicals play with the idea of Christian nationalism, they are playing with the very integrity of Christ's church.

American evangelicals would do well to listen to Abraham Kuyper and accept the fact that America's many faiths are inevitably pervasive, public, and pluriform. When it comes to American Muslims, evangelicals must accept that there is no way to ignore, privatize, or assimilate Islamic faith or culture. Islam is here, Islam is public, and Islam is different. The pluralist project cannot begin until American evangelicals accept this truth. Once evangelicals have done this, they can say with Kuyper, "I know of no other solution than to accept—freely and candidly, without any reservations—a free multiformity."[8]

Once Kuyper accepted this reality, he could finally begin to advocate a pluralistic approach for a nation that was irretrievably divided. For, Kuyper insisted, our pluralistic reforms "do not divide the nation or break society . . . they find the nation divided, conviction against conviction and they reckon with this undeniable fact!"[9] Once evangelicals put down the dream of Christian nationalism and accept Islam's presence in American life, they can begin

7. Kuyper, "Calvinism: Source and Stronghold," in Bratt, *Centennial Reader*, 390.

8. Abraham Kuyper, "Uniformity: The Curse of Modern Life," in *Abraham Kuyper: A Centennial Reader*, ed. James Bratt (Grand Rapids: Eerdmans, 1998), 39.

9. Abraham Kuyper, *Pro Rege*, 3:181–82. Trans. and quoted in Wendy Fish Naylor, "Abraham Kuyper and the Emergence of the Neo-Calvinist Pluralism in the Dutch School Struggle" (PhD diss., University of Chicago, 2006), 147.

the much more interesting process of exploring how they can love their Muslim neighbors with the hospitality, justice, and grace of Jesus Christ.

7. Construct Christian Pluralism

If they believe anything, American evangelicals believe that Christ *alone* is Lord. The logical next step will be asking evangelicals a quintessentially Kuyperian question: if Christ alone is Lord, can Christians continue to claim lordship over Muslims? The answer, of course, is, "No!"

For if Christ—not the Christian—is the only rightful ruler over a Muslim, that has significant consequences for how Christians relate to their Muslim neighbors. If Christ has sovereignly bestowed dignity, rights, and freedoms on Muslim citizens, evangelicals dare not presume to take these sacred rights away. As Abraham Kuyper argued, Christ alone is sovereign over the diverse faiths of a nation. No Christian can dare seize Christ's temporal or spatial sovereignty over a diverse nation.

If evangelicals wish to honor Christ's temporal sovereignty over America, they will have to stop trying to control American history. They will need to relinquish their claims to historical sovereignty over America's past or its future. Evangelicals do not control American history; Christ does. Moreover, Christ will sovereignly decide the time and tenor of his eschatological return. His exclusive temporal sovereignty should greatly humble the apocalyptic predictions and prognostications of evangelical dispensationalists. Finally, evangelical fears about a future clash of civilizations or an Islamification of America betray a fundamental lack of trust in Christ, who is sovereign over American history.

In the same vein, if evangelicals wish to honor Christ's spatial sovereignty over America, they will have to stop allowing the American government to invade, monitor, and control sacred Muslim spaces. Evangelicals will need to actively resist the American government's claims to spatial sovereignty over Muslim schools, charities, mosques, families, media, and so on. They will need to defend these spaces, not out of charity, but because Christ's spatial sovereignty demands that these sacred spaces be honored and respected. As Abraham Kuyper argued long ago, before a government "crosses the boundary" into a faith community, it recognizes that it is walking on holy ground and "respectfully 'takes the shoes off from its feet.'"[10]

---

10. Kuyper, "Sphere Sovereignty," in *Centennial Reader*, 477.

Releasing their imaginary grasp on American time and space will be diffi-cult for American evangelicals. That said, they will experience a great relief in the end. No longer will they bear the imagined burden of American cultural and religious leadership. Instead, they will be set free to serve as one moral minority voice within a pluralistic culture. Their new responsibility will be to embody a faithful witness to the justice and hospitality of Jesus Christ. Rather than dominate American culture, they will seek to be a distinct source of salt, light, and leaven lifting up the whole.

8. Follow the Whole Christ

As we discussed in chapter six, a respect for Christ's exclusive sovereignty over Muslim spaces is not enough. The complex fear, distrust, and division of this historical moment demands more than simply the kingship of Christ. Evangelicals making their way amidst this complex conflict need the whole Christ—every bit of him. In chapter six we explored the public implications of this more complex Christ.

We explored, for example, the public implications of Christ's humble heal-ing and liberation of the slave who came to arrest him on the Mount of Olives. Amidst the chaos and violence of clubs, torches, and swords, Jesus—the king of American evangelicals—quietly kneeled down, picked up the man's severed ear, and healed him—all the while rebuking his followers and commanding them to put away their swords. In this brief encounter with Jesus, American evangelicals are confronted with the power of Christ's humility and healing—not simply for his friends, but his enemies too. Klaas Schilder's reflections on this encounter allow American evangelicals the opportunity to reflect on the power of small acts of healing and vulnerability for friend and foe alike amidst the so-called clash of civilizations.

Moving on to Schilder's more grotesque portrayal of the naked Christ on the cross, American evangelicals are here forced to gaze upon their own naked fear, hatred, and violence. Gazing at Christ's nakedness, evangelicals are forced to finally admit their own propensity for aggression and their own need for mercy. The cross exposes all—including American evangelicals. Looking at the naked body of Jesus, they are forced to admit a humbling truth: "I put him there on that cross. I am capable of this violence. I am looking at my own naked aggression." The evangelical who has gazed upon the naked cross can no longer essentialize the Muslim neighbor as some violent *thing* that is wholly other from him- or herself. On Golgotha, all of humanity—evangelicals and

Muslims—participated in the violence of the cross. This is a hard but stubborn truth. Schilder was right, "We want to avert our eyes, but we may not. We *must* look on." For Christ "made this plundering of His clothes a sign for all ensuing generations."[11]

In the Christology of Hans Boersma, American evangelicals must wrestle with the fact that hospitality is absolutely central to Christ's cross and the knowledge of what it means to carry one. American evangelicals at this historical moment are locked in a massive debate about Muslim refugees escaping the Syrian civil war. Does America have a responsibility to open itself up to the needs, pain, and potential violence of these asylum-seekers? Christ did. According to Boersma, this is exactly what the cross represents—the hospitality of God. On the cross we witness the opening of God's very self to the pain and violence of the world. The outstretched hands of Christ have public implications for how American evangelicals respond to the Syrian refugee crisis. Christ's cruciform hospitality does not promise a romantic rainbow nation of multicultural harmony. Cruciform hospitality lived out amidst deep difference and violence means that there will be pain—even blood. Nevertheless, this is the cost of cruciform hospitality evangelicals must be prepared to pay in a divided nation.

Finally, we examined Herman Bavinck's pervasive vision of Christ's redemptive work in every sphere of social and political life. For Bavinck insisted that the "fruits of Christ's sacrifice are not restricted to any one area of life; they are not limited, as so many people think nowadays, to the religious-ethical life, to the heart, the inner chamber, or the church, but are extended to the entire world."[12] In light of this picture, American evangelicals can participate in Christ's pervasive redemptive work in every sphere of American society.

In other words, the grace that evangelicals have received in their hearts can—and must—be lived out in every aspect of their public lives alongside their Muslim neighbors. As evangelicals interact with Islam at work and school, in politics and business, through the media and the marketplace, the hospitality they have received from Christ must be given to their Muslim neighbors.

Rather than looking at their Muslim neighbors through the lenses of the world (security concerns, cultural clashes and controversies, and so on),

---

11. Klaas Schilder, *Christ Crucified*, trans. Henry Zylstra (Grand Rapids: Eerdmans, 1940), 168.

12. Herman Bavinck, *Reformed Dogmatics*, ed. John Bolt, trans. John Vriend (Grand Rapids: Baker Academic, 2003–2008), 3: 451.

American evangelicals must view their Muslim neighbors first and foremost through their primary lens—Jesus Christ. Christ's sovereignty, humility, nakedness, hospitality, sacrifice, and healing must be the ultimate framework through which American evangelicals not only see but also engage their Muslim neighbor.

9. Go Through Worship Training

It will not be enough, however, for American evangelicals to simply have the framework of Christ; they will need to develop the heart of Christ as well.

In chapter seven we argued that if Christian pluralists were going to form strong and durable hearts capable of resisting the politics of fear, worship would need to play a central role. We argued that durable hearts and lasting affections do not emerge instantaneously. Sturdy and strong hearts require exercise, practice, discipline, habituation, and a supportive community of desire and imagination. This is why we stressed the importance of worship.

However fearful, hateful, or angry evangelical hearts feel throughout the week, they can begin the slow process of redirecting themselves towards the humility, grace, and hospitality of Christ in and through Sunday worship. In the sanctuary, evangelical citizens have the opportunity to hear stories of hospitality, sing songs of justice, pray prayers of humility, assume postures of openness, and look upon images of grace. They can, in short, train their hearts to desire hospitality over hostility.

Of course, heads and hearts are notoriously stubborn, and worship works slowly. That said, if American evangelicals are ever going to serve as a faithful and lasting voice for Muslim rights and dignity in the United States, worship formation will have to play a significant role. For in a fear-filled age, durable pluralists will require formative spaces of confession, lament, encouragement, humility, and direction. For the American evangelical, that space will and must be the sanctuary.

10. Make Pluralism Vocational

Finally, while a few American evangelicals will serve in the elite offices of national politics, media, and the academy, the vast majority of them will lead relatively ordinary lives alongside their Muslim neighbors. If evangelicals are going to be a force for pluralism in America, they will need to do so at both the national and the local level. Evangelicals are going to need a vocational approach to peacemaking and hospitality with their Muslim neighbors. They will need to see their vocational spaces in businesses, schools, hospitals, neighborhood councils, and city halls as sacred spaces of hospitality, justice, and grace. These so-called mundane vocational spaces need to be understood as critically important places in which the love of Christ can be made manifest.

When a coworker is harassed, when a local Mosque is vandalized, when a student requests a space for prayer, when a customer asks for a different meal, or a patient requests a translator, all of these relatively small moments must be seen by everyday evangelicals as treasured opportunities to embody the hospitality of Christ in a fragmenting world. After all, evangelicals follow a God who—during a time of great fear and fragmentation—offered not only his love, but his very self.

The Politics of Holy Week

It is April 2017 and pluralism has fallen on hard times. Just this past month,

- In Sweden, a terrorist hijacked a truck and drove it into a crowd of people, killing four and wounding fifteen more.
- In Syria, US missiles struck military installations in retaliation for Bashar al-Assad's chemical weapons attack against his own citizens.
- In Texas, a group of citizens expressed outrage at the fact that a school provided Muslim students with a place to pray.
- In Italy, Muslim parents punished their daughter for not wearing her hijab—they forced her to shave her head.
- In Canada, a new study was released revealing that nearly half of Canadians now view Islam unfavorably.
- In the United States, President Trump attempted to ban immigration from six Muslim-majority countries in pursuit of his desire for a "total and complete shutdown of Muslims entering the United States."
- In England, a Muslim woman in a city square was surrounded by shouting members of the nationalist English Defence League. The men loudly demanded that she "go home!"
- In the Netherlands, Geert Wilder's anti-Islamic party became the second largest political party in the entire country.
- In France, rising quickly in the presidential polls, the rightwing leader Marine Le Pen quipped that a "multicultural society is a multiconflict society."
- Finally, in Afghanistan, the largest non-nuclear bomb in human history was dropped by the United States.

Perhaps it is providential that I am writing this epilogue during Holy Week. Today, in fact, is Holy Saturday. Here I am—amidst the pain and terror of this past month—tapping away on my laptop, waiting, longing for Easter to arrive. The enemies of pluralism didn't take Holy Week off this year. Six days ago, on the morning of Palm Sunday, two churches in Egypt were brutally attacked by suicide bombers—they killed forty-five and injured another 126. In the aftermath, an ISIS leader quipped that Christians are "our favorite prey." In the face of this horrific terror, what response can Holy Week offer?

Epilogues are the place where we typically ask, "In the light of what we know, what do we do?" Writing these words on Holy Saturday, I feel compelled to reframe the question, "In the light of Holy Week, what should we do?"[1] Of course, such a question assumes that Holy Week, rightly understood, actually has something relevant to say to my twenty-first-century life—that Easter has political consequences for my life and the life of the world. Furthermore, it assumes that my participation in Holy Week should impact the way I see, live, and walk amidst the horrors of this conflict over Islam and the West. Readers who regard Holy Week as a private religious ritual—a spiritual season whose relevance is limited to one's personal life—will, no doubt, find the question silly and inappropriate. My wager, however, is that those readers closed the book some time ago. With that let me restate the question for this epilogue: in light of Holy Week, what should we do?

The Failure of High Walls and Open Doors

At the beginning of this book we explored the two dominant Western voices shaping the debate over Islam in the West. First was the left-wing voice advocating a certain vague openness and generosity, tolerance and diversity, inclusion and multiculturalism. This was the voice of the inclusive and open doors. In reaction to this was the nationalist right-wing voice of law and order, safety and security, nation and culture. For this reactionary voice the political goal was a set of restrictive and high walls.

If the Dutch experience with Islam taught us anything, it is this: political visions that myopically seek either high walls or open doors are not only unsustainable, but they are dangerous. Open doors fail to wrestle with the real costs, challenges, and dangers of deep difference, while high walls make

---

1. A version of the following reflection was published as "Refugees and the Politics of Holy Week," *Public Justice Review* 2 (2017).

the politics of difference even more difficult as they actively increase social distrust, fragmentation, and division on all sides.

The dominant Western rhetoric of open doors and high walls fails to provide citizens with the critical resources they desperately need to live in a globalizing world in which difference is increasingly deep, fast, and close.

The right is certainly correct that a safe house requires walls. The left is certainly correct that a hospitable house requires doors that open. That said, as we have seen time and time again, neither walls nor doors make a house feel at all like a home. A third element is needed—and I think we can find that third element in Holy Week, of all places.

The Alternative Politics of Holy Week

How might Holy Week move us beyond the myopic visions of high walls and open doors? What is this missing third element that Holy Week reveals? Consider for a moment five critical spaces in which Christ's approach to hospitality is made manifest throughout his final week.

First, the streets of Jerusalem. With raucous crowds chanting and singing, Palm Sunday launches Holy Week with a parade of jubilation and political expectation. The crowds of Jerusalem loved the idea of being a part of the Jesus-movement. They waved palm branches and sang loudly for the charismatic leader. They loved the idea of joining a righteous and vibrant movement. But, as we all know, a few days later, when the music died down, when things became difficult and dangerous, when the true cost of the movement was revealed, the followers and their political visions melted like snow.

Today the advocates of the open door love a good protest. There is a pride and an energy that comes from shouting against the evils of restrictions and racism. There is a self-satisfaction that comes from being a part of the morally generous team. Advocates of the open door love the idea of speaking out for cultural diversity, tolerance, and inclusion.

That said, Holy Week is about to ask them a difficult question. It is one thing to shout for the opening of your nation's door; it is another thing entirely to open your home and your life to the deep challenges of difference. Palm Sunday stands as an unwelcome reminder to advocates of the open door that political ideals are fleeting and fragile. For as the week proceeds, Jesus will demonstrate that true hospitality amidst difference that is deep, fast, and close will ultimately cost more than a palm branch—or a protest sign.

Second, the upper room. In preparation for the last supper, Jesus begins the process of embodying the sort of hospitality he desires for his movement. He does not simply open the door for his guests. Rather, he assumes the posture of a servant. He fetches water, disrobes, kneels, and begins to scrub the feet of all twelve guests. His hospitality is not abstract, it is not theoretical; it is embodied. The feet, the objects of his hospitality, are covered in mud and dust, sweat and shit.

As the evening proceeds, Jesus offers each of his guests a seat at the table. He welcomes each of them into a space of intimacy, vulnerability, and relationship. The ultimate host, Jesus ends the evening by offering his guests more than food, more than relationship; he offers his very self. For his guests, Jesus breaks open his body and pours out his blood. To pile scandal upon scandal, Jesus offers this to a group of guests who will reject his gift, deny him, and abandon him.

The hospitality Christ embodies at the table demands more than the opening of a door or the sharing of resources; it involves the offering of one's very self to a group of people who may well reject and abandon the offer.

Third, the Mount of Olives. Following the meal, Jesus goes to the Mount of Olives to pray with his disciples. Soon after, a band of soldiers and servants of the high priest arrives to arrest Jesus. A struggle ensues and Peter attacks a slave of the high priest named Malchus. The slave's ear is severed and falls to the ground. Jesus rebukes Peter, reaches out, and heals Malchus—his captor.

It is not uncommon for high-wall advocates to begin their arguments with the claim that Islam is coming to bind and enslave the West. While their claim about Islam's intentions can be challenged, Malchus's intentions can't. Malchus is clearly coming to bind Jesus, to take his freedom and lead him to death. How does Jesus respond to this clear and present threat? Does he build a wall? Does he seek first his own security? No, amidst the fear, chaos, and violence of the struggle between the disciples and the soldiers, Jesus reaches out his unarmed hand in calm vulnerability and he heals the one who came to hurt. He liberates the slave who came to bind.

Advocates of the high wall might protest that national security in a violent world requires some measure of coercive power—and they are certainly right. However, the story of Malchus still stands. This brief encounter refuses to be ignored or dismissed. Holy Week demands that we wrestle with the healing of Malchus. With integrity, we cannot explain away this vulnerable healing in the face of violence.

The Mount of Olives reminds us that power and security are not political ends in and of themselves. They must serve a deeper purpose—namely the goal of healing and relationship. In the shadow of the Mount of Olives, followers of Jesus can no longer seek an ultimate political goal of security from Muslims.

Rather, Christians may only seek national security for the sake of healing and building a relationship with Islam.

Fourth, Golgotha. While we often think that humanity stripped and exposed Jesus on Golgotha, Klaas Schilder disagrees. He submits that it was humanity who was stripped bare on that forsaken hill outside Jerusalem. On that hill, he argues, humanity is forced to gaze upon the ghastly sight of its own naked aggression, fear, and violence. We Westerners like to paint ourselves as civilized and rational in contrast with Islam, which we paint as uncivilized and irrational. We are safe; they are dangerous. In ghastly detail, Golgotha exposes both West and East as one species united in their mutual capability for grotesque injustice and violence. Beholding our naked aggression every Good Friday, looking head on at all of our exposed ugliness, is a sobering and humbling experience.

That said, Golgotha offers us a word of comfort, as well. Jesus does not leave us naked and shivering in our aggression. Though we stole his clothes in violence, he clothes us with his peace. But even more than that, Jesus promises to clothe our naked aggression with his very self. As pluralists, we can be tempted to imagine that our hospitality emerges from some inherent moral superiority—some reservoir of goodness that we ourselves generate. Golgotha rejects this dangerous lie. Golgotha reminds the pluralist that she can open herself to others only because Christ first opened himself up to her.

Fifth, a tomb, a road, and a beach. If Golgotha demands that we follow Christ in opening ourselves to a dangerous world, the empty tomb promises that this openness is not a fool's errand. It ensures that the final chapter of Christian pluralism is not death, but life. Finally, from Sunday resurrection to Monday reconnection, Easter leads us to a Galilean beach and a dusty road to Emmaus. After his resurrection, Jesus immediately begins the process of reconnecting with his scattered followers. He walks alongside them, joining them in conversation on the road to Emmaus. They don't recognize it is Jesus until he demonstrates his hospitality at the dinner table. Finally, the story ends with Jesus once again preparing a meal. The disciples had been fishing on the Sea of Galilee all morning and they discover Jesus—ever the host—sitting on the beach making them breakfast.

Table Politics

When it comes to Islamic immigration in the West, the myopic politics of either high walls or open doors fails to provide the political humility, hospitality, and relationship that this dire situation requires. Those of us who participate in Holy Week are offered the opportunity to try on an alternative political imagination for this clash between Mecca and Amsterdam. Participating in this holiest of weeks, we begin to see what the politics of walls and doors have been missing all along: a table.

The table politics embodied throughout Holy Week require costly sacrifice, true humility, and real relationship. To be sure, table politics require functioning walls and open doors. After all, tables work best in homes that are both generous and secure, both open and ordered. These five critical spaces of Holy Week insist that the ultimate political goal is not the security of a high wall or the generosity of the open door. No, the ultimate political goal is a well-set table.

After all, if a home is concerned with nothing but high walls, outsiders will not be able to approach the table. Those excluded will come to resent the table or doubt that it even exists. Make no mistake, the order and security provided by walls are a necessary political good. They make the house safe for a table to exist. However, walls, laws, and restrictions are not political ends in and of themselves. The ultimate end of politics is not a wall of security but a table of fellowship. The walls protect the table—the walls serve the politics of the table. If the walls come to inhibit the hospitality of the table, they must be altered.

Likewise, the generosity of open doors is an important political good. In times of war, famine, and immediate danger, open doors are a moral absolute. However, an open door is not a sufficient political end in and of itself. An open door must lead to a well-prepared table. If hosts wish to let people in, they must count the cost of the meal, and they must be willing to vulnerably and humbly take a seat at the table next to their guests.

Finally, table politics will demand that the distinct categories of *guests* and *hosts* ultimately come to an end. Well-functioning tables will not dissolve our differences, but they will dissolve our hierarchies. Well-functioning tables will encourage both guests and hosts to shed their labels and begin to call each other by a new name, a category unknown in modern political theory—friend.

For, after his resurrection, Jesus demonstrates this final aspect and ultimate image of table politics. There, on the shores of Galilee, Christ embodies our ultimate political longing: a free, just, and joyous meal. On that crisp morning by the sea, Jesus sat down in the sand, made a fire, and began to cook breakfast. He lovingly prepared this meal for people who were no longer his guests; he now called them friends.

Bibliography

Ahmed, Akbar. *Journey into America: The Challenge of Islam.* Washignton, DC: Brookings Press, 2010.

Al-Marayati, Salam. "America's Muslim Ghettos." *Washington Post.* August 15, 2005.

Al-Shaikh-Ali, Anas. "Islamophobic Discourse Masquerading as Art and Literature: Combating Myth through Progressive Education." In *Islamophobia: The Challenge of Pluralism in the Twenty-First Century.* Edited by John L. Esposito and Ibrahim Kalin. Oxford: Oxford University Press, 2011.

Ali, Ayaan Hirsi. *The Caged Virgin: An Emancipation Proclamation for Women and Islam.* New York: Free Press, 2006.

———. *Infidel.* New York: Free Press, 2007.

———. *Nomad: From Islam to America: A Personal Journey through the Clash of Civilizations.* New York: Free Press, 2010.

Althusius, Johannes. *The Politics of Johannes Althusius.* Translated by Frederick S. Carney. Boston: Beacon Press, 1964.

An-Na'im, Abdullahi Ahmed. *Islam and the Secular State: Negotiating the Future of Shari'a.* Cambridge, MA: Harvard University Press, 2008.

d'Appollonia, Ariane Chebel. *Frontiers of Fear: Immigration and Insecurity in the United States and Europe.* Ithaca, NY: Cornell University Press, 2012.

d'Appollonia, Ariane Chebel and Simon Reich, eds. *Immigration, Integration, and Security: America and Europe in Comparative Perspective.* Pittsburgh: University of Pittsburgh Press, 2008.

Ashworth, G. J., Brian Graham, and J. E. Tunbridge. *Pluralising Pasts: Heritage, Identity and Place in Multicultural Societies.* London: Pluto Press, 2007.

Baber, H. E. *The Multicultural Mystique: The Liberal Case against Diversity.* Amherst, NY: Prometheus, 2008.

Bavinck, Herman. "Common Grace." Translated by R. C. Van Leeuwen. *Calvin Theological Journal* 24, no. 1 (1989): 35–65.

———. *De algemeene genade.* Kampen: G. PH. Zalsman, 1894.

————. "De navolging van Christus," *De vrije kerk* 11 (1885):101–13, 203–13 and 12 (1886): 321–33.

————. *De navolging van Christus en het moderne leven.* Kampen: Kok, 1918.

————. *Reformed Dogmatics.* 4 vols. Edited by John Bolt. Translated by John Vriend. Grand Rapids: Baker Academic, 2003–2008.

Bavinck, J. H. *The Church between Temple and Mosque.* Grand Rapids: Eerdmans, 1961.

Bawer, Bruce. *While Europe Slept: How Radical Islam Is Destroying the West from Within.* New York: Broadway Books, 2006.

Bellah, Robert N., et al. *Habits of the Heart: Individualism and Commitment in American Life.* 3rd ed. Berkeley: University of California, 2008.

Benhabib, Seyla. *Democracy and Difference.* Princeton, NJ: Princeton University Press, 1996.

————. *Situating the Self: Gender, Community, and Postmodernism in Contemporary Ethics.* New York: Routledge, 1992.

Berezin, Mabel. *Illiberal Politics in Neoliberal Times: Culture, Security, and Populism.* Cambridge: Cambridge University Press, 2009.

Berger, Peter, ed. *Between Relativism and Fundamentalism: Religious Resources for a Middle Position.* Grand Rapids: Eerdmans, 2010.

————. *The Desecularization of the World: Resurgent Religion and World Politics.* Grand Rapids: Eerdmans, 1999.

————. "Sociology: A Disinvitation?" *Society* 30 (1992): 12–18.

Berkvens-Stevelinck, Christiane, Jonathan Israel, and G. H. M. Posthumus Meyjes, eds. *The Emergence of Tolerance in the Dutch Republic.* Leiden: Brill, 1997.

Bhatia, Amit A. "American Evangelicals and Islam: Their Perspectives, Attitudes, and Tractices towards Muslims in the US." *Transformation,* 34.1 (2016): 26–37.

Biggar, Nigel and Linda Hogan, eds. *Religious Voices in Public Spaces.* Oxford: Oxford University Press, 2009.

Bijleveld, Nikolaj Hein. "Voor God, Volk en Vaderland: De plaats van de hervormde predikant binnen de nationale eenwordingsprocessen in Nederland in de eerste helft van de negentiende eeuw." PhD diss., Groningen University, 2007.

Boersma, Hans. *Violence, Hospitality, and the Cross: Reappropriating the Atonement Tradition.* Grand Rapids: Baker Academic, 2006.

Bolt, John. *A Free Church, A Holy Nation: Abraham Kuyper's American Public Theology.* Grand Rapids: Eerdmans, 2001.

————. "The Imitation of Christ Theme in the Cultural-Ethical Ideal of Herman Bavinck." PhD diss., University of St. Michael's College, Toronto, 1982.

Bonney, Richard and D. J. B. Trim, eds. *Persecution and Pluralism: Calvinists and Religious Minorities in Early Modern Europe 1550–1700.* Bern: Peter Lang, 2006.

Boomgaarden, Hajo G. and Rens Vliegenthart. "Explaining the Rise of Anti-Immigrant Parties: The Role of News Media Content." *Electoral Studies* 26 (2007): 404–17.

Borgman, Erik. "Het Westen en de islam: Theologische bijdragen aan een geseculariseerde cultuur." In *Islam in Nederland: Theologische bijdragen in tijden van secularisering.* Edited by Mohammed Ajouaou, Erik Borgman, and Pim Valkenberg. Amsterdam: Boom, 2011.

Bornewasser, J. A. "The Authority of the Dutch State over the Churches, 1795–1853." In

Britain and the Netherlands: Church and State since the Reformation. Edited by A. C. Duke and C. A. Tamse. The Hague: Martinus Nijhoff, 1981.

———. "Thorbecke and the Churches." In *Acta Historiae Neerlandicae: Studies on the History of the Netherlands.* Volume 7. Edited by B. H. Slicher van Bath. The Hague: Martinus Nijhoff, 1974.

Bornschier, Simon. *Cleavage Politics and the Populist Right: The New Cultural Conflict in Western Europe.* Philadelphia: Temple University Press, 2010.

Bosch, Mineke. "Telling Stories, Creating (and Saving) Her Life: An Analysis of the Autobiography of Ayaan Hirsi Ali." *Women's Studies International Forum* 31 (2008): 138–47.

Bowen, John. *Blaming Islam.* Cambridge, MA: MIT Press, 2012.

———. "Europeans against Multiculturalism." *Boston Review,* July/August, 2011.

———. *Why the French Don't Like Headscarves: Islam, the State, and Public Space.* Princeton, NJ: Princeton University Press, 2008.

Bowlin, John, ed. *The Kuyper Center Review.* Vol. 2: *Revelation and Common Grace.* Grand Rapids: Eerdmans, 2011.

Bracke, Sarah. "From 'Saving Women' to 'Saving Gays': Rescue Narratives and Their Dis/continuities." *European Journal of Women's Studies* 19, no. 2 (2012): 237–52.

Brants, Kees and Katrin Voltmer, eds. *Political Communication in Postmodern Democracy: Challenging the Primacy of Politics.* New York: Palgrave, 2011.

Bratt, James D. "Abraham Kuyper, J. Gresham Machen, and the Dynamics of Reformed Anti-Modernism." *Journal of Presbyterian History* 74 (1997): 247–58.

———. *Abraham Kuyper: Modern Calvinist, Christian Democrat.* Grand Rapids: Eerdmans, 2013.

———. "Abraham Kuyper's Calvinism: Society, Economics, and Empire in the Late Nineteenth Century." In *John Calvin Rediscovered.* Edited by Edward Dommen and James D. Bratt. Louisville, KY: Westminster John Knox Press, 2007: 79–92.

———. "Abraham Kuyper's Commentatio (1860): The Young Kuyper about Calvin, a Lasco, and the Church." *Church History and Religious Culture* 87 (2007): 130–32.

———. *Dutch Calvinism in Modern America: A History of a Conservative Subculture.* Grand Rapids: Eerdmans, 1984.

———. "In the Shadow of Mt. Kuyper: A Survey of the Field." *Calvin Theological Journal* 31 (1996): 51–66.

Bratt, James D. and Edward Dommen, eds. *John Calvin Rediscovered: The Impact of His Social and Economic Thought.* Louisville, KY: Westminster John Knox Press, 2007.

Bratt, John H. *The History and Development of Calvinism.* Grand Rapids: Eerdmans, 1964.

Bremmer, Rolf Hendrik. *Kuyper, Hoedemaker en de Doleantie.* Apeldoorn, NL: Willem de Zwitjgerstichting, 1986.

Brooks, Stephen. *The Challenge of Cultural Pluralism.* Westport, CT: Greenwood Publishing, 2002.

Buijs, Govert. "The Promise of Civil Society." In *Civil Society: East and West.* Edited by Peter Blokhuis. Sioux Center, IA: Dordt College Press, 2006.

Buruma, Ian. *Murder in Amsterdam: The Death of Theo van Gogh and the Limits of Tolerance.* New York: Penguin Books, 2006.

Butler, Judith. "Sexual Politics, Torture, and Secular Time." *The British Journal of Sociology*, 59, no. 1 (2008): 1–23.

Calvin, John. "Articles Concerning the Organization of the Church and Worship at Geneva Proposed by the Ministers at the Council January 16, 1537." In *Calvin: Theological Treatises*. Translated and edited by J. K. S. Reid. Philadelphia: Westminster Press, 1954.

———. *Calvin: Theological Treatises*. Translated and edited by J. K. S. Reid. Philadelphia: Westminster Press, 1954.

———. *The Institutes of the Christian Religion*. Edited by John T. McNeill. Translated by Ford Lewis Battles. The Library of Christian Classics. Philadelphia: Westminster Press, 1960 (1559). 4.17.40.

Carlson-Thies, Stanley. "Democracy in the Netherlands: Consociational or Pluriform?" PhD diss., University of Toronto, 1993.

Carney, Frederick S. "The Associational Theory of Johannes Althusius: A Study of Calvinist Constitutionalism." PhD diss., University of Chicago, 1960.

Cavanaugh, William. *The Myth of Religious Violence: Secular Ideology and the Roots of Modern Conflict*. Oxford: Oxford University Press, 2009.

Cesari, Jocelyne. "Islamic Organizations in the United States." In *The Oxford Handbook of American Islam*. Edited by Jane I. Smith and Yvonne Yazbeck Haddad. Oxford: Oxford University Press, 2015.

———. *When Islam and Democracy Meet: Muslims in Europe and the United States*. New York: Palgrave Macmillan, 2006.

Chaplin, Jonathan, Paul Marshall, and Bernard Zylstra, eds. *Political Theory and Christian Vision: Essays in Memory of Bernard Zylstra*. Lanham, MD: University Press of America, 1994.

Cherribi, Sam. *In the House of War: Dutch Islam Observed*. Oxford: Oxford University Press, 2010.

Cliteur, Paul. "De noodzaak van morel en politiek secularism." In *Continent op drift? Europese waarde in de schaduwen van morgen*. Edited by Hans Verboven. Kapellen, NL: Uitgeverij Pelckmans, 2010.

———. *The Secular Outlook: In Defense of Moral and Political Secularism*. Oxford: Wiley Blackwell, 2010.

Clouser, Roy. *The Myth of Religious Neutrality: An Essay on the Hidden Role of Religious Belief in Theories*. South Bend, IN: University of Notre Dame Press, 1991.

Cohen, Job. "Religie als bron van sociale cohesie? Godsdienst en overheid in een postgeseculariseerde samenleving." Public lecture at the University of Leiden, December 19, 2003.

Connolly, William. *Pluralism*. Durham, NC: Duke University Press, 2005.

Cristillo, Louis. "The Case for the Muslim School as a Civil Society Actor." In *Educating the Muslims of America*. Edited by Yvonne Y. Haddad, Farid Senzai, and Jane I. Smith. Oxford: Oxford University Press, 2009.

D'Costa, Gavin. *Theology in the Public Square: Church, Academy, and Nation*. Oxford: Wiley Blackwell, 2006.

Daalder, Hans. "Consociationalism, Centre, and Periphery in the Netherlands." In *Mo-

bilization, Center-periphery Structures, and Nation Building. Edited by P. Torsvik. Oslo: Universitesforlaget, 1981.

————."Dutch Jews in a Segmented Society." *Acta Historiae Neerlandicae* 10 (1978): 175–94.

Dalrymple, Theodore. "A Wiser Holland: The Dutch, Mugged by Reality, Toughen Up on Radical Islam." *National Review*. January 30, 2006.

de Bruijn, Hans. *Geert Wilders Speaks Out: The Rhetorical Frames of a European Populist*. The Hague: Eleven International Publishing, 2012.

de Bruijne, Ad. "Is er ook een kerk in de buurt?" http://www.tukampen.nl/schooldag/2007/ toes praakalthdb.doc (accessed May 5, 2012).

————. *Levend in Leviathan: Een onderzoek naar de theorie over 'christendom' in de politique theologie van Oliver O'Donovan*. Kampen: Kok, 2006.

De Graaf, Beatrice. *Waar zijn wij bang voor? Veiligheidsdenken en de angst voor de ander*. Amsterdam: Forum, 2011.

De Haan, Ido. *Het bange Nederland*. Amsterdam: Bert Bakker, 2008.

de Jong, K. W. *Achtegronden en ontwikkeingen in de eredienst van de Gereformeerde Kerken in Nederland*. Baarn: Ten Have, 1996.

De Leeuw, Marc and Sonja Van Wichelen. "'Please, Go Wake Up!' Submission, Hirsi Ali, and the 'War on Terror' in the Netherlands." *Feminist Media Studies* 5, no. 3 (2005): 325–40.

de Niet, Johan, Herman Paul, and Bart Wallet. *Sober, Strict, and Scriptural: Collective Memories of John Calvin, 1800–2000*. Leiden: Brill, 2009.

Dekker, Gerard and George Harinck. "The Position of the Church Institute in Society: A Comparison between Bonhoeffer and Kuyper." *The Princeton Seminary Bulletin* 28, no. 1 (2007): 86–98.

Dekker, Gerard, Donald A. Luidens, and Rodger R. Rice, eds. *Rethinking Secularisation: Reformed Reactions to Modernity*. Lanham, MD: University Press of America, 1997.

Dénes, Iván Zoltán, ed. *Liberty and the Search for Identity: Liberal Nationalisms and the Legacy of Empires*. Budapest: Central European University Press, 2006.

Dennison, William D. "Dutch Neo-Calvinism and the Roots for Transformation: An Introductory Essay." *Journal of the Evangelical Theological Society* 42 (1999): 271–91.

Doomernik, Jeroen. "Integrating Former Guest Workers and Their Descendants: The Dutch Case." Paper presented at Trans-Atlantic Perspectives on International Migration: Cross Border Impacts, Border Security, and Socio-Political Responses Conference at the University of Texas at San Antonio, March 5, 2010.

Dostert, Troy. *Beyond Political Liberalism: Toward a Post-Secular Ethics of Public Life*. South Bend, IN: University of Notre Dame Press, 2006.

Dudink, Stefan P. "Homosexuality, Race, and the Rhetoric of Nationalism." *History of the Present: A Journal of Critical History* 1, no. 2 (2011): 259–64.

Duinham, David. "Stage, Performance, Media Event: The National Commemoration of the Second World War in the Netherlands." In *Panic and Mourning: The Cultural Work of Trauma*. Edited by D. Agostinho, E. Antz, and C. Ferreira. Berlin: De Gruyter, 2012.

Duke, A. C. and C. A. Tamse, eds. *Britain and the Netherlands: Church and State since the Reformation*. The Hague: Martinus Nijhoff, 1981.

Duyvendak, Jan Willem. *The Politics of Home: Belonging and Nostalgia in Europe and the United States.* New York: Palgrave Macmillan, 2011.

Duyvendak, Jan Willem, Trees Pels, and Rally Rijkschroeff. "A Multicultural Paradise: The Cultural Factor in Dutch Integration Policy." In *Bringing Outsiders In: Transatlantic Perspectives on Immigrant Political Incorporation.* Edited by Jennifer L. Hochschild and John H. Mollenkopf. Ithaca, NY: Cornell University Press, 2009.

Eberly, Don E. *The Essential Civil Society Reader: The Classic Essays.* New York: Rowman and Littlefield, 2000.

Edmondson, Stephen. *Calvin's Christology.* Cambridge: Cambridge University Press, 2004.

Eisinga, R., A. Felling, and J. Lammers. "Deconfessionalisation in the Netherlands." *Journal of Contemporary Religion* 11, no.1 (1996): 77–88.

Eisinga, Robert, Philip Hans Franses, and Marius Ooms. "Convergence and Persistence of Left-Right Political Orientations in the Netherlands 1978–1995." *Econometric Institute Report,* 1997.

Ellian, Afshin. "Emancipation and Integration of Dutch Muslims in Light of a Process of Polarization and the Threat of Political Islam." Middle East Program Paper Series. Washington, DC: Woodrow Wilson International Center for Scholars, 2009: 15–23.

Elver, Hilal. *The Headscarf Controversy: Secularism and the Freedom of Religion.* Oxford University Press, 2012.

Entzinger, Han. "Changing the Rules while the Game Is On: From Multiculturalism to Assimilation in the Netherlands." In *Migration, Citizenship, Ethnos: Incorporation Regimes in Germany, Western Europe, and North America.* Edited by Y. Michal Bodemann and Gökçe Yurdakul. New York: Palgrave Macmillan, 2006.

———. "A Future for the Dutch 'Ethnic Minorities' Model?" In *Muslims in Europe.* Edited by Bernard Lewis and Dominque Schnapper. London: Pinter, 1994.

———. "The Rise and Fall of Multiculturalism: The Case of the Netherlands." In *Toward Assimilation and Citizenship: Immigrants in Liberal Nation-States.* Edited by Christian Joppke and Ewa T. Morawska. New York: Palgrave, 2003.

Entzinger, Han, Martin Martiniello, and Catherine Wihtol de Wenden. *Migration between States and Markets.* Burlington, VT: Ashgate, 2004.

Entzinger, Han and Jelle van der Meer, eds. *Grenzeloze solidariteit: naar een migratiebestendige verzorgingstaat.* Amsterdam: De Balie, 2004.

Eppsteiner, Holly Straut and Jacqueline Hagan. "Religion as Psychological, Spiritual, and Social Support in the Migration Undertaking." In *Intersections of Religion and Migration: Issues at the Global Crossroads.* Edited by Jennifer B. Saunders, Elena Fiddian-Qasmiyeh, and Susanna Snyder. New York: Palgrave Macmillan, 2016: 49–70.

Esposito, John and Francois Burqat, eds. *Modernizing Islam: Religion in the Public Sphere in the Middle East and Europe.* New Brunswick, NJ: Rutgers University Press, 2003.

Esposito, John and Ibrahim Kalin. *Islamophobia: The Challenge of Pluralism in the Twenty-First Century.* Oxford: Oxford University Press, 2011.

Ewing, Katherine. *Stolen Honor: Stigmatizing Islamic Men in Berlin.* Stanford, CA: Stanford University Press, 2008.

Eyerman, Ron. *The Assassination of Theo van Gogh: From Social Drama to Cultural Trauma.* Durham, NC: Duke University Press, 2008.

Fekete, Liz. "Enlightenment Fundamentalism? Immigration, Feminism, and the Right." *Race & Class* 48, no. 2 (2006): 1–22.

Fitzgerald, Timothy. *Religion and Politics in International Relations: The Modern Myth* New York: Continuum, 2011.

Fogarty, Michael. *Christian Democracy in Western Europe 1820–1953*. New York: Routledge, 1957.

Fortuyn, Pim. *Tegen de islamisering van onze cultuur: Nederlandse identiteit als fundament.* Utrecht: A.W. Bruna, 1997.

Fraser, Nancy. *Justice Interruptus: Critical Reflections on the "Postsocialist" Condition.* New York: Routledge 1997.

Galema, Annemieke and Barbara Henkes. *Images of the Nation: Different Meanings of Dutchness, 1870–1940*. Amsterdam: Rodopi, 1993.

Geddes, Andrew. *The Politics of Migration and Immigration in Europe*. London: SAGE, 2003.

Gellner, Ernest. *Nations and Nationalism*. Ithaca, NY: Cornell University Press, 1983.

GhaneaBassiri, Kambiz. *A History of Islam in America: From the New World to the New World Order*. Cambridge: Cambridge University Press, 2010.

Gilhuis, M. *Memorietafel Van Het Christelijk Onderwijs: De Geschiedenis Van De Schoolstrijd*. Kampen: Kok, 1974.

Glenn, Charles. *The Myth of the Common School*. Amherst: The University of Massachusetts Press, 1987.

Gottschalk, Peter. "Islamophobia and Anti-Muslim Sentiment in the United States." In *The Oxford Handbook of American Islam*. Edited by Jane I. Smith and Yvonne Yazbeck Haddad. Oxford: Oxford University Press, 2015.

Goudzwaard, Bob. "Christian Social Thought in the Dutch Neo-Calvinist Tradition." In *Religion, Economics, and Social Thought*. Edited by Walter Block and Irving Hexman. Vancouver, BC: The Fraser Institute, 1986.

Gowricharn, Ruben. *Andere Gedachten: Over de Multiculturele Samenleving*. Amsterdam: Damon/Forum, 2000.

———. *Hollandse Contrasten: Over de Keerzijde van Integratie*. Amsterdam: Forum, 1998.

Graham, Fred W. *The Constructive Revolutionary: John Calvin and His Socio-Economic Impact*. Richmond, VA: John Knox Press, 1971.

Groeneveld, Simon and Michael Wintle, eds. *Under the Sign of Liberalism: Varieties of Liberalism in Past and Present*. Rotterdam: Walburg Pers, 1997.

Haak, Stephen and Geert Hunink. "Veiligheid door gastvrijheid." Proposal submitted to the *ChristenUnie*, March 18, 2010.

Haas, Guenther. *The Concept of Equity in Calvin's Ethics*. Waterloo, ON: Wilfrid Laurier University Press, 1997.

———. "Kuyper's Legacy for Christian Ethics." *Calvin Theological Journal* 33 (1998): 320–49.

Haddad, Yvonne Yazbeck. *Muslims in the West: From Sojourners to Citizens*. Oxford: Oxford University Press, 2002.

Harchaoui, Sadik, Chris Huinder, and Mohammed Benzakour. *Stigma: Marokkaan!: Over afstoten en insluiten van een ingebeelde bevolkingsgroep*. Amsterdam: Forum, 2003.

Harinck, George. "De actualiteit van Abraham Kuyper." *Christen Democratische Verken-*

ningen. Themanummer "Benauwd in het midden." Edited by Marcel ten Hooven, et al. Summer, 2008: 276–80.

———. "CDA: Keer terug naar het pluralistische model van Kuyper!" *Zonder geloof geen democratie: Christen Democratische Verkenningen.* Summer, 2006: 284–95.

———. "Gastvrijheid als sleutel voor een christendemocratische samenlevingsvisie." *Migratie in een open samenleving: Christen Democratische Verkenningen.* Edited by Hubert Beusman, Pieter Jan Dijkman, Ab Klink, and Jan Willem Sap. Fall 2011: 141–47.

———. "Kuyper als medevormgever van de plurale samenleving." *De Reformatie: Weekblad tot ontwikkeling van het gereformeerde leven,* 85, nos. 10–11 (December 5 and 12, 2009): 151–53, 165–68.

———. "Een leefbare oplossing: Katholieke en protestantse tradities en de scheiding van kerk en staat." In *Ongewenste goden: De publieke rol van religie in Nederland.* Edited by Marcel ten Hooven and Theo de Wit. Amsterdam: SUN, 2006.

———. *De tucht van de democratie: Over pluriformiteit en burgerschap.* Amersfoort: Wetenschappelijk Instituut van de ChristenUnie, Mr. G. Groen van Prinsterer stichting, 2005.

Hart, Hendrik, Johan van der Hoeven, and Nicholas Wolterstorff, eds. *Rationality in the Calvinian Tradition.* Lanham, MD: University Press of America, 1983.

Hauerwas, Stanley. *The Truth about God: The Ten Commandments in Christian Life.* Nashville, TN: Abingdon Press, 1999.

Heijne, Bas, ed. *Dromen van Europa.* Amsterdam: Bert Bakker, 2004.

Henderson, R. D. "How Abraham Kuyper Became a Kuyperian." *Christian Scholars Review* 22 (1992): 22–35.

Heslam, Peter S. *Creating a Christian Worldview: Abraham Kuyper's Lectures on Calvinism.* Grand Rapids: Eerdmans, 1998.

———. "Faith and Reason: Kuyper, Warfield, and the Shaping of the Evangelical Mind." *Anvil* 15, no. 4 (1998): 299–313.

Hillson, Harvey. "The Struggle for the Control of Primary Education in the Netherlands 1848–1917." PhD diss., Yale University, 1952.

Hollenbach, David. *The Common Good and Christian Ethics.* Cambridge: Cambridge University Press, 1998.

———. *The Global Face of Public Faith: Politics, Human Rights, and the Christian Ethic.* Washington, DC: Georgetown University Press, 2003.

Holwerda, David, ed. *Exploring the Heritage of John Calvin: Essays in Honor of John Bratt.* Grand Rapids: Baker Book House, 1976.

Hooker, Mark T. *Freedom of Education: The Dutch Political Battle for State Funding of All Schools Both Public and Private, 1801–1920.* Bloomington, IN: LlyFrawr, 2009.

Hopfl, Harro. *The Christian Polity of John Calvin.* Cambridge: Cambridge University Press, 1982.

Howell, Sally and Amaney Jamal. "Detroit Exceptionalism and the Limits of Political Incorporation." In *Being and Belonging: Muslims in the United States since 9/11.* Edited by Katherine Pratt Ewing. New York: Russell Sage, 2008: 47–79.

Huntington, Samuel. *The Clash of Civilizations and the Remaking of World Order.* New York: Simon & Schuster, 1996.

Hussain, Amir. "(Re)presenting: Muslims on North American Television." *Contemporary Islam* 4 (2010): 55–74.

Jellema, Dirk. "Abraham Kuyper: Forgotten Radical?" *Calvin Forum* 15 (1950).

———. "Abraham Kuyper's Answer to Liberalism." *Reformed Journal* 15 (1965).

———. "Abraham Kuyper's Attack on Liberalism." *Review of Politics* 19, no. 4 (1957): 472–85.

Jinkins, Michael. *Christianity, Tolerance, and Pluralism: A Theological Engagement with Isaiah Berlin's Social Theory.* New York: Routledge, 2004.

Johnson, Keith E. *Rethinking the Trinity and Religious Pluralism: An Augustinian Assessment.* Downers Grove, IL: InterVarsity Press, 2001.

Johnson, Kristen Deede. *Theology, Political Theory, and Pluralism: Beyond Tolerance and Difference.* Cambridge: Cambridge University Press, 2010.

Joppke, Christian and John Torpey. *Legal Integration of Islam.* Cambridge, MA: Harvard University Press, 2013.

Juergensmeyer, Mark. *Terror in the Mind of God: The Global Rise of Religious Violence.* Berkeley: University of California Press, 2000.

Jung, Jong Hyun. "Islamophobia? Religion, Contact with Muslims, and the Respect for Islam." *Review of Religious Research* 54, no. 1 (March 2012).

Jusová, Iveta. "Hirsi Ali and van Gogh's Submission: Reinforcing the Islam vs. Women Binary." *Women's Studies International Forum* 31 (2008): 148–55.

Kaplan, Benjamin J. *Divided by Faith: Religious Conflict and the Practice of Toleration in Early Modern Europe.* Cambridge, MA: Belknap Press, 2007.

Kärkkäinen, Veli-Matti. *An Introduction to the Theology of Religions: Biblical, Historical, and Contemporary Perspectives.* Downers Grove, IL: InterVarsity Press, 2003.

Kassam, Zayn. "The Challenges of Migration and the Construction of Religious Identities: The Case of Muslims in America." In *Intersections of Religion and Migration: Issues at the Global Crossroads.* Edited by Jennifer B. Saunders, Elena Fiddian-Qasmiyeh, and Susanna Snyder. New York: Palgrave Macmillan, 2016: 91–122.

Kaya, Ayhan. *Islam, Migration, and Integration: The Age of Securitization.* London: Palgrave Macmillan, 2009.

Kennedy, James C. "Building the New Babylon: Cultural Change in the Netherlands during the 1960s." PhD diss., University of Iowa, 1995.

———. Personal interview with the author. Amsterdam: November 24, 2011.

———. *Stad op een Berg: De publieke rol van protestantse kerken.* Zoetermeer: Boekencentrum, 2009.

———. "The Problem of Kuyper's Legacy: The Crisis of the Anti-Revolutionary Party in Post-War Holland." *Journal of Markets and Morality* 5, no. 1 (2002): 45–56.

Kennedy, James and Jan P. Zwemer. "Religion in the Modern Netherlands and the Problems of Pluralism." In *Bijdragen en Mededelingen betreffende de Geschiedenis der Nederlanden* 125, no. 2/3 (2010): 237–68.

Kidd, Thomas S. *American Christians and Islam: Evangelical Culture and Muslims from the Colonial Period to the Age of Terrorism.* Princeton, NJ: Princeton University Press, 2009.

Kimball, Charles. "The War on Terror and Its Effects on American Muslims." In *The*

Bibliography

Oxford Handbook of American Islam. Edited by Jane I. Smith and Yvonne Yazbeck Haddad. Oxford: Oxford University Press, 2015.

—————. *When Religion Becomes Lethal: The Explosive Mix of Politics and Religion in Judaism, Christianity, and Islam*. San Fransisco: Wiley & Sons, 2011.

Kinnvall, Catarina and Paul Nesbitt-Larking. *The Political Psychology of Globalization: Muslims in the West*. Oxford: Oxford University Press, 2011.

Klausen, Jytte. *The Islamic Challenge: Politics and Religion in Western Europe*. Oxford: Oxford University Press, 2005.

Knitter, Paul. *Introducing Theologies of Religions*. Maryknoll, NY: Orbis Books, 2002.

Kobes, Wayne Allen. "Sphere Sovereignty and the University: Theological Foundations of Abraham Kuyper's View of the University and Its Role in Society." PhD diss., Florida State University, 2005.

Kossmann, E. H. *The Low Countries, 1780–1940*. Oxford: Oxford University Press, 1978.

Krabbendam, Hans and Hans-Martien Ten Napel. *Regulating Morality: A Comparison of the Role of the State in Mastering the Mores in the Netherlands and the United States*. Leiden: E.M. Meijers Institute, 2000.

Kuyper, Abraham. *Abraham Kuyper: A Centennial Reader*. Edited by James Bratt. Grand Rapids: Eerdmans, 1998.

—————. *Christianity and the Class Struggle*. Translated by Dirk Jellema. Grand Rapids: Piet Hein Publishers, 1950.

—————. *Dagen van goede boodschap*. Amsterdam: J. A. Wormser, 1887.

—————. *De Gemeene Gratie*. 3 vols. Leiden: Donner, 1902–1905.

—————. *De Meiboom in De Kap*. Kampen: Kok, 1913.

—————. *De Schoolkwestie I. naar aanleiding van het onderwijs-debat in de kamer*. Amsterdam: J. H. Kruyt, 1875.

—————. "False Theories of Sovereignty." *The Independent* 50, no. 2,613 (December 29, 1898).

—————. "Het Bigeloof." Speech given to Beest Nut van 't Algemeen, January 25, 1866.

—————. *Lectures on Calvinism*. Grand Rapids: Eerdmans, 1953.

—————. *Niet De Vrijheidsboom Maar Het Kruis: Toespraak Ter Opening Van De Tiende Deputatenvergadering in Het Eeuwjaar Der Fransche Revolutie*. Amsterdam: J. A. Wormser, 1889.

—————. *Our Program*. Translated by Harry Van Dyke. Bellingham, WA: Lexham Press, 2015.

—————. *Our Worship*. Translated by Harry Boonstra. Grand Rapids: Eerdmans, 2009.

—————. *Principles of Sacred Theology*. Translated by John Hendrik De Vries. Grand Rapids: Eerdmans, 1954.

—————. *Pro Rege of het koningschap van Christus*. Vol. 3. Kampen: Kok, 1912.

—————. Speech to the Vereeniging voor Christelijk Nationaal Schoolonderwijs in Utrecht, May 18, 1869.

—————. "The Antithesis between Symbolism and Revelation." *The Presbyterian and Reformed Review* 10 (1899): 220–36.

—————. *The Encyclopedia of Sacred Theology*. Translated by Hendrik de Vries. New York: Charles Scribner's Sons, 1898.

————. *To Be Near unto God.* Translated by John Hendrik De Vries. Grand Rapids: Eerdmans, 1928.

————. *Wij, Calvinisten . . . Openingswoord Ter Deputaten-Vergadering.* Kampen: Kok, 1909.

————. *Wisdom and Wonder: Common Grace in Science and Art.* Translated by Nelson Kloosterman. Grand Rapids: Christian's Library Press, 2011.

Kymlicka, William. *Multicultural Citizenship.* Oxford, UK: Oxford University Press, 1995.

Lagerwey, Walter. "The History of Calvinism in the Netherlands." In *The Rise and Development of Calvinism.* Edited by John H. Bratt. Grand Rapids: Eerdmans, 1959: 63–102.

Lahav, Gallya. *Immigration and Politics in the New Europe.* Cambridge: Cambridge University Press, 2012.

Langely, Mckendree R. "Emancipation and Apologetics: The Formation of Abraham Kuyper's Anti-Revolutionary Party in the Netherlands." PhD diss., Westminster Theological Seminary, 1995.

Laurence, Jonathan. *The Emancipation of Europe's Muslims: The State's Role in Minority Integration.* Princeton, NJ: Princeton University Press, 2012.

Laurence, Jonathan and Justin Vaisse. *Integrating Islam: Political and Religious Challenges in Contemporary France.* Washington, DC: Brookings Institution Press, 2006.

Lechner, Frank J. *Globalization and National Identity.* New York: Taylor and Francis, 2007.

————. "Secularization in the Netherlands?" *Journal for the Scientific Study of Religion* 35, no. 3 (1996): 252–64.

Lentin, Alana and Gavan Titley. *The Crisis of Multiculturalism: Racism in a Neoliberal Age.* London: Zed Books, 2011.

Lettinga, Doutje. *Framing the Hijab: The Governance of Intersecting Religious, Ethnic, and Gender Differences in France, the Netherlands, and Germany.* Ridderkerk, NL: Ridderprint, 2011.

Liang, Christina Schori, ed. *Europe for the Europeans.* Burlington, VT: Ashgate, 2007.

Lijphart, Arend. "Consociational Democracy." *World Politics* 21, no. 2 (1969): 207–25.

————. *Democracy in Plural Societies.* New Haven, CT: Yale University Press, 1977.

————. *The Politics of Accommodation.* Berkeley: University of California Press, 1968.

Little, David. *Religion, Order, and Law: A Study in Pre-Revolutionary England.* Chicago: University of Chicago Press, 1984.

Lohman, A. F. De Savornin. *Onze Constitutie.* Utrecht: Kemink, 1901.

Lugo, Luis E. *Religion, Pluralism, and Public Life: Abraham Kuyper's Legacy for the Twenty-First Century.* Grand Rapids: Eerdmans, 2000.

MacIntyre, Alasdair. *After Virtue: A Study in Moral Theory.* 2nd ed. South Bend, IN: University of Notre Dame Press, 1984.

Mahmood, Saba. "Secularism, Hermeneutics, and Empire: The Politics of Islamic Reformation." *Public Culture* 18 (2006): 323–47.

Makari, Peter. "Muslim–Christian Relations in the United States." In *The Oxford Handbook of American Islam.* Edited by Jane I. Smith and Yvonne Yazbeck Haddad. Oxford: Oxford University Press, 2015.

Margry, Peter Jan. "The Murder of Pim Fortuyn and Collective Emotions: Hype, Hysteria, and Holiness in the Netherlands?" *Etnofoor: antropologisch tijdschrift* 16 (2003): 106–31.

Margry, Peter Jan and Henk te Velde. "Contested Rituals and the Battle for Public Space in the Netherlands." In *Culture Wars: Secular-Catholic Conflict in Nineteenth-Century Europe.* Edited by Christopher Clark and Wolfram Kaiser. Cambridge: Cambridge University Press, 2003: 129–51.

Marshall, Christopher D. *Beyond Retribution: A New Testament Vision of Justice, Crime, and Punishment.* Grand Rapids: Eerdmans, 2001.

Mathewes, Charles. *A Theology of Public Life.* Cambridge: Cambridge University Press, 2008.

Maussen, Marcel. *Constructing Mosques: The Governance of Islam in France and the Netherlands.* Amsterdam: Amsterdam School for Social Science Research, 2009.

———. "Pillarization and Islam: Church-State Traditions and Muslim Claims for Recognition in the Netherlands." *Comparative European Politics* 10 (2012): 337–53.

Mavelli, Luca. *Europe's Encounter with Islam: The Secular and the Postsecular.* London: Routledge, 2012.

May, John, ed. *Pluralism and the Religions: The Theological and Political Dimensions.* London: Cassell, 1998.

McGraw, Bryan T. *Faith in Politics: Religion and Liberal Democracy.* Cambridge: Cambridge University Press, 2010.

Mepschen, Paul. "Against Tolerance: Islam, Sexuality, and the Politics of Belonging in the Netherlands." *Monthly Review* 102 (2009).

Mepschen, Paul, Jan Willem Duyvendak, and Evelien H. Tonkens. "Sexual Politics, Orientalism, and Multicultural Citizenship in the Netherlands." *Sociology* 44 (2010): 962–78.

Merleau-Ponty, Maurice. *Humanism and Terror: An Essay on the Communist Problem.* Translated by John O'Neill. Boston: Beacon Press, 1969.

Meyer, Stephen E. "Calvinism and the Rise of the Protest Political Movement in the Netherlands." PhD diss., Georgetown University, 1976.

Monsma, Stephen V. *Positive Neutrality: Letting Religious Freedom Ring.* Westport, CT: Greenwood Press, 1992.

———. *When Sacred and Secular Mix: Religious Non-Profit Organizations and Public Money.* Lanham, MD: Rowman and Littlefield, 2000.

Morey, Peter and Amina Yaqin. *Framing Muslims: Stereotyping and Representations after 9/11.* Cambridge, MA: Harvard University Press, 2011.

Morgan, John H. "Disentangling Religion and Culture: Americanizing Islam as the Price of Assimilation." *International Journal of Islamic Thought* 4 (2013) 28–36.

Morin, Aysel. "Victimization of Muslim Women in *Submission.*" *Women's Studies in Communication* 32, no. 3 (2009): 380–408.

Mouw, Richard. "Baptismal Politics." *The Reformed Journal* 28, no. 7 (1978): 2–3.

———. *Called to Holy Worldliness.* Minneapolis: Fortress Press, 1980.

———. "Public Discipleship and Spiritual Formation." *Catalyst* 38, no. 2 (2012).

———. "A Spirituality for Public Life." *Theology Today* 61 (2005): 471–84.

———. "Virtue Ethics and the Public Calling of Reformational Thought." *Philosophia Reformata* 71 (2006): 3–13.

Mouw, Richard J. and Sander Griffioen. *Pluralisms and Horizons: An Essay in Christian Public Philosophy*. Grand Rapids: Eerdmans, 1993.

Murdoch, Iris. *The Sovereignty of Good*. New York: Schoeken Books, 1971.

Murphy, Andrew R. *Conscience and Community: Revisiting Toleration and Religious Dissent in Early Modern England and America*. University Park: Pennsylvania State University Press, 2001.

Naylor, Wendy Fish. "Abraham Kuyper and the Emergence of the Neo-Calvinist Pluralism in the Dutch School Struggle." PhD diss., University of Chicago, 2006.

Nederman, Cary J. and John Christian Laursen, eds. *Difference and Dissent: Theories of Toleration in Medieval and Early Modern Europe*. Lanham, MD: Rowman and Littlefield, 1996.

Newman, Elizabeth. *Untamed Hospitality: Welcoming God and Other Strangers*. Grand Rapids: Brazos Press, 2007.

Noll, Mark. *Adding Cross to Crown: The Political Significance of Christ's Passion*. Grand Rapids: Baker Publishing Group, 1996.

Nouwen, Henri J. M. *The Genesee Diary*. Garden City, NY: Doubleday, 1976.

Oliner, Pearl, M. Zuzanna Smolenska, and Samuel P. Oliner. *Embracing the Other: Philosophical, Psychological, and Historical Perspectives on Altruism*. New York: New York University, 1992.

Paas, Stefan. *Vrede stichten: Politieke meditaties*. Zoetermeer: Boekencentrum, 2007.

Paldiel, Mordecai. *Churches and the Holocaust: Unholy Teaching, Good Samaritans, and Reconciliation*. Jersey City, NJ: Ktav Publishing, 2006.

Parekh, Bhikhu. *Rethinking Multiculturalism: Cultural Diversity and Political Theory*. London: Routledge, 2006.

Parsons, Craig and Timothy M. Smeeding, eds. *Immigration and the Transformation of Europe*. Cambridge: Cambridge University Press, 2006.

Perry, John. *The Pretenses of Loyalty: Locke, Liberal Theory, and American Political Theology*. Oxford: Oxford University Press, 2011.

————. "The Weight of Community: Alasdair MacIntyre, Abraham Kuyper, and the Problem of Public Theology in a Liberal Society." *Calvin Theological Journal* 39, no. 2 (2004): 303–31.

Platvoet, Jan. "Pillars, Pluralism, and Secularisation: A Social History of Dutch Sciences of Religions." In *Modern Societies and the Science of Religions*. Edited by Gerard Wiegers. Leiden: Brill, 2002.

Po-Chia, Hsia and Henk van Nierop, eds. *Calvinism and Religious Toleration in the Dutch Golden Age*. Cambridge: Cambridge University Press, 2002.

Pohl, Christine. *Making Room: Recovering Hospitality as a Christian Tradition*. Grand Rapids: Eerdmans, 1999.

Post, Harry. *Pillarization: An Analysis of Dutch and Belgian Society*. Avebury, UK: Gower Publishing, 1989.

Proust, Marcel. *In Search of Lost Time*. Vol. 6, *Time Regained*. Translated by Andreas Mayor and Terence Kilmartin. Revised by D. L. Enright. New York: Random House, 2003.

Ramadan, Tariq. *Western Muslims: From Integration to Contribution*. Swansea, UK: Awakening Publications, 2012.

Rath, Jan, Astrid Meyer, and Thijl Sunier. "The Establishment of Islamic Institutions in a Depillarizing Society." *Tijdschrift voor Economisch en Sociale Geografie* 88 (1997): 389–96.

Ratzsch, Del. "Abraham Kuyper's Philosophy of Science." *Calvin Theological Journal* 27 (1992): 277–303.

Rawls, John. *A Theory of Justice*. Cambridge, MA: Harvard University Press, 1971.

Reid Jr., William Watkins. "O God of Every Nation." In *Worship and Rejoice*. Holland, MI: Hope Publishing, 2001, No. 626.

Rentier, Cees. *Europa, het Mekka van de Islam? Evangelisch perspectief op het samenleven met moslims*. Amsterdam: Buijten & Schipperheijn, 2007.

———. Personal interview by author. Amersfoort, the Netherlands, March 21, 2012.

Robbins, Keith, ed. *The Dynamics of Religion and Political Reform in Northern Europe: Political and Legal Perspectives (1780–1920)*. Leuven, BE: Leuven University Press, 2010.

Roy, Oliver. *Secularism Confronts Islam*. Translated by George Holoch. New York: Columbia University Press, 2007.

Sacks, Jonathan. *The Dignity of Difference: How to Avoid the Clash of Civilizations*. London: Continuum, 2002.

Saharso, Sawitri and Doutje Lettinga. "Contentious Citizenship: Policies and Debates on the Veil in the Netherlands." *Social Politics* 15, no. 4 (2008): 455–80.

Said, Edward. *Orientalism*. New York: Vintage Books, 1979.

Sap, Jan Willem. *Paving the Way for Revolution: Calvinism and the Struggle for a Democratic Constitutional State*. Amsterdam: Free University Press, 2001.

———. *The Queen, the Populists, and the Others: New Dutch Politics Explained to Foreigners*. Amsterdam: Free University Press, 2010.

Schama, Simon. "Schools and Politics in the Netherlands, 1796–1814." *The Historical Journal* 13, no. 4 (1970): 589–610.

Scheffer, Paul. *Immigrant Nations*. Cambridge: Polity Press, 2011.

Schilder, Klaas. *Christ Crucified*. Translated by Henry Zylstra. Grand Rapids: Eerdmans, 1940.

———. *Christ in His Sufferings*. Translated by Henry Zylstra. Grand Rapids: Eerdmans, 1938.

———. *Christ on Trial*. Translated by Henry Zylstra. Grand Rapids: Eerdmans, 1939.

Schindler, Jeanne Heffernan, ed. *Christianity and Civil Society: Catholic and Neo-Calvinist Perspectives*. New York: Lexington Books, 2008.

Schinkel, Willem. "The Continuation of the City by Other Means." In *2030: War Zone Amsterdam Imagining the Unimaginable*. *Open* 18 (2009). http://classic.skor.nl/article-4566-en.html (accessed February 6, 2013).

———. *Denken in een tijd van sociale hypochondrie: Aanzet tot een theorie voorbij de maatschappij*. Zoetermeer: Klement, 2007.

———. "The Politicization of Culture in the Netherlands." *Metropolis M* 3 (2011). http://metropolism.com/magazine/2011-no3/realpopulism-the-politicization/English (accessed February 6, 2013).

Schinkel, Willem, and Friso Van Houdt. "The Double Helix of Cultural Assimilationism and Neo-liberalism: Citizenship in Contemporary Governmentality." *The British Journal of Sociology* 61, no. 4 (2010): 696–715.

Schnabel, Paul. *De Multiculturele illusive: Een pleidooi voor aanpassing en assimilatie.* Utrecht: Forum, 1999.

Scholten, Peter and Ronald Holzhacker. "Bonding, Bridging, and Ethnic Minorities in the Netherlands: Changing Discourses in a Changing Nation." *Nations and Nationalism* 15, no. 1 (2009): 81–100.

Schreiner, Susan E. *The Theater of His Glory: Nature and the Natural Order in the Thought of John Calvin.* Grand Rapids: Baker Academic, 1995.

Scott, Joan Wallach. *The Politics of the Veil.* Princeton, NJ: Princeton University Press, 2009.

Scott, John T. "Rousseau and the Melodious Language of Freedom." In *Jean-Jacques Rousseau: Political Principles and Institutions.* Edited by John T. Scott. New York: Routledge, 2006.

Segers, Gert-Jan. *Voorwaarden voor vrede: de komst van de islam, de integratie van mosliims en de identiteit van Nederland.* Amsterdam: Buijten and Schipperheijn Motief, 2009.

Selby, Jennifer A. *Questioning French Secularism: Gender Politics and Islam in a Parisian Suburb.* New York: Palgrave Macmillan, 2012.

Seligman, Adam and Robert Weller. *Rethinking Pluralism: Ritual, Experience, and Ambiguity.* Oxford: Oxford University Press, 2012.

Sengers, Erik, ed. *The Dutch and Their Gods: Secularization and Transformation of Religion in the Netherlands since 1950.* Hilversum: Verloren, 2005.

Sengers, Erik and Thijl Sunier, eds. *Religious Newcomers and the Nation State: Political Culture and Organized Religion in France and the Netherlands.* Delft, NL: Eburon, 2010.

Serhan, Randa B. "Muslim Immigration to America." In *The Oxford Handbook of American Islam.* Edited by Jane I. Smith and Yvonne Yazbeck Haddad. Oxford: Oxford University Press, 2015.

Shadid, W. A. R. *Religious Freedom and the Position of Islam in Western Europe: Opportunities and Obstacles in the Acquisition of Equal Rights.* Leuven, BE: Peeters Publishers, 1995.

Shadid, W. A. R. and P. S. van Koningsveld. *Political Participation and Identities of Muslims in Non-Muslim States.* Leuven, BE: Peeters Publishers, 1996.

Shadid, W. A. R. and P. S. van Koningsveld, eds. *Integration of Islam and Hinduism in Western Europe.* Leuven, BE: Peeters Publishers, 1994.

———, eds. *Intercultural Relations and Religious Authorities: Muslims in the European Union.* Leuven, BE: Peeters Publishers, 2002.

———, eds. *Religious Freedom and the Neutrality of the State: The Position of Islam in the European Union.* Leuven, BE: Peeters Publishers, 2002.

Shryock, Andrew. "On Discipline and Inclusion." In *Being and Belonging: Muslims in the United States since 9/11.* Edited by Katherine Pratt Ewing. New York: Russell Sage, 2008: 200–206.

Skillen, James W. "E Pluribus Unum and Faith-Based Welfare Reform: A Kuyperian Moment for the Church in God's World." *The Princeton Seminary Bulletin* 22, no. 1 (2001): 285–305.

———. "From Covenant of Grace to Equitable Public Pluralism: The Dutch Calvinist Contribution." *Calvin Theological Journal* 31 (1996): 67–96.

———. "Kuyper Was on Time and Ahead of His Time: An Essay on Religion as a Way of Life and Societal Differentiation." *The Reformed Ecumenical Synod Theological Forum* 16, no. 2 (1988): 15–19.

———. *Recharging the American Experiment: Principled Pluralism for Genuine Civic Community*. Grand Rapids: Baker, 1994.

———."Religion in Public Life: A Dilemma for Democracy." *Calvin Theological Journal* 31 (1996): 527–31.

———. "Societal Pluralism: Blessing or Curse for the Public Good?" In *The Ethical Dimension of Political Life*. Edited by Francis Canavan. Durham, NC: Duke University Press, 1983: 166–72.

Skillen, James W. and Rockne M. McCarthy. *Political Order and the Plural Structure of Society*. Atlanta: Scholars Press, 1991.

Skillen, James and Stanley Carlson-Thies. "Religion and Political Development in Nineteenth-Century Holland." *Publius* (1982): 43–64.

Skinner, Quentin. *The Foundations of Modern Political Thought*. Vol. 2, *The Age of Reformation*. Cambridge: Cambridge University Press, 1978.

Smith, Gregory A. "Most white evangelicals approve of Trump travel prohibition and express concerns about extremism." Pew Research Center. February 27, 2017. http://www.pewresearch.org/fact-tank/2017/02/27/most-white-evangelicals-approve-of-trump-travel-prohibition-and-express-concerns-about-extremism/.

Smith, James K. A. *Awaiting the King: Reforming Public Theology*. Grand Rapids: Baker Academic, 2017.

———. *Desiring the Kingdom: Worship, Worldview, and Cultural Formation*. Grand Rapids: Baker Academic, 2009.

———. *Imagining the Kingdom: How Worship Works*. Grand Rapids: Baker Academic, 2013.

———. "Sanctification for Ordinary Life." *Reformed Worship* 103 (2012).

———. "Teaching a Calvinist to Dance." *Christianity Today* 52, no. 5 (2008).

Sniderman, Paul M. and Louk Hagendoorn. *When Ways of Life Collide: Multiculturalism and Its Discontents in the Netherlands*. Princeton, NJ: Princeton University Press, 2009.

Soper, J. Christopher, Kevin R. den Dulk, and Stephen Monsma. *The Challenge of Pluralism: Church and State in Six Democracies*. Lanham, MD: Rowman and Littlefield, 2017.

Sorkin, David. *The Religious Enlightenment: Protestants, Jews, and Catholics from London to Vienna*. Princeton, NJ: Princeton University Press, 2008.

Spykman, Gordon. *Reformational Theology: A New Paradigm for Doing Dogmatics*. Grand Rapids: Eerdmans, 1992.

———. "Sphere-Sovereignty in Calvin and the Calvinist Tradition." In *Exploring the Heritage of John Calvin*. Edited by D. E. Holwerda. Grand Rapids: Baker, 1976.

Stout, Jeffrey. *Democracy and Tradition*. Princeton, NJ: Princeton University Press, 2005.

Stuurman, Siep. *Verzuiling, Kapitalisme, en Patriarchaat*. Nijmegen: Socialistiese Uitgeverij, 1983.

Sullivan, Winnifred Sallers. *The Impossibility of Religious Freedom*. Princeton, NJ: Princeton University Press, 2005.

Sunier, Thijl. "Assimilation by Conviction or by Coercion? Integration Policies in the Netherlands." In *European Multiculturalism Revisited*. Edited by Allesandro Silj. London: Zed Books, 2010.

―――. "Islam in the Netherlands: A Nation Despite Religious Communities?" In *Religious Newcomers and the Nation State: Political Culture and Organized Religion in France and the Netherlands*. Edited by Erik Sengers and Thijl Sunier. Delft, NL: Eburon, 2010.

Sweetman, Brendan. *Why Politics Needs Religion*. Downers Grove, IL: Intervarsity Press, 2006.

Takim, Liyakat. "The Ground Zero Mosque Controversy: Implications for American Islam." *Religions* 2 (2011): 132–44.

Taras, Raymond. *Xenophobia and Islamophobia in Europe*. Edinburgh: Edinburgh University Press, 2012.

Taylor, Charles. *Modern Social Imaginaries*. Durham, NC: Duke University Press, 2003.

Te Velde, Henk. *Gemeenschapszin en plichtsbesef: Liberalisme en Nationalisme in Nederland, 1870–1918*. Groningen, NL: Rijksuniversiteit Groningen, 1992.

―――. "Liberalism and Bourgeois Culture in the Netherlands, from the 1840s to the 1880." In *Under the Sign of Liberalism: Varieties of Liberalism in Past and Present*. Edited by Simon Groenveld and Michael Wintle. Zutphen, NL: Walburg Pers, 1997.

Ten Hooven, Marcel. "Religie verdeelt Nederland: Een oude scheidslijn in een nieuwe gedaante." In *Ongewenste Goden: De Publieke rol van Relie in Nederland*. Edited by Marcel ten Hooven and Theo de Wit. Amsterdam: Verschenen, 2006.

Ter Borg, Meerten. "Fundamentals and Civil Religiousity." In *The Search for Fundamentals: The Process of Modernisation and the Quest for Meaning*. Edited by Lieteke van Vucht Tijssen, Jan Berting, and Frank Lechner. Dordrecht, NL: Kluwer Academic Publishers, 1995.

―――. "Publieke religie in Nederland." In *Religie in de Nederlandse samenleving: De vergeten factor*. Edited by O. Schreuder and L. van Snippenburg. Baarn: Ambo, 1990.

―――. "Some Ideas on Wild Religion." *Implicit Religion* 7, no. 2 (2004): 108–19.

Thorbecke, J. R. *Een Woord In Het Belang van Europa bij het voorstel der schieding tusschen Beligie en Holland*. Leiden: Luchtmans, 1830.

Toonen, Theo, Frank Hendriks, and Th. A. J. Toonen, eds. *Polder Politics in the Netherlands: The Re-Invention of Consensus Democracy in the Netherlands*. London: Ashgate, 2001.

Uitermark, Justus. *Dynamics of Power in Dutch Integration Politics*. Amsterdam: Amsterdam University Press, 2012.

Valenta, Markha. "The Future of Islamophobia: The Liberal, the Jew, the Animal." *Open Democracy* May 13, 2011. http://www.opendemocracy.net/markha-valenta/future-of-islamophobia-liberal-jew-animal (accessed February 7, 2013).

―――. "How to Recognize a Muslim When You See One: Western Secularism and the Politics of Conversion." In *Political Theologies: Public Religions in a Post-Secular World*. Edited by Hent de Vries and Lawrence E. Sullivan. New York: Fordham University Press, 2006.

―――. "The Moral Sadism of the Dutch State." *Open Democracy*. December, 4 2012.

http://www.opendemocracy.net/markha-valenta/moral-sadism-of-dutch-state (accessed February 7, 2013).

———. "Multiculturalism and the Politics of Bad Memories." *Open Democracy,* March 20, 2011. http://www.opendemocracy.net/markha-valenta/multiculturalism-and -politics-of-bad-memories (accessed February 7, 2013).

Valk, John. "Religion and the Schools: The Case of Utrecht." *History of Education Quarterly* 35, no. 2 (1995): 159–77.

Van de Donk, W. B. H. J. et al., eds. *Geloven in het publieke domein: Verkenningen van een dubbele transformatie.* Amsterdam: Amsterdam University Press, 2006.

Vander Hart, Mark. "Abraham Kuyper and the Theonomy Debate." *Mid-America Journal of Theology* 2 (1986): 63–77.

van der Kooi, Cornelius and Jan de Bruijn, eds. *Kuyper Reconsidered: Aspects of His Life and Work.* Amsterdam: Free University Press, 1999.

Van der Kroef, Justus Maria. "Abraham Kuyper and the Rise of Neo-Calvinism in the Netherlands." *Church History* 17, no. 4 (1948): 316–34.

van der Stoep, Jan. "Religie, maatschappelijke orde en geweld." *Reformata Philosophia* 73, no. 1 (2008): 85–99.

van der Veer, Peter. "Pim Fortuyn, Theo van Gogh, and the Politics of Tolerance in the Netherlands." *Public Culture* 18, no. 1 (2006): 111–24.

Van Deursen, Arie. *The Distinctive Character of the Free University in Amsterdam, 1880–2005: A Commemorative History.* Grand Rapids: Eerdmans, 2008.

Van Dyke, Harry. "Abraham Kuyper: Heir of an Anti-Revolutionary Tradition." Paper presented at the international conference "Christianity and Culture: The Heritage of Abraham Kuyper on Different Continents," Free University, Amsterdam, June 1998.

———. "How Abraham Kuyper Became a Christian Democrat." *Calvin Theological Journal* 33, no. 2 (1998): 420–35.

Van Eijnatten, Joris. *Liberty and Concord in the United Provinces: Religious Toleration and the Public in the Eighteenth-Century Netherlands.* Leiden: Brill, 2003.

van Essen, Jantje Lubbegiena. "The Struggle for Freedom of Education in the Netherlands in the Nineteenth Century." In *Guillaume Groen Van Prinsterer: Selected Studies.* Edited by Jantje Lubbegiena van Essen and Herbert Donald Morton. Jordan Station, ON: Wedge Publishing Foundation, 1990.

van Essen, Jantje Lubbegiena, and Herbert Donald Morton, eds. *Guillaume Groen Van Prinsterer: Selected Studies.* Jordan Station, ON: Wedge Publishing, 1990.

van Rooden, Peter. "History, the Nation, and Religion: The Transformations of the Dutch Religious Past." In *Nation and Religion: Perspectives on Europe and Asia.* Edited by Peter van der Veer and Hartmut Lehmann. Princeton, NJ: Princeton University Press, 1999.

Van Til, Henry R. *The Calvinistic Concept of Culture.* Grand Rapids: Baker, 1959.

Verkaaik, Oskar. "The Cachet Dilemma: Ritual and Agency in New Dutch Nationalism." *American Ethnologist* 37, no. 1 (2010): 69–82.

Vink, Maarten P. "Dutch 'Multiculturalism': Beyond the Pillarisation Myth." *Political Studies Review* 5 (2007): 337–50.

Volf, Miroslav. *Exclusion and Embrace: A Theological Expression of Identity, Otherness, and Reconciliation.* Nashville, TN: Abingdon Press, 1996.

————. *Flourishing: Why We Need Religion in a Globalizing World*. New Haven, CT: Yale University Press, 2015.

Vree, Jasper. "The Marnix-Vereeniging: Abraham Kuyper's First National Organization, 1868–89." *Nederlands archief voor kerkgeschiedenis* 84.1 (2004): 388–475.

————. "Petrus Hofstede de Groot and the Christian Education of the Dutch Nation, 1833–1861." *Nederlands archief voor kerkgeschiedenis* 78 (1998): 70–93.

Vroom, Hendrik. *No Other Gods: Christian Belief in Dialogue with Buddhism, Hinduism, and Islam*. Translated by Lucy Jansen. Grand Rapids: Eerdmans, 1996.

————. *A Spectrum of Worldviews: An Introduction to Philosophy of Religion in a Pluralistic World*. Translated by Morris and Alice Greidanus. Amsterdam: Rodopi, 2006.

————. "What Policies towards Islam?" Paper presented at the European Ideas Network and Centre for European Studies. Brussels, February 9, 2011.

Vroom, Hendrik M., Henry Jansen, and Jerald D. Gort. *Religion, Conflict, and Reconciliation: Multifaith Ideals and Realities*. Amsterdam: Rodopi, 2002.

————. *Religions View Religions: Explorations in Pursuit of Understanding*. Amsterdam: Rodopi, 2006.

Vroom, Hendrik, Charles Van Engen, and Inus Daneel. *Fullness of Life for All: Challenges for Mission in Early Twenty-First Century*. Amsterdam: Rodopi, 2005.

Vroom, Hendrik, Michael Weinrich, and Christine Lienemann-Perrin. *Contextuality in Reformed Europe: The Mission of the Church in the Transformation of European Culture*. Amsterdam: Rodopi, 2004.

Waardenburg, Jacques. "The Institutionalization of Islam in the Netherlands, 1961–86." In *The New Islamic Presence in Western Europe*. Edited by T. Gerhold and Y. Litman. London: Mansell, 1988.

Walzer, Michael. "The Idea of Civil Society: A Path to Social Reconstruction." In *Community Works: The Revival of Civil Society*. Edited by E. J. Dionne. Washington, DC: Brookings Institution, 1998.

Westra, Johan. "Abraham Kuyper on Church and State." *Reformed Review* 38.2 (1985): 119–29.

Wilders, Geert. *Marked for Death: Islam's War against the West and Me*. Washington, DC: Regnery Publishing, 2012.

————. "NYC Speech" given in New York on September 11, 2010. http://www.geert wilders.n l/index.php? option=com _contentandtask=viewandid=1712.(accessed February 5, 2013).

————. "Speech to the Gatestone Institute" delivered in New York, NY, April 30, 2012, http://www.geertwilders.nl/index.php/in-english-mainmenu-98/in-the-press-main-menu-101/77-in-the-press/1781-speech-geert-wilders-new-york-april-30 (accessed February 5, 2013).

Williams, Rowan. "Is Europe at its end?" (Forum debate presented at the Sant'Egidio International Meeting of Prayer for Peace, Palais de Congress, Lyons, France, September 12, 2005), http://www.archbishopofcanterbury.org/958 (accessed November 5, 2009).

Wintle, Michael. *An Economic and Social History of the Netherlands, 1800–1920: Demographic, Economic, and Social Transition*. Cambridge: Cambridge University Press, 2000.

Bibliography

Witte Jr., John. "Introduction" in *Christianity and Human Rights: An Introduction*. Edited by John Witte Jr. and Frank S. Alexander. Cambridge: Cambridge University Press, 2010.

———. *The Reformation of Rights: Law, Religion, and Human Rights in Early Modern Calvinism*. Cambridge: Cambridge University Press, 2007.

Witvliet, John. *The Biblical Psalms in Christian Worship: A Brief Introduction and Guide to Resources*. Grand Rapids, Eerdmans, 2007.

———. "The Cumulative Power of Transformation in Public Worship." In *Worship That Changes Lives: Multidisciplinary and Congregational Perspectives on Spiritual Transformation*. Edited by Alexis D. Abernathy. Grand Rapids: Baker Academic, 2008.

———. "Teaching Worship as a Christian Practice." In *For Life Abundant: Practical Theology, Theological Education, and Christian Ministry*. Edited by Dorothy C. Bass and Craig Dykstra. Grand Rapids: Eerdmans, 2008.

———. "A Time to Weep—During Advent." *Reformed Worship* 45 (1997).

———. "We Are What We Sing: Searching for a Balanced Diet." *Reformed Worship* 60 (2001).

———. "What I Learned on Sabbatical: Eleven Things to Celebrate, Ponder, or Lament." *Reformed Worship* 103 (2012).

———. "Words to Grow Into: The Psalms as Formative Speech." In *Forgotten Songs: Reclaiming the Psalms for Christian Worship*. Edited by Ray Van Neste and C. Richard Wells. Nashville, TN: B&H Publishing, 2012.

———. *Worship Seeking Understanding*. Grand Rapids: Baker, 2003.

Wodak, Ruth, Majid KhosraviNik, and Brigitte Mral, eds. *Right-Wing Populism in Europe: Politics and Discourse*. London: Bloomsbury, 2013.

Wolterstorff, Nicholas. "Christian Political Reflection: Diognetian or Augustinian." *The Princeton Seminary Bulletin* 20, no. 2 (1999): 150–68.

———. *Educating for Shalom: Essays in Christian Higher Education*. Edited by Clarence Joldersma and Gloria Goris Stronks. Grand Rapids: Eerdmans, 2003.

———. *Hearing the Call: Liturgy, Justice, Church, and World*. Edited by Mark R. Gornik and Gregory Thompson. Grand Rapids: Eerdmans, 2011.

———. "Imitating God: Doing Justice as a Condition of Authentic Worship." *Reformed Worship* 68 (2003).

———. *Justice: Rights and Wrongs*. Princeton, NJ: Princeton University Press, 2008.

———. *Lament for a Son*. Grand Rapids: Eerdmans, 1987.

———. *Until Justice and Peace Embrace*. Grand Rapids: Eerdmans, 1983.

———. "The Young Person and the Liturgy." *The Reformed Journal* 19, no. 2 (1969): 9.

Wolterstorff, Nicholas and Robert Audi. *Religion in the Public Square: The Place of Religious Convictions in the Public Square*. Lanham, MD: Rowman and Littlefield, 1996.

Yilmaz, Hakan and Çagla E. Aykaç, eds. *Perceptions of Islam in Europe: Culture, Identity, and the Muslim "Other."* London: Tauris, 2012.

Yoder, John Howard. *The Politics of Jesus*. Grand Rapids: Eerdmans, 1972.

Yukleyen, Ahmet. *Localizing Islam in Europe: Turkish Islamic Communities in Germany and the Netherlands*. Syracuse, NY: Syracuse University Press, 2011.

Zwaanstra, Henry. "Abraham Kuyper's Conception of the Church." *Calvin Theological Journal* 9 (1974): 149–81.

Index